PENNSYLVANIA STATE PARKS

A Complete
Outdoor Recreation Guide for
Campers, Boaters, Anglers, Hikers
and Outdoor Lovers

Bill Bailey

Glovebox Guidebooks of America

To our readers: Travel outdoors entails some unavoidable risks. Know your limitations, be prepared, be alert, use good judgment, think safety and enjoy Pennsylvania's terrific outdoors. Be bold!

Special thanks to Roger Fickes and Matt Azeles and to all the staff at all the parks. Pennsylvania has some of the finest parks–and staff–in the nation!

Copyright © 1996 by Glovebox Guidebooks of America/Bill Bailey.

Cover and interior design by Dan Jacalone
Cover photo: Hardie Truesdale
Senior Editor, William P. Cornish
Managing Editor, Penny Weber-Bailey

Published by: **Glovebox Guidebooks of America**
1112 Washburn Place East
Saginaw, Michigan 48602-2977
(800) 289-4843 or (517) 792-8363

Library of Congress, CIP.

Bailey, William L., 1952-

Pennsylvania State Parks Guidebook
(A Glovebox Guidebooks of America publication)
ISBN 1-881139-15-8

Printed in the United States of America

10 9 8 7 6 5 4 3 2 1

Pennsylvania State Parks

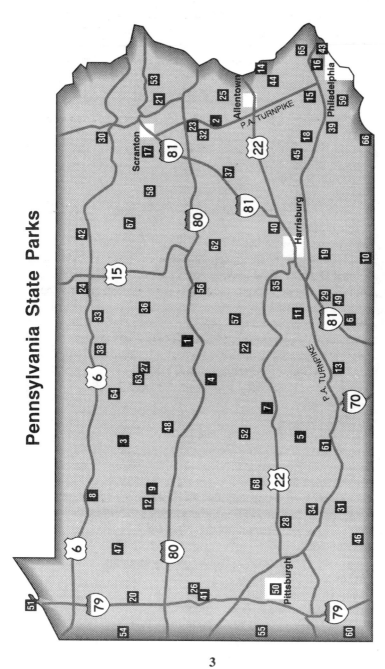

Contents

Pennsylvania State Park locator map 3
Forward 6
Introduction 8

STATE PARK AND RECREATIONAL AREAS

1. Bald Eagle State Park 14
2. Beltzville State Park 21
3. Bendigo State Park 25
4. Black Moshannon State Park 27
5. Blue Knob State Park 35
6. Caledonia State Park 41
7. Canoe Creek State Park 49
8. Chapman State Park 55
9. Clear Creek State Park 62
10. Codorus State Park 69
11. Colonel Denning State Park 76
12. Cook Forest State Park 80
13. Cowans Gap State Park 89
14. Delaware Canal State Park 96
15. Evansburg State Park 99
16. Fort Washington State Park 102
17. Frances Slocum State Park 105
18. French Creek State Park 112
19. Gifford Pinchot State Park 121
20. Goddard State Park 129
21. Gouldsboro and Tobyhanna State Parks 134
22. Greenwood Furnace State Park 139
23. Hickory Run State Park 145
24. Hills Creek State Park 154
25. Jacobsburg Environmental Education Center 160
26. Jennings Environmental Education Center 164
27. Kettle Creek State Park 166
28. Keystone State Park 171
29. Kings Gap Environmental Education and Training Center 174
30. Lackawanna State Park 178
31. Laurel Hill State Park 185
32. Lehigh Gorge State Park 188
33. Leonard Harrison and Colton Point State Park 192

34. Linn Run State Park/Laurel Summit State Park 199
35. Little Buffalo State Park 202
36. Little Pine State Park 209
37. Locust Lake State Park 215
38. Lyman Run State Park 222
39. Marsh Creek State Park 226
40. Memorial Lake State Park 231
41. Moraine State Park 234
42. Mt. Pisgah State Park 238
43. Neshaminy State Park 241
44. Nockamixon State Park 244
45. Nolde Forest Environmental Education Center 250
46. Ohiopyle State Park 254
47. Oil Creek State Park 260
48. Parker Dam State Park 267
49. Pine Grove Furnace State Park 274
50. Point State Park 282
51. Presque Isle State Park 285
52. Prince Gallitzin State Park 293
53. Promised Land State Park 301
54. Pymatuning State Park 310
55. Raccoon Creek State Park 317
56. R.B. Winter State Park 321
57. Reeds Gap State Park 330
58. Ricketts Glen State Park 334
59. Ridley Creek State Park 342
60. Ryerson Station State Park 349
61. Shawnee State Park 353
62. Shikellamy State Park 360
63. Sinnemahoning State Park 363
64. Sizerville State Park 369
65. Tyler State Park 375
66. White Clay Creek Preserve 381
67. Worlds End State Park 386
68. Yellow Creek State Park 393

Foreword

For over a hundred years, Pennsylvania State Parks have continued to meet the needs of all park visitors in a never-ending commitment to quality service. State parks in the Keystone State share a wealth of natural, historical and cultural resources for visitors to enjoy year-round.

Pennsylvania State Parks offer millions of visitors each year over 7,000 family campsites, 285 cabins, nearly 30,000 picnic tables, 56 major recreational lakes, 10 marinas, 61 beaches for swimming, 17 swimming pools, thousands of miles of trails, and much more. Opportunities to fish, whitewater raft, hike, bike, camp, ski, boat, skate, golf, picnic and more, all await enthusiastic visitors.

Breathtaking vistas and landscapes and unique natural areas are a big part of the Pennsylvania State Park experience. Each park harbors a wealth of resources that make visits interesting and enjoyable. You won't want to miss the beautiful and bountiful resources found in the state parks of Pennsylvania. Natural waterfalls, spectacular vistas and overlooks, historic districts, relaxing drives, and vigorous hikes all add their own signature to the character of individual parks.

Pennsylvania State Parks recently began a formalized Natural Areas Program. The program helps meet an ongoing goal to protect and preserve unique resources in our state parks. This program will grow in the years to come and strives to protect these areas of "unique scenic, geologic, or ecological value" for scientific study, environmental educational opportunities, and for future generations. From the 300 year-old white pine and hemlock trees at Cook Forest, to the gorge at Ricketts Glen with its 22 named waterfalls, these sensitive areas provide rare glimpses into nature's curiosity.

Since the establishment of the first state park in 1883, the system has grown through a rich history to its present size of 116 parks. Many traces of this history remain indelibly etched on the features and buildings of the parks. Visitors are often treated to rustic cabin accommodations built by the Civilian Conservation Corps during the 1930s, or walk through historic districts to learn about our state's past which are steeped in history and interpreted through historical presentations and reenactments.

Through a strong commitment to making visitors of all ages more aware of the world around them, the state parks operate four environmental education centers year-round, and many seasonal environmental education programs at various state parks.

It is difficult to sum up the facilities, resources, and programs of the Pennsylvania State Parks in just a few paragraphs. The expanse of the system dictates a diversity that is far ranging and complex. The Pennsylvania Bureau of State Parks also coordinates the Pennsylvania Rails to Trails program, cooperates with American Youth Hostels to provide simple accommodations to overnight travelers, develops comprehensive management plans, oversees an extensive volunteer and intern program, and ensures the safety and security of park visitors. The Pennsylvania State Park system is one of which Pennsylvanians can be proud and which will serve the needs of all Pennsylvanians, both today and in generations yet to come.

Roger Fickes

Director
Bureau of State Parks

Introduction

Pennsylvania state parks are our common ground; they are our core experience, our crown jewels. The 114 parks coming in all shapes and sizes, from the mountains and steep valleys to quiet lakes, freestone streams and fascinating historic sites. The best of Pennsylvania is in our state parks.

There's lots to do in the 277,000 acres of property. You can fish, hike, camp, swim, learn about our environment, picnic, hunt, go boating (or whitewater rafting!), paddle a quiet lake, ski, sled, mountain bike rugged trails, stay in a log cabin or just relax in a shady day-use area. Pennsylvania state parks are outstanding–one of the biggest and best systems in the nation. For family fun in the out-of-doors, start your next vacation–or weekend–in your nearby state parks.

HISTORY

Pennsylvania state parks began in 1893 with the opening of the first park in Valley Forge, which because of its national significance was placed in the National Park Service in 1976 as a National Historic Park.

In the early years, the rapidly developing park system was managed as part of the state's forest resources. During this time an increasing emphasis was placed on preserving and protecting rare, scenic, historic and natural areas. By 1929 the Legislature established the Bureau of State Parks. The agency was charged with providing outdoor recreation facilities in a natural setting, preserving park areas and providing accessible environmental education opportunities. One year later, the bureau managed 13 state parks and was busy preparing a statewide plan for growth and development of the system.

MISSION

"The primary purpose of state parks is to provide opportunities for enjoying healthful outdoor recreation and to serve as outdoor classrooms for environmental education. In meeting these purposes, the conservation of the natural, scenic, aesthetic and historical values of the parks should be given first consideration. Stewardship responsibilities should be carried out in a way that protect the natural outdoor experience for the enjoyment of current and future generations."

The Great Depression jump-started park growth, using the Civilian Conservation Corps in the early 1930s to help build wonderful structures of stone and log while helping the country out of its economic crisis. CCC members worked hard, learned skills, built parks and revitalized and spurred state park development. Thanks to them, the log cabins, stone chimneys, roadways, lakes, dams and trails were built–and still enjoyed today.

After rapid development, a survey taken in 1936 indicated that there was a need for 10 parks near urban areas. The close-to-home parks were built, as were even more day-use parks after World War II. But the greatest period of park growth occurred between 1955 and 1970. In 1955, the Department of Forests and Maurice K. Goddard, director of the department, set a goal of having a state park within 25 miles of every citizen. With the help of two state funding programs and substantial federal funds, the system grew from 45 state parks and five historical parks in 1955 to 87 state parks in 1970.

Today, 37 million enthusiasts annually visit the 114 parks. The system has more than 7,000 family camping sites, 281 cabins, 56 major recreational lakes, 61 beaches for swimming, 17 swimming pools, more than 1,000 miles of trails and much, much more.

OPERATING TIMES

Pennsylvania state parks are open year-round with most facilities staffed and available from Memorial Day weekend to Labor Day. All park day-use areas are open year-round from 8 a.m. - sunset, unless otherwise posted. Swimming pools, swimming beaches, boat rentals and food concessions operate during the summer season.

OVERNIGHT FACILITIES

FAMILY CAMPING

From intimate tent camping sites to full-service hard-surfaced pads for big RV rigs, Pennsylvania state parks have a camping site that's perfect for you. Fifty-five state park campgrounds offer more than 7,000 sites. Some are open year-round, others from the second Friday in April to the last day of antlerless deer season in December and the remaining are open from the second Friday in April to the third Sunday in October.

The maximum camping period is 14 consecutive nights during the summer season. Some parks offer camping for 21 consecutive nights during other seasons of the year. A few areas are limited to tent camping only. Most campgrounds–and most sites–can accommodate any camping equipment. Some parks have limited numbers of electrical hookups. Site occupancy is limited to one family per site and camping fees should be paid upon entering the campground or if no attendant is available, according to the posted procedure.

Reservations are available for all state park family campgrounds, by calling the respective state park offices.

GROUP CAMPING AREA

Many of the state parks offer excellent organized group camping. These areas are typically in isolated areas of the park and have drinking water, pit or flush toilets and can be reserved in advance by calling the respective park offices.

CABINS

Twenty-nine state parks maintain 284 modern and rustic cabins.

Eleven parks provide 147 rustic family cabins that were built during the 1930s of wood and stone. Most of them have indoor fireplaces and/or woodburning stoves. These charming cabins are a testament to the importance of the Civilian Conservation Corps that built them. The quaint rustic cabins sleep between two and eight people, and have no indoor plumbing.

Other furnishings include beds, chairs, tables, a modern range, refrigerator and lights. (Extra cots are not available). Firewood is available, but not guaranteed. Kooser, Parker Dam, Linn Run and World End state parks rent rustic cabins year-round. The other seven rustic cabin parks rent from the second Friday in April until the Friday of the week of regular antlerless deer season. Cabins are only rented by the week (Friday to Friday) during the summer.

Fourteen state parks provide 131 modern cabins constructed by the Pennsylvania Conservation Crops. The modern cabins take the rough out of roughing it for those who enjoy comfortable accommodations. Each cabin features electric heat, carpeting, living/dining room, modern kitchen and bath. The cabins feature a wooden cathedral ceiling in the main living area. They have two or three bedrooms. Each cabin has one double bed and bunk beds for varied sleeping arrangements.

Six state parks offer one-of-a-kind modern cabins that provide overnight accommodations year-round. Keystone, Moraine and Pymatuning have cabins that are handicapped accessible.

Cabin guests should take along the following items: bed linens, towels, pots and pans, dinnerware, an ax for splitting firewood, insect repellent and first aid kit. Pets are prohibited. Virtually all cabins have grills and picnic tables.

DAY-USE FACILITIES AND AMENITIES

PICNIC FACILITIES

Most state recreation areas are accompanied by drinking water, charcoal grills, and many have nearby rest rooms. Many parks rent pavilions that are perfect for family reunions or organization picnics and outings. Most parks have a scattering of handicapped accessible picnic tables.

SWIMMING

Sixty-one state parks have designated swimming beaches and 17 have swimming pools. Swimming is permitted only when lifeguard protection is provided. Some pools charge a small admission fee. Hours of operation are typically 11 a.m. - 7 p.m. Memorial Day weekend to Labor Day unless otherwise posted and depending on the availability of lifeguards. Some beaches (and pools) have access ramps for those visitors with disabilities.

FISHING

More than 35,329 acres of fresh water lakes and many miles of streams provide excellent warm and cold water fishing in 96 state parks. See individual park write-ups for details and tips on fishing each park. Anglers should also seek local fishing knowledge from concession operations and off-park bait and tackle dealers. Many parks maintain shoreline fishing areas and piers that are accessible for those with disabilities.

BOATING

Fifty-four parks offer boating. Overnight mooring of boats is available by permit from April 1 to November 1. Marina and services vary. Some parks have seasonal mooring and limits on power.

SNOWMOBILING

Snowmobilers should request the publication, Pennsylvania Snowmobile Trail Directory (Snowmobile/ATV Unit, P. O. Box 8553,

Harrisburg, PA 17105-8553), for a comprehensive listing and map of trails on state lands. If headed for the north central part of the state ask for the North Central Snowmobile Trails booklet from the same address. It includes trails, rules, information phone numbers, code of ethics, wind chill chart and more. Snowmobilers must operate on designated trails, roads and areas in state recreation lands from the last day of antlerless deer season until April 1 or earlier.

HIKING AND BACKPACKING

There are also at least 1,000 miles of hiking trails in the Pennsylvania state parks. Trails vary in degree of difficulty, some trails traverse steep mountains and across deep valleys, some along cool running streams, while others are perfect for leisure walking at any age.

Oil Creek and Laurel Ridge offer overnight backpacking with shelters located along the trail. Many parks serve as trailhead backpacking and hiking trails on other state lands. Many parks also maintain self-guided interpretive trails. Check with the office for maps and information.

CROSS-COUNTRY SKIING

Many hiking trails (which often connect to other trail networks outside the park boundaries), park roads and open spaces are open to cross-country skiers when weather permits. Many parks have dozens of miles of moderate to difficult trails. Request a copy of "Cross-country Skiing in Pennsylvania State Parks and Forest," from the Parks Bureau. The 12 page booklet describes many trails, offering trail length, trailhead locations and other useful information.

MOUNTAIN BIKING

Bike riding is permitted in state parks only on designated bicycle trails. Many parks have bike trails. For more information on mountain biking on state forest lands contact the Division of State Forest Management, P.O. Box 8552, Harrisburg, PA 17105-8552, or call 717-787-2014. For additional information on mountain biking on state game land by contacting the Pennsylvania Game Commission, Bureau of Land Management, 2001 Elmerton Avenue, Harrisburg, PA 17110-9797.

HUNTING

Many state parks have large tracts that are open to hunting. Hunting is permitted in state parks in accordance with current state game laws on all areas, unless otherwise posted. Call the respective parks for details.

OUTDOOR EDUCATION

State parks are parks for the people. And at the same time they also protect and preserve the natural resources. This wholesome blend of park use, protection and environmental education is a major objective of the bureau. Pennsylvania is a clear leader in outdoor education in the nation, offering a broad menu of seasonal and year-round environmental education programs.

Environmental educators and interpreters conduct guided walks, evening and daytime programs, historical programs on past lifestyles such as ironmaking, milling and lumbering, and teach thousands of school children annually. This talented staff also helps to develop in-service training for teachers, create self-guided nature trails, produce educational brochures and staff visitor centers.

Year-round environmental education and interpretive programs are offered at Nolde Forest, Kings Gap, Jennings, and Jacobsburg environmental education centers. These sites offer a variety of wonderful programs for all ages and interests.

OTHER PUBLICATIONS OF INTEREST

The state produces many publications that can be picked up at state parks or ordered (see address below), they include: Pennsylvania State Parks Recreation Guide (large maps and informational graph); Natural Symbols of Pennsylvania; Animal Tracks; Pennsylvania Geology; Hiking Trails in Pennsylvania (8.5" x 11" map); Camping in State Parks brochure; Campground Tips brochure; Picnic Pavilions brochure; Let's Go Fishing in Pennsylvania (717-657-4518, other fishing-related brochures are also available from this number); Poison Ivy brochure; Guide to Common Freshwater Animals booklet; State Park Access Guide; Family Camping Reservation System brochure and others.

Rules and regulations

All pets are permitted in day-use areas only and they must be on a leash at all times. Plants, animals, minerals, fossils, structures and exhibits must be left undisturbed. Respect quiet times, speed limits and the prohibition of alcohol in the parks.

For more information on Pennsylvania State Parks write Bureau of State Parks, P.O. Box 8551, Harrisburg, PA 17105-8551, call 1-800-63 PARKS (TDD number is 800-654-5984).

1 Bald Eagle State Park
Land: 5,900 acres Water: 1,730-acre lake

First, tune up your power boat, pack a picnic basket, bring your swimsuit, and then head for Bald Eagle State Park. You might also want to bring your binoculars (for bird and butterfly watching), fishing pole (for bass and panfish) and water skis. This park is a high-energy reservoir.

Lying between the Allegheny Plateau and Bald Eagle Mountain Ridge, the park is along the last ridge in the Appalachian Mountains section of Pennsylvania's Valley and Ridge Province. The region is known for tall, narrow forested mountain ridges, high slopes and sprawling green valleys of farms and hamlets.

The park is bordered to the west and north by the Allegheny Plateau and surrounded by hardwood cover that turns to gold and crimson in the autumn. Fall hiking and color touring in and around Bald Eagle are popular autumn activities.

The park and Bald Eagle mountain range were named after well-known Chief Bald Eagle of the Leni-Lenape tribes. Bald Eagle or

14

Wapelanewack, as the chief was referred to in his native tongue, lived in the region near Milesburg until 1720 when his tribe was conquered by the Iroquois. About 250 years later, in 1971, the park was opened to the public.

Bald Eagle State Park was developed cooperatively by the U.S. Corps of Engineers and the Commonwealth of Pennsylvania. The Corps purchased the land and constructed the Foster Joseph Sayers Dam in 1969; recreational amenities were finished in 1971. At this time of dedication, the state of Pennsylvania entered into an agreement to operate the 5,900 acres of the project land for recreational purposes. The unit continues to improve today.

Information and Activities

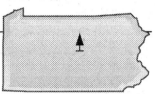

Bald Eagle State Park
149 Main Park Road
Howard, PA 16841-9607
(814) 625-2775

DIRECTIONS: From I-80 depart at exit 26, north on U.S. 220 to SR 150 and continue 13 miles. Traveling east on I-80, depart at Exit 23 and turn left onto Rt. 150, continue nine miles to the main park entrance. The park is midway between Milesburg and Lock Haven. Inside the park office with a wood shingle roof are a small brochure rack that contains information about the bald eagles of the park and butterfly trail, check list, bird list, park map, camping information and more.

EMERGENCY NUMBERS: 911 system; state police 355-8945.

CAMPGROUND: The Russell P. Letterman Campground (101 sites) features a contact station and 17 class A electrical hookup sites scattered along the twin loops. The grounds and landscaping are new, and little shade (bring your sun screen!). All handicapped sites are hard-surface and near the modern washrooms.

The Letterman campground is open from the second Friday in April until the end of antlerless deer season. Virtually any size RV rig can fit on the large pads. Depending on availability, firewood is offered for campers use. All of the sites have hard-surfaced pads, well-maintained picnic tables and ground-mounted fire rings. Site numbers are stenciled on the blacktop pads of each site.

The electric camping sites fill up first. Sites 11 to 27 can be wet, especially early in the year or after considerable rain spells that might cause

15

flooding. Sites 44, 47, 48, 49, 82, 85 and 100 have some shade in the flat campground, which has a distant mountain view and is near open fields. Sites 62-65 are divided by some vegetation.

Thirty-five tent (primitive) and 35 RV camping sites are on the backside (east) of the lake strung along a narrow tree-lined gravel road that's on a wooded ridge line above the lake. Forested ravines and shady tracts surround the oblong walk-in camping loop. Campers should set up before registration. Many of the sites are slightly off the road and nestled under tall trees. Three rest rooms serve the rustic loop, and a footpath connects the area to the lake and mooring docks. Picnic tables and ground-mounted fire rings are on each camping site. Most of the sites are spaced at least 50 yards apart for privacy.

Sites 37 and 41 are two of the nicer spots in the rustic campground. An open sunny site in this loop is 63, while site 61 is also popular. An extra car (or boat trailer) parking area is near the entrance to the wooded tent camping drive.

FISHING: The irregular shoreline of the 1,730-acre Foster Joseph Sayers Dam & Reservoir (the lake has 23 miles of shoreline) offers bass anglers many places to cast buzzbaits and crankbaits, and to explore. These same anglers can find many underwater points and places where depth changes may hold species like crappies, panfish, muskie, catfish and perch. Other species include pumpkinseed, bluegill, walleye, large- and smallmouth bass, sucker, bullhead and common carp.

Local muskie anglers tend to use rattle baits and cigar-sized trolling lures. Smallmouth bass anglers say color and presentation are important on this busy lake. Early and later season fishing are best, before and after motor boats, jet boats and skiers have turned the surface into a foam.

Many anglers like to start their exploration of the lake near Hunter's Run Cove at the northeast end of the lake. The cove can produce good bass fishing in the spring. Although there is no map depicting the underwater structure, underwater materials have been expanded over the years. Visiting anglers may want to watch what the others are doing and where, and copy them, if they are catching fish. Wooden fish cover structure has been installed in the lake.

BOATING: Unlimited horsepower boats are the big draw at Bald Eagle State Park. The six launches at Bald Eagle have hard-surfaced ramps

Near the popular beach is a food concession, bathhouse and play equipment.

and can accommodate cruiser-sized boats. Three launches are open 24 hours a day. Dry mooring for area boaters is available west of the marina. A small yacht club operates out of the newer marina that has eight sets of floating docks. At these long docks, many types of boats bob gently, waiting for their owners to take them for a cruise on the shimmering eight-mile-long lake.

Pontoons, runabouts, Jet Skis, fishing boats, 14-foot rowboats, pedal boats and ski boats are available from the brick boat rental concession. Paddles, ores, lifejackets, ropes, skis and battery jumpers can also be rented. The modern marine store, with large windows overlooking the docks and lake, is on a knoll and also sells coffee, soft drinks, sunglasses, insect repellent, flotation devices, T-shirts, simple fishing tackle, camping necessities and snack foods.

HIKING: The unit maintains 7.5 miles of easy hiking trails. The most popular one of which is the butterfly trail and garden loop. The Lakeside Trail, on the southeast shore of the lake, is very rugged and accessible from the primitive campground or the boat launch at Howard. There are about 7.5 miles of trails south of PA Route 150. On the north side of Route 150, skiers and hikers can use four miles of moderate trails that explore mixed woods and open fields.

DAY-USE AREAS: The unit has two large picnic areas complete with tables, grills, rest rooms, game fields and open spaces near parking. The park has nine rental pavilions.

The Schencks Grove picnic area is on a point of land about one-half mile from the popular beach and busy marina. The grove has many sun-drenched areas and shady clusters of trees with about 200 picnic tables scattered about. Two rest room buildings, two play fields, four volleyball courts and horseshoe pits are also in this day-use area.

The Skyline Drive day-use area is also a ridge overlooking the lake with one picnic pavilion and more than 100 picnic tables and a few pedestal grills. The linear area has four rest room buildings, play fields, volleyball court and mixed open and shady terrain. The view of the lake and surrounding hazy mountains offers picnickers an excellent location for a lunch or family reunion. When you look toward the lake, it's often busy with water skiers, fishermen and pleasure cruisers. Evening is a terrific time to drive, bike, in-line skate or walk Skyline Drive.

SWIMMING BEACH: Along the sandy beach is large and interestingly designed timber-frame play equipment. The bulky climbers and arched elements seem to be as busy as the actual beach, where waters lap against the firmly packed sandy shore. The play equipment is set on a deep sandy surface.

The swimming beach, on a double open cove, stretches about 400 yards long and 25 yards wide. About six acres of mowed, open day-use area is adjacent to the beach. The bathhouse, with a wood shingle roof, serves swimmers and is central to surrounding day-use amenities.

Picnic tables rest in front of the walk-up food concession stand that serves all your favorite snacks including candy, cold drinks, burgers, ice cream (including Scooters and hand-dipped cones), fried foods and lots more.

NATURE: Habitats at Bald Eagle are varied, with large mowed areas and open spaces interspersed with deciduous forest, marsh, old fields, scrub brush, small ponds and the large and deep reservoir lake.

As expected, park visitors can view an occasional migrating bald eagle in the spring (usually in the Greens' Run area), if you are lucky and persistent. A few of the big birds of prey, which have a seven-foot wing-span, can be seen during the fall. Equally impressive are a few golden eagles that bi-annually migrate over the park scanning the shallows, sometimes stopping for rest and feeding. Large rafts of waterfowl and shorebirds also drop into the lake when they are on their migratory course north or south.

About 230 species of birds have been recorded at the park over the past decade, including 28 warbler species.

The butterfly trail at the unit was the first of its kind in the park system, built in the early 1990s. (See the R.B. Winter State Park for details on butterfly gardens and plant material list). The 1.2-mile trail is a former exercise trail that winds through sunny meadows and loops by a large pond. The park began planting wildflowers and shrubs in 1992 and opened the trail in 1993, becoming one of the first interpretive trails in the state to be dedicated to butterflies. The trail is dedicated to teaching about insects, which compose 90 percent of all species on earth–and to better explain their role in the natural world. About 35 species of butterflies have been recorded in the park.

The pleasant trail includes blooms and plants that suit each life stage, plus a shelter to protect fragile butterflies during heavy rains. The garden offers large splashes of color, great for attracting passing butterflies and soothing passing park visitors. There are no steep grades and the trail is suitable for all ages.

Although the park is heavily used, dedicated naturalists can find a number of animals, including the fox, snapping turtles, spring peepers, black rat snake, northern water snake, painted turtle, box turtle, deer, woodchuck, gray squirrel, tundra swan, woodcock, ruddy duck, black duck, osprey, marsh hawk and many others.

Bring your cross-country skis when the conditions warrant and try the 10 miles of trails north of Route 150 or the challenging seven miles of trails in the main park area. Ice skating, ice boating and ice fishing are also enjoyed on the lake. Sledders can also slip and slid at the park when snow conditions permit.

About 4,200 acres in the park are open to seasonal hunting. Deer and small game hunting are popular. Call the park manager for details.

Buy or borrow a butterfly field guide (and binoculars). You'll be amazed at the beauty and diversity of the delicate creatures when you start to examine them.

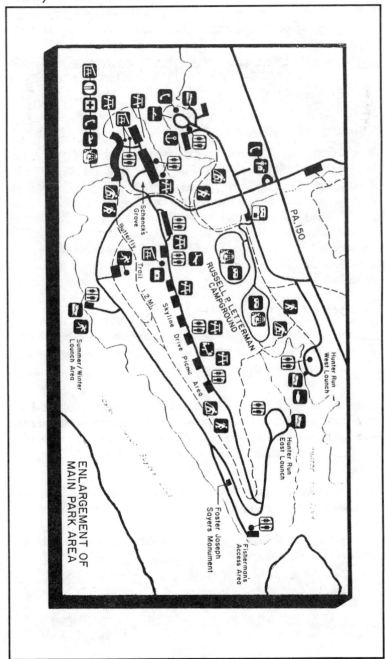

ENLARGEMENT OF MAIN PARK AREA

2 Beltzville State Park
Land: 2,023 acres Water: 949-acre lake

Behind the 170-foot-tall dam is the well-manicured and busy Beltzville State Park. In the summer the park is the playground of speed boats, Jet Skis and all sorts of revving pleasure crafts. Water skiers, fishermen and even human-powered watercraft carve the surface of the lake. There can be hundreds of boats on the lake on a warm summer weekend. This is a high-energy boater's lake, with a large beach.

The Beltzville Dam, built and operated by the U.S. Army Corps of Engineers since 1972, has 1,300 feet wide base. The top of the dam is a mere 30-feet wide. The drainage area of the dam is 96 square miles. The small visitor center at the dam features a diorama of the dam, brochures, a great view of the lake and state park from observation windows. The Philadelphia District, which is responsible for a huge watershed, including the operation of the Delaware River channel, Chesapeake channel, five flood control dams, beach erosion control projects and water supply.

Beltzville State Park is along Pohopoco Creek amid rolling farmlands, woodlots, orchards and pastoral expanses. About eight months out of the year, when the powerboats aren't on the lake, the park is a pleasant place to hike and look for wildlife. Spring and autumn bring rafts of waterfowl to the lake and cheery songbirds to the tree tops and forest floors. Fall is a wonderful, colorful time to view lesser scaup and black duck, Canada geese and birds of prey that often circle the lake and soar over the shoreline and empty parking lots riding updrafts looking for dinner.

The mixture of habitats offer visitors a chance to spot common mammals, such as deer, raccoon, skunks, squirrels, mice, fox and opossums. More woodland creatures that are seen along the trail system might be ruffed grouse, woodpeckers, turkey vultures, screech owls, box turtles and a host of woodland songbirds. The wildlife management area, east of the main day-use amenities offers an excellent place to view wildlife or practice your photography skills.

Information and Activities

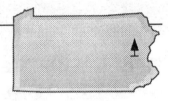

Beltzville State Park
2950 Pohopoco Drive
Lehighton, PA 18235-8905
(610) 377-0045

DIRECTIONS: Five miles east of Lehighton, off U.S. Route 209 in Carbon County. The red-brick office is open 8 a.m. - 4 p.m. Monday - Friday, seven days per week inthe summer. No overnight camping (including boats) is allowed in the park.

BOATING: Large private marinas and boat service facilities, nearby offer sales, service, marine supplies and fuel. A courtesy dock at the beach allows boaters to pull up and stop for one minute to load or unload passengers.

The large boat rental concession offers rooster-tail shooting Jet Skies, pontoon boats, tubes, rowboats and other motorized watercraft. The brick concession that is on a ridge above the lake and looks down on a floating dock, also sells fuel and rents water-skis.

Boaters should obtain a map and talk with park staff, if necessary, to understand the location of the water skiing and no wake zones.

FISHING: Over 19 miles of shoreline offers plenty of places to explore. The best fishing, both for biological reasons and due to crowds (Jet Skis and power boats), is spring and fall. The lake is stocked with

The park is high energy, with plenty of fine day-use amenities.

warmwater species including bass, walleye, muskie and perch. Pohopoco Creek, below the dam, is stocked with trout.

Most of the lakeshore is accessible to bank fishermen.

HIKING: From easy to moderately difficult, the parks 15 miles of trails includes a hike near an old gristmill raceway, water dams and gateways, small ponds and a stream, a slate quarry that was operated in the 1700s.

DAY-USE AREAS: Large open, mowed and wooded picnic areas are in the main day-use area near the beach. Modern rest rooms, water fountains, creative timber-frame play apparatus and temporary boat mooring is provided. Volleyball, horseshoes and other field games can be played in the day-use area.

Some of the most pleasant picnic sites are under conifers, about 100 yards from the busy beach where the aroma of barbecue chicken is intoxicating.

SWIMMING BEACH: Jumbo hard-surfaced parking lots serve the main day-use and beach on the north shore of the long, narrow lake. The beach is one of the largest in the state park system. Lifeguards patrol the designated beach that reaches about five-feet in depth. The lake is tree-lined. A simple handicapped access ramp allows people with disabilities to safely enter the cool waters of the lake.

Along a ridge just above the beach are flush toilets and an open-air changing room near the three-window food concession and park store. The concession and store is in a red brick building and features beach toys, T-shirts, playing cards, mugs, ice cream, soft drinks, popcorn, candy, sandwiches and simple grill items.

Sunbathers will enjoy watching the antics of Jet Skiers and the crowd of boats on the lake. The beach is open 11 a.m. - 7 p.m. Memorial Day weekend to Labor Day.

NATURE: The small visitors center is the focal point for outdoor education programs. Seasonal programs are offered for all ages. Birding is good at the park. About 220 species have been identified since the park opened in the early 1970s. Migrant waterfowl rest and feed on the lake including horned grebe, scaup, bufflehead, common ducks, Canada geese and common loons. Orchard and northern orioles are often seen in fields, while warblers are best viewed from wooded trails at the east end of the park.

WINTER: Bring your ice skates, ice boat, ice fishing rod or cross-country skies to Beltzville. The fun never stops. Nine miles of cross-country ski trails are available.

HUNTING: About 1,700 acres are open to hunting. Call for details.

INSIDERS TIPS: This is a high energy boating lake during the summer. For quieter visits, come during the spring, fall or winter.

3 Bendigo State Park
Land: 100 acres   Water: Swimming pool/river

The day-use park entrance is lined with tall spruce that seem to sway in slow motion when breezes circle their tops.

The 100-acre park was named after the former town of Bendigo by Alfred Truman in 1895. The town was named by the Pennsylvania Railroad after William Thompson, an English boxer who fought under the name Bendigo.

Because the ring fights were illegal, Thompson was arrested 28 times for violating the anti-fighting law. After his boxing career he became a noted Methodist evangelist.

Kinzua Bridge State Park is a famous landmark four miles north of U.S. Route 6 at Mt. Jewett. The park facilities are on the south end of the huge bridge and include picnic tables, interpretive kiosk, group tent camping and a scenic overlook. The long erector-set-like viaduct was placed on the National Register of Historic Civil Engineers Landmarks in 1977.

Information and Activities

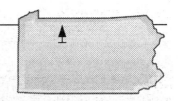

Bendigo State Park
P.O. Box A
Johnsonburg, PA 15845
(814) 965-2646

Bendigo State Park manages Elk and Kinzua Bridge state park.

DIRECTIONS: Four miles northeast of Johnsonburg on Route 24201, off U. S. Route 219. The park office is under the tall communications tower and attached to the maintenance facilities.

EMERGENCY NUMBER: 911 system.

DAY-USE AREA: About 150 picnic tables are scattered around the mowed linear park and along the creek. Most of the picnic sites are very shady. A volleyball court is near the popular pool. Two basketball hoops are on the edge of a large hard-surfaced parking lot that serves the entire day-use area and swimming pool. Picnic shelters are available.

SWIMMING POOL: On the left side of the park entrance road, the 35- by 105-foot swimming pool has a wide concrete deck that extends to the fence. The clapboard brown changing house serves the pool from 11 a.m. - 7 p.m. Memorial Day weekend to Labor Day. Depth ranges from three to five feet.

FISHING: A three-foot-tall dam stacks the stream waters behind it, causing a dark pool to form where local anglers often cast spinning and lures made from live bait. There is about one-quarter-mile of shoreline fishing along the creek, behind the swimming pool. A small fishing pier is also in the main day-use area where families bring smaller children to try their luck in the rushing river.

WINTER: Sledding and tobogganing on designated slopes are open as weather permits.

INSIDERS TIP: The Knox, Kane Railroad travels over the Kinzua Bridge Viaduct at Kinzua State Park. To make a reservation call the railroads' Marienville office at (814) 927-6172. The ride is a thrill.

4 Black Moshannon State Park
Land: 3,394 Water: 250-acre lake

Aside from terrific amenities like the beach, rustic concession stand, CCC structures, campground, fishing and placid canoeing, the delicate bog area may be the most fascinating–and important–attraction at Black Moshannon. The unique natural area can be accessed by the Bog Trail, Moss-Hanne Trail and Star Mill Trail where a long wooden boardwalk greets eager visitors. The boardwalk allows walkers to experience the cool wetland without damaging fragile vegetation or getting their feet wet!

Black Moshannon is a blend of beauty, recreation and delicate natural areas. From the mountain lake that once stored three million feet of freshly cut timber, to rafts of lilies and the history of the old logging boom town Antes, the shores of the lake and environs today attract lazy geese, fishermen and family vacationers.

Some nights it so still in the campground that the campfire smoke fills the air like incense. Nearly 350,000 people annually visit, ranking Black Moshannon in the top 25 parks in the state. The nearest store, other than the friendly, but modest park concession, is eight miles away. There are no malls out here in the sprawling state forest.

In the late 1880s a small lumbering town called Antes was within the park boundaries. The town was on the old Erie Turnpike that connected Philadelphia and Erie and was comprised of a hotel, general store, blacksmith, livery stable, shingle mill, lumber mill, school and a large ten pin bowling alley. The town was a popular stop-off for stage coaches and drivers traveling the dusty turnpike.

Although the first dam was built by beavers, a sawmill later built their own dam to power the lumbering of virgin white pine. The trained eye can still see remnants of this era's activity. In the mid-1930s the area was a Civilian Conservation Corp project site and the park was born.

Information and Activities

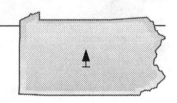

Black Moshannon State Park
R. R. 1, Box 183
Philipsburg, PA 16866-9519
(814) 342-5960
(814) 342-5777 - campground

DIRECTIONS: In Centre County on PA Route 504, nine miles east of Philipsburg. The park office is open 8 a.m. - 4 p.m.

CAMPGROUND: The booth-like contact station is generally open in season, Thursday-Saturday 2:15 -10 p.m. Moshannon's camping area is a on a linear ridge above the lake, near the day-use areas and is rolling and heavily wooded terrain. Most sites have chipped stone and gravel pads, picnic tables and fire rings. Some sites are separated by a thin wall of vegetation. Campers with medium to large RV rigs will need to look around to find sites large enough for their vehicles. The brick showerhouses are modern and have outside sinks that serve all of the 80 camping sites. The campground is full on holiday weekends.

Tent campers will like wooded and private sites 16, 41 and 44. Sites in loop 71-80 are tightly packed, small and not all are level. Grassy and reservable on holidays, site 52 is popular for medium-sized rigs or tents. Sites 68-70 at the end of a spur are private under mature pines. A trail at these sites leads to the day-use area where the popular food concession and other amenities are clustered. These are the choice sites in the campground.

Organized group camping for up to 120 is available in the park.

There are 16 miles of trails in the park.

CABINS: Fifteen of the cabins are open from the second Friday in April until the end of antlerless deer season in late December, the heavily wooded park has 20 rustic family cabins that are reservable. Five cabins are open year-round. The cabins are sparsely furnished, but clean and quiet. Furnishings include a modern stove and refrigerator, electric lights and fireplace. Wood is provided whenever possible in the area. Five of the cabins sleep six.

The roadway back to the loop of cabins off of PA Route 504 is like driving through a living tunnel. The high canopy of tree limbs reach toward each other covering and shading the narrow lane.

Cabins 15 and 18, 19 are notched out of the woods and have a gravel porch-side parking area for two cars. The private spot is ideal for a week-long stay in the newer brown log-style cabins. Most of the other cabins have green roofs and stone chimneys and are old log buildings that are well-maintained and heavily used by families during the summer months. The cabins are scattered along a ridge and have a view of the thickly forested valley and mountains in the distance.

Cabin 1 is private and all of the units have picnic tables and grills. All of the cabins are well shaded and near the modern showerhouses with

29

outdoor sinks. Maybe the most private of the cabins is clapboard-style No. 13. It also has a partial view of the lake in the distance and is next to the Seneca Trailhead.

Cabin 20 is a remodeled ski lodge that is now a popular cabin that sleeps eight and has a view from a wall of windows down the former ski slope into the wooded valley. The modern brick cabin has two-stories, vaulted ceilings, with three bedrooms and modern facilities. This cabin is handicapped accessible and has a large outdoor deck. This cabin is highly recommended for large families that want to be away from other campers, cabins and day-user distractions. There is parking for over 150 cars in the large hard-surfaced parking lot that once served the ski hill. Bring your in-line skates.

FISHING: The warm water lake can be fished from shore or small non-powered or electric powered boats. Panfish and other warm water game fish (pike and bass) can be taken year-round. The best action in the shallow lake is spring and fall, using live bait, bobbers and patience.

Trout fisherman can go off site and explore a number of mountain streams including Six Mile Run, Black Bear Run, Black Moshannon Creek and Bald Eagle Creek. The amber-stained waters of these little rocky streams offer excellent scenery and fair to good fishing. The best access to these streams is by walking in. Regular hatches along the streams include Hendricksons, in early May; brown drakes in late May; with Adam's, light Cahills, caddis, stoneflies and sulphurs working well during the spring and summer season.

Ice fishing is fair to good on the lake.

HIKING/BIKING: Trails for snowmobiles and mountain bikes (non-motorized) are blazed with orange diamonds. Within the state park only the Snowmobile and Dry Hollow trails are open. Most unpaved roads, trails and old woods roads in the surrounding state forest are open. Hiking trails can be challenging, talk with the staff about grades and degree of difficulty. There are 16 miles of trails in the park. Two miles of trails provide access, plus the nearby state forest trail network and unpaved roads.

Bog Trail (.5 mile loop) has a elevated, handicapped accessible walkway that takes hikers out into the bog to examine sphagnum moss, leatherleaf, sedges, blueberries, carnivorous plants, lilies and rushes.

Moss-Hanne Trail (10.7 mile loop) traverses pine plantations, hemlock bottom land, spruce groves, marsh edges and beaver ponds. Two boardwalks help keep travelers dry, but depending on the weather the alder swamp and other areas can be very wet.

Hay Road Trail (1.1 miles) A gentle walk eases through a mature mixed oak forest with a black cherry understory.

Star Mill Trail (2 mile loop) offers fine views of the lake and lake inhabitants, plus a scenic walk through a pine plantation, balsam fir and forest of beech and hemlock. Traces of the century old timber mill can also be seen.

Ski Slope Trail (2.2 mile loop) offers some steep climbs to the top of Rattlesnake Mountain. Chestnut oaks, bracken ferns, sarsaparilla and mountain laurel are found along the way.

Sleepy Hollow Trail (.6 mile) head is only one-quarter mile from the campground. Wild turkey, deer and songbirds are abundant in the areas that are regenerating after some lumber took place in the mid-1980s. The area now offers plentiful food sources for many species.

Dry Hollow Trail (1.7 miles) has a wonderful mountain laurel bloom from May to late June. From rocky sections, along a valley to open woods, the trails is moderately difficult and passes a vernal pond. Dry Hollow is a good way to reach the state forest trails.

CANOEING: Canoes and paddle boats are available for rent from a tan-colored shelter-like building on the lake. Only non-powered or electric powered boats are permitted on the shallow upside-down Y-shaped lake that from the dam at the north, splits into two southern branches. The Black Moshannon lake is within a bog and offers canoeists a fascinating look at an unusual ecosystem. The best paddling is in the southern branches of the quiet lake.

The lake, like the park, gets its name from the Indian word *"Moss-hanne,"* meaning "moose stream." And the name "black" from the tannin-producing sphagnum moss and oak leaves. From the water you will see leatherleaf and thickets of dense blueberries that line the shore. On shore, from a boardwalk, visitors can also see other interesting flora including the carnivorous swollen bladderwort, Northern pitcher plants, round-leaved sundew, sedges and other bog-loving wildflowers.

Quiet paddlers in the early evening might also spot active beavers that venture near the lake and are always busy on their streamside dams near the west side of the lake. When on land, look for signs of beaver that include freshly cut sapling and trees. Staff reports canoeists some-times see bear along the berry patches and on the Moss-Hanne Trail south of the lake. Also in the south part of the lake are rafts of floating yellow and white water lilies.

The isolated wilderness lake is really a biological wonderland of inter-esting plants like the football-shaped water shield plant, large lily beds, bog habitats and the towering white pines that dominate this north woods.

DAY-USE AREAS: Visitors love the friendly park store/concession stand that is outfitted with five wood booths, grill and a picnic table inside. The rustic CCC log building has a log beam high ceiling, large fire-place, cold drinks, crafts for sale, candy, milk, firewood and other sim-ple supplies. The concession looks and fits perfectly into the park set-ting. A small chapel is next to the food concession.

Much of the day-use amenities are near the concession stand including several picnic shelters, tables and open spaces along the water's edge. About 250 picnic tables and eight timber and stone (most constructed by the Civilian Conservation Corps) pavilions are in four areas, open year-round.

BEACH: Fresh yellow sand is trucked in each year and spread out on the 125-yard-long beach. The beach is only open when its guarded, about 11 a.m. - 7 p.m., Memorial Day weekend to Labor Day. The deepest point in the designated area is five feet. The beach is handi-capped accessible. The beach is busy on holidays and about 200-300 swimmers attend on summer weekdays. The tan-colored beachhouse is along the knee-high brick retaining wall that outlines the beach.

TRAP SHOOTNG: Open occasionally, the range is operated by a local club.

NATURE: Seasonal naturalist programs are offered from Memorial Day weekend to Labor Day, featuring trout fishing programs, guided nature hikes and evening campfire programs. In fact, staff believes that the diversity and quality of the environmental education programs are a primary reason park users visit time and again. The park attracts some fine seasonal naturalist staff members from the state university.

Moshannon is on the Allegheny Front. The underlying rock formations are of the Pennsylvania series showing at the surface as part of the Pocono formation. Bituminous coal is mined a few miles west of the park, and at one time clay was also mined near the park.

Common loons (and other waterfowl including old squaw, tundra swans, Canada geese, scaup, etc.) drop into the quiet lake each spring and fall, but not staying to nest. The exposed mudflats are often filled with shorebirds probing the soils for morsel and wading carefully along the ribbons of mud and shallows. Forest dwellers include pileated woodpeckers, ravens, grouse, wild turkey, scarlet tanagers, chickadees and warblers.

The wetlands, surrounded by second growth hardwoods also support box turtles, timber rattlesnakes, wood frogs, water snakes, snapping turtles and deep-voiced bull frogs. Bats also put on a show at dusk darting for their evening feast of flying insects.

The elevation of the park is the big reason for the Canada-like bog and diverse ecosystems.

HUNTING: 3,000 acres are open to hunting. Contact the park superintendent for details. Deer, black bear, wild turkey grouse and squirrel are common game species.

WINTER: This year try some ice sports. Moshannon State Park accommodates ice skating, ice fishing and ice boating (permit required). There are also about 12 miles of cross-country skiing trails.

INSIDERS TIPS: Watch for occasional National Guard aircraft in the area general. They now operated out of a nearby airport and have assisted the park by using their large helicopter to lower a 30-foot-long wooden footbridge. Moshannon has an active fire tower that is manned as conditions warrant. Hike the elevated boardwalk into the bog!

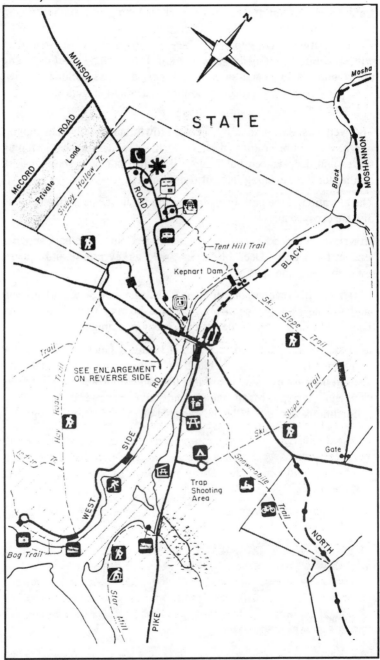

5 Blue Knob State Park
Land: 5,614 acres Water: Streams

Blue Knob State Park is named after the splendid quartzite peak, Blue Knob, the second highest point in the state at 3,146 feet above sea level. The mountain is only 67 feet less than Pennsylvania's tallest mountain, Mount Davis, in Somerset County. But because Blue Knob is on a beautiful spur of the Allegheny Front, its scenic views are much better. The tree-covered ridges, rounded mountaintop that sometimes touches the clouds and lush valleys are the most spectacular in the Commonwealth.

The wilderness park draws people who enjoy a variety of recreational opportunities during all seasons. Some facilities close after Labor Day, but lands are open for use year-round.

In 1936, the former Department of Forest and Waters surveyed the Commonwealth in search of state park sites. The need for a comprehensive park near Altoona and Johnstown was identified. Within a short time, the federal government purchased the land around Blue Knob as a special project area.

The National Park Service, with the able help of the Civilian

Pennsylvania State Parks

Conservation Corps (CCC), began work on what was called the Blue Knob Recreation Demonstration Area, one of several special projects nationally.

On September 26, 1945, the scenic tract was transferred to the Commonwealth and became known as Blue Knob State Park.

Information and Activities

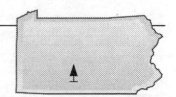

Blue Knob State Park
R. D. 1, Box 449
Imler, PA 16655
(814) 276-3576

DIRECTIONS: The park is in the northwestern tip of Bedford County, west of U.S. Route 220.   Several roads between Bedford and Duncansville serve as access roads.

CAMPGROUND: The wilderness retreat-style campground is the highest in the state. It's also one of the quietest and most secluded. There are no electrical power, showers or water hook-ups in the Blue Knob campground that is open the second Friday in April to the third Sunday in October. There are 42 sites. There is no contact station in the campground. You can go in, pick your site and the rangers will collect the fee, or stop by the office to register. The family campground, rarely full, is not within walking distance to the public swimming pool.

The campground is laid out in two simple loops, with lots of mowed open space in the middle of the loops. Sites 7 and 8 are hard-surfaced and handicapped accessible near the rest rooms. The campground is dimly lit–and that's fine with most campers, especially tent campers, who can set up in the woods near the sites marked, 40, 41 and 42.

Sites 15-18 and 25 are secluded and spread out. In fact, all of the sites are well separated, private and dry. Sites 38 and 39 are sunny. Sites 26-28 are great for small RV rigs or tents. Although play equipment is sparse, the pristine natural areas, walking trails and open spaces will entertain campers for days. Bring your volleyball; there is a court in the campground.

Group camp by advanced registration is available for youth and church organizations.

EMERGENCY NUMBER: 911 system.

FISHING: Many area creeks are stocked with trout, and some have natural reproduction.

The most famous of the area's trout streams is Bob's Creek, which routinely gives up 15-inch browns and brookies. In the upper reaches, in the game lands, access is only steps away. Bob's Creek, and the entire watershed, have suffered from the effects of acid rain and many anglers are worried but willing to work to protect the lovely rock-strewn stream. Bob's Creek offers a delightful mix of meadow and forest fishing.

May and early June can produce some good green drake hatches, huge mayflies also get the big fish to rise well into June. In July and August, slate drakes and blue quills hatch. Stoneflies and caddis are also in good numbers. In fact, rusty caddis is a favorite fly during a large part of the season. Other fly choices should include Adams, Hendrickson, March brown, light Cahills, terrestrials and stoneflies.

Bass anglers might try the junction of Dunning Creek and the Raytowns Branch near the Bedford interchange of the turnpike downstream to the Bedford-Huntingdon county line.

HIKING: The Lost Turkey Backpacking Trail will take the average hiker about two days to complete. Access points to the wilderness trail are few. From the state park you can get on the trail at Herman Point, northwest of the park office about three-quarters of a mile. The trailhead is near the fire town (and various antennas) at the top of the mountain. The first 12 miles of the 26.3-mile-long-trail is difficult, up and down hiking through mountainous terrain. Much of the trail was built in 1977 by the Youth Conservation Corp, with additions and improvements yearly.

To hike Lost Turkey you must register at the office, where you can pick up a topographic map and advice about trail conditions and camping sites. Some of the trail is on an old rail bed. The trail has mileage marked in kilometers, the first metric trail in the country. Much of the meandering trail winds through state game lands. Along the trail you will cover stone steps, remnants of other trails and abandoned roadways, campsites, the Lost Cox Children's memorial caged in a cyclone fence along a wooded creek, powerline swath, creeks, view points and lots of flora and fauna.

Mountain View Trail (5 miles) is the wilderness trail within the park. The first section of the trail is easy walking called the "look out" loop that descends along Beaverdam Creek before extending along the eastern slope of the mountain to the Willow Springs picnic area. From here the trail become difficult, crossing steep and rugged tracts. Use caution due to the high elevation if the weather is inclement.

Three Springs Trail (5 miles) is a wide, gentle mountain trail to the Willow Springs picnic area, with view of the lowlands some 2,000 feet below.

Other trails are generally easy, wooded and dotted with open spaces and great views. The Homestead Trail (1.8 miles) winds through some old homesteads and has some gentle uphill travel that is suitable for the entire family.

BRIDLE TRAILS: A staging area for horsemen is across from the campground entrance at Chappel Field and the pull-off on Ickes Hill. Horseback riding is permitted on open park roads. Groups must register at the park office.

CROSS-COUNTRY SKIING: Blue Knob is one of the few state parks with consistent snow from late November to spring. Many avid skiers use two cars for linear ski trips. Most service roads, closed roads and other trails can be used by skiers. Blue Knob can be a great place for beginning skiers, but steep hills and mountains make it the ideal place for intermediate to experts to ply their skill.

DAY-USE AREAS: Some of the best day-use areas surround the pool. The park has more than 200 picnic tables scattered around the unit, and there are six day-use shelters that may be reserved in advance by contacting the park office. A special handicapped accessible picnic shelter is near the swimming pool.

SWIMMING POOL: The mountaintop swimming pool, which may have the best view of any pool in the state, is two-feet-deep in the shallow end and five feet deep in the other end. There are lifeguard chairs on each end of the blue pool that is open Memorial Day weekend to Labor Day, 11 a.m. - 7 p.m. daily. There are four shinny ladders in the pool and the deck is about 25 yards wide. The entire facility is fenced and clean. There are no diving, food or drinks at the pool. Some of the pool deck is shaded during portions of the day. The brown dressing stockade that looks down upon the pool has several simple benches inside and is open during pool hours. Three benches near the parking lot are restful places to watch the kids frolic in the cool pool waters.

NATURE: Birding records are sparse, but because of the elevation many northern species frequent the park. The park has good migrations and ruffed grouse are commonly seen.

WINTER: Winter sports are encouraged at the state's highest park. Snowmobiling is permitted on marked routes only. The trail system consists of about eight miles of trails and roads.

HUNTING: More than 5,000 acres are open to hunting after Labor Day. Common game species include deer, squirrel, grouse and turkey. Call for details about the spring turkey season. The park is adjacent to the 12,000-acre State Game Area No. 26, one of the largest game land in the Commonwealth.

NEARBY ATTRACTIONS: The marble monument to the Lost Children was dedicated on May 8, 1906. "The Lost Children of the Alleghenies" were found here in 1856, by Jacob Dibert and Harrison Wysong. The monuments represent a sad story of young George and Joseph Cox, wandered from their cabin home one morning. Their tiny, scratched bodies with torn clothes were found several days later.

Legend has it that Joseph, the youngest (5 years old) died first, and that George had put his cap on a flat rock to make a pillow for the little fellow's head. The trail to the monument is off a simple gravel township road.

Blue Knob ski resort, a privately operated slope on leased park lands, is open for downhill skiing. Call (814) 239-5111 for information on snow conditions, ski schools, group lessons, lodging and special events.

INSIDERS TIPS: Six vistas provide a view of the view of the tangled ridges and canyons of the Allegheny Front. Annual snowfall is 12 feet. During the summer, the park is several degrees cooler than surrounding cities—keep that sweatshirt on!

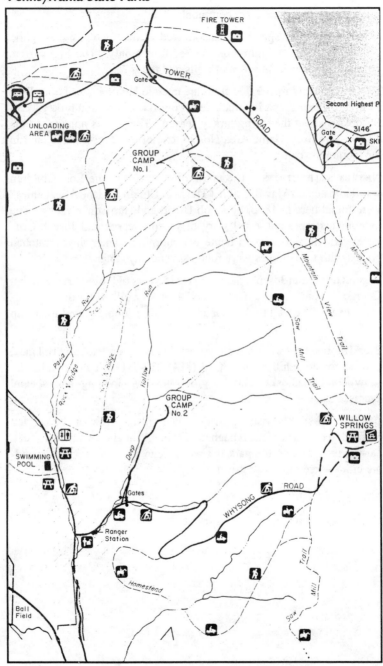

6 Caledonia State Park
Land: 1,130 acres Water' Streams and a pond

Caledonia State Park has as many diversions and attractions as any park in the state. It's hard to slow down. Many visitors want to blast from one feature to the next. Go swimming, play golf, take in a summer stock show, hike, fish and more!

But my advice is to slow down. Don't be in a hurry. Take your time to "window shop" around this full-feature park. Walk slowly, be observant, enjoy nature–then grab your swimsuit, nine iron or fly rod and really *GO NUTS.*

The colorful, varied park is named after famed abolitionist, statesman and father of the public school system, Thaddeus Stevens. He was also the founder of the huge charcoal iron furnace that began operation in 1837.   During the Civil War, the forested region was visited by Confederate troops. The war between the North and the South, and in part due to Stevens' views on slavery, resulted in the destruction of the furnace in June 1863 by Confederate Cavalrymen under the control of General J. A. Early.

Pennsylvania State Parks

The Pennsylvania Alpine Club reconstructed the stack of the old furnace in 1927. A reconstructed blacksmith shop and stack, which stands near the road, are the only visible reminders of the early iron works. The park is second oldest in the system. It was first operated privately and later by transportation companies which promoted and developed it as an amusement park. At one time the lush park hosted carnivals, balloon ascensions and other large events-based activities that drew huge crowds.

Caledonia is also the name given to ancient Scotland by invading Romans. Today the only invaders are peaceful park users.

Information and Activities

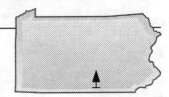

Caledonia State Park
40 Rocky Mountain Road
Fayetteville, PA 17222-9610
(717) 352-2161

DIRECTIONS: Between Adams and Franklin counties midway between Chambersburg and Gettysburg on U.S. Route 30, the park is 13 miles west of Gettysburg. The park office is north of Rt. 233, take the first left. It has a brochure rack and large map that depicts points of interest and amenities.

CAMPGROUNDS: Hosack Run Campground (55 sites) is open from the second Friday in April until the end of antlerless deer season in December. Chinquapin Hill Campground (130 sites) opens the Wednesday before Memorial Day and closes Labor Day. There are no electrical or water hookups in either camping area. Sites 8-73 are reservable on summer holiday weekends. Both camping areas have sites on multiple elevations, creating visual barriers and interest.

CHINQUAPIN HILL CAMPGROUND: Camping sites 1-20 are along the busy campground road. The amphitheater, with wooden seats and a fire ring, is behind site 14. Adjacent sites 18-20 is an excellent choice for a group of three families for a long weekend. Many of the sites at the back of the loop, from 25-36, are elevated about six feet above the roadway, offering extra privacy. Sites 42, 44, 46, 49, 51 and 53 are on a hillside above a wooded ravine. Site 56 is a good choice for those who like to be near the rest room. Sites 71 and 72 are combined, offering two families a convenient camping place.

Sites 74-130 are covered with the swaying branches of mature trees,

42

offering shade all day. The pads are hard-surfaced or gravel in both camping areas. All sites in both campgrounds have ground-mounted fire rings and picnic tables.

Site 95 is elevated and gets quite a bit of afternoon sunshine. Good, dry tent sites in this section include 97, 99, 100, 101, 103, 104 and 111. The sites are flat and you will set up your tent on crunchy leaves in the early spring and late fall. Sites 112-115 are slightly elevated up about three steps to a flat space perfect for a four-person tent.

Hosack Run Campground, which is less popular than Chinquapin Hill, offers a small playground at the back of the loop near site 160. All of the sites have gravel pads. Sites 132, 134 and 135 have some afternoon sun; most of the other sites are well shaded. Sites 137-139 are medium-sized, while 146 can accommodate larger RV rigs. 148-155 is like a common camping area where a group could occupy the entire mini-loop. Site 150-163 and 166-167 are also grouped together where several families could camp together. You can pitch your tent back into the woods a little bit at site 169. Medium-sized RV rigs can fit up against the hillside at site 172. Because 178 is so wide and shady, it is the best single site in this campground. Most of the camping sites in Hosack are on the same elevation, and the general terrain is flat. Hosack is the getaway camping area in this otherwise busy state park.

Organized group camping for 100 persons is offered to qualified groups by advance registration.

CABINS: Two cottages are rented year-round. One cottage features a 1.5-story frame house with modern kitchen, bathroom, central heat, dining room, living room and three bedrooms that sleep ten. The second is a two-story frame house with a modern kitchen, closed-in porch, 1.5 baths, dining room, living room, central heat and three bedrooms that can sleep 10. Reservations are accepted by telephone and on a first-come, first-served basis. Call the park office for information on how you can participate.

FISHING: From the bank, anglers can toss a line and bait at fish that inhabit the triangular-shaped pond. Watch children closely if you fish from the side of the pond near the park road; the road is narrow. Think of the state park as a staging area for adventures to nearby streams, including Conococheague, Rocky Mountain, and Carbaugh Creek, which flows through the park and state forest.

Fly fishermen should try such patterns as woolly bug, black gnats,

Adams, quill Gordon, royal coachman, Hendrickson, minnow imitations and soft hackle nymphs. Midges and terrestrials also work in the narrow rocky local mountain streams.

HIKING: The Whispering Pine Nature Trail has numbered posts along the trail that match the paragraphs on a four-panel guide available from the park office. As you walk, you can read the guide and discover how natural forces have interacted to make this park a special place.

You will learn about geological forces that happened 500 million years ago and how you might have been standing along a shoreline then. Other learning stations teach you about floodplain ecology, and that the park gets about 45 inches of precipitation annually. One-half inch of rain over a square mile is enough water for 600,000 people to take a bath! You'll pass some 200-year-old white pine trees and a dense understory of rhododendron. The trail has 13 stations.

Appalachian Trail (1.8 miles) is a famous hiking trail developed and maintained by the Potomac Appalachian Trail Club. It passes through the park as it traverses from Maine to Georgia. The entire trail is 2,000 miles long. An example of what can be expected along its entire length can be seen as you walk this trail in the park.

Three Valley Blue Blaze Trail (.7-mile) originates at the Ramble Trail, crosses the Chamberburg Water Pipeline, ascends 400 feet to Ore Bank Hill and terminates at the Appalachian Trail. The trail is blazed with blue. When you reach white blazes, you have reached the Appalachian Trail.

Ramble Trail (2.2 miles) is a wide hiking trail that starts at the Trail Visitors Center. It passes through scenic lowlands and returns to the swimming pool area. In its circular route, the trail follows the Old Rolling Mill Race and passes the Rolling Mill Water Falls. Here, one of the oldest white pine plantations can be seen.

Midland Trail (.7-mile) begins at the Trail Visitors Center and rambles around the day-use area. It's an easy family-style trail.

Charcoal Hearth Trail (2.7 miles) is the most rugged trail in the park. The trail starts at the falls on the Thaddeus Stevens Trail, ascends Graeffenburg Hill and terminates at Furnace Dam. About one-third of of bark with wooden rungs nailed to it, plus various anchor wires. This is reputed to have been the first fire lookout in Pennsylvania.

Thaddeus Stevens Historical Trail (.8-mile) takes about one hour and has a terrific 13-page booklet filled with line art available from the park office. The booklet asks that hikers imagine that you are visiting Caledonia in 1837. This is when Thaddeus Stevens' iron furnace community was in full operation. As hikers follow the easy-walking trail, you will see the remains of a once prosperous industrial town and learn what natural resources make it possible to manufacture iron in this area.

The trail is wildly interesting. Using your imagination, it's not always easy to think of roads with no automobiles, only dusty foot and coach travel. Although Thaddeus Stevens was never a blacksmith, but a well-known lawyer and politician, the park's blacksmith shop bears his name. The informative guide will teach walkers about cold-blast furnaces and the Caledonia Iron Furnace built in 1837. You will also see the manmade waterway dug in the 1830s to power iron furnaces, sawmills and gristmills.

The steps in making charcoal are particularly interesting. From the clear hearth and chimney building to controlling the burn and raking out the charcoal, you'll have a new appreciation for your backyard hot dog grill. Other paragraphs in the guide talk about the importance of dams and the power and usefulness of water. Appropriately, the final page of the booklet has Longfellow's classic poem, *"The Village Blacksmith,"* that begins "Under a spreading chestnut tree the village smithy stands..."

DAY-USE AREAS: Some of the picnic tables are streamside under a canopy of cool trees and connected by several wonderful stone and timber footbridges that cross the scenic creek.

TOTEM POLE PLAYHOUSE: "Pennsylvania's foremost summer theatre" features summer stock plays and performances. The professional theater has high-quality and affordable venues (musicals, comedies, reviews, etc.) that run all summer. You may order tickets or get information by calling (717) 352-2164. Or walk up to the two-window box office when visiting the park. The outdoor theater has been in operation for more than 45 years. Children will love to see the two colorful totem poles near the front entrance of the playhouse.

THADDEUS STEVENS' BLACKSMITHING SHOP: A small white stone building with wooden doors on three sides was once Stevens' metal working shop. Here staff interprets blacksmithing and more on Sundays during the summer. A small coal-fired forge and huge English leather bellows, dated 1785, are the central exhibits of the shop. Other tools include a large assortment of tongs, hammers and wares. Products that era smiths might have made include ornate hinges, calipers, ladles, a traveler, shovel plow, hog catcher, farriers' knife and small nails. Examples of carriage axles and buggy springs are also interesting displays that help us understand the lifestyle of these pioneers.

SWIMMING POOL: The rocky Conococheague Creek meanders near the swimming pool, looking every bit as inviting as the large pool with snack bar. A small admission fee gains you entry to the swimming pool, which is surrounded by hard-surfaced decks and grassy sunning areas. Lifeguard chairs stand near the pool, with nearby picnic tables a favorite spot to munch on a snack. The depth of the blue pool is from one to nine-feet-deep. The pool is in the middle of a large day-use area that includes playground equipment, field game areas and open spaces.

GOLF: Cut out of the wilderness more than 70 years ago, Caledonia Golf Club is an unpredictable layout that offers one surprise after another. The course's mountain goat terrain dictated how the course was laid out long ago, and it determines how every shot must be played now. Avid golfers say they use every club in their bag hacking around the 5,154 yards of turf, rough, hills and trees. It's a shotmakers course that rewards consistency. It is nicely maintained with well-kept greens and a cabin-style clubhouse with fireplace and golfing equipment for sale. The 18-hole course/slope rating is 67.1/118. Bring your sticks and some extra balls for this tough but scenic layout. You can rent clubs and carts at the pro shop.

NATURE: A naturalist offers campfire programs, themed nature walks and natural history activities for all ages during the summer.

The gentle mountains, rounded and covered with hardwood and evergreen forest, are separated by valleys and gurgling streams. During the battle of Gettysburg, Confederate troops used the pastures for field hospitals and the cool streams for resting and water. The open spaces around the golf course, fields and forest combine for good birding and wildlife. Some 117 birds have been identified over the years.

From the 10 miles of trails, some lucky hikers have seen flocks of 50 or more turkeys and black vultures overhead looking for their next meal. In the spring and fall migrations, 26 warbler species have been identified. Other interesting breeding birds that live in the park are barred owl (the only owl with dark-colored eyes), pileated woodpecker (they sometimes carve triangular-shaped holes in trees), whip poor will, kingfisher, veery, ovenbird, scarlet tanager, indigo bunting, rufous-sided towhee and many others.

HUNTING: Large and small game are hunted in the state forest only.

INSIDERS TIPS: Try wading the rocky creek. Don't forget your golf clubs.

NEARBY ATTRACTIONS: Michaux State Forest, (717) 352-2211;. Gettysburg National Military Park, (717) 334-6274; Franklin County Council of Tourist Promotion Agencies, (717) 334-1124.

Mont Alto State Park

In southeastern Franklin County, tiny 24-acre Mont Alto is often populated by trout anglers in waders plopping flies in Antietam Creek. The park, surrounded by the 83,949-acre Michaux State Forest, offers hiking, two picnic areas with about 50 tables and comfort facilities for snowmobilers.

Next to the site was the Mont Alto Iron Furnace, built in 1807 by Daniel and Samuel Hughes. Originally, it was 31 feet high, eight feet wide and produced 2-3 tons of iron daily.

In 1864, the furnace and associated holdings were purchased by George Weistling, who started the Mont Alto company. In a short time a railroad was built to connect with the Cumberland County Railroad, 3.5 miles northeast of Cumberland County. The trains brought visitors to the resort that was built in 1875. The park was eventually acquired by the Commonwealth in May 1902, and became the first state forest park.

Specially designed and marked picnic tables are scattered around the regional park.

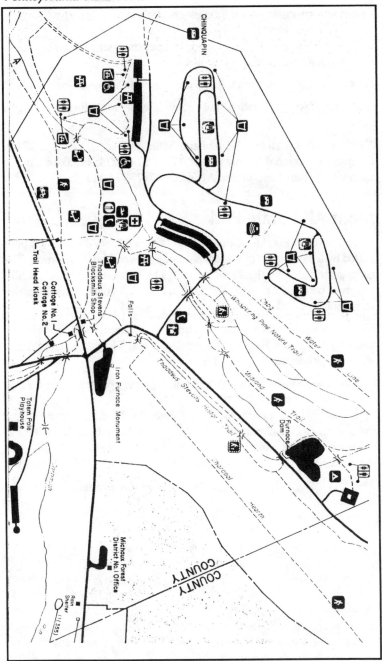

7 Canoe Creek State Park
Land: 958 acres Water: 155-acre lake

Nature lovers come to Canoe Creek for the night life. Some say they have gone batty. Actually, enthusiasts by the thousands are visiting to see bats and participating in nighttime interpretive hikes offered by the staff naturalist. The park shelters the state's largest known bat hibernating population, comprising six species.

Located in the hills of the Allegheny Mountains in the central part of the state, visitors also come for swimming, boating and fishing in the lake. But the bats have made the park famous in recent years.

Bats have hibernated for many years in an old mine at a remote end of the park. They have happily used the abandoned limestone mine that has 2.1 miles of dark tunnels. In 1978 the park, in an effort to protect the public, closed the mine by backfilling the gaping entrances. Fortunately, a biologist at Albright College in Reading learned about the closure in time for park personnel to immediately reopen the cavity where the threatened Indiana bat was known to hibernate. By 1985 the Pennsylvania Game Commission declared the mine a protected area for Indiana bats. Three years later the entrances were fitted with specially designed bat gates.

The installation of the gates and careful backfilling actually warmed the caved slightly, just enough to attract not only Indiana bats, but many little brown bats, eastern pipistrelles, big brown bats, small-footed myotis and northern myotis.

This careful, thoughtful work has created a wonderful resource where upwards to 20,000 bats annually hang out for the winter. Canoe Creek, wedged between Brush Mountain and Canoe Mountain, is comprised of mostly old farm fields, woodlands, wetland, a lake and two streams.

Information and Activities

Canoe Creek State Park
R. R. 2, Box 560
Hollidaysburg, PA 16648-9752
(814) 695-6807

DIRECTIONS: In Blair County, 12 miles east of Altoona off U.S. Route 22. The attractive wood and stone park office is open weekdays 8 a.m. - 4 p.m.

CABINS: Eight modern cabins are available year-round. The carpeted, log-style cabins sleep six people and overlook the oval lake. Cabins have modern bathrooms, a kitchen/living area, dining table with six chairs and electric heat. There are no fireplaces in Canoe Creek cabins. Each cabin does have an outdoor grill, picnic table and lawn-covered side yards.

The gravel road to the cabins can be dusty from baking in the sun. The brown cabins with shake-like roofs have porches and are open and sunny. All of the units are along a gentle rise above the lake where tiny motorless pleasure boats and canoes drift back and forth.

Cabin 5 is private, and cabin 8 has an excellent view of the broad day-use area and the lake in the distance. All of the cabins enjoy a grand view of the lush rounded mountains that wind through this part of the state. There is little shade around the cabins and throughout the entire park.

FISHING: About 20,000 trout are stocked in the lake annually, and soon mingle with a variety of warm water species including muskie, large-mouth bass, catfish, crappies, walleye and other panfish. The lake has an average depth of about 10 feet with a maximum depth of 26 feet.

The north end of the lake is the best fishing area, although many anglers bank fish from the east shore. The park has a lake map that indicates deeps and the location of some underwater structures. Live bait is the standard lure.

BOATING: From the brown-colored boat rental concession, you can rent a boat–or bring your own non-powered or electric powered craft–to enjoy the simple, quiet little lake. Canoeists would enjoy launching from the less developed eastern shore. Go early and sneak paddle to wading birds that work the narrow mudflats or see the waterfowl in the center of the lake. Early in the spring you can often see tiny goslings paddling behind protective parents. Beaver can also be seen from the lake in the shallows near Canoe Creek's mouth. Maybe the best part of canoeing the small lake the 360-degree vista. The large open shore allows paddlers a chance to relish the wonderful views of hills and farm fields that nestle the quiet waters.

HIKING: No mountain bikes are allowed on the trails, but some of the trails can be used on horseback. Most of the hiking trails are at the north end of the park, with Moore's Hill trail running along Canoe Creek and past Hartman's Kiln at the northwest tip of the property.

For a short historical hike, try the loops (Limestone Trail, near the visitor center) that take you near the remains of the Blair Co. Limestone Company, near Mary Ann's Creek. Fisherman's Path, running along the east shoreline, is easy walking and used by anglers and day users.

DAY-USE AREAS: Two volleyball courts and a ball field are near the beach and main day-use area. Canoe Creek has three rentable picnic pavilions, two on the west shore and one in the smaller day-use area on the east bank.

BEACH: Not far from the dam, on the west bank of the lake, is the 430-foot-long, horseshoe-shaped sandy swimming beach that is open 11 a.m. - 7 p.m. from Memorial Day weekend to Labor Day unless posted otherwise. A stone retaining wall outlines the tan-colored concession near the bathhouse which is complete with showers and dressing booths. The clean patio-like area around the food concession is sunny and popular during the summer months in this large, tightly-mowed day-use space.

VISITOR CENTER: The well-designed center is a focal point of environmental education programming. Perched on a ridgeline, looking down on the amphitheater and off in the distance are hazy mountains.

Pennsylvania State Parks

Maybe the most pleasing small nature center in the park system, each display inside is of the highest visual and interpretive quality. Interpretive programming is comprehensive at Canoe Creek, including activities like salamander searches, many children programs, medicinal plant walks, aquatic study, butterflies and hummingbirds, and, of course, bat hikes and evening watches.

The center houses the naturalist's office, hands-on display and a small room set up with a video player that seats 10. A variety of videotapes about bats and other wildlife can be viewed. Displays include "The Dissolving World of Limestone" (when limestone and water mix the result is often caves and sinkholes, rock formations and underground rivers), a simulated bat cave with tiny freeze-dried bat mounts hanging, the beautiful $30,000 vertical limestone kiln exhibit in a huge glass case, quarrymen of Blair County (a small diorama of a man with tools and clothing of the trade of digging and blasting in the quarry), touch table with magnifying glass, soils, mounts and more.

Most impressive is the kiln model and description. Limestone would come from the quarry to a kiln (like the one displayed) in softball-sized chunks and was converted to lime. The stone was heated to temperatures between 1,600 and 2,200 degrees, which drove out the carbon dioxide, leaving quick lime. For every 100 pounds of limestone burned, about 44 pounds of quick lime was produced. This exhibit is great. It shows the trains and chimneys of the giant kiln that once operated in the area.

The company was a subsidiary of the Jones and Laughline Steel Company of Pittsburgh. The preservation and interpretation of an industrial lime kiln site is part of the Path of Progress, a cooperation educational effort that commemorates the significant contribution the region's iron and steel industry played in the growth of the country.

In the lower level of the visitor center is a modern classroom that can easily accommodate six eight-foot tables, chairs and teaching supplies.

NATURE: Rolling open spaces dotted with young trees, small mixed woods and lake shore actually make the park a good birding destination. About 180 species have been identified at Canoe Creek since it opened in 1979. A bird list prepared by the Juniata Valley Audubon Society is available from Paula Ford, author of "Birder's Guide to Pennsylvania," by calling (814) 695-4799.

MORE ABOUT BATS: About 15,000 bats also roost in an old church near a "bat condo" to help accommodate increasing numbers of the tiny insect eaters. The condo is an insurance policy in case the church gets damaged or overpopulated.

About once a month during the summer, park naturalists conduct evening bat programs, including the careful capture of a bat or two using mist nets and light tagging them with small transparent capsules containing a safe florescent dye. The bats are then released over the lake in the dark so visitors can see the nimble acrobats hunt insects by the hundreds. The tiny capsules fall off within a few hours. The naturalists are also beginning a bat banding program that will help biologists understand population density, movement patterns, general health of the colony and so on.

In addition to this bat-related program, staff also lead visitors to a 19th century church on park property near the park entrance where the evening exodus of bats from the attic is observed. Some 13,000-15,000 bats use the attic of the small white church as a roost. As many as 150 people often collect at the abandoned church to watch action. The church has undergone a variety of repairs and improvements aimed at preserving the bat colony.

Canoe Creek is the place to visit to learn about bats. It's a terrific program.

HUNTING: About 550 acres of old farm fields provide good hunting of common species like deer, pheasant and rabbit.

WINTER: Because the park is open year-round, ice skating on a lighted, maintained two-acre portion of the lake is popular. Sledding, cross-country skiing and ice boating are other wintry recreational opportunities at Canoe Creek.

NEARBY ATTRACTIONS: Gallitzin State Forest, Beaver Dam State Game Area, various Altoona attractions, Quaint Corner Children's Museum, Swigart Museum, Horseshoe Curve, Altoona Railroaders Memorial Museum, Baker Mansion, rail trails (814-832-2400) and more. Call the Blair County Convention and Visitors Bureau for additional travel information at 800-84-ALTOONA.

INSIDERS TIP: Plan to participate in an evening bat watch and program.

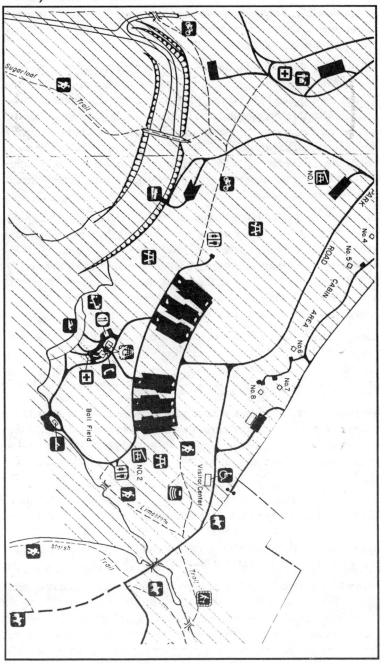

8 Chapman State Park
Land: 805 acres   Water: 68-acre lake

In the midst of the 517,000-acre Allegheny National Forest south of Warren, Chapman State Park is only five miles from Clarendon and open year-round. Chapman is one of the most innovative parks in the country for handicapped accessibility design, from modified drinking fountains with foot pedals, universal signs, kiddy seats on the end of picnic tables and an accessible ramp to the beach and boat launch. The park is leading the way in design and implementation of equipment and facilities that meet the needs of all visitors.

Chapman is a family-style park now being used by the third generation of families that come back to swim, camp, play during the winter, fish or hike the trails. The park has about 300,000 visitors annually.

The park is a great launching point for exploration of the huge Allegheny National Forest. A million years back in time, the misty mountains, deep valleys, beautiful lakes and rushing rivers were formed in this part of the state. Today this scenic heritage has been preserved in the national forest and amenities for public recreation. Vast forest and outdoor recreation opportunities are right next door when you stay or visit Chapman State Park.

The nearby Allegheny National Forest has boat launches in four counties, orienteering trails, elk herds, fish hatcheries, national scenic areas (NSA), nature/visitor centers, cross-country ski trails, snowmobile trails, more than a dozen camping areas), nearby private cabins and campgrounds, backpacking and interpretive trails, fishing, horseback riding, golf, hunting lands, mountain biking and even a scenic railroad trip. Call the headquarters for more information at (814) 723-5150.

The state park opened in 1951 and has been a member of the local chamber of commerce for many years.

Information and Activities

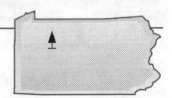

Chapman State Park
Box 1610
Clarendon, PA 16313-9607
(814) 723-0250

DIRECTIONS: In Warren County near Clarendon off U.S. Route 6, adjacent to the Allegheny National Forest and State Game Lands No. 29. The log-style park office was constructed by the Pennsylvania Conservation Corps (PCC).

EMERGENCY NUMBER: 911 system.

CAMPGROUND: The upper loop of the campground is open in early spring and later in the fall, while the lower loop is open during the summer only. The 83-site campground is open April 1 through December 15. Half of the sites can be reserved in advance. Hydrants at the park are for drinking water only; no washing of any kind is allowed at the hydrants. Hand washing sinks are provided at the rest rooms. The park has had some problems with bear getting into food containers and barrels. Plan to seal food containers and use other precautions that the staff can explain.

The upper loop has most of the electrical sites and all of the walk-ins. Electrical sites are the most requested. All of the camping sites are dry and can accommodate medium-sized RV rigs.

Most of the sites have rolled gravel pads, picnic tables and fire rings.

Sites 30-32 are popular for families with younger children who like to be near the playground. Sites 6, 8, 10 and 30 are also popular for the same reason. According to staff, site 43 (tent only) is the most popular

The lake is stocked with brook and brown trout. Most anglers use live bait.

site in the gently rolling and shady campground. Site 27 is a more private site. Many picnic tables in the campground have the unique toddler (booster-type) seats on the end of the tables.

Walk-in tent sites 72-83 are becoming increasing popular (they have been improved in recent years), as is tent camping in general at Chapman. The amphitheater, with a pull-down screen and 10 rows of wood benches with cement supports, is busy during the summer with naturalist programs.

Seasonal recreational vehicle storage can be arranged at the park.

Organized camping is at the foot of the toboggan hill near the creek in an open field. About 100 people can be accommodated with pit toilets, fire rings, picnic tables and water available in two areas. Groups must register in advance.

FISHING: Expert anglers at the popular Warren Bait and Tackle Shop suggest that you will catch the most fish if you use a bobber to cast a meal worm. Keep the meal worm about four feet below the surface. Other anglers use a split-shot above a barbed-hook with a lip hooked minnow. Still other fishermen at the lake swear by Powerbait on a treble hook. Anglers at the shop also suggested minnows as the live bait of choice. The lake is stocked with brook and brown trout. Fishermen tend to fish near the spillway after mid-May. Some anglers also congregate at the 14-foot wide handicapped fishing pier near the boat launch on the west side of the lake.

Besides trout, anglers may catch large- and smallmouth bass, sunfish, yellow perch and bluegills.

Fishing is not allowed within 100 feet of the swimming beach, but there are lots of places for shoreline fishing around the lake.

Ice fishermen use tip-ups, meal and wax worms and minnows for under-the-ice fishing. Local experts say you should move often to find the fish.

Anglers are also near the huge Allegheny Reservoir (a 12,000-acre lake, 7,634 acres in Pennsylvania) that has more than 91 miles of jagged shoreline and hundred of coves and points behind the Kinzua Dam. The entire reservoir, which stretches into New York state, is regulated and managed for sport fishing and other water-based recreation. It is a year-round trout fishery, with many feeder streams that contain rainbow, brook and brown trout, most of which are hatchery raised.

BOATING: Only non-powered and electric boats are permitted on the quiet lake. A small rental concession features canoes and paddles, yellow and white pedal boats and small V-bottom aluminum boats for rent by the hour. It's by the beach.

A small gravel, one-lane ramp and seasonal mooring sites are on the west shore of the lake.

Bring your canoe (or rent one at the park) and enjoy a quiet lake with upper reaches that hold beavers, wading birds and marshy shallows. Much of this area is heavily channeled by beavers, and there are interesting pathways everywhere to explore. A wide variety of shorebirds and waterfowl can be seen along the marshy waterway.

Much of the Tionesta Creek can be paddled, especially in the spring. Even in the summer you can travel up the channel a half-mile or more. In this stretch look for the work of beavers–freshly cut side channels, lodges piled high or snipped vegetation along the watery passage.

HIKING: A 12-mile hiking trail system is in the park. The interpretive trail, which starts in the campground, is an easy walking, shady trail with numbered posts that match a brochure.

Hunters Ridge (2.8 miles) is rugged and hilly with interesting geological features and fossils. At times the trail follows the boundary between the park and the Allegheny National Forest.

Adams Run Trail (2.9 miles) has about half its length in rugged and hilly country.

Lumber Trail (.4 mile) is on an abandoned lumbering road. Evidence of lumber can be seen along the trail, which is suitable for hikers of all ages.

Penny Run Trail (1.4 miles) winds through diverse hardwoods in the park and neighboring national forest. The trail has moderately steep uphill grades. This is a challenging ski trail.

DAY-USE AREAS: Four pavilions and 200 picnic tables are found in the park. The main day-use picnic area overlooks the swimming area. Two sandy volleyball courts are also near the swimming area.

SWIMMING BEACH: Once the sand was very white. But, says the park manager, the yellow sand is cheaper, so now the beach has very nice yellow sand along the east side of the lake. The beach is about 125 yards long and guarded from 11 a.m. - 7 p.m. from Memorial Day weekend (full time after school gets out) until Labor Day. A dressing stockade and small food concession (snack foods and ice cream) serves swimmers.

The swimming area is divided by white floating buoys and patrolled by four lifeguards. At the buoy line, the water is about six feet deep. Chapman was one of the first parks to install handicapped accessible ramp/steps into the water. There are seven steps on the ramp covered with green indoor-outdoor carpeting, which allows persons with disabilities to gently proceed into the clean lake waters.

NATURE: Seasonal naturalist programs for youth, campers and the general public are offered at Chapman. Outdoor education programs might include day hikes, night hikes, kids' hour and other interpretive programs.

Chapman has a bird checklist with about 120 species recorded in the park, with 21 confirmed breeders. Three acres of marshland, streams, mowed areas and mixed woods offer good birding. Nine species of warblers, 10 species of hawks and owls and 34 types of songbirds are seen during the year.

Tree species in the region include hemlock, black cherry, oak and ash.

Pennsylvania State Parks

HUNTING: About 400 acres of the park are open for hunting. Call the park for details.

WINTER: About two acres of the lake are shoveled off for ice skating, but as the winter goes on the size of the skating area often gets smaller. Cross-country skiers may enjoy 4.4 miles of trails that connect with numerous trials in the adjoining Allegheny National Forest and other state lands.

Seven acres of slopes are lighted and open until 10 p.m. daily for sledding and tobogganing. Staff reports that on a good wintry weekend, there can be many more visitors doing winter activities than during a nice summer weekend. The park is known for its variety of winter events, sled dog races and other cold season events.

Activities during the winter festival include bocci on the ice, golf (using tennis balls, one club, and water hazards painted on the snow with food coloring), ice fishing, skating, cross-country skiing, internationally sanctioned sled dog races, warming stations, foods and lots more fun stuff.

Winter activities are so popular, Chapman is the only state park in the system with lighted skating, sledding and tobogganing hills, parking lots and rest room areas. Lights are on until 10 p.m. when conditions warrant.

INSIDERS TIP: The park has many innovative features for persons with disabilities.

NEARBY ATTRACTIONS: Struthers Theatre in Warren, a summer stock and professional quality theater. The region has lots of attractions; for more information call (800) 624-7802.

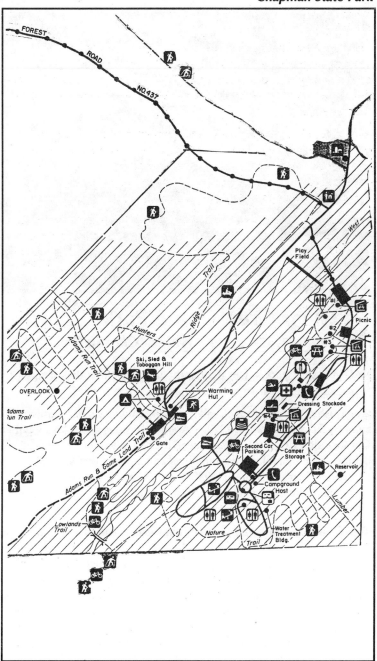

9 Clear Creek State Park
Land: 1,676 acres   Water: Clarion River

At last, a state park where the family can play while dad or mom fly fishes an almost year-round cold-water stream system.

Good fishing, hunting, cool valleys and scenic vistas brought the first campers to the park in 1922. About 10 years later, the Civilian Conservation Corps (CCC) expanded the recreational facilities and left behind some marvelous log buildings and shelters that are still in use today. By their departure in 1938, the CCC had built the family vacation cabins, the swimming areas, food concession building, comfort stations, trails, bridges and roads.

Today visitors still come to fish, hunt, camp and absorb the scenic beauty. The cold stream that runs through the valley, a tributary of the Clarion River, offers many unique habitats for mammals including gray fox, river otter, mink, chipmunks and birds. During the spring and summer, spotted fawns are often seen nibbling sprouts along wooded edge areas with their alert mothers. May is a great time to view migrating warblers that often nest in towering conifers, low saplings, shrubs and on the ground in many places around the rolling park.

Wildflower lovers will appreciate the 180 species inventoried. Early bloomers include Jack-in-the-pulpit, mayapple and painted trillium. The mixed broadleaf-coniferous forest also offers mushrooms and a wide assortment of wildflowers that enjoy the moist summer woods and valley floors.

If all of this nature isn't enough, nearby Clear Creek State Forest comprises 9,089 acres in northern Jefferson County, 3,165 acres in Venango County and 1,012 acres in southern Forest County. Like the state park, the vast state forest (and national forest) is named after the sparkling clear creeks that flow from valley to valley. The state forest has a variety of amenities including overnight camping, a trail system, swimming, day-use areas, fishing and lots more. In Venango County, the tract has more than six miles of frontage on the Allegheny River. A green-colored brochure/map is available at the park office or from the District Forest Office, 158 S. 2nd Ave., Clarion, PA 16214-1904. Call (814) 226-1901

Information and Activities

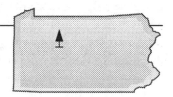

Clear Creek State Park
R. D. 1, Box 82
Sigel, PA 15860-9502
(814) 752-2368

DIRECTIONS: In Jefferson County, 12 miles from Brookville. From I-80, take exit 12 or 13 and follow the signs.

CAMPGROUND: The popular 53-space campground is almost always filled on holiday weekends and busy on summer weekends. Half of the sites are reservable during the summer season. The campground is open from the second Friday in April until the end of antlerless deer season in December. The park chaplain offers nondenominational worship services each Sunday morning during the summer.

Clear Creek has a few very private camping sites on a spur that includes 39-43. Sites along the river and creek are the most popular. Towering conifers and large open spaces also help make the small campground feel larger than it actually is.

If you like open camping sites, consider sites 10-13. They also have an excellent view of the river and the opposite shoreline at the base of a mountain. Sites 31-39 are only partly shaded and narrow, good for smaller RV units along the Clarion River. Site 53 is a favorite, located on a small ridgeline surrounded with rock outcroppings and lots of tall trees. Sites 49-52 are above sites in the 30s that stretch along the river-bank. These flat, private sites are excellent for tent camping. Generally speaking, families will love this campground. Parents can see much of the campground from any spot, making it a little easier to keep track of their youngsters.

CABINS: Clear Creek has the second-most cabins of any state park in the Commonwealth–and they are great Civilian Conservation Corps-style rustic cabins. They are open from the second Friday in April until the third Friday in December. Cabins have minimal furnishings that include bunk beds, chairs, tables, electric range, electric refrigerator and lights. Frost-free water faucets are provided outside of the cabins. About 1.5 miles from the park office, the first group of one-room cabins 1-9 and 20 (two rooms, sleeps three) are the small cabins near the tiny log cabin-style CCC-built museum at the foot of a hill and heated by wood stoves. According to staff, the most popular cabins are those along the loop above the river. A small canoe launch is next to cabin 14.

Cabins 10 and 11, perched on a mossy bluff near cabins 12 and 13, look down upon a busy day-use area. Cabins 10-23 are much more private than cabins 1-9 and 20. Heat for these cabins are provided by wood stoves and/or fireplaces. Most of the cabins sleep three or four. Because cabins 18 and 19 are quite close to each other, they would be an excellent choice for two-family vacations. Bring your mother-in-law. The compact amenities makes this park user friendly and great for kids.

EMERGENCY NUMBER: State police, (814) 938-6060.

HIKING: Think of Clear Creek as a gateway to many adjoining trail systems in the neighboring state and national forest. Inside the park are about 15 miles of maintained trails that are easy to moderate in difficulty. They pass thick patches of rhododendron and mountain laurel and through diverse habitat good for wildlife viewing. A self-guided nature trail is near the nature center/museum by cabin 20.

Clear Creek Trail (1.5 miles) an old logging trail, is the most popular, well-maintained trail in the park. The trail meanders east and west along or near the south bank of Clear Creek. The trail starts in the south beach parking lot and runs the entire length of the park. The trail ends in the camping area. The trail is easy, except at about the halfway point where a steep grade levels off in a pine and hardwood forest. The trail offers splendid views of the babbling creek and fly fishermen who wade among the slippery rocks and foam.

Hunter Trail (1.9 miles) marks the boundary between the hunting and non-hunting areas of the park. This is a wonderful trail to ski or view the yellow and crimson colors of fall. The trail is difficult in places.

River Trail (1.6 miles) is a long loop aligned in a north and south direction that follows the Clarion River on two levels. The upper level is some distance from the river while, the lower section follows the placid river at bank level. The trail is generally easy. Wear bright colors or avoid these trails during the hunting season.

Radcliffe Trail (.8 mile) begins at shelter 4 and takes walkers around the central part of the park. It is an easy walk.

Other short trails include the Ridge Trail (1.8 miles) which offers a steep climb and eventually follows Truby Stream through a cool rhododendron-covered valley to National Fuel's Pipeline near the south boundary. Truby Trail (1 mile) also follows the rich valley and has one steep hill and an expansive viewing point.

FISHING: Clear Creek, which bisects the campground, is stocked with brook trout, some of which enter the Clarion River. Nearly year-round, trout fishing is a popular draw at Clear Creek. The water temperature rarely drops below 62 degrees in the summer. Thus, a strong fishery is retained in the park. See Cook Forest State Park for additional information about fly fishing the Clarion River and neighboring cold streams.

Some bass, pike and walleye are also taken from the river and creek. Bass anglers have good luck on the Clarion at Halton downstream to Piney Dam (access from Rt. 36 and 899), at Kyle Dam (a 150-acre lake off Rt. 830 at Falls Creek) at Mahoning Creek in Jefferson County, and from Punxsutawney downstream to the Mahoning Dam.

CANOEING: Belltown Canoe Rentals (814-752-2561), Cook Forest Canoe Livery (814-744-8094), Cook Riverside Canoe Rental (814-744-8300), Love's Canoe Rental (814-776-6285) and Pine Crest Mountaintop Canoe Rentals (814-752-2200). The downward flow of the Clarion is about four miles per hour. One of the most popular trips is the 10-mile float from Clear Creek to Cook Forest State Park.

DAY-USE AREAS: The 390-foot-long beach (open 11 a.m. - 7 p.m.), on

The 53-space campground is a favorite for families with small children.

a cove, is sandy with two lifeguard chairs along a small manmade lake. It is served by a vending machine-only concession and is near the park office, which is open Memorial Day - Labor Day. Scattered picnic tables near the beach and under shade are equipped with grills, pit toilets and shelters. There are about 300 tables in the park and four shelters that can be reserved for a fee. When not reserved, they are on a first-come, first-served basis.

MUSEUM: The cozy lumbering museum, under a flapping American flag, is charming with a creek in the rear and small landscaping and educational elements on two sides. Wood floors house displays that interpret the fascinating lumbering era. Heated by wood, the museum is open seasonally and offers examples of large logging tools, CCC work projects, historic photos, wrought nails and fasteners, the dam and much Clear Creek history, along with a bird's nest, snake skins, mammal mounts, geology and an example of how a white-footed rat can chew through a thick electric wire. Zap! The Oz Shoe Self-Guided Historical Trailhead is next to the tiny museum.

NATURE: Thick woods and rolling terrain dotted with laurel cover a large part of the park. For an excellent view of the forest lands, travel to the Beartown Rocks vista, southeast of the park off Corbett Road. The Beartown outlook is actually in Clear Creek State Forest, the eastern forested neighbor of the park. On the northeast side of the park is a large tract of Allegheny National Forest.

A large rock outcropping offers amateur naturalists a diverse, sometimes difficult terrain to survey for a wide variety of wildflowers and fauna. Birders can strain their necks searching the tree tops, understory and leaf litter for some rare visitors which include Northern goshawk, little blue heron, eagles (bald and golden), orange-crowned warbler, lark sparrow and other accidentals. A birding checklist is available from the naturalist or park office.

Seasonal naturalist programs offered for campers and visitors typically include themed hikes, nature films, youth programs and flora walks.

HUNTING: 627 acres are open to hunting. Call the park manager for details.

WINTER: A lighted ice skating rink and cross-country skiing are popular in the park as weather permits. Most skiers use the Sawmill Trail, but there is an extensive network of trails on park and neighboring forest lands. Sledding and tobogganing the two-acre slope areas is popular with all ages.

NEARBY ATTRACTIONS: Cook Forest State Park, call (814) 744-8407; Clear Creek Stare Forest, call (814) 226-1901; Allegheny National Forest, call (814) 723-5150.

INSIDERS TIPS: The mountain laurel blooms in mid-June are some of the most accessible and best in the state. There is an annual laurel fest about the third week in June. Enjoy the many nearby cold-water scenic creeks.

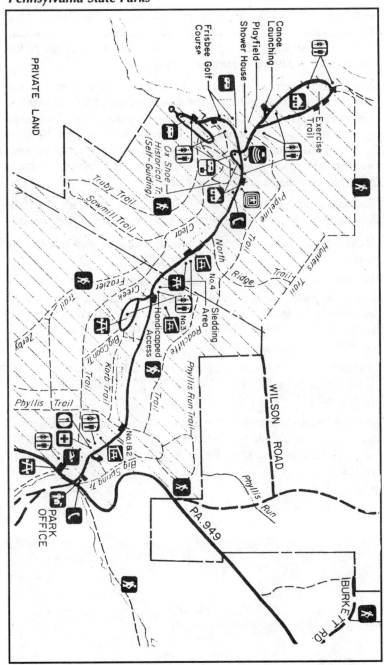

10 Codorus State Park
Land: 3,326 acres Water: 1,275-acre lake

Codorus State Park has one of the biggest swimming pools in the state and some overlapping natural habitats that attract many kinds of birds and other mammals. The newer park has many open spaces, offering plenty of day-use amenities and heavy activity on the lake.

Lake Marburg is a cooperative project of the Commonwealth and the P. H. Glatfelter Paper Company in Spring Grove. The purposes of the joint effort were to provide quality recreational lands for the public and a water source for the paper mill. The undertaking was the first in the state serving both private and public needs. The effort has proven to work very well.

The $5.5 million earthen dam was built by the paper company in the mid-1960s. The dam is 109 feet tall, 1,690 feet long and 750 feet thick and is located on Glatfelter property. The state acquired the adjoining property in 1965-66 and development began of roads, day-use areas and other structures. The park was first known as Codorus Creek State Park, and finally as Codorus State Park.

Pennsylvania State Parks

The region has many attractions for park visitors to enjoy. People have been coming to the area for decades to relax, but at one time they visited the region only to keep moving deeper into the pioneer wilderness. Monocacy Path, from Wrightsville to Frederick, Md., crossed over Codorus Creek several miles north of the park at the city of York, and then followed it upstream, crossing again at Spring Grove. This well-worn trail was one of the primary thoroughfares taking settlers from Pennsylvania through Maryland, Virginia and North Carolina to the Cumberland Gap and Kentucky.

Many of the park's facilities were dedicated in the spring of 1970.

Information and Activities

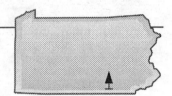

Codorus State Park
1066 Blooming Grove Road
Hanover, PA 17331-9545
(717) 637-2816

DIRECTIONS: In the southwest corner of York County, three miles southeast of Hanover along PA Route 216. No swimming is allowed in the lake. The two-tone brown park office building looks like a ranch-style house and is open 8 a.m. - 4 p.m., with weekend hours added in the summer.

CAMPGROUND: The 198-site campground is open the second Friday in April to the third Sunday in October. Certain sites are reservable and there are 13 walk-in tent sites. There are no on-site hookups, but four beautiful round-shaped, shake-roofed showerhouses with exterior sinks serve the loops. The gently rolling campground is connected to the busy swimming pool via a walkway. The campground is often full on holiday weekends and is busy or nearly full on many other weekends. All sites have hard-surfaced pads (except the 13 walk-ins), picnic tables and ground-mounted fire rings.

The campground has four loops. Three are shaded, with D loop in a grassy area. The east half of the A, B and D and all of C loop are flat, while the remainder of the sites are sloping. Campers with a boat can choose the D loop because it is the closest to the small launching ramp.

Campground staff says C loop is the most popular, largely because it's close to the pool. Other campers want open sites in the 150s (D loop). Popular shady sites are 57-59, which are close to the play field and are often requested by large families. Sites 60, 61 and 63 are very open,

You can reserve some of the 198 sites in the rolling campground.

near a play field and popular with large RV pilots.

Sites in the A loop are deep and big enough for larger RV units. Sites in the B loop, 43-80, are heavily wooded. In the C loop, sites 81-144 are heavily used, flat and dry. Many of the sites are separated by vegetation. D loop is completely open with no shade. The walk-in sites are off the D loop, where campers park and camp under a thick canopy of mature trees.

FISHING: Lake Marburg is a good sport fishery. Muskie, pike and bass are the most sought after game fish, while early season anglers cast for trout and walleye and later in the season focus on panfish, including crappies, yellow perch and bluegills. Many anglers concentrate on the shoreline near the three bridges. You may not fish from the bridges. Fish deep for trout past June.

Codorus Creek, which means "*rapid waters,*" has its headwaters near the village of Sticks, north of the Maryland line. Some of the upper waters are stocked with brown and rainbow trout. Stretches of the main branch (the west branch of the creek feeds the lake at the park) are broad and surrounded by scenic farmlands, fine old houses and mills, rocky outcrops, and cool woodlands of elder and birch.

Pennsylvania State Parks

The region has some interesting history, much of it resulting from the strong creek and early settlement along it. From historic land purchases by the Penns of "All lands lying on the West side of the said river (Susquehanna) to the setting of the Sun" to the influx of Scotch-Irish and German immigrants. Nearby Hanover was also the first Civil War battle fought above the Mason-Dixon Line. Even George Custer fought in the area.

Part of the main branch of the creek stays cold year around. Even in the middle of summer the freestone creek stays in the low 60s.

Today anglers will find the creek equally fascinating. Try caddis flies in the early summer, while some of the following might also cause a rise. Hendrickson, minnow imitations, sulphur duns, spinners, adult mayfly, small streamers, soft-hackle nymphs, coachman, terrestrials and midges worked slowly. Bring your short rod; many of the better pools are surrounded by low tree limbs.

BOATING: Seven launching ramps are scattered around the irregularly shaped lake. Two boat rental concessions rent canoes, rowboats, pedal boats, motor boats, and pontoon boats. Boats can be rented by the hour or for an eight-hour day. Call the larger Inland Watercraft Marina (main marina area) at (717) 632-6896 for details. Sailboats and seasonal mooring are popular on the lake. The park also operates a small dry dock for sail craft. Many of the sailboats operate out of Hidden Cove on the north side of the lake.

The stone and timber marina concession is open 8 a.m. - 7 p.m. daily during the season and sells live bait, cold soft drinks, limited marina supplies and, of course, boat rentals.

HIKING: The wheelchair accessible trail is a four-foot-wide hard-surfaced loop that is half wooded and half shady, with the trailhead off the campground road to loops C and D. The park has a total of five miles of easy trails. Most of the trails link day-use areas and park amenities.

BRIDLE TRAILS: A gravel staging area (parking lot) is provided for equestrians to park trucks and trailers, and prepare for a ride on the seven miles of bridle trails. The trailhead is on the same peninsula as the band shell, east of the marina.

DAY-USE AREAS: Expansive mowed areas are near the pool, marinas, visitor center and along the winding shoreline of the lake. Two pavilions and more than 750 picnic tables are throughout the park.

BAND SHELL: On the lake shore, the angular-shaped stone and wood band shell is the site for many concerts and other events. Many summer concerts are set for Sunday evenings. The band shell, dedicated to the citizens of Pennsylvania, is made possible by the P. H. Glatfelter Company. Mowed open spaces and day-use areas are adjacent to the band shell.

SWIMMING POOL: Codorus State Park's pool (small fee, twilight rates and children under 38 inches are free) has three lobes (cloverleaf-like) and an island in the middle where a lifeguard is perched. The pool is one of the largest in the state (25,000 square feet) and is busy with organized groups, campers and day-use visitors. The huge pool is open 11 a.m. - 7 p.m. Memorial Day weekend to Labor Day, unless otherwise posted. There are special admission rates for overnight campers and organized groups.

Poolside, visitors will find an elevated patio-like area with picnic tables. The pool is partly surrounded by a low stone wall that tapers and outlines many segments of the deck area. Bicycle parking is near the pool.

NATURE: The unit is comprised of mixed hardwoods, pines, old fields reverting to woodlands, marshland, open meadows, shrubby border areas and mud flats. These diverse habitats often converge along some of the park's hiking trails, offering wildlife watchers an excellent chance to see shorebirds, waterfowl, songbirds and common mammals. About 240 species of birds have been identified and recorded.

Because the park has considerable open spaces, visitors will often see bluebirds and northern orioles. Along the woodland foot trails, it is common to see red-bellied woodpeckers, brown creepers and downy woodpeckers working up and down tree trunks looking for insects. Others include kinglets, scarlet tanagers, ovenbirds, veery, rufous-sided towhees and fair to good populations of spring and fall migrant warblers.

Black tern are sighted on Long Island. Other good sightings include Ross's gull, cattle egret, nesting osprey (as many as nine have been seen at a time), common loon and avocets. The park is divided into 10 sectors. Area birders are developing a census and checklist using the grid.

The park has a strong dedication to birding and environmental education programming. In fact, a monument erected near the marina reads,

Pennsylvania State Parks

"In the interest of preservation of wildlife, we here dedicate this monument to the ill-fated passenger pigeon which from earliest pioneer days until the 1880s flocked to these pigeon hills. The migratory bird, which is now extinct, once darkened the sky." The six-foot-tall monument was dedicated on Oct. 12, 1947 by the Boy Scouts of America.

ENVIRONMENTAL CENTER: The newer single-story nature center is on a ridge near the park office overlooking the lake near Route 216. The air-conditioned center features natural history displays, wall posters, blue birds, a touch table, magazine rack and tweed carpeting. A gravel parking lot is behind the building.

Behind the center is an interesting terraced garden on five levels built with landscaping timbers. The demonstration butterfly garden features a number of labeled plant materials including catnip, weigala, butterfly bush, purple cornflower, Jupiter's beard, beebalm, selfheal, lemonbalm, feverfew, oxeye daisy, hyssop, butterfly milkweed, liotris, rue, goldenrod, aster, ironweed, phlox, silky dogwood, red trumpet vine and more.

SNOWMOBILING: About 100 acres of the park are open for snowmobiling after the antlerless deer season.

CROSS-COUNTRY SKIING: About 300 acres of mixed fields and woodlands are heavily used by Nordic skiers when weather permits.

WINTER: Ice skating takes place on a small portion of Chapel Cove. The rest of the lake is open for ice fishing.

HUNTING: More than 2,900 acres are open for hunting. Contact the park office for complete information.

INSIDERS TIP: Windsurfers will find good winds and beach launching places.

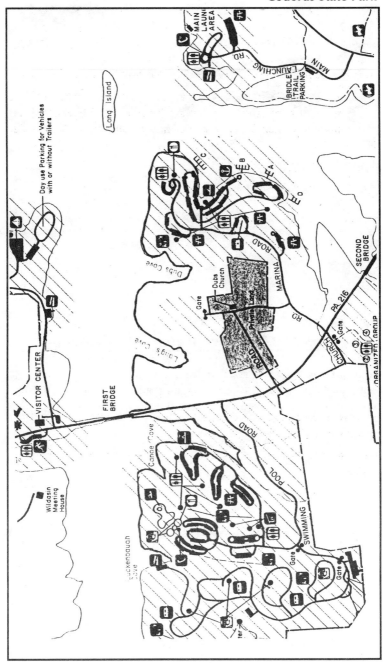

11 Colonel Denning State Park
Land: 273 acres   Water: 3.5-acre lake

Colonel Denning State Park is in Doubling Gap, so named by the "S" turn where the rounded Blue Mountain doubles back on itself. The scenic feature can be seen from Doubling Back Vista on nearby state forest lands.

William Denning (1737-1830), a Revolutionary War veteran for whom the park is named, was never a colonel, but he was an innovator and manufacturer deserving of a place in history for his role in developing and making an improved wrought iron cannon. Denning, who was a sergeant, served his country from March 1788 to April 1780 in Nathaniel Irish's Company of Artillery Artificers in Benjamin Flower's Regiment.

Denning's company was stationed near Carlisle, Pa., at Washingtonburg Forge, now Carlisle Barracks. Washingtonburg Forge was a large manufacture of armaments for the Continental Army, including huge cannons. It was at Washingtonburg that Denning developed a technique to make wrought iron cannons using a process of welding gads (strips) of wrought iron in successive layers, producing a much lighter cannon. The durable weapon could also resist dangerous failures when firing. None of the cannons exists today.

No one knows when or who added the Colonel to Sergeant William Denning's name. Denning settled in Newville, Pa., after the war, where he is buried near his son and daughter. His monument reads: "Blacksmith and Forger of Wrought Iron Cannon."

The scenic tract became a state recreational area in 1930 and was developed and opened formally in 1936. Much of the work in the park was done by the Civilian Conservation Corps (CCC) in Perry County.

Information and Activities

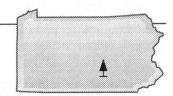

Colonel Denning State Park
1599 Double Gap Road
Newville, PA 17241-9756
(717) 776-5272

DIRECTIONS: In north central Cumberland County, along PA Route 233. The park is eight miles north of Newville and nine miles south of Landisburg.

EMERGENCY NUMBERS: 911 system; state police, 249-2121.

CAMPGROUND: All 52 family hilltop camping sites are full on holiday weekends in the cozy facility. Entrance to the campground is over a wood-plank bridge to the single loop, with three spur-like camping areas. Sites have gravel pads, picnic tables and fire rings. Each site has a trash barrel.

Mini-loop 1-11 has small sites, except for site 3, 4, 5, 10 and 11 which are wide, near a stream and at the end of the quiet loop. Through a thin wall of vegetation are a swing set and a connection to the day-use area.

Sites 13-18 are shady and near a drinking fountain and the campground host. On a curve of campground road, site 22 is large enough for a big RV rig and is private. Many of the other sites in the 20s and 30s (except for the walk-ins) are much smaller, ideal for tents or pop-up campers.

A wide, well-worn pathway climbs a small hill to shady, rustic sites 27-32. The walk-in sites are heavily wooded. Sites 42-45 are on a lower elevation and look down into a wooded ravine. Site 47 is deep enough for a medium to large RV unit, with plenty of shade and privacy. Site 50 is a hard-surfaced handicapped accessible camping site near the brown rest room with skylights (no showers). Across the lane is site 52, which can accommodate a large motor home or travel trailer.

FISHING: There is shoreline fishing only on the small lake and in Doubling Gap Run Creek. Some trout are planted seasonally. Local anglers catch some panfish and bass from the mostly open shoreline and near the dam.

BOATING: No boating is allowed on the small lake.

HIKING: Colonel Denning's terrain is hilly to mountainous, featuring 18 miles of trail accessible form the park and access to the 105-mile Tuscarora Trail.

Tuscarora Trail is part of the National Trail System. The long and rugged trail has orange-colored blazes along the entire length. You may access Flat Rock Trail from the park.

All park trails, unless noted otherwise, are blazed in red and range from moderate to difficult.

CROSS-COUNTRY SKIING: There is no formal trail system for skiing. Skiing is permitted on existing roads and trails in all areas of the park.

DAY-USE AREAS: Sand volleyball and some small play apparatus are in the day-use area, as are some picnic tables and open spaces. Directly across from the beach is the nicest day-use area, complete with picnic tables, nature trail and shoreline fishing.

BEACH: Only 75 yards long, the sandy beach is guarded by three life-guard stations and open 11 a.m. - 7 p.m. Memorial Day weekend to Labor Day. The maximum depth is five feet. Park benches and the tiny dam are south of the 30-yard-wide beach that's on the east shore of the small lake.

Four picnic tables surround the concession stand that is open seasonally. Rattlesnake Trail departs from the small concession stand.

NATURE: A tiny rustic outdoor classroom at the foot of a large hill is a converted picnic shelter with eight bench seats. The little pavilion-like lecture center has natural branches and large twisted twigs forming the railing around the enclosure.

Also in the interpretive area is a small pond where various animals are kept for a short time to be used in educational programs. Box turtles are often kept in the enclosure. The box turtle, can withdraw its head and legs completely into its shell by folding both halves of its pastron to form a tight box. Male box turtles have red eyes—I know the feeling. Females have yellow eyes. The females lay about 35 eggs after mating in June. Box turtles are often found on land and may spend their entire life in an area the size of a football field. They can live to be 60 years old. Some say they are the original mobile home.

Other small buildings in this area have interpretive displays and regional natural history information. Hikes on the weekends and other programs typically begin in this area or near the concession stand. Evening programs are also offered each Saturday during the summer beginning at 8:30 p.m. The 24-foot square log nature center has only one window and a low roof line, and is open on the weekends during the summer. The Flat Rock Trailhead is also located in this small-scale outdoor education compound.

The 91,700 acre Tuscarora State Forest virtually surrounds Colonel Denning State Park. It features huge tracts of second-growth forests, the Hemlock Natural Area (virgin hemlocks), fertile valleys and a trail system.

HUNTING: Certain areas of the park are managed for hunting. Call the park manager for information.

WINTER: Ice skaters may use Doubling Gap Lake when ice conditions permit. About two acres are maintained and lighted. Hours are 8 a.m. - 10 p.m.

INSIDERS TIPS: Hike the three miles of trails at the nearby 120-acre Hemlocks Natural Area (717-536-3191) in the Tuscarora State Forest, 10 miles east of Blain in Perry County. The largest tree has a diameter of more than 51 inches the average age of the trees is between 300-500 years old. Hemlocks are the official state tree of Pennsylvania.

12 Cook Forest State Park
Land: 6,668 acres Water: Clarion River

National Geographic Traveler magazine once chose Cook Forest State Park as one of the top 50 state parks in the nation. The prestigious magazine understands what a diverse selection of vacation options are in, and near, the only true remnant of the original "Penn's Woods."

Few places on earth have 300-year-old forests like the ones near Cooksburg, which is one of the largest and most accessible virgin stands of white pine and hemlock forest in the eastern United States. The trees, some five feet in diameter and more than 200 feet tall, scrape the sky and create an inviting canopy for a variety of wildlife. These towering trees and many other wonderful natural features are along 30 miles of trails, near a terrific campground and charming log cabin visitor center.

From a refreshing day trip to a week-long stay in rustic cabins or the campground, the area offers dozens of specialty shops, cottages industries and family-style attractions.

Even Hollywood loves Cook Forest. It was the site for the filming of

"Unconquered," the Cecil B. deMille film depicting the battle and siege at Fort Pitt. The famed director chose the park because of the huge stand of virgin pine, which appears today in much the same condition it existed in the middle of the 18th century. Gary Cooper, Paulette Goddard and Boris Karloff starred in the epic movie.

Cooksburg, the small community on the park's edge, was founded in 1828 by John Cook, who started a sawmill along Tom's Run. John's son, Andrew Cook, took over the business in 1857 and it continued to prosper for many years. In the 1920s the Cook Forest Association was formed to help preserve the large tract of virgin timber. The dedicated group raised money to help the Commonwealth purchase the land from the Cooks for the purpose of developing a park. The park was dedicated in 1927.

Information and Activities

Cook Forest State Park
P.O. Box 120
Cooksburg, PA 16217
(814) 744-8407

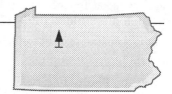

DIRECTIONS: At Cooksburg. From the east take exit 13 off I-80 then take PA Route 36 north to the park. From the west take exit 8 off of I-80, then take PA Route 66 north to Leeper. From Leeper follow PA Route 36 south seven miles to the park. Inside the green clapboard park office are a brochure rack and a small black bear and other mammal mounts. The canoe livery is directly across from the park office.

CAMPGROUND: Virtually every one of the 226 family camping sites in the rolling terrain is very good and near one of the four showerhouses. Drinking fountains are scattered throughout the shady, wooded camping area. Staff reports that the most popular sites are those on the outside of the loop, which back up against natural areas and benefit from slightly more privacy than interior sites. The bathhouses in Cook Forest are newer, modern and have slate-like roofs. Extra vehicle parking is also available in the campground for boats, trailers or extra cars.

Inside the campground gate next to the contact office is a wide open space with play fields, amphitheater and timber-style play apparatus. All of the camping spots have picnic tables and fire rings. Sites 38 and 39 have a great view of the mowed open space area where children play. These sites and 36 and 37 would be excellent choices for families with small children. In this loop, site 19 is the best for tent camping. The Ridge Trailhead is at site 30.

Sites 114-120 are good for larger RVs and as hard-surfaced handicapped sites. They are somewhat isolated from the larger loops.

Sites 141 and 198 are good for tent camping, complete with shade. Sites numbered 152-170 are smaller, but plenty large enough for pop-up or pickup truck campers. Loop 189 to 208 is airy and on higher ground, but still shady from stands of evergreens and mixed deciduous trees.

Sites 7 and 8 can be easily combined for two families who would like to share a shady camping place.

A small creek runs through the campground near the entrance, close to site 24. Sites 118 and 120 are the most sunny and open sites in the park and are good for medium to large RV units. There are a few pull-through sites including 129, 179 and 181.

Organized group tent camping is offered in two areas. Contact the park office.

CABINS: Twenty-four rustic family cabins are open from the second Friday in April until the end of the antlerless deer season in late December. Twelve of the cabins sleep four; six sleep six; and six sleep eight people. During the summer, the cabins are rented by the week, Friday to Friday. During the rest of the season the log-style cabins can be rented by the half week.

Log-style with white chinking, the small cabins have stone chimneys and brown roofs and are across a small bridge near the fishing pond. The 12 smallest cabins are all in cozy, shady locations, ideal for small families and vacationers.

The larger log-style river cabins, east of the park office on River Road, are scattered along a shady hillside. Cabins 15 is especially private. All of the cabins in the area are near the large day-use area along the Clarion River. Cabins 6 and 7, also very private, have large porches and parking for two or more vehicles. Cabin 5, with a big stone chimney, has the nicest covered porch. All of the cabins have a picnic table, grill and a view of the slow-moving river and picnic area below.

ELDERHOSTEL: Elderhostels are for age 55-plus students who want to expand their knowledge and cultivate new interests. More than 400,000 seniors have participated in an Elderhostel adventure at more than 1,500 sites across the United States and in more than 40 countries.

You can learn more about the program by contacting Elderhostel, 75 Federal St., Boston, MA 02110-1941. The educational experience at Cook Forest can include arts and crafts, theatre and many other activities.

FISHING: The children's fishing pond, sponsored by a local rod and gun club and the Cook Forest Vacation Bureau, has an improved shoreline for wheelchair accessibility and is stocked with trout. Persons with disabilities and children 12 and under may use the pond.

There are trout, warm-water game fish and panfish in the Clarion River, which flows alongside the park. There are also many mountain trout streams and reservoirs in the area.

Mayfly hatches are down on the Clarion, so most fly anglers have tied on caddies and midges in an effort to raise trout. The Clarion River is, however, an interesting fly fishing experience. The river is wide and slow, and has many deep runs. If you are willing to travel a bit, try Bear Creek for good green drake hatches or Spring Creek. Mill Creek has a special one-mile-long fly fishing only section and Tom's Run, Big Mill Creek and the stocked Toby Creek can be fair to good, if you hit the hatches.

When the Clarion warms, move to Pine Creek and fish the deep pools with cool water on the bottom.

CANOEING: The Clarion River is a scenic trip for beginning canoeists under normal conditions. A number of private canoe rentals serve the growing numbers of visitors who come to the area for a relaxing float trip. In fact, the canoe rental area is rapidly growing to include an ice cream shop, old time photographer and other amusement-type services.

HIKING: Cook Forest has 16 marked hiking trails equaling about 30 miles. The extensive network of trails go off in every direction, with Seneca and Indian trails being the only very difficult ones in the park. Bikes are not permitted on the trails.

Longfellow Trail is the most popular walking trail in the park. Only 1.2 miles long, the easy trail can be used to reach other trails which lead deeper into the forest. Beginning from the log cabin visitor center and passing Memorial Fountain, the trail heads to the Forest Cathedral where 200-foot-tall trees stand, uncut and preserved for all time. The primeval white pine and hemlock stand is the largest virgin forest of its type in Pennsylvania. The area is registered with the National Park Service as a National Natural Landmark. The impressive trees are more than 300 years old, although with some of the oldest and largest were destroyed in a 1956 storm. Don't miss this trail!

Rhododendron Trail, which enters the forest at Tom's Run near the north end of the Indian Cabin area, winds through the main stand of timber and emerges on Forest Drive. The primary point of interest on this 1.5- mile-long trail is the swinging bridge over Tom's Run creek.

Mohawk Trail, 1.8-miles-long, begins on Route 36 above the fork in the road. It's a moderate climb, taking hikers along hemlock covered slopes above the Clarion River to cross the Fire Tower Road and Deer Park trails. The trail passes some impressive hardwoods and songbird habitats. Spring wildflowers are also considered excellent on this trail.

Seneca Trail leaves the highway at Cooksburg at the northern end of the Clarion River bridge along a ridgeline of hemlock forests and past a mineral spring.

Baker Trail is a 140-mile trail maintained by the American Youth Hostels and links Freeport, Pa., and the Allegheny National Forest. Visitors hiking solely the Cook Forest should ignore the Baker Trail signs.

The CCC (Civilian Conservation Corps) Trail is a self-guided trail of 1.5 miles. Deer Park Trail starts at Route 36 opposite Hemlock Trail and winds about one mile through a mature forest of hardwoods and virgin hemlock to an area that was damaged by a tornado in July, 1976. When the rhododendron are in bloom (late May), Hemlock Trail is a wonderful trail spiced with palm-sized blooms and hungry butterflies.

BRIDLE TRAILS: Two bridle trails north and east of the park office totaling 4.5 miles are available for equestrians. A private horse rental concession is nearby. Hikers are also invited to use these trails.

SAWMILL CRAFT CENTER: Begun in 1975, the Sawmill Center for the Arts celebrates the arts with more than 500,000 visitors annually. Staffed by professional and volunteers, the center is a healthy example of John Ruskin's famous quote: "A man who works with his hands is a laborer, a man who works with his hands and brain is a craftsman, and a man who works with his hands, his head and his heart is an artist." The Sawmill Center is where nature meets the arts.

While the dream of a rural-based art center within a state park seemed impossible to many, the parks system and dedicated artisans have cooperated to offer a wonderful showroom sales outlet for locally-produced handwork. Open seven days a week, 10 a.m. - 5 p.m. from May to October, the large building is filled with textiles, games and toys, woodcrafts, T-shirts, small country crafts, jewelry, dolls, quilts, rugs, wall hangings, baskets, carvings, wearable art and much more. A second Sawmill Craft Market, on Route 36 between Leeper and Cooksburg, is only 10 minutes away and is open year-round.

The center also offers an ambitious schedule of arts and crafts classes. Some courses are one-time; others are week-long classes featuring some of the top instructors in the area. A variety of weekend festivals is also offered including a woodcarving competition, doll shows, quilt shows, dulcimer round-up and a harvest fest. The center has a meeting/classroom.

VERNA LEITH SAWMILL THEATRE: In 1981, the Sawmill Theatre was first introduced in what was the museum section of the old sawmill, using church pews and camp chairs for seating. Soon the need for a larger theatre was evident and, in 1994, the Verna Leith Sawmill Theatre was constructed with money from the Appalachian Regional Commission and a Commonwealth appropriation. First of its kind in the Eastern United States, the theatre's unique hexagon shape, awning entrance and harmonious blend with the natural setting earned its designer, William Snyder, the 1994 Design Award from the Arts Architectural Commission of Pennsylvania.

Final details such as professional lighting, side decks, ticket office and interior rest rooms were added in 1988. Theatre patrons find themselves seated on historic seats from the Old Silver Fox Theatre.

The attractive facility offers a blend of mystery, comedy and major Broadway-style musicals. Performances are scheduled from late May through mid-September on Thursday through Saturday evenings. Reservations are recommended; call (814) 927-6655. The theatre can seat about 200.

DAY-USE AREAS: Shelter No. 1 is a busy, large day-use area with plenty of parking for family reunions and group outings. There is one other rentable shelter in the park and several areas where tables are clustered.

SWIMMING POOL: Northwest of the park office near the Sawmill Craft Center is the large rectangular-shaped public pool, surrounded with red benches and a green bathhouse. The pool depths range from 2.5 feet to five feet. A round kiddies' wading pool is busy on hot days with splashing toddlers. The pool is open Memorial Day - Labor Day, 11 a.m. - 7 p.m. for a small fee. Vending machines are at the pool.

NATURE/VISITOR CENTER: The creaking, rough-sawn floors in the former Log Cabin Inn with bright white chinking are soon forgotten as visitors begin viewing displays and reading about the park's natural history. The large center is in the main picnic area. Under the beam ceiling are free-standing displays, maps, touch table, labeled tree trunk sections and mammal and bird mounts near a huge hearth of a stone fireplace. Theater-style seating in rustic wooden chairs are used during programs and presentations. A variety of public nature programs begin at the center, with about 10,000 participating annually. Nature walks often have 60 or more people attending. Pick up a schedule of environmental education programs at the office or visitor center.

One of the more interesting displays is a stump puller. During the 1800s area farmers used these big machines to clear Jefferson County pine forest. A huge chain wraps around each long arm of the T-like structure, and the stump is attached to the lifting bar. Pumping the long hickory handle would raise the lifting bar slightly, with each pump similar to a car jack. At times, three men worked the handle at once. Most of the white pine and pencil-straight stands of hemlock were cleared using homemade devices like this one on display. Clearing the lands was a major struggle that took ingenuity and perseverance.

The twisted stumps were often used to made strong fences.

The Forest Cathedral natural area contains one of the largest old-growth stands of white pine and eastern hemlock in the state. Many of these magnificent pine and soft-looking hemlock exceed three feet in diameter and can be best viewed from the Longfellow Trail (1.2 miles). Some of the tree approach 200 feet in height. Tree of this size are often more than 300 years old, dating to the era of William Penn, the first governor of "Penn's Woods." They are often refereed to as "William Penn trees."

It is perhaps fitting that the forest remains in the midst of an area that saw the greatest logging boom in the Commonwealth in the late 1800s, when thousands of acres of old-growth were cut for ship building and the construction industry. The Forest Cathedral area is registered as a National Landmark and has been set aside for protection.

BIRDING: The bird habitat at Cook Forest is mostly deep conifer forest of white pine and eastern hemlock. Interspersed among the deep woods are a few smaller areas of less dense second growth timberland and a few areas opened for recreational use. The Clarion River, which borders the park and numerous small streams, provides habitat for waterfowl and species typical of wet areas. The park has a bird checklist that details seasonal abundance and lists species sighted by group.

Some species of interest include little blue heron, bald eagle, gold eagle, Nashville warbler, yellow-throated warbler, pine warbler, hoary redpoll and Henslow's sparrow.

FIRE TOWER: The long, winding, one-way road to the fire tower is surprisingly busy on weekends. The road, in the Demonstration Area, is about a three-mile loop under a wonderful forest canopy. Halfway out is a small day-use area with comfort station, where you begin your short hike back to the green steel tower and the Seneca Point Overlook.

HUNTING: More than 4,000 acres are open to hunting, dog training and trapping. Call the park office for details and seasons.

WINTER: From a lighted ice skating pond to 20 miles of snowmobile trails, Cook Forest can be a busy place if the weather cooperates. Kids will love the 10 acres of sledding hills and three cross-country ski trails.

NEARBY ATTRACTIONS: Canoe rentals, miniature golf, amusements, go-carts, bumper boats, riding stables, antique mall and flea markets.

INSIDERS TIPS: This is one of the few parks in the country where you can climb a fire tower. Check the course schedule at the Sawmill Art Center and take a class. Also, hike to the rare virgin timber on the Longfellow Trail.

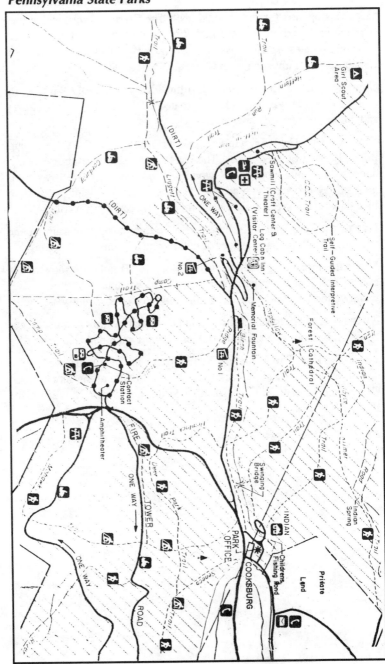

13 Cowans Gap State Park
Land: 1,085 acres Water: 42-acre lake

Cowans Gap sits in the middle of 70,242-acre Buchanan State Forest in a wind gap surrounded by deep valleys and steep mountains.

The tidy park takes it name from Maj. Samuel Cowan, a British soldier who fell in love–and eventually eloped–with the daughter of a Boston merchant during the Revolutionary War. Cowans' future father-in-law supported the colonists and forbade him to see his daughter, forcing Cowans to return to England alone. But, like any great love, he could-n't forget his American sweetheart. He returned to Boston and married.

The happy couple remained for several years until they–like many during that era–decided to move west. Like two other famous Pennsy-lvanians, Daniel Boone and John Jacob Audubon, they wanted to move to Kentucky. Plagued by difficult travel, the intrepid couple's journey ended far short of the Bluegrass State. The family made it only as far as the next county, when their rickety wagon broke down and they trad-ed it to an Indian Chief in exchange for the land now known as Cowans Gap.

Pennsylvania State Parks

The park's first facilities were constructed by the Civilian Conservation Corps (CCC) and opened in 1937. The CCC built the lake and dam, picnic shelters, stone and log cabins, trails and roads. The charming cabin colony was placed on the National Register of Historical Places in 1987.

Information and Activities

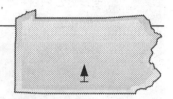

Cowans Gap State Park
HC 17266
Fort Loudon, PA 17224-9801
(717) 485-3948

DIRECTIONS: From the Pennsylvania Turnpike, take exit 14 (Willow Hill) and drive south on Route 75 for 14 miles, then turn west (right) onto Richmond Road at the park sign to the park, about three miles. It takes about 25 minutes once you leave the turnpike to reach the park.

CAMPGROUND: Cowans Gap has 233 deep camp sites in two gently rolling areas. Some sites can be reserved on holiday weekends. Towering white oaks shade many camp sites, which are equipped with picnic tables, ground-mounted fire rings and gravel pads. Many out-of-staters come to Cowans Gap to camp.

Camping sites are well separated, often by a wall of dense vegetation, and sit against the mountainside. The main campground loop is nearly two miles in length, incorporating the areas where the log cabins are located near newer showerhouses.

Smaller camping sites are 160-174–great for popup campers.

Sites 131-134 are extra private sites, backed up against a natural area near the end of the main loop. Site 136 enjoys some mid-afternoon sun.

Area B, which is north of the larger camping area, is up against the mountain and along an area where large trees were blown down during a strong storm. This blown down area is rapidly regenerating and is behind sites 203 and 218. This area has rustic camping sites shaded by pine. Carved into the mountain, sites 204 and 205 are sought-after locations. Many of the sites are notched out of natural areas; others are in the pine plantation, where needles are underfoot and cool breezes blow among the tall trees. The plantation allows slips of sunshine to peek between the trees. All of the sites in this rustic camping section have gravel pads, picnic tables, nearby rest rooms and fire rings.

Cooling off at the 500-foot-long beach is popular all summer.

The walk-in tent camping sites are scattered in a lovely wooded area on the mountainside. Your tent can easily nestle into the shady, private surroundings and still only be a short walk from the rest rooms and other campers.

CABINS: The setting where the 10 family cabins are perfectly suits the Civilian Conservation Corps-built stone and log three-room cabins that are open spring, summer and fall. The classic cabins, built in 1937, are mixed into the camping area on varying elevations along narrow ribbon-like mini-ridges. They sleep four in bunk beds. Cabin G is handicapped accessible.

There is no indoor plumbing in the cabins. However, a water faucet is located outside and a central comfort station has showers and flush toilets.

Cabin A is secluded, with a one-lane driveway down to it.

Cabin K is the prettiest cabin. It has lots of stonework, a large porch and natural landscaping that makes it attractive and reserved much of the season.

HIKING: The 1.5-mile-long Lakeside Trail is the most popular of the

10 miles of hiking trails. Part of the Lakeside Trail is accessible by wheelchairs. Many of the park's trails and those in the neighboring state forest are difficult and not for beginners. Experienced hikers will love the steep, winding trails with linear ridge lines and plunging valleys that bottom out at small rocky streams.

Some of the 105-mile-long Tuscarora Trail in Pennsylvania and Maryland connects to the Big Blue Trail that starts in northern Virginia. The Tuscarora Trail runs parallel to the Appalachian Trail, and junctions with it and the Darlington Trail near Deans Gap, north of Carlisle. The Tuscarora Trail is marked with rectangular orange blaze marks painted on trees.

FISHING: Cowans Gap lake is a mountain lake that stays cold until early summer. Early and later season trout fishing are considered good. When the water warms up bass, perch and panfish go on the bite. There are places in the small lake that are up to 21-feet-deep. Local experts advise using ultralight line in the clear water.

Trout anglers can try their luck on the Little Aughwick Creek, which means *"little brushy creek."* It is a classic ridge and valley mountain stream running along the top of Tuscarora Mountain to eventually join the Juniata River in northeast Huntingdon County. It's a stocked creek. Try the following flies on the creek: various colored caddis, Hendrickson, stoneflies, coachman, light Cahills and Adams.

A wooded plank fishing pier with railings is handicapped accessible.

BOATING: It won't take long to paddle around the 42-acre lake in a rented boat or in your own cartop craft. Two small launching areas are near each other, where 70 small boats can be moored seasonally. Electric motor-powered boats are permitted.

The cool and calm mountain lake is an ideal place for family canoeing and paddling. Large enough to maneuver and get some healthful exercise, the 42-acre lake is named for Major Samuel Cowans, a British officer during the Revolutionary War.

DAY-USE AREAS: Some of the finest CCC picnic shelters in the region get a workout at Cowans Gap. Made of log and stone, day-users scurry to reserve or claim the shelters that are surrounded by picnic tables and other amenities. Picnic shelter No. 4 is the most attractive in the park. About 400 picnic tables are scattered in mostly wooded areas. Many handicapped accessible tables are also in pleasant areas of the park.

VISITOR CENTER: Brightbill (like the author) Interpretive Center teaches a number of natural history themes to casual day-use visitors, campers and school children. One of the major education themes is the wind gap, which is important historically. The first road passed this way, the trail used by settlers to help develop Pennsylvania.

NATURE: From the overlook you can view a fault line, where the north and south ranges of the Tuscarora Mountains separate abruptly, forming the gap.

Chestnut oaks and hickory dominate the area, with a few maples and scattered planted pines. Autumn colors stay a long time in this type of woods, showing off golden colors for weeks. Fall hiking is very popular at the remote park.

Beavers are often seen along the lake buzzing off sapling and chewing the bottoms of larger trees. Bobcat and spotted and stripped skunk are sometimes seen along the trails.

Visitors can learn about forestry, wood cutting, charcoal making, bird identifying, see children's books, Scotch-Irish heritage, a library of nature books, a display of seldom seen animals at Cowans Gap, CCC crews and camps and nature touch boxes for students. The visitors center is open during the summer and offers programs like the magic of sprouts, up and over, life's of change and a variety of nature-oriented programs at the amphitheater. Many flora and fauna hikes are also led by the staff naturalist.

BIRDING: From mixed forest to wetlands and groomed shorelines of the small lake, Cowans Gap has diverse habitat. Scarlet tanagers and rose-breasted grosbeak are summer residents. Pine siskin and redpolls often visit during the winter. The common raven is a year-round resident, while brown creepers and red-breasted nuthatches are migrants.

Local birders often see spotted sandpipers, black- and yellow-billed cuckoos, yellow-bellied sapsuckers in the spring and fall, and good numbers of red-bellied woodpeckers year-round. Yellow-crowned night herons have also been identified in the summer. Both turkeys and black buzzards can be seen soaring effortlessly along the mountaintops and into the valleys during many seasons of the year.

BEACH: Nearly 500 feet long and 35 feet wide, the sandy beach is open for swimming and sunbathing. Swimming takes place at the guarded beach between 11 a.m. and 7 p.m. daily, Memorial Day weekend to Labor Day. Near the bathhouse along a patio-like area is a lively green-colored concession stand with a small gift shop, souvenirs, beach toys and snack foods, cold drinks, and limited camping supplies and grocery items (eggs, cereal, etc.).

HUNTING: More than 600 acres are open seasonally for hunting. Turkey and deer hunting is considered very good. Call the park office for additional information.

WINTER: Bring your ice skates, but double check the ice warning signs that are posted during unsafe times before venturing out on the lake. Sled riding can be done on Knobsville Road, which is closed to all motorized vehicles.

NEARBY ATTRACTIONS: Burnt Cabins Grist Mill, Fulton House, Fulton County Courthouse and more. Call the Fulton County Tourist Promotion Agency at (717) 485-4064. Buchanan State Forest, R. D. 2, P. O. Box 3, McConnellsburg, PA 17233.

INSIDERS TIPS: View the fault and gap from the overlook west of the developed areas. Stay in Cabin K.

Buchannan's Birthplace State Park

The memorial and grounds occupy 18.5 acres. The large stone, pyramid-like memorial was constructed in honor of James Buchannan, once president of the United States. The grounds are his boyhood home. Two pavilions, two picnic tables and comfort stations are at the scenic historical park.

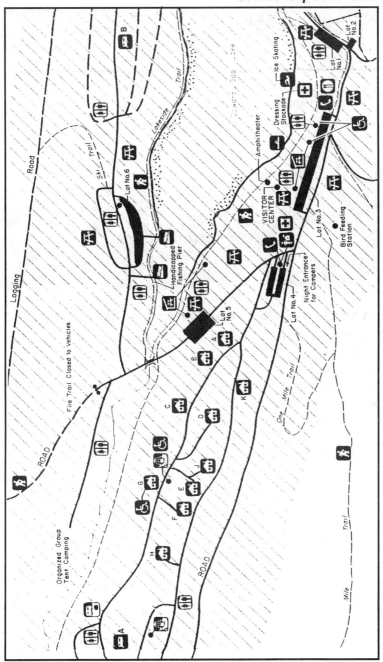

14 Delaware Canal State Park
Land: 556 acres   Water: canal

Access points are scattered along the entire length of the 60-mile canal, which parallels the Delaware River north of Philadelphia. Runners, bicyclists, bank anglers, canoeists, cross-country skiers, equestrians, walkers and sightseers can use the parking lots and the long, flat trail that courses the banks of the elevated canal.

The Delaware Canal is the only remaining continuously intact remnant of the great towpath canal building era of the early and mid-19th century. The canal remains today with virtually all of its features including 23 locks, 10 aqueducts, 4 river islands, lock tender's houses and spillways. With the exception of the last .7 mile, the canal retains all of its engineering and operational structures. The canal passes through a series of village and historic towns including Washington Crossing, Lumberville, Centre Bridge, New Hope, Bristol, Yardley and Piegelsville, where some excellent inns, restaurants and historic homes are located.

Visitors can also use bridges between the towpath of the Delaware canal in Pennsylvania and the Delaware Raritan Canal in New Jersey.

For long stretches, the smooth walking path that borders the Delaware River offers terrific views. The towpath is grass and dirt, easy walking and bicycling with mountain-type bikes. Heavy rains can make the path slippery and small flooded areas might be tricky to cross. Dogs must be on a leash on the tow paths. Children on bikes should be old enough to steer steadily. In many places poor bike control could lead to a plunge into the canal or down a steep embankment or over a vertical wall into the Delaware River.

The Delaware Canal served a primary function in development of the anthracite coal industry in the Upper Lehigh Valley. The manmade waterway provided a convenient and economical means of transporting coal to New York, Philadelphia and the eastern seaboard. Suddenly, coal was available to thousands of homes and businesses, replacing the dwindling wood resources. Maybe most importantly, coal replaced charcoal in the operation of the iron furnaces, stimulating the expansion of iron industry along the Delaware and Lehigh River valleys.

The short but busy life of the canal was a major boost to the area. During the active years the canal transported approximately 33 million tons of anthracite coal and about 6 million tons of miscellaneous cargoes. Much of the latter consisted of food and durable goods for the communities along the canal.

People also used the canal for recreation. Fishing and canoeing were popular sports, and when a suitable scow or canal boat was available, groups of people organized boating parties for a ride and a picnic. Today, the linear park offers many recreational opportunities.

The Delaware Canal tracks through the counties of Bucks and Northampton and offers visitors a wonderful insight into our heritage and the impact of the industrial era. A walk along the towpath is a stroll in American history. The canal is a National Historic Landmark, the towpath is a National Heritage Trail, and is the backbone of the D & L National Heritage Corridor and State Heritage Park.

Information and Activities

Delaware Canal State Park
Box 615A, R.R. 1
Upper Black Eddy, PA 18972
(215) 982-5560

Delaware Canal also manages Ralph Stover State Park.

DIRECTIONS: The park office is at Lodi, Lock No. 19, north of Uhlerstown and Frenchtown on Route 32. Eleven children were raised in the white lock tender's house that is now the park office, which was designated a National Historic Landmark in 1978.

Duckweed floats in the canal near the locks by the park office. The well-maintained office area is a pleasant place to inspect a lock. A private campground is near the park office.

VISITOR CENTER: Purchased in 1989, the tiny lock house near New Hope is outfitted with interpretive and historical information. The building is restored inside and out, with the downstairs room furnished in 1840s style and the other room with interpretive display panels, wood stove and a counter.

The Friends of the Canal (a volunteer support group) operates the visitor center and offers weekend hours and educational programming.

FISHING: In the river, striped bass on eels at night is a local favorite. Some largemouth are taken from the canal itself, along with common warm-water rough fish like catfish and carp. The southern one-third of the canal is stocked with trout, a put-and-take-style fishery in the spring.

DAY-USE AREAS: Eight picnic areas are scattered along the canal. Six, three-sided interpretive kiosks (with photos of canal boats, information about mules and men, passenger boats, heritage information, etc.) are located in day-use areas that teach about the canal. Ten more descriptive signs are also scattered in the public area that detail the canal history or engineering elements of the canal.

INSIDERS TIPS: Try a canoe/tubing trip or ride the 4.5-mile long passenger mule barge between Eagle Island and New Hope. Route 32 (River Road), which parallels the canal, is a narrow, scenic drive.

15 Evansburg State Park
Land: 3,349 acres Water: Skippack Creek

Evansburg State Park is a multi-purpose unit, but is best known for spring creek fishing for trout and hunting in more than 1,000 acres of mixed habitat for deer and small game. The park was originally going to be a dammed, lake-based state park typical of many Keystone parks, but the effort never happened. Today, the unit is a day-use park with potential for historic site development and programming.

The park is eight miles long, following the Skippack Creek ("Skippy," as its known locally) that carves its way through a combination of northern and southern hardwoods in various stages of growth.

Aside from routine day-use amenities and activities, especially hiking, the park's fine golf course is popular—and challenging. Surrounded by rolling farmlands, pastures, open fields and woodlots, the mostly tree-lined course attracts a steady stream of players throughout the season. In fact, the course is so busy, slow play is not tolerated and a starter helps keep golfers moving on weekends. Many duffers use carts, and if you keep the ball out of the trees, your round will go well.

Remember to keep carts 30 feet from the greens and off the fairways. Fix ball marks, level footprints in the traps, replace divots and get in a little practice on the driving range before your round.

Information and Activities

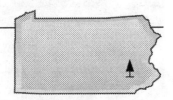

Evansburg State Park
851 May Hall Road.
Collegeville, PA 19426-1202
(610) 489-3729

DIRECTIONS: Five miles northwest of Norristown, reached via U.S. Route 422 in Montgomery County. The park is only 25 miles from center city Philadelphia, via the Schuylkill Expressway. The park office has a handicapped accessible ramp. Bicycles are permitted on roads open to motor vehicles.

FISHING: Brown and rainbow trout are heavily stocked in the easy running Skippack Creek. About five miles of the creek are stocked. The creek waters warm rapidly in early summer. Anglers should be on the stream early in the season for the best chance at catching a trout. The creek attracts the purist fly fisherman, bait fishermen, families and spin casters.

Anglers love the sand and gravel bottom of the creek and the flat-water pools that offer subtle riffles. The gentle creek has no rocky pockets or gushing white water. Fly fishermen should try minnow imitations, soft hackle nymphs, Adams, royal coachman and terrestrials.

YOUTH HOSTEL: The hostel, located in a ranch-style house, provides overnight accommodations supervised by house parents. The hostel operates under the self-help system and provides a place to sleep, eat, shower and meet interesting people. Membership passes are required and can be obtained from the American Youth Hostel national office. You should plan to arrive between 4:30 p.m. and 8 p.m. and leave by 9:30 a.m. Stays are limited to a three-night maximum.

VISITOR CENTER: The white, two-story stucco facility is called the Friedt Visitor Center and was built in the early 1770s on a wooded ridge line. The building has a split-shake roof and interprets natural history and the lifestyles of German Mennonites who owned the home 190 years ago. Surrounding the country home, now a visitor center, are a garden of day lilies outlined by a picket fence, cedar-style wildlife feeding station, towering walnut tree, root cellar and a strong 18th century atmosphere. A variety of seasonal programs are offered, many starting from the center for youth groups, day visitors and organized groups.

HIKING: Walk the gentle six miles of park trails or wander at large along the creek, park roads or day-use areas.

The Skippack Creek Loop (5 mile) passes a variety of trail intersections. Hikers will pass some picnic areas along a bluff, descend to bottomlands, cross the creek and meander along the water's edge. Follow the white blazes through hemlock woods (there is one steep section in the hemlocks), fields and open spaces. The trail and footbridges are maintained by volunteers. A map is available from the park office or the visitor center.

EQUESTRIAN TRAILS: Beginning at a parking lot where horsemen can state, more than 15 miles of open and wooded trails are available.

DAY-USE AREA: The long linear park has four softball fields (on Skippack Road) that are used by area leagues, over 150 picnic tables and open spaces for non-organized family games like badminton, horseshoes and frisbee.

GOLF: The park owns the rolling and treed property, but the outstanding Skippack Golf Course (584-4426) is operated by a private vendor. It's a par 71, 5,697 (white tees)-yard course with a rating of 66.5 and a slope of 106. The pro shop is in a three-story colonial building with black shutters. Inside, hungry golfers can snack on cold drinks and sandwiches. There are only six tables in the food eating area. Most golfers seem to prefer to wander around munching on hot dogs, looking at golfing equipment or watching others putt out on the 18th green.

KEYSER MILL: Buildings built in 1835 on the ground originally were owned by Abraham Funk. The historic building were stabilized in 1984 by the state and are ready for future interior renovations and possible use. The mill was originally built by Joshua Croll and rebuilt by Peter Keyser. It served the area for 95 years, until 1930.

HUNTING: Because Montgomery County has little hunting land, the hunting pressure at Evansburg State Park is high. Deer and small game hunting attract the largest attendance of any seasonal activity. From Sept. 1 to the end of December, the park averages 5,000-6,000 visitors monthly.

16 Fort Washington State Park
Land: 493 acres Water: Wissahickon Creek

History buffs will find the park–and the region–abounding with sites of local and national significance including old mills, Revolutionary-era homes, public museums and other landmarks. Day-users will find game fields, easy hiking trails, picnicking sites and fishing along the Wissahickon Creek, which offers good spring trout angling and summer cat- and pan fishing.

Fort Washington State Park was developed, at least in part, as a result of George Washington's encampment during the Revolutionary War. After the Battle of Germantown Oct. 4, 1777, the Continental Army moved into the Whitemarsh Valley and beyond, nursing their wounds and reorganizing.

By Nov. 2, Washington had established his camp in Whitemarsh Valley. Here occurred the nearest approach to a battle in Montgomery County, when the British marched out from Philadelphia with the plan to attack the Continental Army in December. General Howe abandoned the plan, once he realized how strongly the American Army was posted. Washington had received reinforcement from the north. The Redoubt on Fort Hill, now a part of Fort Washington State Park was an American victory with very little bloodshed. A contingent of Redcoats reached Church Hill, but was unable to seize Fort Hill. Their cannons fell short of the target.

Winter set in with great severity, and it was impossible for the poorly clad and poorly fed troops to survive in tents. Washington chose Valley Forge for his winter quarters. There he ordered warmer log cabins and shelters built. He assured the soldiers that he would cheerfully share their hardships and inconveniences. The American Army, roughly 1,800 officers and men, left Whitemarsh on Dec. 11 and arrived at Valley Forge on the 18th.

In 1981 the Pennsylvania Sons of the Revolution erected a marble memorial stone near the Fort Hill Redoubt along Bethlehem Pike. It reads:

"About 700 feet south of this stone is an American Redoubt and the site of Howe's threatened attack on December 6, 1777."

These lands became a state park in 1953.

Information and Activities

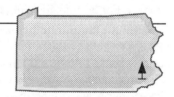

Fort Washington
500 Bethlehem Pike
Fort Washington, PA 19034
(215) 646-2942

DIRECTIONS: Between the towns of Fort Washington and Flourtown along the Bethlehem Pike. It is about two miles from PA Turnpike exit 26.

Fort Washington State Park and the surrounding community take their names from the fort built here by American Revoluntary soldiers in the fall of 1777. Whitemarsh, as the area was called then, was the scene of the encampment of General Washington's soldiers from Nov. 2 until Dec. 11, 1777. Although Whitemarsh Valley saw only skirmishes, the importance of this phase of our War of Independence should not be underestimated.

DAY-USE AREAS: Organized group camping is available on Ridge Road by advance registration. Skiers and hikers may also use about 3.5 miles of trails in the park.

The area is rich in old homes, mills, Hope Lodge and Georgian architecture. One of the most popular features of the park is the Wissahickon Creek, which means "the stream of yellow catfish," located off West Mill Road.

The Militia Hill area is mostly wooded with a variety of mature trees. The hillsides are dotted with dogwood, a beautiful sight in both spring and fall. The pleasant day-use area also has an observation deck on the park road, where a historical marker is set. The area west of Joshua Road remains undeveloped.

The Fort Hill area has scattered plantings of dogwood, sassafras, oak, maple, yellow poplar and sycamore. One old poplar there is 375 years old. The historic site also has a flagstone and a horseshoe-shaped speakers stand that overlooks a grassy space in the center of the park. A plaque dedicates the area to "those who have served their country." Picnic tables are scattered in the mowed area.

NEARBY ATTRACTIONS: Hope Lodge, south of Fort Hill on Bethlehem Pike on a grassy knoll, is a wonderful example of early Georgian Colonial architecture. Built circa 1750, the building is owned by the Pennsylvania Historical and Museum Commission, and is open to the public. For information call (215) 646-1595.

The three-story stone Clifton House, north of Fort Hill on Bethlehem Pike, was built in 1801. Formerly the Sandy Hill Tavern, it now houses a valuable library and museum of local importance. The museum also maintains a collection that includes maps, deeds, leather-bound books, brass lanterns, portraits, swords and other artifacts. The elegant facility is open the first and third Sundays of the month and Wednesdays, 2 p.m. - 4 p.m. Planting beds with annuals and picnic tables surround the library/museum.

NATURE: A bird list is available from the park office. A good number of interesting accidental species have been seen in the park's tracts over the years.

The Militia Hill Hawk watch is from September 1 - November 30 each year. More than 25,000 hawks pass through the area on their fall migration.

INSIDERS TIPS: While in the area, plan a visit to the Valley Forge National Historical Park, just 15 miles to the south. One of the finest evening displays of fireflies is in the Militia Hill tract.

17 Frances Slocum State Park
Land: 1.035 acres   Water: 165-acre lake

The horseshoe-shaped 165-acre lake is lined with day-use amenities, foot trails along the lapping waters, a family campground, dam and boat launches. Pedal boat riding, fishing with kids from the shore and family reunions are popular activities at the green rolling park.

On Nov. 2, 1778, while men and older boys were at work in a field, two boys by the name of Kingsley were sharpening a knife in front of the Slocum family cabin. Sometime earlier these boys and their mother had been given a home by Mr. Slocum when their father was captured by the Indians. Mrs. Slocum heard the sharp report of a rifle, rushed to the door and was horrified to see one of three Indians scalping the elder Kingsley boy, who had been shot. Mrs. Slocum slammed the door, grabbed her infant son and ran off into the swamp, instructing the others to follow.

The Indians, who historians believed were still reeling from the ravages of the Battle of the Wyoming Valley between the American patriots, British and American Indians, ransacked the tiny cabin. One of the invaders saw little Frances Slocum hiding under the stairs. He grabbed her and slung her onto his back, taking the remaining Kingsley boy by the hand and made off into the thick woods. Frantic, Mrs. Slocum tearfully begged for their release as the Indian disappeared. Although Mrs. Slocum never lost hope that her little girl and the Kingsley boy lived and were all right, the curly head of the little 5-year-old girl as it rested on the shoulder of the Indian was the last she ever saw of tiny Frances. The family never stopped looking for Frances, who became known as the "Lost Sister of the Wyoming Valley."

But this wasn't the end of the story. A gentleman named Colonel Ewing turns out to be the real hero of this story. He was traveling through a remote section of Indiana in 1835 during a storm and asked for lodging in the home of a prominent Indian woman of Deaf Man's Village. As the night grew late, the old woman of the lodge asked him to sit with her a while by the fire. She eventually told him she was a white women and her father was a Quaker, and that she remembered having seven or eight brothers and sisters who also lived by a river. She even remembered that her name was Slocum and that the family lived on a farm.

Frances had never told the story before because she had found a rich and happy life among the Indians and knowing no other way of life, did not want to leave. In fact, at one point she asked the Indians to pass a rumor that she had been killed. She was quite content living with her new family.

Colonel Ewing was so moved by the story that he wrote a letter to a Lancaster newspaper, thinking it to be the largest city in the area which Frances thought she came from. The letter went into print and it reached the Slocums in Wilkes-Barre. The family immediately traveled to see the old woman. Instead of a grown white Quaker woman, they found an old wise Indian woman with little resemblance to the child they lost decades before.

At first, Frances was fearful the family wanted her to come with them, but when she realized they understood and honored her wish to remain who and where she was, she imparted her incredible story. It is reported she felt great relief–and that she could now die in peace–knowing her biological family understood and would never try to force her away from her land and Indian family.

After being captured the first day, the party of Indians quickly traveled into the woods to avoid capture and stayed under a rock overhang (located in the present day state park). They continued on to a village of Delaware Indians, where she was adopted by a chief. She was brought up well and cared for as one of their own. As white encroachment became worse, her family began to move west. In her travels she met and married a Miami chief and moved to Indiana. She bore two sons and two daughters, and became a prominent member of the tribe and village. Her people called her "Maconaquah," meaning "Young Bear," because of her great strength and vitality.

At the time of the family visit, she had much land, many horses and a large herd of cattle. She was happy and wished to remain with her children and grandchildren. Members of the Slocum family saw her many times afterward. She died in 1847 at the age of 74 in the presence of her Miami family. She is buried on a knoll on the banks of the Wabash River. Frances lived a remarkable life–happily, she wasn't lost. She found a full and happy life among the Indians.

The park opened in 1968. Flood refugees lived in 262 federally provided mobile trailers set up at the park, which closed to the public during the time, when it served as a housing facility after the devastating tropical storm Agnes in June 1972.

Information and Activities

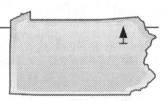

Frances Slocum State Park
565 Mt. Olivet Road
Kingston Township
Wyoming, PA 18644
(717) 696-3525

DIRECTIONS: In northeastern Luzerne County, I-81 to Exit 47B (309 North). Five miles from Dallas and 10 miles from Wilkes-Barre. Follow the signs off of Rt. 309.

EMERGENCY NUMBER: 911 system.

CAMPGROUND: A 100-site family campground, with 15 walk-in tent sites and 85 tent/trailer sites, is open from the second Friday in April to the third Sunday in October. The rolling campground has three loops along the east bank of Slocum Lake. Some of the sites are very private; others are along old stone walls and scattered about varying elevations against the shady hill side. The park check-in station has a pay phone and bulletin board.

Stoney Point, sites 1-54, is slightly rolling and about 50 percent shady.

About one-third of the sites in the loop have electrical hook ups. Sites 1-4 are sunny, while sites 5, 7 and 9 are shady. Many of the sites are separated by vegetation and all sites have gravel pads, picnic tables and ground-mounted fire rings. Site 15 allows campers to pitch a tent under a grove of conifers. Sites 16-19 are open, while sites 22-24 have a lake view. A timber play apparatus with two swings, climbing structure and benches for mom and dad in the campground. Site 37 is both private and sunny. Site 49 is oversized, and great for a large RV rig.

Hemlock Hills, sites 55-87, is a little higher ground and along a ridge line. This small loop also has smaller sites than the Stony Point loop, and not quite as private. Sites are grass and gravel and semi-walk in-style, where you climb several steps, then back a few yards to the flat tent camping pad under a canopy of trees. Many of the sites are scattered along different elevations. Sites 69 and 70 are the highest of the sites, along the top of a hill. Sites 73 and 75 are along a stone wall and nestled under some tall pines. A playground with a tiny slide and four swings serves the loop.

Rocky Knoll, sites 86-100, are walk-in tent sites along the top of the knoll. Some mowed spaces are scattered in the wooded section that tent campers use heavily. Campers park on the hard-surfaced parking area and lug tents and equipment many yards to the numbered sites back into the airy woods. A comfort station serves the walk-in sites.

Organized group tent camping for 40 people is available by advance registration. The group tent area has drinking water, flush toilets and showers, fire rings and picnic tables.

FISHING: Thick stands of trees meet the shoreline much of the way around the lake, yet there are also many bank fishing opportunities, especially in the main day-use areas. The warmwater fishery has common species that include bluegills, large- and smallmouth bass, walleyes and panfish. Live bait suspended under bobbers is the lure of choice most of the year. Ice fishermen like small jigs tipped with minnows gently bounced on the bottom for walleye, and wax works on tear drops for panfish.

Some good-sized muskie are taken from the lake, usually by accident, according to local bait shop clerks. Serious muskie anglers would need to troll big plugs and minnow imitators for many days to get a strike.

BOATING: Red and white, and blue and white pedal boats and other human-powered craft are popular on the 165-acre lake. Canoes, rowboats and electric motors can be rented by your family to frolic on the relaxing lake. If you forget your fishing pole, you can rent that too. Senior citizens receive a 25 percent discount. The boat rental also has snacks and is open 8 a.m. - 7 p.m. most days during the season, Memorial Day weekend to Labor Day.

HIKING: Hiking is easy at Frances Slocum. Five trails (plus connectors) total about 12 miles of trails.

The Deer Trail features a 12-page interpretive booklet that describes places along the trail from the treetops to the lake bottom. The booklet, called *Field Notes,* has a quality map, guidelines and plenty of information for the casual nature lover. The text details the shore zone, which extends from the water's edge outward as far as rooted plants will grow and the life cycle and animals that live and use this area. The open water zone is the most productive part of the lake, where millions of microscopic plants and animals (plankton) provide a nutrient base for all other life. Turtles, fish and waterfowl are found here.

Walkers can explore a disturbed area, a tract that has been altered by man from its natural condition and left to regenerate. You will see many birches and aspen, shrubs and wildflowers in this area. Other parts of the trail teach about watersheds, hemlock stands, aquatic insects, mixed woodlands, woodpeckers, nuts, sedges, submerged plant habitats, beavers and animal tracks.

The park also features a handicapped accessible trail and four-page guide that details quaking aspen trees, raspberry bushes, grapevines (did you know grapes are more than 40 millions years old?) and wildflowers.

DAY-USE AREAS: The open, tightly mowed main day-use areas are long flat lands along the horseshoe-shaped, shallow lake. Game fields, visitor center, trailheads, pool, boat launch, ice skating and parking are concentrated in the area. About 400 picnic tables with nearby sanitary facilities, drinking waters and pavilions are also in the main day-user area.

SWIMMING POOL: The guarded swimming pool is on a knoll looking down on the lake and surrounded by tan-colored showerhouses. The pool deck is both concrete and grass. Two walk-up food concession windows serve swimmers with routine snack foods from the grill and freezer. The shallow end of the pool is 1.5 feet deep.

A controlled diving area, supervised by lifeguards, is open during regular hours, 11 a.m. - 7 p.m. Memorial Day weekend to Labor Day.

NATURE: Unique in the state park system, Frances Slocum naturalists not only interpret natural history concepts and themes, but also the lifestyles of Native Americans. Many programs detail the lives and times of North America's first inhabitants. Topics of discussion at the lakeside visitor/nature center include hunting techniques, foods, tool making, clothes, sewing techniques, farming and gathering, and family lifestyles. Cultural and natural history programs are offered seasonally. Staff also teaches and leads many school groups during the spring and fall. Day and evening programs are offered for campers and park visitors from about March to November.

The wood-frame visitors center is carpeted and complete with a classroom-like teaching area. The facility is open seasonally, Saturday 1-5 p.m. and Sunday 1-5 p.m.

The park is comprised of mixed hardwoods, pine, hemlock and old fields. Migratory warbler populations are good and the viewing can be excellent in early May and mid-autumn. Loons and bald eagles also pass through the park on their seasonal ventures. 207 bird species have been recorded and a birding checklist is available from the park naturalist.

The center also features display materials about Native Americans, geology, animal mounts, butterflies, scavenger hunts, predators, Frances Slocum and more.

WINTER: Sledding and tobogganing on a five-acre slope are popular when snow conditions are good. Ice skating on the lake and snowmobling on a seven-mile trail system.

HUNTING: About 300 acres of the park are open to hunting. Call for details.

INSIDERS TIP: Frances Slocum State Park is one of the first in the state to develop an Adopt-a-Trail program where volunteer groups, families and organizations take responsibility to clear two-mile sections of hiking trails.

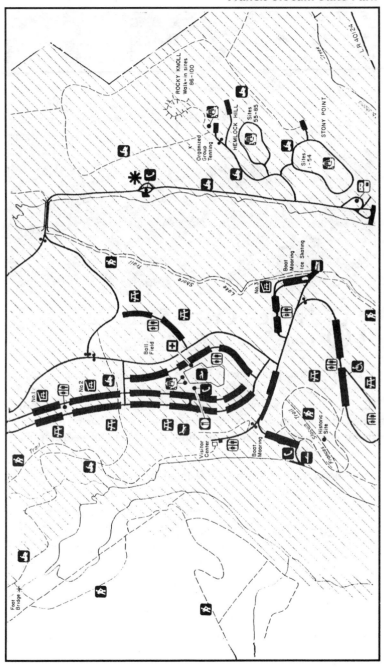

18 French Creek State Park
Land: 7,335 acres   Water: Two lakes

The heavy forests and scenic hills of French Creek State Park wrap around more than half of the 848-acre Hopewell Furnace National Historic Site. These two excellent adjacent recreation facilities offer living and cultural history of the iron furnace era, camping, fishing, swimming, paddling, cabins, hunting, hiking, outdoor education and much more.

Large poplar, oak, hickory, maple and beech trees cover much of the park, with a sparse understory of mountain laurel, rhododendron and bushy plants. Wetlands and pristine streams flowing through rich, damp creek valleys offer great habitats and chances to view wildlife. French Creek is a pleasant retreat.

Neighboring Hopewell Furnace preserves an industry and lifestyle once common, but now nearly forgotten. It is the finest example of an early American "iron plantation," forerunner of today's iron and steel industries.

Hopewell's first ironmaster, Mark Bird, chose the site because of its proximity to roads which linked the furnace to nearby markets and to the raw materials of iron ore, limestone and forest for coal. The charcoal-fueled furnace produced pig iron and finished castings from 1771 until 1883 making it one of Pennsylvania's most important furnace operations. During the Revolutionary War, Hopewell employees cast cannon, shot and shell for the patriot forces. Reaching their peak of prosperity from 1820 to 1840, furnace workers produced pots, kettles, machinery and grates. In 1826-27 doors and door frames were made for the new Eastern State Penitentiary in Philadelphia. Though Hopewell cast many items, the most profitable were beautiful coal- and wood-burning stoves.

Here, you can experience a 19th century iron community, its lifestyle and operations. The restored furnace, waterwheel, blast machinery, ironmaster's mansion and numerous other structures are now quiet reminders of the thriving industry which once flourished in this small rural community.

French Creek was the fifth of five federal demonstration parks turned over to the state government on Nov. 25, 1946. In early 1982, an additional 493 acres were added to the park.

Information and Activities

French Creek State Park
843 Park Road
Elverson. PA 19520-9523
(610) 582-9680

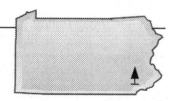

DIRECTIONS: Take SR 724 east of Reading to Birdsboro and turn right onto Route 345 to the park.

CAMPGROUND: The campground has 201 family sites along four similar, mostly wooded loops. Half of the sites are reservable on summer holiday weekends. The modern sites, mostly shady are near flush toilets and shower building. Each clean bathhouse building has exterior sinks. All of the sites have picnic tables and ground-mounted fire rings of steel or cement. The campground has a feeling of safety and extra space at and between camping sites.

Loop A is on a knoll with a thin forest towering over the hard-surfaced camping pads. Sites 9 and 45 are oversized. A little more light filters through the trees in this loop onto good, high and dry sites. Many sites allow tent campers to get back off the road several yards. Site 32 is one of the few in the entire campground that gets sunlight most of the day. Lush walls of vegetation often separate individual camping sites. Sites

49 and 51 are also open and sunny and can hold a medium to large-sized RV rig.

Loops B and C have many larger sized sites, with virtually all of the sites shady and many good for private tent camping. Loop B is very pleasing, with many sites having almost a side yard to spread into. Site 25 receives some mid-day sunshine. Sites 29-35 are on a slight incline, while sites 37 and 38 are near the shower house.

Loop D is a rolling wooded tract of 51 hard-surfaced sites. Site 18 offers campers large boulders scattered around the pad where you can sit and watching other campers, kids and walkers. Site 21 is small, site a good choice for a popup camper. Some of the other sites in this loop, like site 24, are slightly oversized, offered an enlarged area behind the pad where an additional tent or lawn furniture might be placed. Sites 26 and 27 are perfect tent camping sites, located away from the road and private. Like most loops, sites along the outside perimeter have a bit more privacy to their rear and are often up against natural areas. A telephone pole-type play structure with three swings is at the entrance of Loop D.

Organized group tenting north of Scott Run Lake, along a dry gravel spur offering primitive sites. There are two group camping facilities. The group camp (open April 15 -Sept.) area has a dining hall, central washhouses, camper cabin and staff quarters. Camp capacity ranges from 68 to 135. Applications for use are available from Jan. 1 to March 1 each year.

CABINS: Up a gentle hill, into a young mostly deciduous forest, are 10 furnished family cabins, a pleasant alternative to state park camping. Each cabin features sleeping for six, electric heat, fully equipped kitchen, private bath with shower and wall to wall carpeting. The modern cabins are reservable year-round.

The cabins are log-style, built from cedar. Cabin 1 has boulders outlining the front yard and an inviting barbecue grill near the porch and picnic table. Many large boulders line the cabins, which are on slightly varying elevations. Many of the cabins are notched out of the surrounding woodland and set back from the road about 100 yards. They are also spaced about 100 yards apart. Cabin 6 is off the road the farthest, offering cozy privacy and canopy-like trees overhead. Cabin 8 is the closest to the road with a picnic table in the front yard-like area. Cabin 10 is the most private, surrounded by a lawn that gives way to trees at the end of the gravel road.

FISHING: Shoreline and fishing from small boats on Hopewell Lake are popular. The 63-acre lake is a warmwater fishery offering northern pike, chain pickerel, muskie, bass and a variety of panfish. This lake is a big bass lake, and local anglers claim good-sized bass are taken on rubber worms and light-colored spinners in the spring.

Scotts Run Lake, a cold 21-acre body of water that is surrounded by tree-lined shores, offers good trout fishing. The small, intimate lake is stocked preseason, during the season and in the winter. Powerbait is preferred bait here. A single-lane boat ramp is next to the dam spillway. Local anglers say that you should wait for the fish to rise. When they are poking their nose to the surface, they are active, "on the bite" and feeding, often taking live bait (meal worms, waxworms and red crawlers) and dry flies. Shoreline fishing is popular near the dam. Some anglers also wade the small lake, waving a flyrod or using very small spinners cast into a fan-shaped pattern.

BOATING: Non-powered and electric powered boats are permitted on Hopewell and Scotts Run lakes. Each lake has a launching ramp and seasonal mooring.

The boat rental, near the single-lane ramp and connected to the pool complex, is often visited by a large flock of resident Canada geese and park visitors. The facility is on a shady cove with a tan-colored comfort station. Pedal boats, aluminum canoes and V-bottom boats are rented from Memorial Day weekend to Labor Day.

Paddlers can try "two for the price of one." Both Hopewell and Scotts Run lakes are inside park boundaries and combine to provide easy, family-style canoeing.

Hopewell Lake was made in the early 1800s to power the iron furnace's blast. Along the small cove and quiet bays, paddlers may discover a variety of birds and mammals, aquatic life and good fishing. The marshy area in the northwest corner, where Scotts Run enters the lake, is a cool section of thick woods on the shore and shallow waters beneath.

The almost square-shaped Scotts Run Lake can be busy with trout anglers, but usually it is quiet and cool, a favorite drop zone for waterfowl and other birds that glean the shoreline and flock along the banks. This is a terrific lake for a morning paddle.

HIKING: French Creek and Hopewell Furnace National Historic Site

Pennsylvania State Parks
have a combined 30-mile-long trail system covering more than 8,000
acres. The trails allow visitors to reach most of the facilities without
driving a car. Along many trails you will see dogwood, northern hardwoods (oak, hemlock and hickory), pink azalea and mountain laurel.

THERE ARE FOUR SHORT HIKES:

Lenape Trail (2.4 miles) crosses the parking lot near the campground
contact station and is marked in green blazes. The easy hike tracks
near the lake–bring your fishing rod and a couple of sandwiches.

Hopewell Furnace (2 miles). an easy trail that crosses a dam and tours
the historical area.

Miller Point (3.5 miles) is actually a large rock formation that is fun
to scramble on. The trail is marked in white blazes with a red strip.

THE TWO FACILITIES HAVE EIGHT LONG HIKING TRAILS:

Boone Trail (6 miles) is a loop that connects to all major attractions of
the state park. It begins at the Hopewell Lake boat ramp or the
Hopewell Furnace visitor center. Several sections of the trail are steep
and rocky.

Turtle Trail (4 miles) circles through the western side of French Creek
offering easy hiking mixed with some challenging sections.

Lenape Trail (5.5 miles) begins from the campground contact station.

Other interesting trails include, Six Penny (3 miles); Mill Creek Trail
(6 miles), a back country-style trail; Buzzards Trail (3 miles); Raccoon
Trail (1.7 miles) and Horse-shoe Trail (6 miles), a hiking and equestrian trail. The entire Horse-shoe Trail is more than 130 miles long connecting Valley Forge to the Appalachian Trail near Harrisburg.

MOUNTAIN BIKING: Eleven miles of mountain biking trails are maintained at the rolling park. Some of the trails are on park roads. The
routes are spur and loop. Check with the office for regulations on
mountain bike use.

ORIENTEERING: Orienteering is a foot race, a puzzle-solving thought
race, a cross-country running sport and a potentially rugged event that
can take participants over land, through forests and along, sometimes
through, creek beds. Competitive orienteering is a treasure hunt and
track meet combined. Participants use a map and compass to cover the

The park has two excellent fishing lakes.

course in the fastest time possible. The Orienteering Course at French Creek is a permanently marked course, as opposed to the portable markers used in competition. The course allows participants to find orange and white markers in the woods by using a compass and map. Check with the park office for a map and details. Orienteering is a great way to teach map reading skills to children.

HOPEWELL FURNACE: The high-quality living history facility is open 9 a.m. to 5 p.m. daily, 362 days a year. Aside from the wonderfully preserved structures, the historic site also offers special events and programs. Some of the interesting and fun programs include moulder (casting iron) for a day, molding and casting skills, miners and maids and guided tours. For more information call (610) 582-8773 or (610) 582-2093 (TDD).

One of the most interesting aspects of the iron plantation is the people who lived and worked at the site. A traditional hierarchy governed furnace operation. At the pinnacle was the ironmaster–director of the enterprise and often an owner. A good ironmaster had to be a financier, technician, bill collector, marketing analyst, personnel director, purchasing agent, and host to prospective buyers. He had a volatile pro-

117

fession: bad luck or poor judgment usually meant failure; success often brought great wealth.

The ironmaster was assisted by a clerk who kept the books, ordered supplies, served as paymaster, and managed the store office. This job was often a stepping stone to ironmaster, if performed well. The quality of the iron was the founder's responsibility for keeping the furnace blowing at peak efficiency. The founder supervised the other workers at the furnace. Keepers helped him monitor the furnace and took the night shift. Fillers charged the furnace with raw materials. Guttermen directed the molten iron as it left the furnace. Moulders, the highest-paid workers, performed the exacting job of casting the iron. The colliers (charcoal makers), miners and woodcutters provided raw materials for the furnace. Other important members of the workforce included teamsters, who drove the wagons carrying raw materials and finished products; and cleaners, often women and children, who finished the cast products and teachers. Women supplemented family income using traditional skills–sewing, providing lodging and board for single workers and laundering. Some augmented their income working as woodcutters and miners. Farmers, some of them furnace workers part of the year, fed the community. The workforce included people from diverse ethnic backgrounds including African-Americans–first as slaves and later as temporarily employed runaway slaves and free blacks.

You will also learn about raw materials, the casting house, finished products (including beautiful iron stoves), moulding and furnace operations. Buildings include the furnace, charcoal hearth, sheds, office, blacksmith shop, barns, springhouse, cast house, cooling shed, mansion, waterwheel and other buildings that appear today much the way they were more than 100 years ago.

DAY-USE AREAS: Picnic Area 1 and other day-use sites around the park are equipped with tables and play apparatus. Maybe the nicest family picnic area is at Scott's Run Lake, north of the big lake, which is private and scenic. The cool breezes off the 21-acre lake are pleasant.

A very pleasant and well equipped day-use area is above the swimming pool. From here, you have a good view of splashing and aquatic fun in the sparkling pool.

Bring your flying disc for a round of Frisbee golf. Located along the mowed day-use areas are cage-like baskets on poles which are the "holes" for the course.

Other amenities include ball fields and open spaces.

SWIMMING POOL (SMALL ADMISSION): At the lake's edge, the clean and modern pool has five terraced parking lots above it and a narrow, cement sunning deck surrounding it. A large portion of the pool side area is grassy, sloping to the green wire fence that outlines the facility. The pool features a handicapped access ramp with railings and a diving well. The vertical-sided bathhouse is fully equipped, including a concession with four walk-up windows that sells snacks (the fudgesickles are great!), ice and firewood. About 10 picnic tables outside the food concession are available for munching your hot dog or ice cream treats.

The pool is open 11 a.m. - 7 p.m. Memorial Day to Labor Day. The attractive pool is the focal point of the park.

NATURE: Black turkey vultures nest in a nearby quarry and can often be seen by hikers and other visitors. The lakes are magnets for migratory waterfowl, and the hardwoods of the park are a year-round home to pileated and other species of woodpeckers. Also of interest is the geology of the park. Many rock outcroppings are seen along trails and roadways. Check with the park office about scheduled nature walks, evening talks and demonstrations.

HUNTING: More than 5,000 acres of diverse habitat are open to hunting. Call for details.

INSIDERS TIP: Spend the morning at the Hopewell Furnace and the afternoon hiking the state park trails.

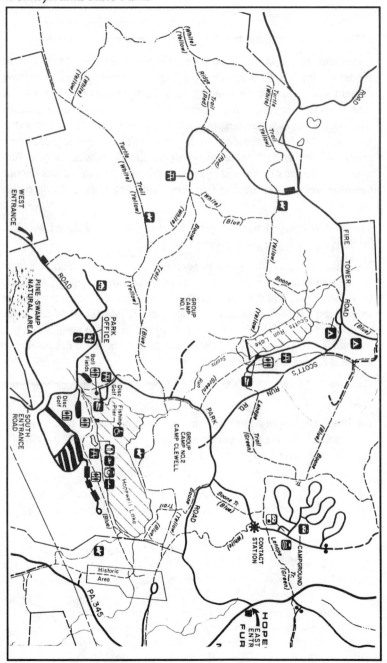

19 Gifford Pinchot State Park
Land: 2,338 acres Water: 340-acre lake

Gifford Pinchot was a true humanitarian. Born to wealth and endowed with imagination, foresight and a love of nature, he shared his possessions and intellect with his fellow Americans to preserve and protect our natural world. For 50 years, Pinchot was America's leading advocate of environmental conservation. In just two decades of his 81-year-long life, he propelled modern forestry and resource management from an unknown experiment to a nationwide movement.

Pinchot used good science and quality environmental management principles to make conservation a public issue and change national policy. In fact, he brought the word conservation into everyday usage.

Twice governor of Pennsylvania, Pinchot got his conservation philosophy from his father, James Pinchot, when in the 1880s at Grey Towers, he often discussed the relationship of forests and natural resources to the welfare of a strong nation with his sons. It was during these formative years that James urged young Gifford to study forestry, an unknown profession at that time. After graduation from Yale, he eventually studied in Europe under prominent foresters, returning home as

Pennsylvania State Parks

America's first professional forester.

In 1898, Pinchot was appointed chief administrator of the Division of Forestry in the Department of Agriculture. Soon the growing agency became the Bureau of Forestry, then the USDA Forest Service. Many large land tracts became rechristened National Forests. With Pinchot in the lead, the agency set about developing effective protection and administration programs for the public properties. The properties were to be managed for the "greatest good of the greatest number in the long run." More than 200 million acres of forests became professionally managed under Pinchot and Teddy Roosevelt.

Soon national and state cooperative projects were underway and at Pinchot's urging, President Roosevelt called a Conference of Governors in 1908 to foster international forestry and natural resources cooperation. Pinchot served two turns as governor and never stopped his crusade for forestry. At the time of his death in 1946, he was still working on forestry plans and urging international conservation.

The state park, named in his honor, was dedicated in May 1961. Gifford Pinchot State Park was the first park specifically designed to serve metropolitan areas–to help give major communities quick access to rural recreation facilities.

Information and Activities

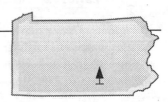

Gifford Pinchot State Park
2200 Rosstown Rd.
Lewisberry, PA 17339
(717) 432-5011

DIRECTIONS: From Harrisburg take I-83 and depart at exit 15 to PA Route 177 south to the park. A relief-map of the area depicting park facilities is outside the log-style park office.

CAMPGROUND: Many sites can be reserved by calling (717) 292-4112. The 340-site family campground is open from the second Friday in April to the third Sunday in October. The facility is along a cove, with each site having hard-surfaced pads, picnic tables and fire rings. The campground's one-lane boat launching ramp is across from site 281. The campground is usually full on holiday weekends, pets are prohibited.

Site 222 is slightly oversized with room for casual seating next to your rig or tent. An amphitheater with scheduled nature programs and a chapel is also nearby, up a narrow footpath near site 225. If you like big boulders, site 228 (and others) has three of them to climb or sit on. Sites 255 and 256 are in the open and campers here would enjoy some sunshine. Sites 333 and 334 offer boulder-strewn additional space behind the camping pad.

Along the cattail lakeshore are sites 161-179. The shoreline in this area is soft, but the view is pleasant. These pads are large enough for medium-sized RV units only. About 207 of the 340 sites in the campground are capable of parking rigs larger than 36 feet in length.

Open sites are 188, 189,190 and 191, near a one-acre mowed area and the showerhouse. Sites 182 and 183 share an open space where campers can set up additional chairs and enjoy some extra space.

Many of the sites, especially those in the 240s, are well separated by vegetation. Campers in this area are near a volleyball court, play field and small play apparatus. Families with smaller children will enjoy site 246 next to the play area. Sites in the 280s and 290s are semi-open, allowing sunshine in during parts of the day. There is also a non-swimming sandy beach-like area where children can dig in the sand and play near sites in the 290s.

Site 315 is airy and open and faces the sandy lake shoreline. Many of the sites between 300-335 have a view of the lake. Sites along this cove-like area are a good combination of openness and shade and are highly recommended. Sites 322 and 324 are good tent sites not far from the shoreline.

Campers who like more open sites might take at look at 1-8 and 141-148. Site 137 has some extra space behind it, and is near many sites along the cove (sites 114-120s) that have a lake view. The shoreline in this area is soft and cattail-lined. Many sites on the tip of this short peninsula are small, good for tents and popup-style campers. Many of these sites look big on the map, but they are actually quite compact. Nevertheless, sites 114 and 115 have excellent views across the lake to the tree-line shore and low hills beyond.

The organized group camping area, unlike most, has regular sites and pads, just like the rest of the campground. Call for details about reserving the group camping area.

CABINS: Southeast of the remodeled park office, 10 furnished family cabins are open year-round. The popular cabins have a living area, kitchen/dining room, toilet/shower room, and two or three bedrooms. Guests should bring their own bed linens, toiletries, kitchenware and utensils. Cabins have a boat mooring area along the lakeshore. Advance reservations are required for the cabins.

The small log-type cabins, built in 1985-86, are scattered along a gravel lane on the northwest side of the lake on a ridge line 50 feet above the lake. Each cabin has doorside parking for two cars, a picnic table and grill.

Cabin 3 is close to the water, while cabins 1 and 10 are fairly secluded. Cabin 9 is notched out of the woods and has its own mini-parking area. By far the most private, tidy cabin 8 is 40 yards from the park road, while cabin 5 has a tiny lawn area and partial lake view. Cabin 6 has a slightly larger mowed area, and is close to the road. Six of the cabins have a partial lake view.

Cabins 2 and 3 share a driveway and would make an excellent choice for a couple of vacationing families. Cabins 1 and 10 are handicapped accessible.

FISHING: Big bass regulations are in effect on the lake. The 8.3-mile-long shoreline hosts bass tournaments and serious anglers who patrol the edge casting lures. The lake is also known for fair to good fishing for pike (spring is the best time), muskie (keep trolling!), crappies from shore in the evening, and good numbers of largemouth and black bass.

Occasional catches of stocked walleye and high-bred striped bass have been reported in the spring and fall, and at nighttime carp and catfish fishermen do well according to local bait shop proprietors. A handicapped accessible fishing pier is at boating area No. 2.

Nearby Codorus and Yellow Breeches Creek are stocked with trout. Taking the time to find the access point when in the area can be worth the effort. The creeks has a native population of brown trout and many anglers discover good hatches along the strong flowing creek. Streamers and nymphs produce throughout the year; otherwise fly fishermen should try matching the hatch or use traditional flies like Hendrickson, brown caddis, Cahills and minnow imitators.

BOATING: Two small boat rentals face each other across the lake, each vying for customers to pedal or paddle canoes, rowboats or pedal boats. You can also rent an electric motor by the hour or day. Seasonal mooring for canoes, small fishing-type boats or sailboats are available in three mooring areas. Non-powered or electric powered boats are allowed on the lake. The lake has three public launches that are open year-round.

At launch No. 2, near the cabins, some small sailboats covered with colorful tarps rest moored near a small fishing peninsula. A number of upside-down aluminum fishing boats are also chained to a green pipe, waiting for weekend warriors to come fishing or paddling.

The Pinchot Sailing Club (established in 1974) operates on the lake with the purpose of encouraging sailing and careful boat handling on the lake. They offer a number of safety, educational and racing programs annually. Races are held on weekends throughout the summer. Call (717) 838-6213 for additional information.

HIKING: Hiking at Pinchot is easy, and most trails connect to amenities and wander near the lakeshore. The Lake Side Trail and Quaker Race Trail on the northwest side of the long lake are popular and gentle walking areas. The Pinchot and Old Farm trails traverses the Straight Hill Natural Area east of the campground. A good network of trails can be accessed from the family campground, ultimately connecting to the Conewago Day-Use Area.

Most trails take between 10 and 30 minutes to complete. Some meander through thick cedar stands and around rock outcroppings, while others explore gentle hills and travel along gravel surfaces.

The Mason-Dixon Trail (200 miles) runs through the park connecting Delaware, Maryland and Pennsylvania. The Mason-Dixon Line was originally surveyed to settle a boundary dispute between Pennsylvania and Maryland, but is best known as the most prominent divider between the northern and southern states.

BRIDLE TRAILS: At the north end of the park, off Alpine Road, riders may use the parking lot near the overlook for staging and saddling. The loop of trails is easy riding and mostly open. Bring your own horse.

DAY-USE AREAS: About 1,000 picnic tables are scattered around the park and down to the lakeshore's edge. Staff reports that the day-use and other areas of the park are packed on holiday weekends. Amenities include play fields, grills, modern rest rooms, water, parking lots, four pavilions (reservable for a small fee) and play equipment. The unit gets some corporate and large group use of the picnic areas. Some picnic tables and facilities are handicapped accessible.

SWIMMING BEACH: Follow the signs to the Quaker Race Day-Use Area and you'll discover the beach, picnic pavilion No. 4, open spaces and plenty of parking. The changing building is a light-green wooden building that is very busy on hot days. The beach is open from Memorial Day weekend to Labor Day, 11 a.m. - 7 p.m., unless otherwise posted.

The 350-yard-long swimming area is subdivided by orange and white buoys and surrounded by lifeguard chairs. Three lifeguard chairs are in the deep part (five feet deep) of the controlled swimming area. The sandy part of the beach is small, but plenty of closely clipped grassy areas are nearby that are great for picnicking and free play. A small green-colored snack food concession stand with walkup windows is open during beach hours.

NATURE: Pinchot is comprised of an abundance of open oak-hickory groves, thick cedar stands, mixed deciduous forests and overgrown open fields. Along with miles of soft shoreline, wildlife watchers can view many species. Osprey and eagles are frequently spotted over the lake.

Seasonal environmental education programs are offered to campers and visitors. Evening programs, pontoon tours of the lake, interpretive walks and demonstrations are popular outdoor education activities. The small visitor center, a focal point for many programs, is at the Conewago Day-Use Area on the south side of the lake.

Common wildflowers, viewed best during the spring, cover wooded and some open spaces around the park. Some of the best wildflower displays are in the Straight Hill Natural Area (near the family campground). Thick aquatic plants along the cattail-lined shore offer excellent nesting and resting places for all types of wildlife, including egrets, American bitterns, herons, waterfowl and songbirds.

Ribbon-like migrations of birds in the skies above the park beckon birders and waterfowl hunters. Some good waterbird sightings include common loons, great egrets, pied-billed grebe, rails, horned grebe, red-throated loon, black-crowned night heron, tundra swan, black duck, widgeon, gadwall, white-winged scoter, old squaw, ruddy duck and others. Good numbers of owls and raptors are also seen hunting the fruitful shoreline and open fields.

The marshy shoreline is a good place to view migrating shorebirds like semipalmated plover, yellowlegs, various sandpipers, dunlin, short-billed dowitcher, 29 species of warbler and six types of vireos.

Grey squirrels, gray and red fox, skunk, deer, raccoon, voles, rabbit, chipmunks, and occasionally mink are seen in the park along the wetland's edge-type habitats. Map turtles, eastern hognose snake, northern water snake, queen snake, eastern ribbons snake and others can also be found, if you look hard and long enough.

STRAIGHT HILL NATURAL AREA: Accessed by trails from the campground or Conewago area, the tract contains abandoned farm fields that are being replaced by eastern red cedar–and the cedar stands are slowing being replaced by deciduous forests dominated by red and white oaks. The successional area also has some interesting geological features.

HUNTING: More than 1,780 acres of the park are open to hunting from the fall archery season through Jan. 31 each year. Call the park office for details since special regulation apply.

WINTER: When conditions permit, ice boaters and skaters take to the frozen water, striking blades against the ice and chilly winds. The best ice for skating is usually in the coves near the visitor center at the Conewago Day-Use Area. Ice fishermen also share lake spudding holes at random, looking for schools of walleye or "on the bite" panfish. Live bait and small jig heads are the rule for all species, according to bait shop owners.

Sledding and cross-country skiing are permitted throughout the park. Many trails are suitable for skiing when snow conditions permit.

NEARBY ATTRACTIONS: Contact the Visitors Bureau at (800) 673-2429.

INSIDERS TIPS: Look for the painting and plaque commemorating Gifford Pinchot displayed in the park office. Pinchot Road, which forms the northwest boundary of the park along Route 177, which is the first hard-surfaced farm-to-market road in the state designed to "get the farmer out of the mud."

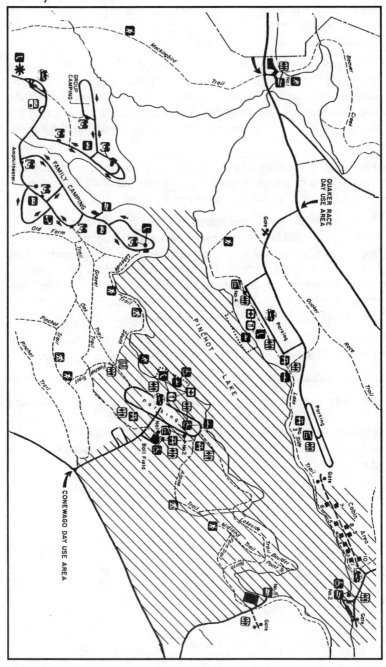

20 M.K. Goddard State Park
Land: 2,856 acres   Water; 1,860-acre lake

Goddard State Park, initially named Sandy Creek State Park, honors Maurice K. Goddard, the Pennsylvania state parks legendary visionary, leader and builder. Goddard, who eventually served as a cabinet officer for more governors than any other person in the history of the Commonwealth, became Secretary of the Department of Forests and Waters for Pennsylvania in 1955, and in 1971, director of the Department of Environmental Resources.

His accomplishments were sound and progressive. Goddard helped to begin a major shift toward better government, insisting on hiring professionals (foresters, civil engineers, park superintendents and degreed people) instead of political patronage, developing comprehensive master plans and setting long-term departmental goals. The one-time professor also found solid funding sources, reorganized personnel and built a professional staff that began the job of statewide park development and modernization.

Goddard's ability to be apolitical allowed him to build support and establish credibility for the state parks system.

Pennsylvania State Parks

In the late 1950s, he commissioned a study and report to the General Assembly that outlined four fundamental criteria that have served as a guideline for Pennsylvania state park development. Within this report, Goddard outlined desirable criteria for new park location, such as, 1) clean bodies of water to serve as the centerpiece of a park, with adequate size and flow, suitable for swimming; 2) reasonably level ground for picnicking, camping, and construction of roads, parking areas and boat ramps; 3) historical or scenic values, and enough area to accommodate 25,000 visitors a day; 4) and a location reasonably near population because, in the end, the report noted, "Parks Are For People."

While statewide park improvement and development were underway, Goddard also championed a movement inside government to improve service and leadership, decentralize power and develop a state park within 25 miles of every Pennsylvania resident. Goddard was one of the first to argue that parks contributed greatly to the economy and that "we've never built a conservation activity that has not raised the local tax base." He was also a strong leader on the Project 70 bond issue that pumped millions into park development and land acquisition.

Information and Activities

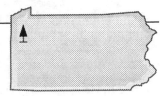

Maurice K. Goddard State Park
684 Lake Wilhelm Road
Sandy Lake, PA 16145-8715
(412) 253-4833

DIRECTIONS: From I-79 in Mercer County, take exit 34, drive west on Route 358 about one-half mile, follow signs to the park. The park office is sometimes closed during lunch time.

FISHING: Lake Wilhelm is a narrow nine-mile-long flood-control lake that is tree-lined and has many small coves and a restricted "Propagation Area" at its west end.

The lake has had about 3.5 million walleye fry planted each year. Other species planted in the lake since 1971 were channel catfish, tiger muskie and muskie. About 15,000 redear sunfish were planted in 1972.

The deepest parts of the lake are less than 20 feet deep. The lake is based on glacial soils and drained farmland. The lake bottom was cleared before flooding. Underwater structures include sunken roadbeds, submerged bridge and abutments along an old stream channel. There are a few stumps and felled trees along the coves. Over the years some structures have been added including tire bundles, Christmas trees and wood lattice cribs known as porcupine brush cribs.

Other fishing hot spots include north of the dam along felled timber; across from launching ramp No. 2 around some sunken Christmas trees; east of launch No. 2 along the shore near some felled timber; directly across from launching ramp No. 3; in front of the handicapped fishing access; and east of ramp No. 4 around the sunken wooden cribs. There are also some good evening panfishing sites along the extensive shoreline of the lake, especially along Creek Road on the south side of the park.

The lake is very good for panfish–perch, bluegill and crappies. Spring is the best time, in the shallows when the fish are on the beds. Small minnow on small white and yellow jigs are a hit combination for panfish. Yellow twister tails, white jigs and minnows are local favorites for spring and summer walleye. Use stinkbaits and scented doughballs at night for big catfish.

BOATING: Plenty of slow-moving pontoon boats cruise the narrow lake, some for pleasure, other for fishing. Seasonal mooring at the marina can accommodate motorboats, fishing boats and pontoons. The newer brown brick marina store is open at 6:30 a.m. to about 8:30 p.m. daily during warm weather offering live bait, a limited assortment of tackle, cold drinks and snack items. There is a tiny dining space inside the store equipped with a picnic table.

Lake Wilhelm has a 10-horsepower limit and there are five launching ramps. The marina has 200 docks, 179 rented by the public, 19 rented by the watercraft concessionaire and two for patrol boats. There is a waiting list for seasonal docks at Goddard's clean and busy marina. The park also operates a 48-space dry land mooring area from May 1 - Oct. 31.

A variety of watercraft can be rented by the hour, including 14-foot-long fishing boats and motors, pontoons and life jackets.

HIKING: Hiking is easy to moderate on Goddard's 21 miles of trails. The Wilhelm Trail circles the lake through alternating meadows and patches of woods, up and down many hills and along the wavy shoreline. Sections of the trail are mowed, and in the fall the meadows are filled with colorful goldenrod and asters. This trail is popular in the winter for cross-country skiers.

You may also hike the Falling Run Trail at the south end of the lake.

The self-guided trail (pick up a brochure at the office) takes about 45 minutes of easy walking to discover the life of a tree, woodpecker holes, bracken fungi, hemlock stands that tower above the forest floor and information about the leaf litter on the ground that decays and becomes rich soil to support the many types of trees, shrubs and wildflowers in the area. The handy brochure also has a line drawing of yellow birch leaves, American chestnut leaves, Indian cucumber root, tree clubmoss and wild grape.

BEACH: A swimming beach is proposed for future development. Its likely location is across from launching ramp No. 2 on the north shore.

NATURE: The McKeever Environmental Education Center is at the south end of the park, near the dam off of Route 358. The residential learning center specializes in ecology programming for school-age children. The center can house and feed up to 120 people in three dorms. The area has excellent, heavily used trails, an auditorium and discovery/interpretive building. Call (412) 376-7585 for additional information.

Birding at Goddard is very good, with 219 species on the checklist and an additional 25 accidentals seen. Many waterfowl species stop at the lake during migrations, such as pied-billed, lesser and greater scaups and hundreds, if not thousands, of Canada geese. Other species of interest include northern waterthrush, grasshopper sparrow, Lapland longspur, northern goshawk, broad-winged hawk and the lightning fast Cooper's hawk. Warbler migration numbers are average.

WINTER ACTIVITIES: Goddard has six miles of trails marked for cross-country skiing. Boat launch areas 3 and 4 are access point for snowmobilers. There are about four miles of snowmobile trails inside the park that connect to additional trails and roads outside the parks boundaries.

Ice fishing, ice boating, skating at launch 3 and sledding at the dam are also popular winter activities.

NEARBY ATTRACTION: State Game Lands No. 270, a 2,027-acre rolling, wooded area include a 420-acre lake. For more information call (814) 432-3187.

INSIDERS TIP: Ask the marina store for a lake photocopy map that indicates where the underwater structures are that often hold fish.

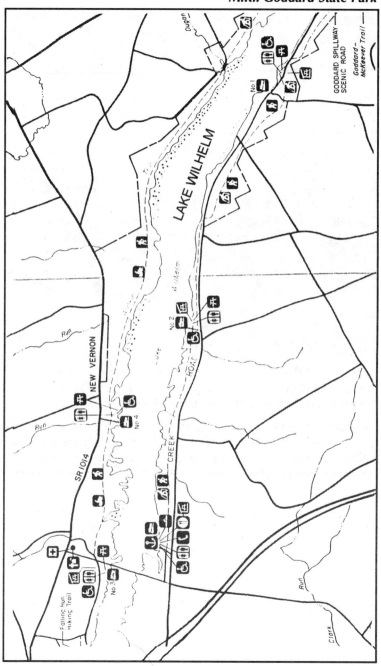

21 Gouldsboro and Tobyhanna State Parks

Land: 8,240 acres Water: 345 acres, two lakes

Gouldsboro is a day-use park. Tobyhanna (which means *"stream whose banks are fringed with alder"*) has day-use areas and family and organized group camping. Each park has swimming beaches, hiking trails, fishing and excellent day-use and picnic facilities. And both parks are a terrific balance of manmade outdoor recreation and nature. They share tracts of mature hardwoods and conifers, open meadows and successional wetland.

The parks also share black bear that live in thick swamps and come out during berry time to gorge themselves on blueberries and beechnuts. Occasionally, bear ramble through the campground and picnic areas sniffing around for food and poking their heads in trash barrels. Woodcock are also inhabitants of the wetlands and woods. The mating flights and eerie calls can often be seen and heard in the spring and summer, especially along the railroad bed in Gouldsboro State Park.

Logging was the first major industry to the area, sending tens of thousands of board feet of sawn lumber south to Philadelphia. By the late 1800s the timber resources of the area had been depleted, and the harvest and shipment of clear clean ice began to dominate the local economy. Many early residents cut and worked the ice business through the winter to fill large barn-like storage buildings. In the summer the ice was used to cool rail cars shipping perishables all over the East Coast.

Also during this era and in the early 1900s, the railroad system brought vacationers from Philadelphia and New York to enjoy the cool mountain air in summer and the snowy mountains in winter. A variety of large and small resorts were built to accommodate the increasing number of visitors. To this day the Pocono region is one of the best known and finest vacation spots in the country.

In 1948 the state acquired title to a portion of the former Tobyhanna Military Reservation. Since before World War I, the military had used it for various purposes, including artillery training for West Point cadets and housing for German prisoners-of-war in World War II. The federal government retained part of the site to create Tobyhanna Army Depot, while the rest of the 2,600-acre area was divided into Tobyhanna and Gouldsboro state parks. That same month, the Legislature authorized the acquisition of land for Bendigo State Park north of Johnsonburg, in Elk County.

Information and Activities

Gouldsboro and Tobyhanna State Parks
P.O. Box 387
Tobyhanna, PA 18466-0387
(717) 894-8336

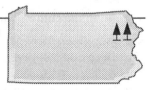

These two parks have adjacent land, and main facilities are only minutes from each other.

DIRECTIONS TO GOULDSBORO: In Monroe and Wayne counties in northeastern Pennsylvania. The park entrance is one-half mile south of the village of Gouldsboro on PA Route 507. PA Route 507 intersects with I-380, two miles south of the park entrance. About 70,000 people visit the park annually .

DIRECTIONS TO TOBYHANNA: Also in Monroe and Wayne counties. The park entrance is 2.1 miles north of Tobyhanna on PA Route 424. PA Route 423 intersects with I-380 2.5 miles south of the park entrance. About 80,000 people visit Tobyhanna annually .

EMERGENCY NUMBER: 911 system.

CAMPGROUND: The 140-site campground at Tobyhanna is open from the first weekend in April to mid-December. Flush toilets and showers are not provided. The campground, which is about 2,000 feet above sea level and shady, is on a single one-way loop near Tobyhanna Lake. Twenty-three of the 140 sites are for trailers at least 21 feet in length. Sites have gravel pads, large-size fire rings and picnic tables.

Sites 1, 3, 5 and 7 are notched out of the woods and most sites on the outside perimeter are against natural areas. Oversized sites include 18 19, 20, 21 and 23. Sites 61 and 67 catch a bit of the sun and are pleasant camping sites for tent or medium-sized RVs. Gravel pathways wind through the campground connecting the sides of the loop. Some of the quietest sites are 133-140, a short connector land between the linear sections that make up the larger loop.

Beginning at site 98 to 132, campers will have a through-the-trees view of the lake. Site 111 is one of the closest to the water's edge, only about 15 yards from the somewhat soft bank. A sand volleyball court is near site 108, which is near an overflow parking lot, camper's boat mooring area and tiny boat ramp. Site 125 has a partial lake view and is high and dry. Sites 130 and 131 are excellent grassy places for family tent camping.

Limited RV storage is available at Tobyhanna.

FISHING: Bank fishermen like the dam and near the shallow camper's boat ramp and mooring. There are also many other shoreline fishing opportunities in the park.

Gouldsboro anglers often bring their bass boats, standing and casting spinners and crankbaits at underwater points and other patterns. Gouldsboro Lake is a good to very good warm-water fishery, offering good populations of largemouth bass, muskie, panfish and pickerel. Some excellent evening crappie fishing is done during the spring and early summer using wax and red worms and small jigs.

BOATING: The Tobyhanna boat rental concession has canoes and V-bottom aluminum boats at the newer dock . The dock is one of the finest rental boat facilities in the park system and offers boats for rent by the half-hour and by the hour. Electric boats are permitted on the lak.

Tobyhanna Lake was once extensively used for harvesting ice. Ice from Tobyhanna also made its way to Florida and was used in hospitals and other places. Ice fishing and ice skating are still popular on the lake; harvesting ice is not. Tobyhanna is a pleasant lake to canoe. The south shore is wooded with beech, birch and maple, and the shallow headwaters of the Tobyhanna Creek are open to explore.

Gouldsboro Lake (250 acres) prohibits all but electric and human-powered boats. Small watercraft are available to rent. Paddling Gouldsboro Lake is a pleasant and interesting surprise. At first glance the lake looks routine, especially if you evaluate it from a map. Once on the lake, paddlers will find many small islands at both the north and south end, rafts of vegetation and emergent stumps everywhere. At the north end of the lake, a swamp can be penetrated when water levels are high. This area is characterized by alders and other wetland species. This is an excellent birding area.

HIKING/BIKING: Five miles of the park's trails are hard-surfaced and suitable for hiking or biking. About seven more miles of gentle trails are in Tobyhanna park, including the 3.7-mile Frank Gantz Trail that connects to Gouldsboro. Part of the Tobyhanna Lake Trail is wheelchair accessible.

The Tobyhanna and Yellow Trail (4 miles) wind northward along the Tobyhanna Creek and through Bender Swamp. Much of the trail is wide and flat, passing through the swamp, past downed and water-dead trees, through lush forests, along fields and by a low stone wall.

Gouldsboro maintains 8.5 miles of trails that encircle the northern end of the park by way of the old entrance road, old Route 611 and Prospect Rock Trail. Portions of Prospect Rock are difficult. The old road portions of the trail are suitable for bicycling.

DAY-USE AREAS: About 300 picnic tables are in Tobyhanna, many in the main day-use area, with some other scattered along the east shore of the lake. The main shoreline is extensive with playgrounds, pavilions and other amenities. The smell of barbecued chicken can fill the air on weekends. Tobyhanna is a very popular family day-use park.

Gouldsboro also maintains about 300 picnic tables from which lots of potato salad and watermelon has been served. You can often hear the clacking of steel horseshoes as players compete after a hearty outdoor feast. The beach is about 100 yards from the parking lot, so travel light when you visit the Gouldsboro beach.

Paddling Gouldsboro Lake is interesting. Both the north and south sides have many small islands, rafts of water vegetation and emergent stumps. A watercraft concession rents canoes and other small boats.

SWIMMING BEACH: Tobyhanna's beach is guarded, sandy and about 125 yards long. It's open Memorial Day weekend to Labor Day, 11 a.m. - 7 p.m. A pleasant grassy area surrounds the beach and has many picnic tables scattered throughout the area. The simple vertical-sided changing rooms are open air. The water is divided by floating buoys into three patrolled areas. Benches are on site.

Gouldsboro's swimming beach is guarded. The narrow band of sand about 170 yards long next to a four acre mowed day-use area is dotted with mature trees and plenty of picnicking areas. The open spaces around Gouldsboro invite impromptu softball games and touch football matches.

NATURE: Tobyhanna offers seasonal naturalist programs; for example, nature hikes, summer wildlife, beach hikes, lakeside guided walks, Tobyhanna falls, color, and patterns in nature.

Both parks are comprised of mixed hardwoods, some softwoods, coniferous forest, meadow edges and wetlands. These habitats are suitable for a wide range of birds. Good numbers of spring and fall migrant waterfowl drop into the lake to feed and rest while many spring warblers can be seen in their breeding plumage during early May.

Bald eagles are sometimes seen, but more common are turkey, killdeer, waxwing, hummingbirds, several kinds of sparrows, woodpeckers and ruffed grouse.

WINTER: Ice fishing is popular on both lakes. Cross-country skiers and snowmobilers have about five miles of trails Tobyhanna State Park. Ice skaters can dress warmly and use a one acre area near Parking Lot 3 (unheated rest room) at Tobyhanna.

INSIDERS TIP: There's plenty of quality Poconos-area attractions nearby.

22 Greenwood Furnace State Park

Land: 423 acres   Water: Six-acre lake

Today Greenwood Furnace is a quiet forested park nestled in the mountains of northeastern Huntingdon County. But it was once a bustling community, the site of Greenwood iron furnaces that produced some of the best charcoal iron in America to help feed the appetite of the developing industrial nation. The huge furnaces operated from 1834, when the Pennsylvania Canal opened to Pittsburgh, until 1904.

No one knows for certain how Greenwood Furnace was named. The area was once called "the lordly evergreen forest," which it is. And the nearby town of Belleville was at one time known as "Greenwood." The mystery, according to the park's cultural interpreter, will likely continue. What isn't a mystery is the history of the furnace town, including considerable information about individuals and families that lived and worked here.

For 70 years, furnaces dominated the landscape. The town vibrated with life. From the roar of the towering furnaces, the shouts of workmen, the hiss of a steam engine, the creaks and groans of heavily laden wagons and the twice-daily shrill of the steam whistle—all signaled prosperity in the iron town.

Greenwood Furnace Public Camp was established in 1925 when the state began a camp around the lake formed by the old ironworks dam. During the Great Depression of the 1930s, the Civilian Conservation Corps built many of the park facilities and improvements to the surrounding state forest lands. In 1989, the Greenwood Furnace National Historic District was established by the National Park Service due to the historical and architectural significance of the former ironworks community.

Information and Activities

Greenwood Furnace State Park
R.R. 2, P.O. Box 118
Huntingdon, PA 16552-9006
(814) 667-1800

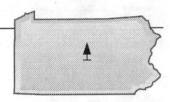

DIRECTIONS: In Jackson Township, Huntingdon County, along Route 305, five miles west of Belleville and East of McAlevys Fort. The park is a 40-minute drive from Huntingdon, Lewistown or State College. Summer hours for the visitors center are 9 a.m. - 5 p.m. daily. From the park you are five miles to the closest town.

CAMPGROUND: The 51-site family campground is outfitted with a showerhouse that has flush toilets and outside dish-washing sinks. Site 1, which is often occupied by the campground host, has electrical and sewer hookups. When the host is not on the site, it is open for first-come first-served campers. Staff says that many of the sites that are close together are often used by multiple families for long weekend stays.

The east branch of Stone Creek is behind sites 1-18. It is classified as a wild trout stream, offering good spring fishing. Sites 32 and 44 are pull through sites offering additional space for large families. Tent campers that want seclusion will want to inspect sites along a ridge - 45, 46, 47, 48, 49 and 50. Site 24 is the handicapped site with a hard-surfaced path that connects to the bathhouse.

FISHING: There is no boating on the small lake, but anglers will discover plenty of shoreline access points and an accessible fishing pier. Brook trout and cold-water-tolerant brown trout are in the small lake.

Staff stays the scenic little lake is one of the coldest in the state parks system because it is spring fed. In addition all of the contributing streams are in tree cover, supplying very cold, oxygen-rich water.

The lake is about 15 feet deep with steep banks and little underwater vegetation.

The East branch of Standing Stone Creek still gives up some good stocked holdovers and native trout. The lower section is quite warm, offering fair to good smallmouth bass angling. Trout anglers should stay in the upper reaches after Memorial Day.

HIKING: The self-guided historic walk takes about one hour of easy walking An accompanying foldout brochure describes the company-town life of workers, clearing of the forest at the rate of one acre per day, rates of pay (30 cents per cord of wood cut), what colliers did (charcoal makers), the making of pig iron, a slag dump (caution: slag is a crude glass and can be very sharp), the company store, grist mill operation, the church (which still holds weekly services in the summer), school house, and finally the cemetery.

More traditional hiking includes many short trails and connectors to the Mid-State Trail and state forest trail network. The Greenwood Spur of the 171-mile Mid-State Trail leads past the Greenwood Forest Fire Lookout Tower and through the Alan Seeger Natural Area. Check with the park office for information about the Link Trail, a rugged 65-mile long link to the Tuscarora Trail near Cowans Gap State Park.

For more information about the Mid-State Trail, write MSTA, 227 Kimport Ave., Boalsburg, PA 16827.

VISITOR CENTER/MUSEUM: The surprisingly large barn-like (post and beam) museum that was probably built in the late 1860s, interprets the cultural and industrial history of the Greenwood furnace. Blast furnaces reached temperatures of more than 3,000 degrees. There is great emphasis on the lifestyles of the workers and their families who lived and worked in the iron town. Outside, surrounding the facility are a split-rail fence, brick walkway, three small demonstration gardens and examples of old wagons (the undercarriage of one was built here). Several benches are also placed near the outdoor exhibits and landscaped areas.

Interpretation and programming at the museum often try to answer the questions, "What was it like to live in the iron community? What was daily life like? What were the workers and their families lifestyles like? What were their hardships?"

Inside the rectangular-shaped museum are a variety of artifacts. From an archaeological dig, bits of metal, bottles, pieces of shoes, dishes, houseware items, thimble, keys, sleigh bell, pocket knife, clay pipes, ice skate, harmonica and more.

One of the more interesting research projects that the staff is engaged in is reconstructing and organizing the census records of the town and furnace company. Part of the history of the furnace is that many of the work force were drawn from families who were already settled in the valley. So there is a strong ancestral tie to the region. Many visitors to the museum come to find ancestors who once lived or worked in the community. Much of the genealogical information is in a free-standing display and much more is computerized. Staff stands ready to help visitors who are seeking relatives who might have worked for the iron company. The list includes more than 300 families and 2,300 individuals.

The museum building, originally a wagon and blacksmith shop, features some interesting structural elements that helped serve those functions. For example, king trusses (one horizontal member and two triangular shaped beams) that support large cross beams were installed in half of the building and were used to lift the huge wagons. An empty wagon bed could weigh up to two tons, so the beefed up truss system made it easy to install the beds on the wagon frames. The iron company began building its own wagons merely to save the cost of buying them from outside vendors.

The back portion of the building features a working blacksmith shop complete with forge, tongs, hand-operated blower, anvil and other tools. Other displays include examples of pig iron, charcoal and iron ore. In one corner of the open space section of the museum are a shaving horse, many examples of woodworking tools and a wood craftsman's bench. Here handles, wagon wheels and other wood items were made by hand to supply the needs of the workers.

The museum also has a short videotape presentation about the iron-making furnace and the community that made it work. About 25 seats are lined up in front of the television in the first half of the building.

FURNACE: Outlined by a split-rail fence and red brick pavers, the looming stack is described by a nearby kiosk. The interpretive sign has historical photographs of workmen and sketches of how the iron-making process worked, showing the blast furnace and casting shed, bellows and casting floor. In just five minutes of reading the sign, visitors will understand the basic process of making charcoal iron. Additional information includes a cross-section drawing of the furnace showing the crucible (fire pit), air ducting systems, stone work and charcoal.

Visitors can actually step inside the furnace, stand next to the crucible and peer up the tall brick chimney to the sky above. Many of the bricks that make up components are marked with the word "Queens." Today the furnace is surrounded by towering evergreens near a stream where chattering squirrels and birds are often seen.

Furnace workers were paid $24-30 per month for six 12-hour shifts per week. This was during the most prosperous time during the 1850s and 1880s. About 300 (the total peak population in the community was about 750) men were employed at the furnace during this era. The town consisted of 127 buildings, with the majority being homes, many of which rented for $3 per month.

Greenwood families were self-sufficient. Almost every family owned a cow, pig and chickens and tended large gardens. Only staples like sugar, cloth or coffee were purchased from the company store.

DAY-USE AREAS: Many day-use areas are outlined by rail fences and are well-kept, inviting places for a picnic or slow walk. Reservable shelters are available for family outings.

SWIMMING BEACH: Open Memorial Day weekend to Labor Day, 11 a.m. - 7 p.m. The small beach of imported yellow sand is about 100 yards long and 20 yards wide and is surrounded by a beautiful CCC-built stone wall. The water is divided by yellow buoys and has a maximum depth of about five feet. Two or more lifeguards patrol the beach. A timber-frame play structure and handicapped accessible fishing pier and ramp into the water are in the general area. Even in the middle of summer the water temperature rarely rises above 65 degrees.

The newer dressing building is sided with weathered Western cedar in a board and batten design. It is near the small food concession that sell traditional snack foods, ice cream and soft drinks.

INSIDERS TIP: The park maintains a three-ring binder called the "Host Book" filled with the brochures of local attractions, restaurants and other useful information.

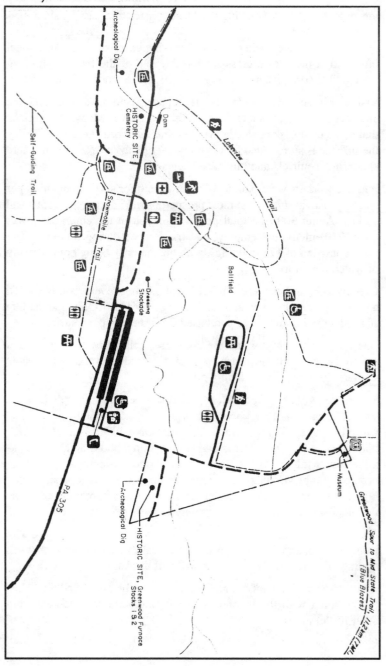

23 Hickory Run State Park
Land: 15,500 acres Water: Small lakes/streams

Hickory Run's boulder field, a huge valley filled with stones, is one of the most striking natural features in the entire state park system. After only a minute or two, when your eyes have scanned the wide field of stones, you'll sense how starkly quiet the gray crag is. The cobble-like noises of sure-footed walkers and their whispers and talk are gobbled up by the vast sea of rocky space. The boulders act like an acoustic sponge, absorbing much of the noticeable sound. It is both an eerie and beautiful place to visit.

The sprawling park, in the western foothills of the Pocono Mountains, was once part of an immense tract of land which, by treaty, was acquired by the Commonwealth from the Indians. But long before the treaty, the first cave-dwelling humans arrived in the region more than 11,000 years ago. They lived in dark forests of spruce trees and boreal bogs filled with sphagnum moss. These bogs were formed as the glacier left behind large chunks of ice that melted into pools that filled with moss.

These early settlers knew nothing of agriculture, only wandering, hunting and gathering on the scenic lands. By the arrival of Columbus to North America, Native Americans had evolved into the tribes that are known today, with rich customs and traditions. When Pennsylvania was settled, the Lenni Lenape, named by the Europeans the "Delaware," held the territory that would become known as Hickory Run. For many decades to follow the land was developed slowly. The government eventually gave 400-acre tracts, called warrants, to anyone who would settle on the land and pay taxes.

Before the Civil War, the area was known as the "Shades of Death" because the entire area was thickly covered with a growth of virgin white pine, hemlock, oak, maple, and also because refugees fled the battle of Wyoming in 1750. They crossed the rugged area and many died. After 1835, towns arose along the banks of Hickory Run, loggers pillaged, mills hummed, a brick factory (just below the current park office) worked and homes sprang up. Three buildings from the town of Hickory Run still stand.

Forty-five years later, the entire region was cut over and dams that were built to supply powers were all that remained. In 1918, Colonel Harry C. Trexler, an Allentown businessman, purchased several tracts of land in the area of what is now the park. After his death, trustees of his estate made 12,908 acres available to the National Park Service. The Hickory Run National Recreation Demonstration Area was built by the National Park Service with the help of the Works Progress Administration during the 1930s. In 1945, this outstanding recreation area was given to the Commonwealth and became Hickory Run State Park.

"The earth is dressed in beauty and all around us it sings in quiet song. In nature, as in life itself, we must listen closely so that we may hear the magnificent melody found within its whisper." L. W. Gilbert.

Information and Activities

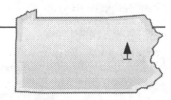

Hickory Run State Park
R. R. 1, Box 81
White Haven, PA 18661-9712
(717) 443-0400

DIRECTIONS: In Carbon County. From I-80 take exit 41 at the Hickory Run State Park exit, and drive east on PA 534 for six miles. The park is two to three hours from Harrisburg, Philadelphia and New York City, and one hour from Allentown, Scranton and Wilkes-Barre.

CAMPGROUND: Sites 1-277 are open the second Friday in April until the third Sunday in October. Sites 278-381 are open the second Friday in April until the end of antlerless deer season in December. Forty-five of the total 381 sites are for tents and many sites are reservable on holiday weekends. Take a drive through the campground, inspecting sites for damp, low sites, size and flatness.

The light green camp store, complete with a neon "open" sign flickering in the window, has roof top flags and lots of camping supplies. From fishing equipment to campfire cooking utensil, the store is crammed with toys, food items, used paperback books, sunglasses, candles, bug spray, hats, T-shirts, sleeping mattresses, lanterns, propane fuel, novelties, firewood, rope, frozen pizzas, basic grocery items and corn cob pipes. Packed from floor to ceiling, this is the best campground store in the Keystone state's system. Hours vary, but they are open until 7 p.m. or 9 p.m. daily during the season.

The hilly campground is shady and heavily wooded with gaps, ravines and thickly covered valleys. Shower houses have exterior sinks for dishwashing. Some sites are on a slight incline. Vegetation separates many sites. All sites have fire rings and picnic tables. Some of the sites in the campground are oversized; others are near patches of ferns and rhododendrons with hard-surfaced pads.

Favorite sites include 58-60 (near a mowed day-use area), 94, 117,119, 127, 141, 152, 158, 189, 196 and 103-105. Sunny sites include 17, 19, 21 and 24. In a hollow are some good tent sites 3-5.

Organized group tent camping for up to 500 people is available by advance registration. Two group camps with cabins can accommodate 129 and 149, respectively. Cabins are available only to organized, non-profit groups.

FISHING: Fishing is offered at Hickory Run Lake. Stream trout fishing is exceptional in the area. Stocked streams include Sand Stream Run and Fourth Run. Mud Run is a fly fishing only stretch in the park. The stream has difficult access. Try to get on the stream from Hawk Falls Trail or Orchard Trail. Hawk Falls Trail is just beyond the turnpike overpass on the right side of Route 534. Orchard Trail is about one-quarter mile east of Hawk Falls Trail. Well-shaded Mud Run (the prettiest creek in the region, offering a wilderness-like fishing experience) has a good population of native brook and brown trout. Midge patterns and emerging caddis patterns are good choices.

Sand Spring Run is behind the park office. It has three dams, Civilian Conservation Corps, Number 5 and Stametz, along its length. The stream is stocked with brooks and browns.

Fourth Run is beyond Group Camp No. 2. Access is by Fourth Run Trail. From the park office, follow Route 534 east to the main park entrance. Make three left turns. When you see the dam on your left, continue straight on the dirt road through the field to Fourth Run Trail. The small stream is stocked with brook and brown trout.

Hickory Run (the warmest creek in the park) from the junction with Sand Spring Run to the Lehigh River is a catch and release area. Artificial lures and barbless hooks may be used. All fish in this year-round stream must be returned.

Francis Walters Dam, about 20 minutes from the park, offers warm-water angling and boating. Trout are taken at the dam.

The Lehigh River was once a productive trout fishing river. From the 1930s to the 1950s, strong hatches and good catches prevailed. For more than 25 years the waters suffered from indiscriminate spraying and the great green drake hatches ceased. Today, however, good hatches bring the noses of stocked trout to the surface. The April Hendrickson hatch is very good. The river has various conditions that include long deep pools with riffles above, side channels and numerous tributaries (many being good trout streams in their own right) flowing into the main stream.

HIKING: The park maintains about 36 miles of trails, some easy, others difficult, all scenic and interesting.

Boulder Field Trail (3 miles) seems longer than three miles due to the rocky going. The popular trail runs from Hawk Falls on Route 534, just east of the turnpike to Boulder Field. The rocky path is a steady uphill slope. When you reach a rocky area with old hemlocks and spruce, you are almost to the end. Going back down the trail is great fun!

Hawk Falls Trail (.75 mile) takes hikers past a very pretty 25-foot waterfall. The trail crosses a stream on stepping stones and circles upstream to Mud Run.

Stage Trail (4.5 miles) is easy walking along an old stage route between Allentown and Wilkes-Barre. The trail intersects the Boulder Field Trail.

The beach is almost as impressive as the sprawling boulder field.

Manor House Trail is an old logging road. Many birders find the trek through mixed woods rewarding. Deer Trail (.5 mile), which runs from the day-use area, is also a good birding hike.

Fire Tower Trail (.25 mile) is a road of crushed shale leading to the Bureau of Forestry fire tower. If open, visitors may climb up, but not into the tower.

Other easy trails include Lake Trail (.5 mile), Stone Trail (1 mile) and Gamewire Trail (1.75 miles).

BOULDER FIELD (National Natural Landmark, 1967): People trudge across the flat boulder field, head down, stepping carefully from one boulder to the next examining each for different textures, colors and quartz. This is the largest boulder field in the eastern United States. Walkers can also listen carefully for the sound of water running beneath them during the spring. Kids love to look for the largest and smallest boulders in the sprawling 400 feet by 1,800 feet field of stones. Some of the boulders measure 26 feet long; many are the size and shape of a basketball.

The boulder field is one of the most striking geologic features in the state and a true relic of the past. The field has not changed much for more than 15,000 years. The field occupies a flat valley near the head-waters of Hickory Run. The broad valley trends east-west and has low ridges on either side which rise more than 200 feet above the surface of the rugged field.

Visitors will see that the boulder field is very uneven, and in many places the relief from one boulder to the next is as much as four feet. The field is made up of a jumbled assortment of loosely packed boulders generally less than four feet in diameter, but some as large as 26 feet in length. There is no fine material such as sand or clay filling the spaces between the boulders. The boulders are mainly red sandstones in the northern half of the field and pock-marked red conglomerates with white quartz pebbles in the southern part. Walking across the field, you will notice a change from rounded boulders near the parking lot to angular boulders near the east end of the field. Boulders at the east end have not received as much scouring from glacial action and the weather like the others part of the craggy field.

The end moraine of Laurentide Continental Glacier straddle the park from the southwest corner up to the northeast corner. This is the ending point of the glacier. Seasonal melting released huge amounts of water which deposited rocks, sand, soil and debris. Chunks of ice also washed into the moraine and when they melted, created boreal bogs.

When the glacier neared the park and Boulder Field, the climate was very cold and harsh. It is comparable to Greenland today, near the Arctic Circle. The ground was so cold it froze, which is called permafrost. The great change in temperature, frequently fluctuating above and below freezing, drove the processes that created Boulder Field.

Given this harsh climate, we can begin to understand how the field was formed. The ridges north and south of the field are red conglomerates, sandstones and siltstones of the upper part of the Catskills Formation and match those found in the boulder field. These nearby ridges, therefore, represent the probable source for all material in the field. A close examination of the rocks in these ridges also shows them to be fractured in a block-like manner. These fractures are natural planes of weakness in the rock and when water seeps into them and freezes, it causes the rock to break away from the outcrop. During glacial times, repeated breakup of rock by freeze and thaw resulted in a pile of angular boulders at the base of these ridges.

Mixed with other boulders and with sand and ice, during each summer thaw the ice in the upper part of this mass melted, and the water-saturated material slid slowly down the slopes on the underlying frozen ground. As these boulders moved along, they were constantly grinding against each other, and their angular corners were gradually worn away to produce the rounded boulders seen in the western part of the field. This ongoing process and their movement was repeated many times over thousands of years and resulted in the large flat boulder we also see in the field.

In 1994 the Boulder Field was declared a State Natural Area.

DAY-USE AREAS: Nearly 500 picnic tables and plenty of play equipment, water fountains and trash barrels are scattered throughout the park. Picnic sites under small groves of maple trees near the beach are very popular and pleasant. Many handicapped picnic tables are mixed in with others throughout the park.

SWIMMING BEACH: Near a gravel walkway across the dam, the coveside beach is guarded and a focal point for the large Sand Springs Day-Use Area. The sandy beach is 175 yards long and 40 yards wide.

The shake-sided concession stand serves foot-long hot dogs, cheeseburgers, French fries, soft pretzels, snow cones and soft drinks. Other items include T-shirts, lighter fluid, bug repellent, paper plates, charcoal, small toys and other small necessities. The concession stand is surrounded by large mowed areas and looks down upon the beach.

NATURE: Seasonal environmental education programs (nine months a year) are popular at Hickory Run and might include a boulder field walk, campfire programs, sing-a-longs, beach games, a brook trout program and nature films at the amphitheater.

The small, almost plain-looking, rough-sawn-sided nature center has a bat box at its gable end and indoor exhibits that include sections of native trees (oak family, hemlocks, black walnut, locust, American elm, etc.), live tanks with salamanders and other aquatic animals and other interpretive displays. The center offers guided outdoor education programs for youths and adults. The kids' corner touch table is loaded with many hands-on nature artifacts and items (skulls, antlers, pine cones, bones, skins and feathers).

The large park is a myriad of forests. Northern hardwoods dominate, but there are sections of climax forest which are composed of mostly hemlocks and pine trees. There is also a section of black spruce near Boulder Field. A variety of animals can be seen along the 36 miles of hiking rails, including deer, bear, porcupine and squirrel. Also rarely seen are bobcat, mink coyote and snowshoe hare.

There are a few hickory trees left on the property. Starting in the 1830s, the area was extensively lumbered and accounts claim that the area had many large hickorys. Because hickory wood is so strong and useful, the logger's ax got to just about every one. The name hickory comes from the Native American word *"pawcohiccora,"* an oily food made by pounding kernels steeped in boiling water. Sweet hickory milk was used in cooking corn cakes and hominy.

There are at least 10 species of hickory in North America (five species exist in Pennsylvania). Colonists used the hardwood for a variety of purposes including tool handles and fuel. Today baseball bats, flooring and furniture are favorite uses of the dense wood. It is also the preferred wood for smoking hams. Yellow dye can be made from the nuts of the shagbark hickory, while lamp oils have been made from the nuts of the bitternut. The oil, it is said by some pioneers, cures rheumatism.

General Andrew Jackson earned the nickname "Old Hickory," because he was as "tough as hickory." You can see Jackson on the $20 bill.

Birders will enjoy seeing and hearing dozens of songbird species, a variety of deep-woods warblers, grouse, Goshawk, a breeding pair of red-shouldered hawks, Cooper's hawk and sometimes rare sightings like nesting saw whet owls, rusty blackbirds and alder flycatchers. Wetland areas away from the crowds produce the best birding opportunities. The Mud Run gorge is a popular birding area, more for the scenery than avian variety.

The uncommon beauty and peace of the park are enhanced by nearby state game lands equaling more than 28,000 acres.

WINTER: Cross-country skiers can enjoy 13 miles of designated trails. Snowmobilers can use 16 miles of marked trails, and ice skaters also visit during the winter season.

HUNTING: A huge section of the park is open for hunting. Call ahead for details.

INSIDERS TIP: The Boulder Field is one of the most scenic and interesting features in the state.

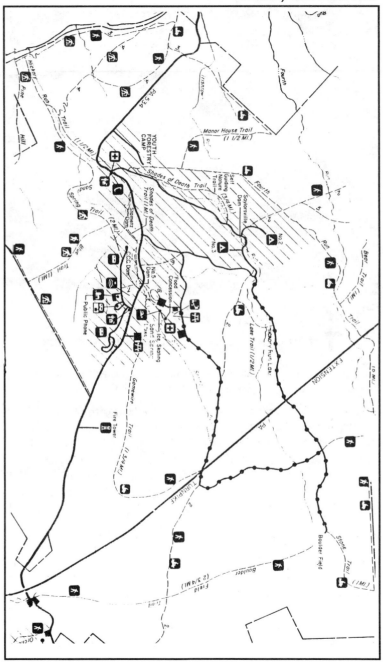

24 Hills Creek State Park
Land: 406 acres   Water: 137-acre lake

The large rolling hills–interspersed with farmlands and pastures, small towns and woodlots–surround the tidy year-round state park.

Backed by a 34-foot-high dam, the 137-acre lake is the focal point of the park built in the early 1950s. Prior to the construction of the earthen dam, the area was known as Kelly Swamp, a sizeable wetland that was often naturally dammed by industrious beavers. Today, man has built the permanent dam, but the beavers are still trying. In fact, Hills Creek is one of the best locations in the state to observe beavers.

North America's largest rodent is constantly chiseling stumps, felling trees and weaving smaller dams and lodges throughout the lake. Although the active areas change from year to year, picnic area No. 2 and the north end of the lake are usually excellent places to spot the busy brown beavers. Late dusk is the best time to scan the surface and shoreline for the aquatic mammals. They are mostly nocturnal, doing much of their feeding, breeding and building at night. They are also most visible in the fall as they store food and prepare for the long winter season.

From land or in a small boat, visitors will likely see other wildlife when looking for beavers. Osprey and bald eagles are often seen in the distance, while waterfowl, resident Canada geese, black-crowned night herons, belted kingfishers, mink and muskrats might also be in or near the waters.

The park opened in 1953 and was named for the creek that runs through it. The small stream was named after Captain Will Hill, who settled in the area around 1820.

Information and Activities

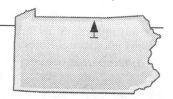

Hills Creek State Park
R. D. 2, P.O. Box 328
Wellsboro, PA 16901
(717) 724-4246

DIRECTIONS: In north central Tioga County, north of U.S, Route 6 and midway between Wellsboro and Mansfield. The park is accessible from PA Route 287 between Tioga and Wellsboro. The park office is open 8 a.m. - 4 p.m. weekdays.

EMERGENCY NUMBERS: State police, 662-2151; and the 911 system.

CAMPGROUND: A small wetland is busy with birds and other animals near the 110-site campground entrance. The camping facility is open from the second Friday in April to the third Sunday in October. The gently hilly campground is comprised of four loops and a couple of small spurs, with sites nicely spaced and airy. Hills Creek has one of the better designed–and maintained–campgrounds in the state.

Loop A is triangular with sites 1-26 under heavy shade and gently rolling terrain. Site 11 is oversized with extra space for kids to play or for setting up an extra small tent or lawn chairs. Most of the sites (and the loops) are well-separated by vegetation; they are dry and level. Site 19 has a lake view and is near the campers' tiny one-lane boat launching ramp. The grassy ramp is for very small boats that are light enough to be hand-launched into the shallow, weedy cove. Campers can bring their small boats and moor them here during their stay. The 2.5-mile Lakeside Trail meanders near the campground.

Site 50, in loop B, is large and easy for trailers to back into. It also has some open mowed spaces nearby. Many sites are on different elevations, offering visual interest and quiet camping. Good sites for bigger RV units are sites 27-29–these sites are open and sunny. Sites 44, 46 and 47 have a lake view.

Loop C is more open than the rest of the spreadout loops and sites. There are many mowed areas and buffers zone-type spaces. Aside from site 63, which is under a big maple tree, the other sites in the 60s are very sunny, breezy and open. Site 54 is large, grassy and open, while 53 and 55-60 are narrow. Sites 74 and 77 shady, nice and near grassy open spaces for kids to play. Sites 80-82, in a single-lane spur, are oversized and especially good for larger RV rigs.

Loop D is heavily wooded with conifers, offering excellent shade and good site separation. Many sites in this loop are appealing. Site 85 is notched into the woods and private. Site 84 and 86 are sprinkled with a thin layer of pine needles. Tent campers couldn't do much better than site 89, which is set back into the woods, level and scenic. Site 91 is one of the most private sites you will find in the park's system. You can pull back off the gravel park road behind a row of trees and enjoy solitude. Sites 93 and 94 are much the same, making the D loop the best in the park and one of the finest camping areas in the state.

CABINS: Hills Creek has 10 modern log-style cabins that are booked solid Memorial Day weekend until Labor Day. Each cabin has parking for two cars, a picnic table and a steel fire ring near the porch and main entrance. All of the cabins are scattered along a gravel lane and back up against lush natural areas.

Cabin 1 is set back into the woods with a tightly mowed lawn and (my favorite) surrounded by a thick stand of mixed trees. Cabin 4 might be the best choice for a family. It has a large yard-like area for informal play and places for outdoor games and activities. Cabins 7 and 8 are close together, separated by a thin wall of vegetation and ideal for two families to share a peaceful vacation with each other.

Cabin 5 is defined by a split-rail fence near the end of the bumpy lane. Cabin 6 is also at the end of the loop, making these two units the most private.

FISHING: The upper end of the lake is stump-filled, offering holding structures for a variety of warmwater species including muskie, walleye, large- and smallmouth bass, bluegill, crappie, yellow perch and lots of bullheads that kids often catch from the shoreline. The lake occasionally suffers from algae blooms and increasing underwater vegetation. Nevertheless, the rich waters often produce four-foot muskies and six-to-eight pound bass. A few dead trees (usually hemlocks that the beavers have girdled) are placed in the pond during the winter, offering some structure in the lake.

In the spring, the flooded stumpy area offers a good place for bass anglers to run spinner baits. Later in the season some anglers flip rubber worms against the stumps and bounce yellow and white jigs along the bottom. Crayfish-type imitators are popular on the lake, according to local tackle shop owners. Live bait is sold at the concession near the swimming beach.

Anglers may request a fishing guide and map to Tioga County by calling (717) 724-0635. The handy map details 40 area fishing locations, species found there and general and special regulations. Fly fishermen should consider trips to Pine Creek, Slate Run, Cedar Run and Kettle Creek. Float fishing the Pine Creek at the gorge is one of the most spectacular experiences any angler can have.

BOATING: Two single gravel-lane launching ramps serve the placid little lake, and one other tiny ramp is reserved for campers. Gasoline-powered motors are prohibited, but electric and arm-powered small boats and canoes are welcome. V-bottom aluminum boats and green canoes are rented at the concession stand's walk-up window at the beach. About 65 seasonal mooring sites are for rent at the park.

Canoeists may have the best chance to see the many beavers that have made Hills Creek popular. Paddle gently along the shoreline, watching fireflies, and virtually every evening beavers can be seen swimming and diving, working and feeding. The northern end of the lake, along the wide coves, is the best place to spot the jumbo rodents doing their construction thing or munching on lily pads and pond weeds.

Maybe the most fun is to very gently drift toward them, until "wap," their tails slap the water, they give you an icy stare and then disappear under the dark surface. The lake, once known as Kelly's Swamp, supports an active population of beavers and fish. Bring your rod and reel, binoculars and camera.

HIKING: Skiers and hikers can receive additional information about outdoor recreation in the Tioga State Forest by calling (717) 724-2868. Tioga County has something for everyone.

Hills Creek has three trails totalling nearly five miles in length.

Lakeside Trail (2.5 miles) offers trekkers a leisurely walk along the lake past at least two beaver colonies and ends at the dam. Along the trail are white spruce, red-osier dogwood and viburnums that dominate the moist area.

Tauschers Trail (1.5 miles) circles the northeast section of the park, arriving at the cabin area from either direction. It winds through a pine plantation, dense stands of alder and fields containing wildflowers. This can be a good bird and wildlife watching trail.

Yellow Birch Trail (.5 mile) is short, but diverse. It leads through areas of natural succession from stands of hardwoods to hemlock swamps and open wetlands.

BIKING: A handy bikers' tour guide map to Tioga County is available at the park's contact points or by calling (717) 724-1906. The map depicts a variety of tours, including a scenic route that passes the park.

VISITOR CENTER: Surrounded by a wood deck, the wood-frame center is next to the large amphitheater that has about 50 metal-frame seats. Seasonal environmental education programs begin at the center and include many natural history lessons, guided hikes, a junior naturalist program, beaver watches, wildlife trivia, park fur-bearers and much more. Inside the center are a natural history display, animal mounts, posters and information. The visitor center is almost in the middle of the campground and very convenient for campers to use. An octagonal picnic shelter is next to the visitor center.

DAY-USE AREAS: Thick patches of conifers are broken up by wide mowed areas that often contain picnic tables and grills. The park has four reservable pavilions, some of them quite interesting. For example, pavilion 3 is on a peninsula near the campground entrance. It's a walk in shelter in a stand of large hemlock, beech, maple and ash trees. Day-use area 2 is north of the beach along a large cove, near an active beaver lodge. Many of the well-kept picnic areas have pedestal charcoal grills.

SWIMMING BEACH: One of the best views of the 80-yard-long beach is from the roadway across the dam along Spillway Road. The changing building (outside cold-waters showers) and concession stand are about 40 yards apart. The small food stand specializes in cold drinks, ice cream and grill items (the grill closes at 6:30 p.m. daily during the season) and has five picnic tables with umbrellas on the adjacent patio. The concession also sells ice, firewood and live bait (meal worms, crawlers, salted minnows and red worms), and rents small boats.

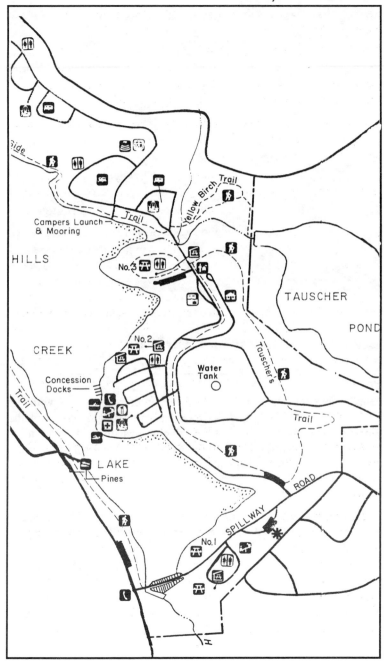

25 Jacobsburg Environmental Education Center

Land: 1,168 acres   Water: Bushkill Creek

"Environmental education is a learning process concerned with the interrelationship within and between the various components of the natural and human-made world, producing growth in the individual and leading to responsible stewardship of the earth," says the Jacobsburg's mission statement.

Jacobsburg is a creative, heavily used center for outdoor learning.

The original land (which is part of the Pocono Mountains) for Jacobsburg State Park was bought by the state from the city of Easton in 1959. In 1969, additional land was purchased. At this time a traditional park was planned–a facility with a dam, reservoir, sprawling day-use areas, swimming pool, family campground, hiking trails and so on. Fortunately, I believe, this development never occurred.

It took time, but slowly the value of undeveloped historic resources was realized. Today, the busy education center accommodates quiet, passive recreational activities and fine learning opportunities near major population areas. The center is now a highly respected learning center, visited by thousands of students annually.

"The mission of state environmental centers is to develop a citizenry that is aware of, and concerned about, the total environment, and its associated problems, and which has the knowledge, attitude, motivation, commitment, and skills to work individually and collectively toward solutions of current problems and the prevention of new ones," says the state's Environmental Education Master Plan.

The center began operation in October 1985. It is one of four environmental learning centers in the state.

Information and Activities

Jacobsburg Environmental Education Center
835 Jacobsburg Road
Wind Gap, PA 18091
(610) 746-2801

DIRECTIONS: In Northampton County. The center is accessible by taking PA Route 33 to the Belfast exit near Nazareth. There is no indoor classroom or nature center-type building. All classes are taught outside. The center is open year-round, 8 a.m. - sunset.

EMERGENCY NUMBER: 911 system.

ENVIRONMENTAL EDUCATION: The staff at Jacobsburg offers an exciting and creative menu of outdoor education programs for most ages. Interesting program include water quality monitoring with high school students, a GREEN program (Global Rivers Environmental Education Network, an effort to improve the quality of watersheds and rivers; using rivers to link people within and between watershed.), teacher training (unique partnerships have been formed), discovery and junior naturalist programs, a conservation week (weeklong sessions), seasonal outdoor education/hikes for students and a variety of special events and summer programs.

In addition, many programs are off-site at area schools. The center has done a terrific job of creating learning partnerships and involving school districts and volunteers in their outdoor education effort. A number of projects are constantly being developed, refined and offered.

FISHING: Rocky Bushkill Creek is stocked with trout and scenic. Two and one-half miles of the creek meander through the park. Bushkill is one of the 10 largest limestone streams in the state. The rushing waters hold lots of native browns and a few brook and rainbow trout. Over the years, the stream has been dammed, diked, dredged, drained and filled with waste. Happily, the stream has benefited from conservation work by Delaware Trout Unlimited and the Bushkill Conservancy. The groups have dedicated time and money to protect and improve the stream. They have planted trees, purchased land for public use and monitor the stream.

The Bushkill actually starts as a freestone trickle near the Northampton/Monroe county line on the slopes of Blue Mountain. This rugged ridge line reaches across Pennsylvania to Virginia's Appalachian Mountains. For about half its length the stream is undistinguished. But as it nears the park, by Easton, the water becomes pristine trout waters. The section of the stream that runs through the park may be the prettiest along its entire length. It seems every speculator, investor and entrepreneur has tried, succeeded and failed along the heavily-used stream.

In short, don't expect a wilderness experience as you search for access along the stream. In fact, you may find many New Jersey and New York anglers elbowing each other for space, especially after the hatchery truck pulls away.

HIKING: Mountain bikers and equestrians share the same 10 miles of designated trails. The network of 12.5 miles of trails make the center's field, woodlands and peaceful stream accessible to both students and casual visitors.

The short Henry Woods Nature Trail winds along Bushkill Creek along upland forests and is coated with stone chips that are wide and flat.

DAY-USE AREAS: Henry Woods has 10 picnic tables and a few grills in the old village day-use area.

JACOBSBURG NATIONAL HISTORIC DISTRICT: The historic village is programmed by the Jacobsburg Historical Society. Programs include ironmongers, house tours, a Civil War encampment, craft fairs and more.

The historical society was founded in 1972 preserve and present the history of the Jacobsburg District. Aside from a variety of public history programs, it also supports and fosters archaeological research and living history activities.

Pennsylvania State Parks

The society administers one of the most significant and picturesque historic sites in the Lehigh Valley. In 1812 Henry Homestead, which is on the 7.48-acre tract leased from the state, was restored in 1980 following a successful fund-raising campaign. In 1989, the group acquired the 1832 John Joseph Henry House and surrounding 22 acres from the Mary Henry Stites estate. Both homes are open to the public on the fourth Sunday monthly from April through October, 1 p.m. - 5 p.m.

The National Historic district lies almost entirely within the state park. The colonial village, of which only foundations remain, was named for the area's first settler, Jacob Hubler, who arrived here in 1740. Through the enterprise of the Henry family, the people of Jacobsburg made a significant contribution to the development of the nation. In 1792, William Henry II built a gun factory at Jacobsburg and in 1824, his son Matthew erected the Ann Catherine Iron Furnace, the first cold blast iron furnace in Northampton county.

NATURE: The rolling park consists of upland forests (mostly oak), old fields (in various stages of succession), cultivated fields, virgin hemlocks, two ponds, two streams and emergent and forested wetlands. About 105 species of birds are sited annually at the Jacobsburg Big Day Bird Count. About 145 total species have been identified and recorded over the years. A bird list is available that details the count. Thirty-five warbler species, 21 types of finches and sparrows, king fishers, flycatchers, ruby-throated hummingbird and four species of hawks can be seen at the learning center.

Henry Woods, a 100-acre climax forest of white oak and hemlock and scenic slate cliffs cut by the Bushkill Creek, is the most significant natural resource in the park.

HUNTING: Limited shotgun only hunting is offered on about 1,000 acres. Call for details.

26 Jennings Environmental Education Center

Land: 352 acres

Man's relationship to nature is the overriding theme at Jennings Environmental Education Center. In fact, Jennings was the first natural preserve in the state to be developed for the protection of an individual plant species–the blazing star. The tall, purple plant is disjunct in the region, but abundant in a small prairie at the education center in Butler County. The blazing star blossoms in early August.

The center's prairie has more than 200 varieties of wildflowers, including tall coreopsis, blue vervain, bowman's roots and others. The various habitats also offer visitors a chance to see the endangered mild-mannered massasauga rattlesnake, woodcock, wild turkey, barred owls and songbirds.

The mission of Jennings is to provide environmental education and interpretive programs which explore a wide variety of ecological and environmental topics to area students and park visitors. A schedule of public programs is available.

Information and Activities

Jennings Environmental Education Center
2951 Prospect Road
Slippery Rock, PA 16057-8701
(412) 794-6011

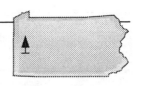

DIRECTIONS: Jennings is located at the junction of PA 8, PA 173 and PA 528, about 12 miles north of Butler and five miles south of Slippery Rock.

INFORMATION: The office is open from 8 a.m. - 4 p.m. Monday through Friday year-round. The grounds are open 8 a.m. to sunset.

Established in the late 1950s by the Western Pennsylvania Conservancy, the facility is named for Dr. Otto Emery Jennings, a famed botanist and naturalist who discovered the blazing star prairie.

The small relict prairie is the focal point of the center and is in the midst of an eastern deciduous forest, one of the few remaining extensions of Western prairie lands. A self-guided interpretive trail follows the Blazing Star and Prairie Loop trails and provides information on the relict prairie ecosystem..

In addition, fascinating wetland area has been developed to treat mine drainage. Of the 5,000 miles of stream in state, about one-third are polluted. Even though the state is a leader in model strip-mine legislation, the cleanup continues. Wetlands may be the most cost-effective and practical way to treat the runoff. Jennings is leading the way in testing and implementing the concept of using wetlands to treat drainage from mines.

Interesting flora include the tiny spike rush, once thought extinct in the state, and the American Colombo, a bizarre plant that reaches six feet with whitish-green flowers that have purple blotches. It's related to the more common century plant.

The center, which features a large multi-purpose classroom and hands-on exhibit, also offers many programs for the general public that includes nature walks, birding hikes, seasonal ecology-themed outdoor activities and much more.

The Wood Whisper Trail is hard-surfaced and suitable for strollers and wheelchairs. This is the only environmental education center in western Pennsylvania. In addition to the self-guided trail, there are about seven miles of wooded trails on the property.

27 Kettle Creek State Park
Land: 1,793 acres Water: 160-acre lake

Kettle Creek is named for the meandering stream that flows through it. According to legend, the creek derives its name from two Indians who floated down the rain-swollen stream with a prize kettle in their canoe. It's said the heavily laden canoe tipped over and lost the kettle–but the duo managed to swim to safety. The park was almost named Tipacanoe–just kidding.

The shadows and reflections of steep mountains can be seen on the surface of the quiet tree-lined lake where canoes and small non-powered fishing boats glide about looking for fish–or just looking at the scenic terrain.

I dream about striking it rich all the time. But Dorcie Calhoun, a Kettle Creek area native, did it. "This notion about gas come to me in a dream," said the now deceased but legendary Calhoun. "It was like a vision." This husky old farmer was responsible for the discovery of a well in what is now the Leidy gas storage field, a multi-million dollar producer.

Pennsylvania State Parks

The well came in with a whoosh and a roar the afternoon of Jan. 8, 1950 and money soon flowed into Dorcie's pockets as effortlessly as the gas flowed from the big-money well. Although he continued to wear farm clothes, Dorcie had a flair, which contributed to his legend of buying new Cadillacs (which he treated like common trucks!) and carrying around as much as $50,000 in a suitcase. He even cashed pay-checks "for the fun of it." Dorcie was quite a character, making–and eventually spending–huge sums of money that captured national attention and media coverage by Collier's magazine many years ago.

Early on, Dorcie's ability to tinker and fabricate Rube Goldberg-like drilling machines added to his reputation as a real world "Jed Clampit." Like Jed, Dorcie paid cash for everything while he was riding high. At one point, he pealed off thousands of dollars for a bulldozer, when only a few years earlier he struggled to make any payments.

He went on to drill "too many dry holes" and spent much of his fortune, living out his life with more normal means in the Kettle Creek valley.

Information and Activities

Kettle Creek State Park
H.C.R., P. O. Box 96
Renovo, PA 17764
(717) 923-0206

DIRECTIONS: On SR 4001, seven miles north of Westport and PA Route 120 in Clinton County, 14 miles northwest of Renovo. The park office, on a ridge above the day-use area and beach, is open 8 a.m. - 4 p.m. weekdays.

EMERGENCY NUMBERS: 911 system.

BUSH DAM: From the top of the 1,350-foot-long dam built in 1962, visitors can look down to the water's surface and tree-lined shoreline 165 feet below. The dam cost more than $7 million for the U. S. Army Corps of Engineers to build. At this viewing area are two small stone monuments in memory of Simeon Pfoutzand and his wife Susannah, the first white settlers on Kettle Creek. He selected this site in 1813, cleared the land, built a log house and went to Perry County for his wife and 2-year-old son, Simon. They returned in 1814 and spent the rest of their days here. The pioneer couple reared nine children in the valley. The cemetery where many of the family members rest is north on the stream. Unfortunately, Simeon died from the bite of a rattlesnake he was handling. Many of his descendants still live in the immediate area. Few go near rattlesnakes.

CAMPGROUNDS: No reservations are taken at the two Kettle Creek campgrounds. The park has an upper and lower campground. Both can be busy, but the lower campground with its 38 electric sites is often the most populated by RV rigs. The lower campground is open April through December, while the upper campground is open from April through October. According to staff, campers tend to "stay awhile" at Kettle Creek.

The upper camping area has no hook-ups, but is popular with small RV units and tent campers. Site 71 is very secluded, located down a short gravel lane offering a terrific mountain view. Mixed open spaces and deep shade greet campers in this tract, with camping sites on multiple elevations.   Site 50, tucked into the mountainside, is about 30 yards from the road and quite private. Sites 52-54 have a view of the gentle lake. Sites 60-70, on a ridge overlooking the lake, are the nicest sites in the area, getting some sunlight during the day.

A babbling stream runs along the lower campground that was once the central portion of the state park. Today, many electrical sites are maintained and some campers stay for many days at a time. More than half of the sites are near the usually slow-moving creek. The area offers a good mixture of sun and shade. There are two short loops connected by a footbridge in the lower campground. Sites 3-5 are parallel to the creek; most of the other sites are just right for medium-sized RV rigs. About every other site has a bench that faces the dark gentle creek. A small dam toward the end of the spur holds back the creek's full flow. A simple playground is on the nearby shore.

FISHING: Rainbow trout are stocked in the stream and lake by the state, and several sportsmen's clubs stock browns and brook trout. About 25 porcupine (pyramid-style) cribs have been installed in the lake to improve the underwater habitat. The cribs provide safety for smaller fish and structure for larger denizens to relate to. The lake is considered a very good smallmouth bass fishery, giving up three-and four-pounders with some regularity. Regional bass tournaments are conducted on the lake, and the best bass fishing is in the fall. It is classified as a cold water fishery.

Spring-time anglers often troll the narrows near Sugar Lake Road. Ice fishing is very poplar at the park, with most anglers using live baits and small colorful jig heads.

Species in the lake include, large- and smallmouth bass, golden shiner, rock bass, white sucker, black crappies, yellow perch, pumpkinseed, bluegill, rainbow and brook trout, and bullheads.

BOATING: Sixty-two numbered seasonal mooring spaces near the beach are available for local boaters and a courtesy dock is set for temporary mooring of small electric and muscle-powered watercraft. Overnight mooring for campers is also available.

Kettle Creek has a single-lane gravel launching ramp that can be busy during good fishing times.

Canoeists will find the scenery of the L-shaped reservoir worth the trip. The two-mile-long lake has a sheer mountainside along about half of its length that is covered with towering hemlock and oak forests that meets the water's edge. Paddler can travel a couple of miles of Kettle Creek and explore rich marshlands that connect the lake to the stream.

HIKING: A small nature trail can be accessed at the north end of the upper campground or the park office.

Short day hikes abound in the park, while backpackers can trek the 53-mile Donut Hole Trail with an access parking lot across from the lower campground. A trail map is available that details this rugged back-packing trail.

MOUNTAIN BIKING: Bring your mountain bike and wear your helmet for a moderately difficult ride on five miles of natural trails. The main trail starts at the day-use parking lot and travels onto state forest trails and roads before returning to the park.

EQUESTRIAN TRAILS: Horse clubs can make advance arrangements to camp in the park and use the 17 miles of trails that start at Beaverdam Run travels through Sproul State Forest before returning to the trail-head. The availability of water along the trail for a horse is a big asset for riders at Kettle Creek and the state forest tracts. A trail map is available at the park office.

DAY-USE AREAS: These are mostly near the beach in front of the park office. Amenities include a play area, ballfield, about 200 picnic tables, pedestal grills, hot coal disposal and water hydrants. The Pine Grove Picnic Area is available for group and family picnic outings at no charge.

SWIMMING BEACH: The swimming area is outlined by a rope and buoys with two lifeguard chairs, one in the five-foot-deep water and the other on the 75-yard-long sandy beach. A brown block changing building serves the beach and mowed day-use areas that surround it. The humble beach is open 11 a.m. - 7 p.m., daily Memorial Day weekend to Labor Day.

NATURE: In the evening, especially when the park is quiet, bald eagles are sometimes seen in the distance riding the thermals, peering downward, hoping to spot a fish near the water's surface for a quick meal.

Some environmental education programming is offered at the park.

Birding is very good at the unit. About 125 bird species have been recorded including common loon, osprey, many waterfowl species, blue-gray gnatcatcher, scarlet tananger and indigo buntings in the spring.

WINTER: Open year-round, Kettle Creek typically gets plenty of snow and cold temperatures for winter sports.

HUNTING: Deer, squirrel, turkey, bear and other small game are hunted in the park and the 278,000-acre Sproul State Forest, which surrounds the park. Call the park superintendent for details. Archery deer hunting is popular at the unit.

INSIDERS TIPS: The nearest store, gasoline and garage services are 10 miles northeast of the park along Route 144. Visit the overlook, 3.5 miles west on Sugar Camp Road.

Ole Bull State Park
(814) 435-2169

Kettle Creek bisects the small, 125-acre park that has two separate flat and wooded campgrounds. One of the campgrounds has some electric sites, pit toilets and hydrants. There are a total of 81 sites at the park. Staff says repeat campers are their biggest customers. The park has a lodge and similar areas as Kettle Creek.

Ole Bull operates a 50-yard-long guarded beach just north of the day-use area. The 85-mile Susquehannock Trail System passes through the unit.

28 Keystone State Park
Land: 1,182 acres Water: 78-acre lake

Along the water's edge at Keystone Lake are medium-sized trees and long, busy day-use areas. Farther away from the shoreline are large mowed open spaces, fields, forest, marshes and streams.

Open since 1945, the lake was built many years earlier to supply water for a coke plant several miles downstream. In 1945, about 796 acres of land were acquired from the Keystone Coal and Coke Company by the state for park development. The remaining lands were eventually acquired from the Atlantic Crushed Coke Co. and from the Benedictine Society.

Today the park is busy with family day-users, campers and spring-season trout anglers. Open year-round, ice fishing, ice skating and sledding are popular winter sports. Snowmobile and cross-country skiing trails are maintained on the southeast and northwest tracts. The park is a good example of land reclamation. Some research on acid mine drainage continues on the site in an effort to protect water quality and continued enhancement of the region's natural areas.

Information and Activities

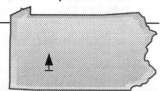

Keystone State Park
R.D. 2, P. O Box 101
Derry, PA 15627
(412) 668-2939

DIRECTIONS: From U.S. 22 east to SR 981, turn left (south) to Derry Road, and travel two miles to the park office. The park is open 8 a.m. - dusk, daily. The office is open 8 a.m. to 4 p.m., sometimes longer during the summer. The small brown park office is near the lake and main day-use areas that stretch along the north shoreline.

CAMPGROUND: A total of 100 camping sites are open from mid-April to October. The area is rolling and wooded, with 40 sites near the lake and 60 sites in a more private area west of the lake. The campground is comprised of two loops, 1-40 and 41-100. There is a washhouse in each loop, with the campground host set up at site 34 and 56.

Sites 1-40, are very shady. Even-number sites are right on the lake, but all of the sites have a lake view. Each site has a hard-surfaced pad. Even-numbered sites from 22-30 are quite small, and best for pop-up-style campers. Sites 33 and 37 are excellent tent camping sites.

In the large loop, away from the lake, sites 41, 43, 45, 47, 49, 51, 53, 55, 57, 59, 61, 63, 65, 67, 70, 71, 72, 74 and 75 are very open. These sites, with hard-surfaced pads, are great for sun-lovers or camping on during the shoulder (early spring and later fall) times of the season.

Excellent shadier and smaller sites include 82, 83, 85, 87 and 88 which are back into the woods. Site 88 is very close to the washhouse that has a phone. Sites 81 and 95 are great spots for smaller RV units.

The campgrounds are mostly shady, gently rolling and equipped with picnic tables and grills. Drivers of larger RV units should inspect sites for size and grade. Also near the park is a private campground called Keystone Corner Family Campground.

CABINS: Adjacent to the family campground is a group of 11 log-style cabins that face the lake and generous open fields. The cabins enjoy scattered shade and privacy along the southwest shore near the dam and trailheads. The brown cabins have large porches and doorside parking for two vehicles, picnic tables and grills. The cabins are two bedrooms, with modern bath and kitchens, and a living room with cathedral ceilings. The cabins are open year-round and can be reserved by calling the park office. The cabins are the most popular in the summer; plan your trip early!

Cabin No. 1 is the coziest.

FISHING: With virtually all of the shoreline open for fishing, anglers can set up near picnic tables or on turf surfaces. Some panfish and bass are taken from the 78-acre lake, but it is best known for good trout fishing in the spring. The lake is regularly stocked and anglers use "Powerbait," a doughball-like mixture, red worm and other live bait on small hooks. Most local anglers choose shoreline fishing locations on the south side of the lake near the dam. Baits shops (and ice cream shop!) are conveniently located near the park. Ice fishing is also popular on the lake with mealworms, tiny jigs and minnows dipped into the icy holes.

BOATING: Rowboats and canoes are rented from the north side of the lake near the dam. Electric boats are also permitted on the lake. A small, one-lane concrete launching ramp and mooring area are next to the boat rental concession stand. Seasonal mooring sites are available; call the office for rates and availability.

HIKING: Some of the best views of Keystone are from the four miles of easy to moderate hiking trails on the south and northeastern tracts. Snowmobilers, horses and cross-country skiers also share large portions of these trails. Snowmobling is allowed on an eight-mile network of trails, but is not during antlerless deer season. The unit has two miles of bridle trails.

DAY-USE AREAS: Keystone has taken great care to offer large open areas near the lake, from the sandy guarded 1,000-foot beach to shoreline fishing and game field areas. There are a bathhouse and small food concession at the beach. More than 400 picnic tables are scattered around the lake, and two newer stone and wood pavilions are available for rent.

NATURE CENTER: Near the twin-loop family campgrounds is a beautiful stone building on a ridge that serves as a visitor and nature center. Operated seasonally, it features natural history displays about wetlands, bluebirds and other subjects. A large room with movable seating is used for programming and other meetings. The center is directly across the narrow lake from the beach and boat rental.

Birders should look for wading birds, great crested flycatchers, various swallows, rufous-sided towhee scratching in the leaf debris, and orchard orioles.

29 Kings Gap Environmental Education and Training Center

Land: 1,443 acres Water: Streams

The Pennsylvania Bureau of State Parks has one of the strongest and most active commitments to environmental education than any state in the country. Kings Gap Environmental Education and Training Center (William C. Forrey Training Center) is a major element in the system's effort to teach about the natural world, critical environmental issues facing society, and skills for appreciating and enjoying the outdoors. The scenic center provides a wide variety of educational services in an effort to bring quality outdoor education to all ages.

The center is dedicated to helping school-age children and adults to better understand the natural and human-made worlds. Since 1977, the center has provided a broad menu of outdoor education programs to individuals, civic groups, teachers and students of all ages.

There may be no such thing as a normal day at Kings Gap, but many days are filled with visiting classes that participate in a discovery-learning approach to environmental studies. Together, teachers and students explore the natural work, learn concepts and deepen their awareness of nature.

Kings Gap has built some wonderful cooperative ventures with area colleges and universities, sponsoring teacher in-service training, special events and college-level workshops on many environmental-related topics.

Aside from a busy schedule of school groups, college programs and staff training, the center also offers some terrific community programs. The full-service learning center is certainly one of the finest in the nation, serving more than 30,000 visitors annually.

Information and Activities

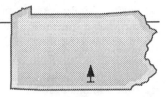

**Kings Gap Environmental Education
and Training Center
500 Kings Gap Road
Carlisle, PA 17013
(717) 486-5031**

DIRECTIONS: In Cumberland County, 25 miles south of Harrisburg. The entrance is on Pine Road, one mile east of the Huntsdale Fish Hatchery. From I-81 take exit 11, then south on Route 233 for 2.5 miles, and left on Pine Road for 2.5 miles. The center is open 8 a.m.-4 p.m. weekdays.

There is no picnicking or camping at the environmental learning center. Bring a small snack and enjoy the trails and terrific mountain views.

The 24-room mansion at 1,280 feet above sea level on South Mountain and 650 feet above the valley floor. South Mountain, formed about 600 million years ago, marks the terminus of the famous Blue Ridge Mountains. In the distance to the north is the much younger Blue Mountain. The rocks there are only 400 million years old. Blue Mountain is part of the Appalachian range.

HISTORY: The mansion and adjoining grounds were built as a summer home for James McCormick Cameron, the grandson of wealthy Simon Cameron, a well-known U.S. Senator and founder of the Republican party in Pennsylvania. Like his father and grandfather, James was a successful businessman with holdings in land and interests in coal, steel, lumber and railroads.

The younger Cameron began acquiring land in Cumberland County in 1904, and by the following year, he owned 46 tracts totaling more than 2,700 acres. The construction phase of the road and buildings took four years to complete at Kings Gap, and Cameron used these facilities until 1946. Five years later, C. H. Masland and Sons Carpet Company of Carlisle purchased the home and nearly half the land of the estate. The carpet company operated and maintained the property as a guest house and meeting center for 20 years. For many of these years, a brightly lit cross was erected on the mansion each Easter. The cross was visible all over the valley and annual Easter sunrise services were held on the front lawn.

In 1973, the Department of Environmental Resources (working with the Nature Conservancy) purchased Kings Gap for one-half the assessed value (the remaining half was donated by the Maslands), and four years later the Kings Gap center opened. The flagstone-surrounded mansion is one of the most picturesque estates in the Cumberland Valley. The view of the valley is magnificent. In the distance you will see Blue Mountain, McAlisters Gap, Double Gap, Kings Gap and the Cumberland Valley.

The mansion, built of stone, brick and cement, is decorated in the "wealthy hunting-lodge style." Slightly ornate, the spangled mansion features colorful overstuffed furniture, floral draperies and thick wool rose-colored carpeting. In short, it's a wonderful, heavily used meeting and training facility.

RECREATIONAL OPPORTUNITIES: Day visitors can hike, use the 12-point orienteering course, cross-country ski, visit a pond or the wonderful pine plantation. The fine self-guided trails and outdoor classrooms with benches are worthy of modeling at other centers of this type.

PINE PLANTATION: The straight-row plantation, composed of eastern white pine, Douglas fir and tamarack trees, is a dramatic contrast to the deciduous forest that surrounds it. Visitors love the aroma, silence and cooling experience of the conifer forest near the entrance to the center. A self-guided trail three-foot-wide, hard-surfaced, wheelchair accessible trail winds through the interior of the plantation past a small 1850s two-story cabin and fenced garden, and small open field.

THE GARDEN: Once a wide front lawn, an impressive educational garden was developed by a group of master gardeners in 1992. The almost football field-sized area, surrounded by a knee-high stacked stone wall, features annual and perennial flowers.

POND AREA: About two miles from the entrance is a series of interesting elevated manmade ponds and constantly moving streams. The Watershed Self-Guided Trail winds through the lush area, examining and interpreting the watershed and its flora and fauna.

White Oaks Trail (.25 mile) is hard-surfaced and wheelchair accessible. It interprets the thick deciduous forest using script and Braille signs. A small outdoor classroom with benches is near the trail.

OTHER HIKING TRAILS: Along the center's 15 miles of wide, mostly easy to moderately difficult trails, are excellent places to spot wildlife and view birds. Whitetail deer, woodchuck, red squirrels and chipmunks are common mammals. Wildflower watchers will find good blooms of columbine, wild sarsaparilla, bergamot and many small spring wildflowers and ferns. Some of the huge black gum trees are spectacular.

Hikers should also look for the jumbo ant mounts, built by Allegheny mound-building ants. The energetic ants choose sandy soil conditions and open areas to patrol and protect the queen ant. Interestingly small trees can be killed by the bite of these otherwise mild-mannered ants. The ants have formic acid in their mouths, and their bite on a tree prevents nutrients from flowing to the roots, killing the trees and keeping the nest in the warming sunlight. The mounds can reach two feet in height.

Short hiking loops include Forest Heritage (1.6 miles) with many dead chestnuts along the way; an oak forest by barren charcoal hearth; and Pine Plantation (.6 mile, see above). Many of the trails have small wooden boardwalks that help hikers cross the network of rocky mountain streams in the park.

Long hiking trails are Watershed (1.8 miles) of easy walking past ant mounds a stream and through an oak/pine forest; Ridge/Rock/Kings Gap Hollow (3 miles), a more difficult hike around large boulder outcroppings and scenic vistas, along a stream and through a mature oak and pine forest; and Scenic Vista/Kings Gap Hollow (4.2 miles) of great overlooks and shady pine forests near a small stream.

HUNTING: About 700 acres in the area are open to hunting. Call for details.

30 Lackawanna State Park
Land: 1,411 acres   Water: 210-acre lake

Lackawanna State Park is an all-purpose park, complete with an excellent campground, visitor center, outdoor education programs, winter sports, a gentle lake for small boating or fishing and easy trails suitable for all ages. The unit is one of the newer parks in the system. Construction of the park's day-use facilities began in 1968 and opened in 1972. Campground construction began in 1974 and opened during 1975. The park is very busy–near large cites. The campground is always filled on holiday weekends and many weekends all of the summer.

Hilly Lackawanna is a hub for fishing and family camping in this part of the state. This park also manages Archibald Pothole and Salt Spring State Park.

Archbald Pothole was discovered in 1884 by coal miners who encountered a mass of rounded stones weighing one to six pounds each, making a barrier for their underground efforts. The miners worked around the stones, leaving an oval pillar of rounded stones. When they eventually removed the stones, they discovered the mass of cobble extended through the rock to the surface 40 feet above. After removing all of the cobble, the pothole was apparent. The small park with a play and picnicking area also offers a small hunting area.

Salt Spring State Park is a day-use unit with hiking through giant 600 to 700-year-old hemlocks and overlooks to the three falls on Fall Brook Stream. The roar of the water is heard along much of the winding trails. The facility has about 200 picnic tables, 300 acres of hunting land and trout fishing in area streams (Fall Brook and Silver Creek). The Nature Conservancy purchased the land in the early 1970s with the understanding the state would buy it later, which it did.

Sometime around 1813, efforts were made to mine the salt from the area. Efforts continued by various owners and users of the land until 1865, when the Susquehanna Salt Works Company sank a well 650 feet, where they found a vein of brine and subsequently manufactured about 20 tons of high quality salt–which was not enough to keep the company solvent. Salt Spring has an interesting history that includes oil drilling, milling and various other attempts to use the natural resources. Today the hemlock forest is safe from miners and millers, salt tycoons and sharp axes.

Salt Spring opened as a small, but scenic, state park in the summer of 1973.

Information and Activities

Lackawanna State Park
R. R. 1, Box 230
Dalton, PA 18414-9785
(717) 945-3239 (main office)
(717) 563-9995 (campground office)

DIRECTIONS: In Lackawanna County, 10 miles north of Scranton. The park is easily accessible off I-81 by taking exit 60 and traveling three miles west on PA Route 524. Visitors coming via U.S. Route 6 and 11 should take PA Route 438 north about three miles to PA Route 407, then east.

CAMPGROUND: The family campground has 96 sites–many of them semi-walk in-style; 10 sites for rigs under 20 feet in length; 10 for rigs up to 50 feet in length; and the rest for medium-sized RV units. The three-loop campground is open from the second Friday in April to the third Sunday in October. Some sites can be reserved in advance.

The round swimming pool is near a quiet lake cove.

Carpenter Town Loop, sites 1-50, like the entire facility, can be packed with small children and family campers enjoying the many amenities of Lackawanna.

The campground is so heavily wooded, it can almost appear dark if the sun ducks under the clouds. Pads are hard-surfaced and equipped with picnic tables and fire rings. Hard-surfaced pathways also connect the loops and wind back and forth between the showerhouse and play spaces. Many sites are oversized, with additional space at the rear for additional chairs, tents or other camping equipment. The oversized sites are the most popular. Sites 28, 29 and 46 are such sites. Site 18, a handicapped accessible site, is the sunniest of the sites in this loop.

The Tall Timbers walk-in tent sites 31-38 (33, 34 and 38 are reservable) are in a densely wooded hillside with beds of ferns adding patches of light green to the brown forest floor. Sites are highly identifiable. Merely choose a level place around the designated area and set up your camp. Some of the sites are as far away as 50 yards off the hard-surfaced campground road.

Fox Run Loop, sites 51-65, is a thickly wooded tract with tall maples and conifers. Sites are often divided by vegetation. Some of the sites are small. Sites 55 and 57 are for smaller RV units, but they have a pleasing view of a wooded ravine. Sites 61 and 62 share rock outcroppings, while sites 63-65 are on a hillside and dry.

Maple Lane, sites 72-82, are on various elevations. All are shady and back up against a natural area. Several walk-in tent sites, 83-91, are adjacent to this loop and feature wooded sites in a hollow.

The Little Fern Loop, sites 92-96, are the most private sites on a narrow wooded spur. Site 96 is on a knoll and one of the best tent sites in the park. Many trailheads are at or near this camping spur.

Two group camping areas can accommodate up to 110 people. They are open April - October.

FISHING: Hilly shorelines with trees to the water's edge greet anglers and boaters on the J-shaped, 210-acre lake. The 2.5-miles lake has more than 7.5 miles of shoreline. Both warm- and coldwater species are taken from the lake—depending on the season. A variety of species including trout, muskie and walleye are occasionally stocked. Local experts say the depths change quickly in the lake, with the deepest waters near the dam. Many coves are excellent spring and early summer spots to try.

The lake is a big bass lake. Bass must be 15 inches or longer to keep. Bass anglers love to fish over the old roadway and submerged bridge. Scuba divers who dive in the lake report that you can still see the traffic lines painted on the old submerged bridge, and that good-sized bass are also seen scattering from the area upon their slow-motion approach.

These and other structures hold bass, walleye and panfish. Stream inlets are also excellent locations for anglers to try spinner baits, jigs, crankbaits and live bait rigs. Many anglers also fish near or under the vehicular bridge. Maximum depth of the lake is about 30 feet. Plenty of bank fishing spots are especially good for evening panfishing with bobber and worms. A fishing pier by the bridge also accommodates young and disabled anglers.

BOATING: Two launching ramps serve the lake. Only non-powered and electric boats are allowed on the lake. Cartop boats can be launched from some of the lakeside parking lots. Seasonal boat mooring is offered at the park.

Canoeists should explore the feeder streams (including Kennedy Creek) for a hemlock and pine lined corridor of narrow and shallow water, up for a chance to see shorebirds and great blue herons stalking minnows and sleeping frogs. Bullhead Bay, just north of Kennedy Creek, is an excellent marshy cove to see aquatic vegetation, kingfishers making their rattling call and ducks motoring around the stickups.

The boat concession rents small craft by the hour during the summer. Call (717) 945-5113 for boat rental information. The concession, which has a soft drink machine out front, is open Monday, Tuesday, Thursday and Friday 11 a.m. - 7 p.m., Wednesday 11 a.m. - 6 p.m., Saturday 9 a.m. - 7 p.m. and Sunday 1 p.m. - 6 p.m. Types of boats available include black canoes, pedal boats and V-bottom aluminum boats.

The small store/boat rental is crammed with all types of stuff, including nose clips for swimming, goggles, air mattresses, ear plugs, fishing supplies, live bait, flashlights, tools, novelty items, propane, hunting supplies, camping necessities, squirt guns and all types of fun items for kids to beg mom and dad for. There are lots of colorful plastic toys and gadgets in the lively but tiny park store.

A topo map of the lake bottom is also displayed on the store wall, and fishing information is freely dispensed.

HIKING: Bikes and horses are permitted on some of the parks five miles of trails. Most of the easy walking trails are on the east side of the lake, linked in concentric circular paths.

Equestrians can use Abington Trail. Horse trailer parking is available in the northern section of the park along Wallsville Road (PA Route 438).

DAY-USE AREAS: More than 200 picnic tables are tucked under evergreens in view of the lake. The main day-use area is near the pool and features trails, play equipment, open spaces, grills, drinking water and rest rooms. One of the more modern play structures with plastic play slide and elevated climbers is near the pool. Several open spaces are defined with a neatly stacked stone wall.

SWIMMING POOL: Near a quiet lake cove, youthful swimmers can often be heard shouting with joy across the flat day-use areas that surrounds the 160-foot-diameter round pool with a green deck. Four lifeguard chairs circle the pool with depths from one to six feet deep. The pool is open 11 a.m. - 7 p.m. Memorial Day weekend to Labor Day.

The changing house is a brown board and batten-style building that can be very busy. A walk-up food concession serves both the inside of the pool and the day-use area serving ice, ice cream, hot pretzels, snow cones, candy, lighter fluid, simple grill items and cold drinks. The foot-long hot dogs are killers.

NATURE: Several old beaver dams dot Big Bass Pond near the Woodland Ponds Self-Guided Nature Trail. Summer outdoor education programs, hikes and campfire programs are featured at Lackawanna.

WINTER: Ice skating on the frozen lake and cross-country skiing on the hiking trails are popular winter activities. Ice fishing is permitted, and sledding on the gentle slopes is great fun when weather conditions cooperate.

HUNTING: More than 500 acres are open to hunting. Common game species include ring-necked pheasant, ruffed grouse, turkey, deer, and rabbit. Call for more details.

INSIDERS TIPS: Sport diving is available on the lake. The coal mine tour in nearby Scranton is one of the area's biggest educational attractions. Manning's Dairy on Rt. 524 has the world's best ice cream!

NEARBY ATTRACTIONS: For area tourist information, call (800) 245-7711.

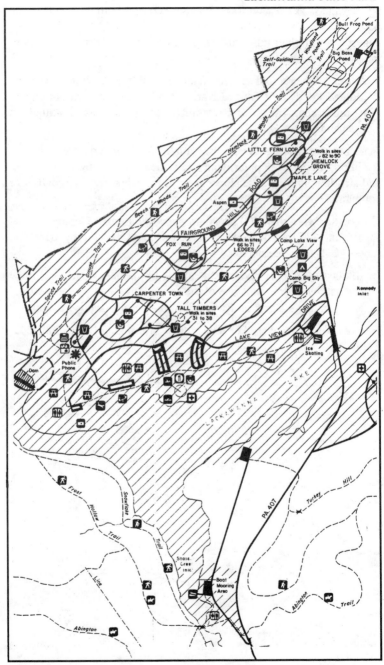

31 Laurel Hill State Park
Land: 3,935 acres   Water: 65.5-acre lake, 15 miles of streams

George Washington slept here, along with his troops during the Whiskey Rebellion of 1794.

Lots of other travelers, many in the 1800s, have also stayed within the park boundaries. In fact, in the area where Group Camp No 8 now stands, an inn once stood just below an active grist mill that kept busy for many years grinding local farmers' wheat and rye. At the head of the lake, a pottery factory and iron forge also once operated.

It wasn't until the mid-1930s when the Works Progress Administration (WPA) and the Civilian Conservation Corps (CCC), under the supervision of the National Parks Service, began construction of the first recreational facilities at Laurel Hill. Much of this development was completed in 1938, and in 1945 the federal government ceded this outstanding recreational demonstration area to the Commonwealth of Pennsylvania.

Laurel Hill, in Somerset County, is mountainous. The topography of the park is typical of the Allegheny plateau province. The thick oak and hemlock forest also includes laurel, rhododendron, sugar maple, birch, cherry, tulip poplar and hemlock. There is a small stand of virgin hemlock on the Hemlock Hiking Trail.

Information and Activities

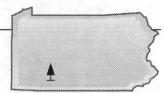

Laurel Hill State Park
R. D. 4, P.O. Box 130
Somerset, PA 15501
(814) 445-7725

DIRECTIONS: From the Pennsylvania Turnpike, take exit 10 (Somerset) west on PA Rt. 31 from Somerset 10 miles and follow directional signs.

CONTACT STATION/OFFICE: Adjacent to the campground entrance, a tan-colored remodeled farmhouse (visitor center) has a small natural history exhibit and learning area. Displays, in what was once the living room, include black and white photographs of the old CCC camp, examples of bird nesting boxes, a hands-on touch box display, kids' corner, animal mounts including a fox and pileated woodpecker, and other small learning exhibits. The park office is open 8 a.m. - 4 p.m. weekdays, and seven days between Memorial Day and Labor Day.

CAMPGROUND: The Laurel Hill family campground has 270 sites for tents and RVs with flush toilets, hot water showers, sanitary dump stations and drinking water. The mostly shady and gently rolling campground is open from the second Friday in April until mid-October.

The campground road and some camp sites are hard-surfaced, while some sites are gravel and outfitted with picnic tables and grills. Laurel Hill has some of the more private camping sites, separated by vegetation, in the system. Amenities in the campground include a play field and play apparatus, small amphitheater and five rest rooms. Laurel Hill has group tent camping areas for about 125 people. The group camping area is open year-round and equipped with pit toilets, fire rings, drinking water and picnic tables. One of the organized group areas (No. 5) is an old CCC camp with wooden cabins. This unique area of old buildings includes flush toilets, central showerhouse, large dining hall and kitchen, and is available to rent by the night.

FISHING: In the spring, trout anglers use "Powerbait," the doughball-like substance that comes in a small jar. Other local anglers use small live bait for panfish, and some bass are taken with spring season top-water lures, jigs and rubber worms. Crappies from the shoreline in the evening are considered good fishing. Use live bait and a bobber.

There are 15 miles of streams in the park. Laurel Hill Creek and Jones Mill Run are considered good trout streams. A small pond behind the dam is also a favorite, quiet fishing spot where panfish can be taken in the early morning and evening.

BOATING: At the foot of the dam, near the southern boundary of the park, is a small, narrow boat launching ramp. The other launch is at the north end of the lake near picnic area No. 4. Registered non-powered boats and electrical powered boats are allowed to cruise the quiet lake.

HIKING: About 12 miles of hiking trails, mostly north of the day-use area, form one large loop with many connecting trails branching from the Bobcat, Hemlock and Tramroad trails. The northermost Bobcat Trail is a narrow trail receiving minimal maintenance and light use. All trails are interesting, most offering examples of history. On Lake Trail, hikers can visit an old shelter of chestnut logs built by the CCC nearly 60 years ago. Remains of a logging railroad can sometimes be seen along the Tramroad Trail, while virgin timber may be seen along Hemlock Trail.

DAY-USE AREAS: The day-use area is stretched along the shady western banks of Laurel Hill Lake. In this heavily used area is the 1,200-foot-long guarded beach that is open 11 a.m. - 7 p.m. Memorial Day to Labor Day. It has changing rooms, several hundred picnic tables, grills, pavilions, play fields and shoreline fishing. One of the pavilions is in a wooded area; picnic area No. 3 is near the beach.

NATURE: Interpretive programs are offered in the park each summer featuring ecology-based lessons, campfire talks and hikes. For information about environmental education programming, contact the educators in the visitors' center. Call (814) 352-8649.

SNOWMOBILE TRAILS: With parking and a staging area near the trailhead, 10-miles of trails in the park connect to about 60 miles of trails in the neighboring Forbes State Forest. This trailhead area is just west of the day-use area.

WINTER: Ice skating, ice boating and fishing are popular on the lake. Cross-country skiing is also available on the park's trails.

32 Lehigh Gorge State Park
Land: 4,548 acres Water: River/gorge

The rugged, boulder-strewn Lehigh River carves an exciting course through the mountains from its outlet at the U.S. Corps of Engineers' Francis W. Walter Dam at the northern end to Jim Thorpe at the southern end. The entire park is characterized by its deep gorge, steep walls and thick vegetation. Rock outcroppings appear throughout the area. The river is a popular whitewater boating site.

More than 26 miles of abandoned railroad grade follow the river, offering wonderful opportunities for hiking, bicycling, sightseeing and photography. The rail trail is closed to motorized vehicles. Parking areas at access points are in White Haven and Rockport. Very limited parking is at Lehigh Tannery and Leslie Run. Request a park map; it details access points and offers directions to public places along the meandering river.

The river has an interesting history that started in earnest after coal was discovered at Summit Hill in 1791 that launched intense development and settlement of the upper Lehigh Valley. The need to transport large quantities of coal drove the development of a series of locks, dams and

Pennsylvania State Parks

canals built between 1835 and 1838. The Lehigh Coal and Navigation Company built 20 dams and 29 locks over the 26 miles between Mauch Chunk (now Jim Thorpe) and White Haven. More than five miles of canals were also built. Devastating floods destroyed the canals in 1862.

Hikers and bike riders can still see remaining locks, dams and a towpath, which is being preserved for historical interpretation. White Haven and Coalport offer Education opportunities.

Information and Activities

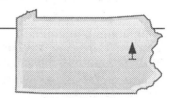

Lehigh Gorge State Park
R.R. 1 Box 81
White Haven, PA 18661
(717) 443-0400

DIRECTIONS: The long, lineal park follows the gorge (Lehigh River). Exit 40 of I-80 at White Haven provides access to the northern end of the park. The southern end is reached by taking exit 34 on the Northeast Extension of the Pennsylvania Turnpike, and following U.S. Route 209 south to Jim Thorpe. The A-frame park office with a flagstone porch is next to a rushing stream in the tiny village of Rockport.

FISHING: With all of the pressure on the Lehigh River, the scenic river holds good numbers of stream bred, carryover and stocked browns and rainbows. Most of the Lehigh River is clear, hurrying over gravel beds and small boulders and under fallen trees. Other stretches of the river are quiet.

Hatches on the winding river include quills, stoneflies, Hendricksons, sulphurs, caddis and green and brown drakes from mid-April to late May. Summer patterns include caddis, terrestrials, green drakes and others.

HIKING/BIKING: Pedal or hike between two mountains along an easy 2 percent grade. The park has 26 miles of excellent, scenic rail trails.

RAFTING: Whitewater boating is the major attraction at the gorge. Depending on the river conditions (call 800-431-4721 for flow information). The waters can froth and roar, challenging the most experienced and fit kayakers or whitewater rafters.

One of the best access sites is at Rockport near the park office. The area has a broad gravel parking lot, rubber launching ramps down the steep banks, stairs, rest rooms and access to the riverside trail at the mountain's base. All boaters must enter and leave the gorge at designated access areas. Mid-March to June is usually the best time for rafting.

Inexperienced boaters should not attempt the Lehigh River without qualified guides. Outfitted trips are available from concessionaires who provide transportation to and from the river, rafts, guides and all appropriate safety equipment. Licensed outfitters operating in the gorge and Lehigh Gorge State Park include:

Whitewater Challenges - (717) 443-9532
Pocono Whitewater Adventures - (717) 325-3656
Jim Thorpe River Adventures - (717) 325-2570
Whitewater Rafting Adventures - (717) 722-0285

These outfitters adhere to controls and capacities so that the gorge doesn't become overpopulated with rafters.

All boaters are required to wear a U. S. Coast Guard approved personal flotation device. Persons in canoes and kayaks should wear helmets as well. Wetsuits and drysuits are often necessary because the best water levels for boating occur when air and water temperatures are low. All inflatables must be at least seven feet long.

RIVER TRIPS ARE OF THREE LENGTHS: White Haven to Rockport, 8.7 miles; Rockport to Jim Thorpe, 15.4 miles; or White Haven to Jim Thorpe, 24.1 miles.

GLEN ONOKO ACCESS AREA: Near Jim Thorpe, the area offers day-use, trailheads and a boat take-out area.

HUNTING: Most park lands are open to hunting. Call for information.

WINTER: The rail trail is wonderful for cross-country skiers. A 15-mile section between White Haven and Penn Haven Junction is open to snowmobling.

Pennsylvania State Parks

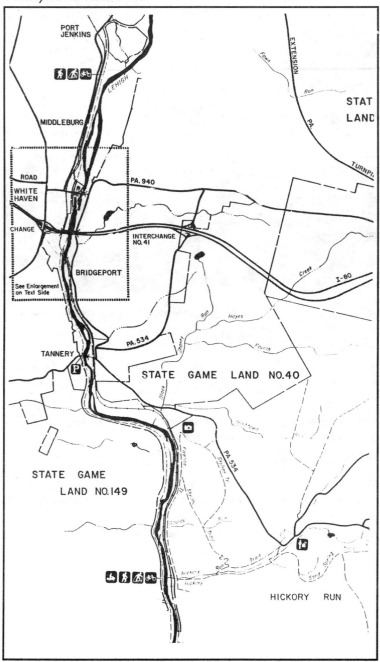

33 Leonard Harrison and Colton Point State Park

Land: 953 acres combined Water: Pine Creek

Leonard Harrison and Colton Point face each other across the 1,000-foot-deep, 47-mile-long "Grand Canyon" (Pine Creek Gorge) of Pennsylvania in Tioga County. Laced with deep valleys and rock-tumbled streams, the scattered lookouts at each park along the canyon's rims furnish an awe-inspiring view. Bring your camera. The canyon (and state parks) is in the 159,466-acre Tioga State Forest that has many features worth exploring, including waterfalls, scenic vistas, backpacking, camping, cabin rentals and much more.

Year-round scenery is the attraction at these two neighboring state parks. Hardwood trees offer a wonderful display of crimsons, golds and tones of red during the autumn, while lush green foliage surrounds you–high and low–during the spring and summer. Early October is the best time of the year to visit Pine Gorge to view the fall colors. The parks are perched on opposite mountain tops, each offering many overlooks of the sprawling open canyon.

From either side of the canyon, you can see hazy mountain tops in the distance. On very quiet days you can hear the moving water below.

In geologic terms, Pine Creek Gorge, whose depth can reach 1,450 feet, is "modern." Before glaciers advanced to this area, Pine Creek flowed in a northeasterly direction near Ansonia. But as the huge glaciers retreated, a dam of sand, gravel and clay plugged the creek's flow north of the two state parks. This natural dam forced broad Pine Creek to carve a new path southward. The exposed rock seen in the gorge is more than 350 millions years old.

Pine Creek's long set of rapids, Owassee, about three miles south of Ansonia, can reach class three rating in high water (whitewater rafting rating system). Kayakers and canoeists challenge the whitewater and also find magnificent scenery throughout the rocky gorge. Travelers on the river after snow melt or heavy rains below Tiadaghton will see the highest waterfall in the region. Falling Springs, which plunges over a nearly-vertical rock wall of the West Rim, is easily photographed from a small camping area on the east bank of the creek.

About 300,000 outdoor lovers annually visit the sister parks. Leonard Harrison, a wealthy businessman, donated all the land, which opened in 1922. Harrison maintained a summer home in the early 1900s just across the creek from the Harrison lookout near Four Mile Run.

Information and Activities

Leonard Harrison State Park
R. R. 6, P.O. Box 199
Wellsboro, PA 16901-8970
(717) 724-3061

DIRECTIONS: To reach the 585-acre Leonard Harrison State Park on the eastern rim, take PA Route 660 west from Wellsboro for 10 miles. Leonard Harrison has the, most complete brochure racks in the parks system. Information about many nearby attractions can be picked up at the office. Leonard Harrison is complete with park office, visitor center and terrific patio-like viewing area along a ridge over the canyon.

The 368-acre Colton Point State Park, on the western rim, is five miles south of U.S. Route 6 at Ansonia. Colton Point has a seasonal contact office only, with limited camping.

EMERGENCY NUMBERS: state police, 662-2151, and 911 system.

CAMPGROUND: Colton Point has 12 tent sites, 10 of which are walk-ins, and 13 shady places for small to medium RV rigs. Each gravel site has a ground-mounted fire ring and picnic table. The single loop also has two group camping areas in semi-open areas near gravel parking lots. The forest floor is covered with large expanses of ferns that seem to reach for the sunlight in many parts of the campground. Some sites have landscape-like timbers that outline the place where your tent should be pitched. This wilderness campground, with a canopy of mixed conifers, is not heavily used. Sites on slightly higher ground are 12-14. Safe, rustic tent camping for families is the major attraction at Colton Point.

The geometric-shaped log and field stone composting toilet has some a viewing panel that allows visitors to see the collection chamber and learn how they work. In fact, inside the toilet, hung on the tan-colored wall, is a brief interpretive sign that details its inner working.

Leonard Harrison State Park operates 30 mowed, highly-manicured camping sites along a single loop, two of which can accommodate trails more than 36 feet in length. On a typical non-holiday week, six to 10 camping sites are in use. Sites 15, 17 and 18 get about a half-day of sunlight. Site 20 can handle a big RV rig and is quite private. A limited amount of firewood is available in the campground. Site 23 is oversized, half shady and large enough for big travel trailers. Many of the sites are on a lawn-like area and very open. The rest room has three outdoor sinks and is near site 30.

Both campgrounds are a great secret. Shhhh!

Parents may want to check out sites 1-3, which are closest to the playground. About half of the sites are wheelchair accessible, offering a handicapped accessible picnic table and a pedestal grill at the right height for persons in wheelchairs to use.

FISHING: You can fish at the twin parks, but it's a long climb down, and seemingly longer back up. Trout, smallmouth bass and panfish are taken from Pine Creek. But it's worth the effort! The trail may be steep, but the scenery is probably the best in the state. On the water there are long deep pools, tidy riffles, swift chutes, boulders and shallows where many 20-inch browns are taken yearly. Most of the trout in Pine Creek are stocked.

Freestone Pine Creek, more like a river than a creek, warms up quickly without the benefit of cold limestone springs or a heavy canopy to shade the rushing water. Typically, at least near the state parks, the trout fishing slows dramatically by June. It is often difficult to fly fish in April and May when the rafters and kayakers are out in full force, especially on the weekends. Nevertheless, early morning angling equals some great match-the-hatch action–especially in the very early part of the season. During the first half of May, you can fly over hatches like light Cahill, slate drake, gray fox, brown drake, blue-winged olive dun and green drake.

Trout fly fishermen may want to try other nearby streams including Marsh Creek, Asaph Straight and Four Mile Run.

FLOAT TRIPS: The 1,000-foot-deep gorge, carved by the southern flow of the Pine Creek, is an excellent place to try a family float trip. Four outfitters operate guided trips on a 20-mile section of Pine Creek, from Blackwell to Ansonia. Trips are offered from about mid-March until mid-June when water levels are high. Although the degree of difficulty is moderate, Owassee and Split Rock rapids provide a sampling of whitewater excitement.

Pine Creek, named a National Wild and Scenic River in 1968, is a combination of moderate whitewater, long quiet pools and outstanding scenic views. The fast-flowing water, framed by towering palisades and dramatic rock outcrops crowned with evergreen forests and cathedral-like hardwoods, is best viewed from the water.

Saturdays are the most popular days for float trips. The number of boaters on Sundays is about one-third that on Saturday. Early or late in the season, boaters should consider wearing a wet suit.

All four outfitters make the trip in standard river rafts. Call Pine Creek Outfitters, (717) 724-3003; Western Wilderness Service, (717) 724-5921; Frome Floats (814) 435-9977; and Canyon Cruises, (814) 435-2969.

HIKING: Turkey Path Trail, all 332 steps (I counted and sweated on the way back up!) of it, take visitors to the bottom of the gorge. It took nine years to build the scenic trail. The Turkey Path winds one mile to the canyon floor and parallels Little Four Mile Run for about half its length. Section of the trail are narrow, steep and hazardous. Once you reach the creek, you can explore along its edges and if the water is low you can cross the creek and hike a steep mile and one-half up Turkey Path through Colton Point. Proper footwear should be worn.

The facilities can be rustic, but the natural features are grand.

The old railroad bed along the east side of Pine Creek is now trackless and may be used by hikers, bicyclists, cross-country skiers and equestrians. It is closed to all motorized traffic. The rail trail, crushed limestone over blast, actually is on two elevations, one for horses and bikes and the other exclusively for walking. Like many of the trails in the park and vicinity, trekkers will pass ferns growing on rocky ledges and mossy spots, past cucumber trees, along a wide variety of wildflowers, and through areas under a canopy of trees and undergrowth.

West Rim Trail (30 miles), orange blazed, generally follows the west rim of the Pennsylvania grand canyon from Ansonia to Route 414, two miles south of Blackwell. The trail elevation is 850-2,020 feet; most of it is 1,600 to 1,900 feet above sea level. The steepest section is near the south terminus, 300 feet in one-quarter mile. The rugged trail features a variety of forest types, frequent vistas of the canyon and surrounding plateaus. The trail requires either two vehicles or a shuttle. The average backpacker can do the trail in three days. Most hike north to south. Private shuttle service is available by calling (717) 724-3003.

BIKING: The areas surrounding the grand canyon contain an interconnected network of innumerable gravel forestry roads, ATV and cross-country ski trails offer seldom-traveled places to explore atop two wheels. A biker's guide to Tioga County available at the park office details a number of trails in the vicinity. There are also mountain bike trails in the Tioga and Susquehannock state forests.

DAY-USE AREAS: The Civilian Conservation Corps built many of the bulky timber and stone shelters and grills at both parks. At Colton Point, day-users often need to park and carry their picnics to the shady pavilions near the rim of the canyon. Larger families may want to check out pavilion number 4 at Colton Point. It has a four-foot-wide stone fireplace and room for four picnic tables under the overhang.

A playground and pavilion are behind the newer park office at Leonard Harrison. There are about 90 picnic tables at this unit. Colton Point has more than 120 picnic tables scattered along the canyon rim.

VISITOR CENTER/VIEWING AREA: At Leonard Harrison, the small visitor center is only one-quarter-mile from the park office and at the entrance to the well-kept and designed viewing area. It has flagstone under foot, and coin-operated binoculars and interpretive signs scattered along it length. From here visitors will get the best view of the canyon. The terrace-like viewing area with chunky wood railing complements the panoramic view.

A nine-minute slide-tape presentation shown on demand at the visitors center tells the story of the park from the ice age to the present. The park's interpreter can also answer questions of the gorge's geological history, flora and fauna. The staff also help to host an annual CCC workers reunion.

Near the visitor center are some small day-use areas and places to park bicycles. ·

Interpretive signs talk about melt waters that formed the area, ice sheets that covered the area and creeks that have shaped the region. Other signs talk about Pine Creek, Indians, forest management, recreation and habitat use. Inside the visitors center are a variety of displays and educational information.

NATURE: In many ways, the grand canyon of Pennsylvania is the crown jewel of Pennsylvania scenic wilderness areas and one of the last and most expansive between New York and Chicago.

Nesting bald eagles and river otters are the marquee mammals in the park. Also seen are strong migrations of warblers and the presence of a variety of birds of prey. The gorge became a Registered Natural Landmark in 1968.

The joint parks have a bird list with 87 species, including four winter-only species and 13 migrators. Mammals in the canyon region include 54 species, such as nine species of bats, seven types of shrews, five types of mice, black bear, river otter, two types of flying squirrels, coyote, deer, three species of mole, porcupine, three kinds of weasels, rabbits and others.

Reptiles and amphibians of Leonard Harrison and Colton Point include nine species of snakes – the timber rattlesnake, black racer, eastern milk snake, red-bellied snake, eastern garter snake and others. Four species of turtles are found in the park including wood turtle, snapping turtle, box turtle and painted turtle. Amphibians that live in the rugged area are two types of toads, seven species of frogs and nine types of salamanders and newts.

Eighty-three tree and shrub species can be found on the mountainsides and valley bottoms. The park also publishes a spring wildflower checklist that details 21 families.

HUNTING: Call for details.

WINTER: Cross-country skiing and snowmobiling are popular on neighboring state forest trails and roads.

INSIDERS TIPS: Take a plane ride over the canyon from Grand Canyon Airport, eight miles from Leonard Harrison State Park. Animal Land, a 12-acre roadside zoo with gift shop, is along the road to Harrison Leonard.

The Tioga (Tioga means *"the meeting of two rivers"*) County Tourist Promotion Agency features all types of visitor attractions, camping, fishing, a state forest, shopping and other information about the area. Call (717) 724-0635.

OTHER ATTRACTIONS: U.S. Fish Research Center, Robinson House, candle-making outlet, golfing, horseback riding, Corning Glass Co. tours, and Sunset Ice Cream store.

34 Linn Run State Park/Laurel Summit State Park

Land: 570 acres

Linn Run and Laurel Summit state parks are within the huge Forbes State Forest. The scenic area features mixed hardwoods and evergreen forests, rolling terrain and meandering, rocky streams.

The parks are a gateway to the Forbes State Forest, nearby skiing areas and to the 70-mile Laurel Highlands Hiking Trail. There are also extensive snowmobling trails that criss-cross the varied terrain of this highlands region

Forbes State Forest is part of the Laurel Ridge mountain range and is composed of 20 separate tracts of land with elevations ranging from 1,300 feet to 3,213 feet. The area is rich with diverse natural communities, including a bog, cold clear streams, rocky surfaces, ridge and rhododendron-covered creek bottoms.

The area teems with wildlife including bear, wild turkey, deer and many species of songbirds and raptors. Even more obvious are the wildflowers that bloom much of the season, but are most spectacular from late April to mid-May. Common and colorful species include Canada mayflower, trilliums, trout lilies, spring beauties and wild hydrangea.

Information and Activities

Linn Run/Laurel Summit State Parks
P.O. Box 50
Rector, PA 15677-0030
(412) 238-6623

DIRECTIONS: From Ligonier take U.S. Rt. 30 east for two miles. At the intersection of PA Rt. 381, turn south for four miles. Turn left on Linn Run Road at the small town of Rector. The office, at the base of a mountain, is open 8 a.m. - 4 p.m. weekdays and is complete with a pay phone, bench and flagpole.

CABINS: Linn Run has 10 rustic cabins nestled in a shady valley with towering trees and mountains above and a boulder-strewn creek. The wooden cabins with porches and fireplaces (but not indoor bathrooms) are open year-round. All of the cabins are within easy walking distance of the park office and showerhouse.

During the fall, winter and spring, the cabins may be rented by the week and half-week. During the summer season the cabins are rented by the week only, starting on Fridays.

All of the cabins are shady and have a picnic table. Cabin 7 is one of the more private of the group in the first loop. Cabins 9 and 10 are tucked along the wood line, across a small plank bridge. These two cabins are the most private.

EMERGENCY NUMBERS: State police, 911 or Laurel Hill State Park at (814) 445-7725.

FISHING: Linn Run offers good trout fishing and is part of some major efforts to correct and protect stream waters and the cold-water fishery.

Restoring trout to Linn Run has been reasonably successful. No trout had lived in the cold waters year-round since 1970. Acid rain mixed with natural acidic soils and bedrock make the stream too acidic to support aquatic life. Researchers thought if they could neutralize the acid waters, fish could live in it again. So they drilled three wells into the ground water table and began pumping cleaner water into the streams. Groundwater beneath flows through loyalhanna limestone and acts as a anti-acid, making the groundwater alkaline.

In the spring of 1985, researchers pumped well water in to Linn Run to combat the acid rain and snow melt. They also stocked trout, and for the first time since 1970 anglers could catch trout in this section of the mountain stream.

Unfortunately, this project offers just a short-term solution. The high power costs of pumping have kept the project small, and researchers worry about drying up the groundwater. Fish left in the stream after the pumps are turned off move to less acidic streams. These wells and an aerator can be seen at the park along with interpretive display boards.

Pennsylvania's rain water is some of the most acidic in the nation. More than 5,000 miles of the state's streams are vulnerable to acidification. While success at Linn Run is heartening, it can not be applied across the state. The best overall solution to improving the watersheds it to 1) car pool, 2) ride a bus, 3) keep your car tuned up, 4) turn off your car when parked, and 5) preserve power in your home.

HIKING: Five miles of hiking trails in the park connect to the network of trails in Forbes State Forest.

DAY-USE AREAS: The Grove Run Picnic Area is the park's largest day-use area, offering more than 100 picnic tables, drinking water and a comfort station. The spacious and shady area is on a ridge north of the park office. No alcoholic beverages are permitted. A small timber-frame play apparatus and grills are in the area. The day-use area is open 8 a.m. to sunset daily.

A wooden pavilion, grills, picnic tables and additional playground equipment are in the Adam's Falls day-use area.

HUNTING: About 400 acres in the park are open to hunting. Common game species are squirrel, turkey, deer and black bear.

LAUREL SUMMIT STATE PARK: Along a rugged gravel road, the small 6-acre picnic area has about 50 tables, a pavilion, grills and small comfort station. The area is 2,739 feet above sea level and is often several degrees cooler in the summer than neighboring towns. If you are looking for a secluded picnic site, under the canopy of mature trees, Laurel Summit is a good choice. To find the park, go past the park office on Laurel Summit Road about four miles to reach Laurel Summit Par.

35 Little Buffalo State Park
Land: 830 acres Water: 88-acre lake

Deriving its name from the Little Buffalo Creek that flows through the park, the unit was comprised of several active farms and homes prior to the state purchasing the property in the 1960s. The open fields are slowly reverting to woodlands, with evidence of the tillable lands still seen in the rolling hills and young forests.

Because of the new woodlands, open spaces and landscaped areas, the park is an excellent place to see wildlife. Many such viewing opportunities are in or near Holman Lake, a long, narrow reservoir along which park amenities and day-use areas are scattered. SR 4010, commonly known as Little Buffalo Creek Road, runs the entire northern length of the lake, very close to the shoreline from which park visitors can often observe an assortment of waterfowl.

From the roadway, especially during late October and early November and late March and April, visitors often see sprawling rafts of noisy waterfowl stopping on the lake from their long journey for resting and feeding. Large flocks of Canada geese are common and so are goldeneye, scaup, mallards, wood ducks, grebes, buffleheads, pintail, blue-winged teal and many others.

Little Buffalo is an active day-use unit. The focal point of the park is the lake, but upon further exploring visitors will find a number of wonderful recreational opportunities including a swimming pool, large working grist mill, covered bridge, 450 picnic tables, a beautiful outdoor stage, playgrounds, fishing, boating, information about a narrow-gauge railroad that once served the area and lots more.

The park was opened to the public and dedicated in 1972.

Information and Activities

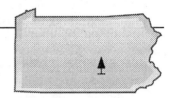

Little Buffalo State Park
R. D. 2, Box 256A
Newport, PA 17074-9428
(717) 567-9255

DIRECTIONS: The park can be reached from PA Route 34 and exiting to the west between New Bloomfield and Newport. The park office, with bright blue doors, is open 8 a.m. - 4 p.m. and often closed for lunch. A ranger is on duty when the office is closed. The park is on the 911 emergency system.

There is no overnight camping at the park.

SHOAFF'S MILL: A restored and working grist mill is open on many weekends, grinding corn and offering educational tours and programs. Restoration efforts on the mill began in 1975 (the state purchased the mill in 1966 form Earl Shoaff) when local craftsmen repaired the, huge steel wheel and other components of the facility. Mills in general are an engineering feat, but Shoaffs is especially pleasing and impressive. You'll love it "down by the old millstream." The mill is open 1-3 p.m. most weekends from mid-April through mid-October and by appointment.

Not so long ago, a grist mill was as necessary to a farm village as a gasoline station is to your hometown today. Hundreds of mills once dotted the land, serving farmers who traveled old highways by wagons to have their corn (or wheat) turned to meal using the power of a giant waterwheel. Flour milling was one of the original industries in Pennsylvania, yet iron making was probably responsible for the formation of Shoaff's Mill.

Shoaffs' Mill was built in 1840 and was part of the Juanita Furnace community west of the park. The mill later ground grains for the general market, stores and local farmers. After William Shoaff's death in 1888, his wife operated the mill. In 1900, Ellis Shoaff purchased the mill from his mother at a public sale and operated it at full capacity grinding wheat, buckwheat, cornmeal and animal feeds.

Ellis replaced the wooden wheel with the present 32-foot steel wheel from Hanover. The wheel, which makes a pleasant sound when running, was used until the three-story mill closed in the 1940s. The wheel was rumored to be one of the largest east of the Mississippi River.

Programs at the mill teach visitors about the dynamics of water power, grinding techniques (wheat is much more complicated to grind then corn), sifting, the miller's toll, huge gearing systems, grooved millstones and much more. The brick house across the road was built by Shoaff in 1861.

FISHING: Holman Lake is stocked with trout and other species by the fish commission on a regular basis and a map is available from the office that depicts some underwater features that hold and attract these denizens. The biggest underwater features are an old pond (near the swimming pool) and the old creek bed that winds under the water's surface from one end of the lake to the other. Many anglers, both shoreline fishermen and boaters, test their skills near the dam. Some sunken tires, structures and Christmas trees have been placed in the lake to provide hiding habitat also.

THE FOLLOWING SPECIES ARE IN THE WATERS: trout, bass, perch, crappies, bluegill, walleye, muskies, suckers, carp and catfish.

BOATING: Two launching ramps serve the lake, with the main ramp and 60 site mooring area at the east end of the lake near the breast of the dam. Wind conditions are good on the lake for windsurfing. Prevailing winds out of the northwest follow the long axis of the lake making for long runs. Only non-powered and registered electric-powered boats are permitted on the lake.

HIKING: If you hike all of the trails, you will have traveled about 10 miles along gently rolling and wooded terrain.

Hikers can construct an interesting five-mile trek that circles the lake, passes a covered bridge, travels along an old rail bed, past a functioning grist mill, along a self-guided trail, near bluebird nesting boxes, in heavy woods that give way to a stream bank and through meadows.

The easy walking, well-graded trail is a combination of the North Side Trail, small connector trails and the self-guided spur on the south.

The self-guided interpretive trail has 25 learning stations along a ridge which forms the southern boundary of the park. The trail is well-marked and rocky in areas. It takes 1 1/2 hours to hike. You will learn about and see pencil-straight young hemlock trees, soil erosion along switchback trails, areas where succession is taking place, signs of wildlife, plants growing among rocky areas, mountain laurel plants, the story a stump can tell and lots more.

VISITOR CENTER: Looking like a converted garage, the gray-colored center has four benches in front that are often used to orient visitors and as a staging area for educational programs and classes. The center is open 1-3 p.m. on weekends from mid-April to mid-October. Small natural history exhibits inside the visitor center include a binocular microscope, touch box, Earth Day information, animal mounts, posters and an outdoor feeding station. The covered bridge is between the visitor center and the grist mill.

The old rail bed of the Newport and Sherman narrow-gauge train that served this area from the 1890s to 1929 is near the visitor center and part of the park's hiking trail system and includes one of the original railroad cars that is being restored by the park's staff.

DAY-USE AREAS: Significant day-use areas are around the busy swimming pool and equipped with picnic tables, grills and nearby rest rooms. The main day-use area is north of the pool, along the lake and offers shady and open mowed recreation spaces. A small boat rental concession in a gray-colored building is along the lake edge east of the swimming complex. V-bottomed aluminum boats, yellow and red pedal boats and canoes are launched from a large wooden dock.

Picnic pavilions can be reserved.

SWIMMING POOL: Little Buffalo has the second largest swimming pool (small fee) in the state park system. The pool is operated by private concessionaires. The guarded pool is a very popular feature of the park and open Memorial Day weekend to Labor Day, 11 a.m. - 7 p.m. daily, unless otherwise posted. Group rates and season passes are available. Children under 3 years are free. Some special evening hours are offered during the hot season. There is very little shade inside the pool, except around the planting pockets that dot the flat cement deck. The unheated pool is 5 feet deep in the middle and 1.5 feet deep at the shallow edges. Depending on the attendance, the pool can be roped off into smaller sections that are easier to patrol. Swimming lessons are offered during the summer.

The attractive rough-sawn and stone bathhouse defines the spacious, heavily used swimming pool. A wood sculpture rests on a small island in the middle of the pool next to a lifeguard stand. Little Buffalo has huge sunning decks with picnic tables and bulky benches scattered about. A smaller wading pool for children is near the big pool and is 1.5-foot-deep. A access ramp with stainless rails to assist the disabled into the pool.

The food concession serves both swimmers and walk-up guests. The concession serves more than small snacks; you can get sandwiches, hot dogs, pieta, pizza, cold drinks, ice cream (which includes rocky road flavor!) and soft pretzels.

MOORE PAVILION: In 1993, when the state park system was celebrating its centennial year, the beautiful Moore Pavilion was dedicated during the annual festival of arts. The 24 x 48-foot performance stage was built by 60 dedicated volunteers starting the project following the 1992 arts festival. Large stripped and varnished hemlock columns support the bulky trusses that frame the roof line above the broad wood deck of finished planks. The performance pavilion is a wonderful example of public/private collaboration involving many partners. Today the structure is valued at $200,000, but it's a priceless addition to this fine park.

The elegant pavilion honors Senator William J. Moore.

BLUE BALL TAVERN: Operated by volunteers from the historical society of Perry County and open on a random basis (some Sunday afternoons), the inn contains the Edwin L. Holman Library and Joseph G. Darlington Museum. The mostly restored wood frame building has floral wallpaper, small baskets hung on the wall, artifacts, static displays and old photographs. The museum is almost astride Little Buffalo Creek. Opened on Sunday afternoons from 1 p.m. - 4 p.m., Memorial Day to Labor day.

NATURE: Naturalist programs are offered, featuring outdoor education programs for all ages. Many programs are also historical in nature. Special events like the Cider Squeeze, Festival of Arts, Halloween night and Christmas trail are offered to the general public at Little Buffalo.

At the narrow end of the lake are some interesting wetland areas that attract waterfowl and wading birds. Many turtles can be seen in southeast corner basking in the sun. The occasional bald eagle and osprey are seen at the park in the spring and fall. Other birds seen in the park include sandpipers, killdeer, green herons, orioles, bluebirds, indigo buntings, wild turkeys and ruffed grouse. Mammals that call the park home are woodchucks, deer, gray squirrel and muskrats. Wildlife viewing in the summer is best in the early morning before day-users crowd the shoreline, picnic areas and pool.

HUNTING: About 300 acres of Little Buffalo State Park are open to hunting. Call for details.

WINTER: About seven miles of trails are open for cross-country skiing. Ice skaters zoom around a one-acre area of the lake that is maintained on the east end of the lake at the main boat launch. Strict rules apply for safety if you plan to ice fish. The park requires at least four inches of ice before anglers may venture out on the lake. A map depicting the location of springs (that can be dangerous) and other underwater structures is available from the park office.

Sledding and tobogganing are encouraged along a 300-yard-long length on the west end of the park.

NEARBY ATTRACTIONS: Along the park border is a private campground. Call the Campground of Truth at (717) 567-7370 for details. The park office has a list of 10 other nearby campgrounds.

INSIDERS TIP: Visit when the grist mill is grinding corn on the weekends, and take the stone step in the stream to reach it.

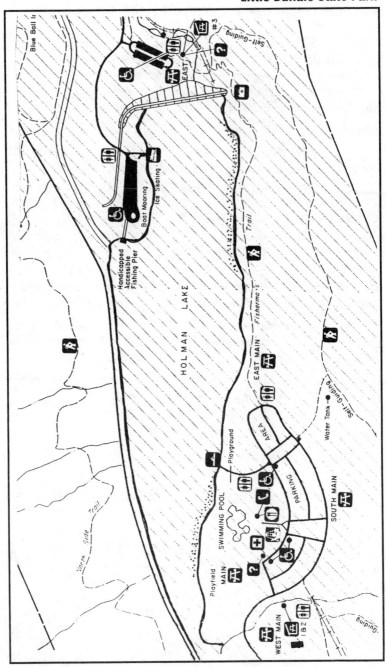

36 Little Pine State Park
Land: 2,158 acres   Water: 94-acre lake

Little Pines State Park rests in a narrow rugged valley in the middle of the 214,973-acre Tiadaghton State Forest. The sprawling and jagged state forest is one of 20 forest districts created for the protection and management of the state's forest resources. The state forests of Pennsylvania cover more than two million acres in 48 of the Commonwealth's 67 counties. That's about one-tenth of Pennsylvnia's entire area.

The purpose of the state forest–which often has state parks in them– is "To provide a continuous supply of timber, lumber, wood and other forest products; to protect the watersheds, conserve the water and regulate the flow of rivers and streams of the state; and to furnish opportunities for healthful recreation to the public."

Like the state parks, the state forests belong to the people of Pennsylvania for whom they are managed and protected. As in Tiadaghton State Forest, most have picnic areas equipped with tables, fireplaces, water and parking. More than 4,000 campsites are leased to individuals and organizations. Access to the state forest is provided by more than 2,600 miles of roads and 2,500 miles of trails. More than five million tree seedlings are also produced and sold to citizens for reforestation of their lands.

Over the past few decades, 62 natural areas within state forest covering 69,429 acres have also been established. These areas are set aside to provide sites for scientific observation of natural systems, protect examples of typical and unique plant and animal communities, and preserve outstanding examples of natural beauty. Sixteen wild areas are spread over 110,341 acres and are managed to retain the undeveloped character of the area for persons who enjoy such activities as hiking, hunting, fishing and the pursuit of peace and solitude.

Thirty-five municipalities have either all or a large part of their watersheds within the state forests. Eleven municipalities have water supply impounding dams within the state forests. Many of the best hunting grounds, finest fishing streams and grandest views are within the grand state forests.

Many Little Pine facilities were built by the Civilian Conservation Corps in the 1930s. Much of this and other years of work were destroyed by raging flood waters resulting from hurricane Agnes in June 1972. Many of the modern buildings at the park were constructed under a federal disaster assistance program.

Information and Activities

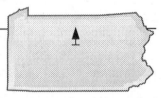

Little Pine State Park
H.C. 63, Box 100
Waterville, PA 17776-9705
(717) 753-8209

DIRECTIONS: Four miles north of PA Route 44 at Waterville and eight miles south of PA Route 287 at English Center in Lycoming County. Part of the drive along Route 44 is along a sheer rock wall, with the road notched out of the mountain ridge.

Little Pine State Park manages Hyner Run, Hyner View and Upper Pine Bottom State Park on North Route 44 (a small picnic/day-use park with shelter on a small ridge overlooking a pretty, narrow cascading stream that is spanned by a small wooded bridge).

EMERGENCY NUMBERS: 911 system; local hospital 398-0100.

CAMPGROUND: During the season, the contact station is open 8 a.m. -

4 p.m. Little Pines is a 104 site (six hillside tent sites) campground that's about 65 percent wooded, with gravel sites scattered along the park road that forms two irregularly-shaped loops in a valley along the Little Pine Creek. Actually, the Little Pine Creek isn't so little. It can be 30 yards wide in many places throughout the park. The Mid State Trail cuts through the campground behind site 17. Every neat and clean camping site has a picnic table and fire ring.

In 1989, hurricane-like winds leveled hundreds of mature trees in the campground, opening up section to sunlight and offering the park a chance to replant and improve certain tracts along the campground. Many of the blown-down trees were originally planted in the 1930s. The wind damage caused thousands of dollars worth of restoration work. Fortunately, no one was injured, even though 20 sites were occupied at the time of the storm. The blow down was part of nature's way of generating new growth. However, since the area is a high-use recreation area, the park can't wait for nature to heal it. To ensure continued operation, repairs to landscaping will take place in phases. Meanwhile, the camping area offers variety. Sun-loving campers and shady dwellers will have plenty of places to pick from in the fine family campground at Little Pine.

Sites 1-8 and 18-21 are open and quite sunny. Sites 11, 12, 13, 14 22, 23, 24, 25 and 27 also enjoy at least one-half day of full sunlight. A large section of the campground (sites 47 and 58 and others) rest on a bed of fragrant needles and under impressive pencil-straight pines that offer an airy but shady camping experience. The light that filters through the sentinel-like pines seem yellow-colored in the morning and much softer at dusk.

The tent sites are especially inviting, nestled into the mountainside and private. They are short walk-ins, off the park road, into the forest a handful of yards, and extremely shady, level and dry. Sites 30-35 are highly preferred sites, according to park staff. An old fenced-in cemetery is behind these sites and shaded by tall conifers.

Beginning at about site 98, you can see and hear the cascading spillway and huge dam that holds back the 94-acre lake. English Run, a small creek, also runs parallel to this row of camping sites. Site 94 is right in front of the tall gray dam and spillway. From your fishing rod if you camp in this area, anglers report some success in the pool. Camping sites in the 70s and 80s are large and can accommodate big RV rigs.

Church services are offered at 10:30 a.m. every Sunday during the summer. Limited seasonal storage for recreational vehicles is available at the park. A timber-style play structure is behind site 42, an excellent area for families–you would also be near the rest rooms. Other amenities include volleyball and basketball courts, amphitheater, benches and rest rooms at the foot of the bridge that accesses the pleasant campground.

Organized group tent camping in three areas is available for church or youth groups by advance registration. The areas are served by paved parking, rest rooms, picnic tables and fire rings.

FISHING: Anglers like to work the breast of the dam from a boat or carefully from the shoreline. Many boat fishermen also work the steep 3.3 miles of shoreline looking for both cold and warm water species that include stocked trout, large- and smallmouth bass, pike, panfish, catfish, carp and suckers.

Many anglers concentrate on stocked trout in the lake using Power Bait, salmon eggs and live bait.

Above the dam, Little Pine Creek is a very good trout stream that in many areas is up to 40 feet wide. It has solid hatches, cold waters and considerable natural reproduction. One of the most productive sections of the stream is the first four miles above the dam, especially during the early spring, when water temps are 50 degree or so. Trout rise often, snapping at emerging duns during this time. In May, the freestone creek can offer some spectacular hatches of green drakes and sulphurs in the evening. Slate drakes and cream Cahills often work in early June. From early June to October, use terrestrials like ants, beetles, grasshoppers and crickets. Fall anglers can have luck with attractor flies, blue-winged olives, streams, flying ants or nymphs. Check with local fly-fishing shops for up-to-date information.

Little Pine Creek runs for nearly 50 miles through canyon country along the Pine Creek Valley. Many mountains tower 1,000 feet above the cool, lush valley floor.

BOATING: Paddle boats are rented and 60 seasonal mooring spaces are available on the multi-use Little Pine Lake. Only non-powered or electric boats may ply the quiet waters.

Like many lakes in the region, Little Pine was dammed after the devastating 1936 flood that damaged Williamsport, Jersey Shore and neighboring communities. But unlike some of the impoundments,

Little Pines is very pleasing, offering great scenery and recreation opportunities along its two-mile length. Canoeists might enjoy the tree-lined lake the most. The waters are gentle and there are many channels and coves to slowly explore. In the spring, canoeists can paddle nearly four miles of the feeder creek.

HIKING: Backpackers can access the Mid State Trail in the family campground. The Mid State Trail goes from Juniata County to Tioga County.

Spike Buck Hollow Trail (2 miles) is a difficult, steep trail. Be ready for some vertical and switch-back hiking through steep grades and past groves of dogwood. But the sweeping vistas, large rock outcroppings and forested areas dotted with tan and gray flagstone make the hike worth the effort. The Mid State Trail shares this section of the trail in the park. Be in shape before attempting Spike Buck. Stone quarries are common.

Lake Shore Trail (.5 mile) is easy walking. It parallels the lake into the upper part of the park and is a good place to view wildflowers.

Panther Run Trial (2.7 miles), like Spike Buck, is steep. Many believe this to be the most scenic trail in the park.

Love Run Trail (3.1 miles) passes by some large hemlock stands and rushing mountain streams that wind through the cool valleys and gaps.

Button Ball Trail (.5 mile) is a short, easy trail.

Carsontown Trail (.88 mile) is short and easy.

DAY-USE AREAS: Picnic shelters with translucent roofs, plenty of picnic tables and grills dot the lakeside day-use areas. Some of the pavilions have oversized grills for group use. You can cook plenty of chicken on them! The park has about 300 picnic tables, a volleyball court, open mowed areas and plenty of parking.

At the top of the dam is a small viewing area with benches and a reader board that describe the logging era and Little Pine Creek's role in transporting logs to mills on the spring's high waters. It also talks about the pre-dam floods and the damage that was caused by overflowing waters.

VISITOR CENTER: Serving the beach and entire park, the block visitor center has changing rooms and vault toilets. Many environmental education programs begin here, including slide presentations, nature games, interpretive hikes, programs for campers and youth activities. The visitor center is open 3 p.m. - 6 p.m. Saturday and 4 p.m. - 7 p.m. Sunday.

NATURE: Diverse habitats of marshes, mature hardwoods and others (sycamore, white and paper birch, maple, poplar, hickory hemlock, white and red pine), dense barberry thickets, open meadows, evergreen plantations and cool valleys equal many opportunities to see birds and other wildlife. Woodland and semi-woodland birds include redstarts, scarlet tanagers, ovenbirds, kingbirds, indigo buntings, rufous-sided towhees and hummingbirds. Common loons are one of the best and regular sightings in the park during the spring as they wing to and from placid lakes of northern New England and Canada.

Bobcat, deer, river otter, fox and black bear also visit the park occasionally.

SWIMMING BEACH: Across from the park office is the beach complex, which has a wonderful view of the surrounding mountains and richly textured Tiadaghton State Forest. The mostly grass beach was built in 1958 and is open, weather permitting, 11 a.m. - 7 p.m. Memorial Day weekend to Labor Day. The deepest part of the guarded waters is five feet. This is a flood control lake and the water levels can fluctuate daily.

Hikers and park users might also spot deer, porcupines and the smaller New England rabbit, which has a spot between its ears. Eastern cottontails are also seen in the field and edge areas of the park.

HUNTING: About 1,700 acres in Little Pines are open to hunting. Call the park manager for details.

WINTER: When the snow flies, bring your skis, sled or snowmobile. There are more than 100 miles of snowmobile trails in the surrounding Tiadaghton State Forest. Ice fishermen can also try to entice trout to their lure...and up through the hole during the wintertime. Hockey players also use the lake ice for informal play.

NEARBY ATTRACTIONS: Algerine Swamp Natural Area, a glacial bog, is a wonderful side trip. The area supports black spruce, balsam fir and other northern plant communities. The "Grand Canyon" of Pennsylvania is also only minutes away.

INSIDEERS TIPS: Camp in the pine grove and walk across the trail over the high dam. Several deer can often be seen at dusk along park roads and trails.

37 Locust Lake State Park
Land: 1,144 acres Water: 52-acre lake

With the exception of 60 acres near the dam, the entire park is forested and nestled in the foothills of Schuylkill County. Locust Lake is a camper's park. There are virtually no day-use amenities (except for hiking and biking). Campers enjoy a quiet facility, shade, good fishing, a bike path, hiking trails, camp store and play equipment for kids. Parking is limited, even for visiting fishermen.

The park, in a deep valley, is comprised of thick stands of northern hardwoods, hedgerows, successional fields and open spaces and wetlands. The oak and hemlock-covered mountains that surround the park plunge to the lake surface, where boulders jut into the water and small points of land welcome shore-bound anglers.

The land was purchased with "Project 70" funds and developed under the "Project 500" program, as a family tent and trail park. The park opened to the public in 1972, with the formal dedication July 10, 1972.

Tuscarora and Locust Lake state parks are jointly managed and only six miles a part.

Information and Activities

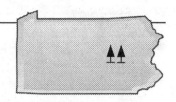

Locust Lake State Park
c/o Tuscarora State Park
R. D. 1, Box 1051
Barnesville, PA 18214-9715
(717) 467-2404 - office
(717) 467-2772 - campground (seasonal)

DIRECTIONS: In Schuylkill County, seven miles north of Pottsville, three miles south of Mahanoy City, and six miles west of Tuscarora State Park. The park is two miles southwest of the PA Route 54 interchange of I-81 - SR 1006 from Saint Clair to Mahanoy City.

CAMPGROUND: Locust Lake has 282 family camping sites (120 are tent only) in a rolling, mostly wooded tract. The campground is clean and well-maintained. Most of the tent sites are on the north side of the lake. The campground is open the second Friday in April to the third Sunday in October. After Labor Day, sites 1-88 are open until the end of the season. Seventy of the sites are reservable. Staff says the most popular sites are the beachside sites 269, 270, 272 and 274. Sites 11-18 are walk-in tent sites. The small campground store (with great ice cream) sells snacks and simple foods. The store also has ice, candy, cookies, lighter fluid, propane, firewood, tissue, limited fishing tackle, soft drinks, diapers, cleaning supplies and other staples.

The adjacent twin tent camping loops have terraced sites with two showerhouses. Some of the best sites are against the hill, shady and away from the regular pad and campground road. Sites in 220s are off the roadway, up the hill and private. Site 234 is on a curve and near a wood shingle-sided shower building.

Sites 244 and 246 are deep, perfect for campers with large rigs or extra equipment. Site 250 is a popular site for tent campers. It's in a hollow nestled under a grove of conifers away from the campground road.

Families with children should consider site 282 (and sites 22, 24, 26, 34, 35, 37 and 38 because they are near the lake and bike path), which is near the interesting bulky timber-style play apparatus.

On the south side of the lake is a shady family camping area that can accommodate small- to medium-sized RV rigs. Loop 1-88 has some sunny camping sites. Sites 60-64 have a lake view. Many sites are separated by a wall of vegetation. The hard-surfaced bike path tracks between the camping sites and the lakeshore. Sites 70 and 83 are over-sized. Site 73 is handicapped accessible and gets strong mid-day sunshine. The spur with sites 76-88 is a very private mini-loop.

Loop 89-161 (Pine/Birch Area) has gravel pads, a beach trail, nearby playground, shade and sites on varying elevations. The north outside part of the loop is backed up against a natural area. All of the sites have ground-mounted fire rings and picnic tables. Most sites are shady all day and well drained. Wooded sites 114 and 115 are two of the more interesting sites in this section. Sites 112-122 are on a slight incline, which make them difficult for medium RV rig use.

At the entrance to the Oak Loop (sites 90-126), a large timber-style playground is heavily used by children.

Loop 162-212 (actually two loops, Dogwood and Laurel) is attractive, shady and often terraced. Sites on the outside of the loop have more privacy. Campers with travel trailers or motor homes should inspect sites carefully; many are on an incline. Tent campers can usually find a level and dry place to pitch a tent. Site 184 and 186 are perfect, shady sites for hot weather camping. Site 197 is in a hollow and a pleasant place for tent campers.

FISHING: The lake is heavily fished and stocked often. Species caught include trout, largemouth, bluegill, catfish, pickerel pike and suckers. The park store and a small bait shop (Tarc's Bait) just outside the park sell live bait and can offer local knowledge of the lake. Directly across from the swimming beach is a stumpy area with a soft shoreline and aquatic vegetation sticking up through the surface. Bass anglers often work rubber worms doused with fish attractor liquids there.

Local anglers recommend casting spinners and jigs at the breast of the dam and in the shallows at the opposite end of the lake. Trout fishermen can also follow Locust Creek upstream, seeking pools and riffles where trout may be lying.

An accessible fishing pier is near the boat ramp by the park store, which jets into the lake about 25 yards.

BOATING: From the camp store, small boats are rented by the hour or day. The 52-acre lake has two boating launching ramps. Boaters and fishermen who are not campers must launch their boat, then park their trailers in the fishermen's parking lot. Much of the shoreline is wooded to the water's edge and offers paddlers a quiet-water trip along the usually windless lake.

The two small launches actually face each other across the small lake. Each launches has courtesy docks.

HIKING: Three loops of easy to moderate hiking trails are northwest of the campground. The Ridge Trail (.75 mile) winds through a mature forest. The Hemlock Trail (2 miles) travels through a mature stand of hemlock and along a woodland stream (Locust Creek rushes off the mountain through a narrow cut along the trail). The Oak Loop (4 miles), the longest trail, encircles a ridge and passes through a deciduous forest.

BIKE TRAIL: A 1.2-mile bike trail circling Locust Lake is extremely popular with families and children. In fact, many campers choose sites that are near the trail. Several fitness stations are also along the trail. The trail is also the quickest way to get to the beach.

DAY-USE AREAS: Locust Lake is a camping park. Since there are virtually no day-use facilities at Locust Lake, day-users are referred to nearby Tuscarora State Park.

SWIMMING BEACH: The narrow 70-yard-long sandy beach is a focal point of summer activity from Memorial Day to Labor Day. It is open 11 a.m. - 7 p.m. daily unless otherwise posted. The swimming area is confined to an area of the lake marked by buoys and has a maximum depth of 5.5 feet. The capacity at the beach is 1,200 people. A few benches are also along the strip of sand where adults or children can rest and watch the watery action.

NATURE: A seasonal naturalist offers weekend and other fun outdoor education programs for campers, students and the general public. Wildflowers at the park include mayapples, jack-in-the-pulpit and many woodland varieties.

Hikers may see raccoon footprints in the mud along the lake or wetland, hear woodpeckers banging on standing dead timber, discover skunk cabbage or find a crayfish building a "chimney-like" home in the moist soils. Wildlife include deer, grouse, some shorebirds, a variety of songbirds (including rare sightings like Louisiana waterthrush, brown creeper and rose-breasted grosbeak and indigo bunting) and migrant waterfowl.

WINTER: Ice fishing is popular on the lake, with anglers using small jigging spoons and live bait to attract the attention of trout that are sluggish and often suspended in various depths.

INSIDERS TIPS: The region has many attractions. Call the Schuylkill County Visitors Bureau at (800) 765-7282. Try a round at the nearby Mountain Valley Golf Course. The 600-acre Weiser State Forest borders the state park to the south, offering numerous trails for hiking, snowmobiling and cross-country skiing.

Some of the beach at Tuscarora is shaded by a tree canopy.

Tuscarora State Park

A golf course (27 holes) lies at the gateway to the park, where a tiny two-story office can supply visitors with information about the park and Locust Valley. Tuscarora, only six miles from Locust Lake, serves the day-use needs of the area. In fact, many golfers play a round and then eat a picnic lunch at one of the 250 tables scattered around the park. There is no camping at the unit.

The dam at the lake was constructed in the 1960s by the U.S. Soil Conservation Service; the Commonwealth provides flood protection and recreational activities.

DIRECTIONS: Two miles west of Tamaqua, the park is south of

Barnesville, on PA Route 54 between the Hometown exit 37E of I-81 and PA Route 309.

DAY-USE AREA: Along the north side of the long 96-acre lake are day-use amenities including a guarded beach, picnicking with pedestal grill, well-stocked food concession that is surrounded by a large wooden deck, and shoreline fishing. The gently lapping waters at the beach make it a focal point of the park during the warm weather season.

The brick food concession is one of the best in the park system, offering gifts, water toys, T-shirts, hats, inflatable toys, goggles and food items that include cold drinks, hot pretzels, sandwiches, pizza, hot dogs, onion rings, French fries, candy and picnic supplies. From the elevated deck, where a handful of picnic tables are set, you can snack and view the mostly grassy shoreline and children playing at the swimming beach.

SWIMMING BEACH: Guarded and sandy, the "Tusk" beach is popular, even though it's quite shady under a canopy of tall trees. The narrow band of sand is only 15 yards wide. The beach is served by a changing stockade that is also elevated, standing on top of huge timbers with a surrounding deck. Benches along the beach offer a splendid view of the lush mountains and shining lake.

BOATING: Non-powered and electric boats are permitted. Simple, human-powered boats are rented and the park maintains 155 seasonal boat mooring spaces. Call the boat rental at (717) 467-3506 for details on renting tobbie boats, pedal boats, canoes, kayaks and rowboats.

FISHING: Muskie, small- and largemouth bass and an assortment of panfish are taken from the small lake.

HUNTING: 82 percent of the park is open to hunting. Call for details.

WINTER: Ice fishing is popular on the lake, with anglers using small jigging spoons and live bait to attract the attention of trout that are sluggish and often suspended in various depths.

INSIDERS TIPS: The region has many attractions. Call the Schuylkill County Visitors Bureau at (800) 765-7282. Try a round at the nearby Mountain Valley Golf Course.

Near the park office is the nifty Tuscarora Flying Field for remote-controlled model aircraft.

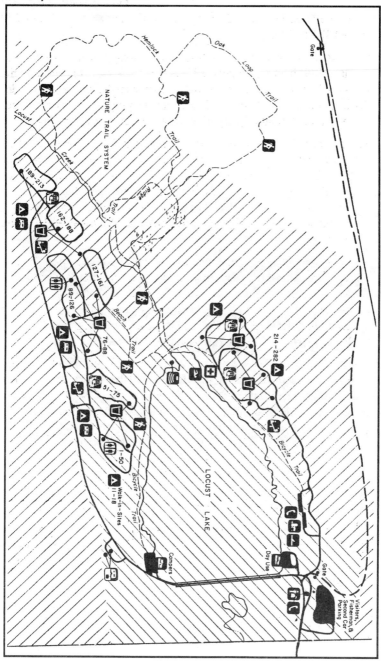

38 Lyman Run State Park
Land: 595 acres Water: 45-acre lake

The best way to see wildlife–or wildflowers, for that matter–is by foot. Lyman Run is in the middle of the 264,000-acre Susquehannock State Forest and has connector trails to the region's 500 miles of sometimes rugged foot trails that criss-cross the mountainous tract. The 85-mile-long Susquehannock Trail also passes through the park and winds into the deep valleys, along wild trout streams and through cool hemlock woods. Lyman Run is a great starting point to discover the area's fishing, hiking, wild areas, ATV trails, snowmobiling, 180 miles of state forest roads, hunting, camping, wildlife viewing, winter sports and lots more.

Lyman Run borrows its name from the mountain stream of the same name. Several beer companies do the same. The well-known mountain trout stream originates at the Eastern Continental Divide which separates the Susquehanna Watershed from the Allegheny Watershed. The land along both banks of the stream remained a wilderness throughout most of the 19th century.

The majestic surrounding Susquehannock State Forest derives its name from the Susquehannock Indian Tribe that once claimed practically all of the land in this region. The original forest, including Lyman Run, was cut over from the late 1800s through the 1920s. During the years since the area was logged and often burned, a new forest of hardwoods has emerged.

Lyman Run and Potter County have a different face for each season. In the fall a spectacular rainbow of colors with hills covered in brilliant red, orange and yellow gleams against the blue skies and crisp crystal-clear nights. Winter blankets the hills in snow, beckoning cross-country skiers and snowmobilers, hunters and hikers for a day or weekend of wintry outdoor fun.

Spring and summer burst forth with hatches on the streams for fly fishermen, and mats of wildflowers with riots of colors against the intense green hills and blue waters of the lake and stream. Summer is also a great time for nature photographers, birders, hikers and campers. The festivals and various events in the small towns around the region are family-oriented and a delight to explore.

Lyman Run dam was completed in 1951. Most of the park facilities opened soon thereafter.

Information and Activities

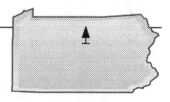

Lyman Run State Park
R. D. 1, P.O. Box 136
Galeton, PA 16922
(814) 435-5010

Lyman Run administers Patterson State Park, Cherry Hill State Park and Denton Hill State Park (ski area and facilities are privately operated).

DIRECTIONS: Fifteen miles east of Coudersport and seven miles west of Galeton in Potter County. The park office is up a single gravel lane on a ridge that overlooks the lake near the dam.

EMERGENCY NUMBERS: 911 system; state police, (814) 274-8690.

CAMPGROUND: The 60 percent shady, 25-site lower campground has smaller sites best used by pop-up campers, tents and smaller travel trailers. Each site has gravel pads and older picnic tables, and the area is served by pit latrines. Many of the sites are on varying elevation, making for visual interest and reasonable privacy. A very small play area serves this campground.

Electric sites and other campground improvements are planned to be phased in over the next few years. Many of the sites will be re-oriented, leveled and eventually outfitted with hookups.

In a cool hollow, on a spur, the 21-site upper campground is known as Daggett Run Campground. Lots of grass, picnic tables, ground-mounted fire rings and small sites welcome campers at Daggett Run. Sites 7 and 8 are next to the cedar-sided latrine and shady. Most sites receive about a half-day of sunlight, and they are dry and well-drained. Site 12 is probably the shadiest, while 21 is the most open. Sites 14-20 are elevated and you must walk up a low hill to reach them. Site 4 has a wooded view along the lip of a valley. A timber-frame play structure and various day-use elements are near the entrance to this loop.

FISHING: Staff says–and fly fishermen agree–that Lyman Run is one of the top fly fishing spots in the state, maybe the region. The park's lake is also an excellent trout fishery with a maximum depth of 28 feet. The spring stream-fed Lyman Lake are stocked with about 20,000 good-sized rainbow trout (up to 300 of them 20 inches in length!) annually. Downstream is also stocked, with upstream the selective harvest area (artificial lures only). Stream-bred brookies and browns are also found in the rushing streams in the area–some anglers say this is one of the best places in the state to experience "wild" trout fishing. Try terrestrials and attractors in mid-summer.

Many streams in the area wind their way down from the mountain tops, producing colorful native brook and brown trout. Fly fishermen should try Cross Fork Creek in southeast Potter with its 5.4 miles of fly fishing-only section.

Lake anglers will have good luck using colorful Powerbait for rainbows. The lake is tree-lined, with little underwater structure. Shoreline fishing is limited, the best being off Lyman Run Road that runs along the north shore of the lake. You can park on the shoulder and walk down to the ribbon-like shoreline to cast and retrieve your lure. After June, the best fishing is from a boat in the deepest waters.

Fishing the entire Potter County area is terrific. More than 800 miles of streams await trout fishermen. About 150,000 fish are stocked annually by sportsmen's groups and the state fish commission, making the sparkling waters even more attractive.

BOATING: Leave your gas-powered engine at home; only non-powered and registered electric boats are permitted on the small lake. A single gravel lane ramp on the north side of the lake serves the narrow, wind-sock-shaped lake. The small seasonal mooring area where tiny fishing boats spend most of their time is on the cove where the beach is.

CANOEING: The tiny lake, with towering mountains in the distance, tree-lined shore and gentle surface, is the perfect place for family canoeing. With plenty of creature comforts nearby, like the guarded beach, food concession and rest rooms, canoeing with small children can be fun.

HIKING: Lyman Run has a spur that connects to the 85-mile Susquehannock Trail System. The backpacking trail is a linkage of old railroad grades, logging trails, roads and fire trails marked in orange blazes. Overnight camping is permitted. For those planning a circuit, allow 7-10 days. The system is for foot travel only.

A two-color map and additional information about the trail system is available by writing: Susquehannock Trail Club, P.O. Box 643, Coudersport, PA 16915.

DAY-USE AREAS: Sixteen bench seats are lined up in rows in front of the amphitheater that is used seasonally for a variety of programs.

SWIMMING: The newer cedar-sided changing house at the small sandy beach has flush toilets, drinking fountains, changing rooms, boat, lifeguard quarters and food concession.

The guarded beach next to the dam open, 11 a.m. - 7 p.m. Memorial Day weekend to Labor Day

WINTER: Trout through the ice is a fun challenge at Lyman. If the fish aren't biting, try ice skating near the swimming area. And if your ankles aren't up to a few triple jumps and camel-backs, take a spin on the 43-mile-long snowmobile loop that passes through Denton Hill State Park.

HUNTING: The park has 505 acres of land open for hunting during the season(s). Bear, deer and wild turkey are among the game hunted. Call the park for details.

INSIDERS TIPS: Lyman Run is a wilderness getaway park, with top-quality trout fishing in the lake and nearby mountain streams. Because of its size and location, Lyman Run maintains a good fishery late into the summer. Finding access points is worth the trouble.

39 Marsh Creek State Park
Land: 1,705 acres   Water: 535-acre lake

The pressure of surrounding development is making Marsh Creek an increasingly important natural and outdoor recreation area. The diverse and protective habitat provides a retreat for wildlife species and a welcome oasis for thousands of day visitors annually (there is no camping at Marsh Creek). The park's neighbors include old farmsteads that are reverting to woodlands, patches of hardwoods and housing developments.

In many ways, dam and watershed management (330 square miles) allowed the park to develop and now the entire area benefits from flood control and improved water quality. Before flooding the reservoir, Milford Mills, a small settlement at the intersection of former Old Covered Bridge Road and Lyndell Road, was the only concentration of dwellings inside what is now the park. Its site is now under 30-50 feet of water.

The tiny village had some local notoriety, dating to the 1930s when Max "Boo Boo" Hoff, reputed to be Philadelphia's top bootlegger and gangland figure during Prohibition years, bought the 44-room Murphy mansion in Milford Mills. He spent the summers of 1930-1935 there. Several unsolved murders took place in the area at the time.

The Murphy mansion, a Chester County showplace, had been owned by Mike Murphy (president of Pure Oil Co. and the United States Pipeline Co., and director of Keystone Telephone) until his death in 1917. In addition to his 169-acre estate, the mansion, barns, stables and tenant houses comprised almost the entire village of Milford Mills when he, his wife, seven children and an enormous staff resided there, raising and training race horses. The remains of the Murphy mansion and the rest of Milford Mills were demolished during park development.

Besides Milford Mills, the present park was populated by those living on scattered small farms. About 72 properties were affected by park land acquisition, including 42 residences and 70 barns. Four residences remain occupied within park boundaries.

The recreational facilities were fully operational in 1979.

Information and Activities

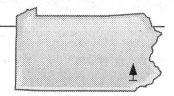

Marsh Creek State Park
675 Park Road
Downington, PA 19335
(610) 458-5119

DIRECTIONS: In the rolling hills of northcentral Chester County, 35 miles from Philadelphia. The park is two miles west of Eagle on PA Route 100 (take Route 100 exit off the Pennsylvania Turnpike). No swimming is allowed in the lake. The park office is open 8:30 a.m. - 4 p.m. all summer.

YOUTH HOSTEL: On the west side of the lake, near the boat landing, an American Youth Hostel operates in a charming 200-year-old farmhouse constructed with native Pennsylvania stone. The hostel is enhanced by a wonderful patio, large fireplaces in the kitchen and dining room and a lovely view of the lake. The hostel has 18 beds in three dormitory-style rooms, with separate accommodations for women and men. Family rooms are available with prior arrangement.

For more information write AYH, P.O. Box 376, East Reeds Road, Lyndell, PA 10354, or call (215) 458-5881.

FISHING: Mowed shorelines, shady respites and good fishing bring families to the lake for panfish and rough fish action. The lake is a big bass lake, and area bass clubs have been active placing underwater structures. The park publishes a map that details their locations. The submerged structure include catfish spawning devices, porcupine cribs of various sizes and many felled trees along the shoreline. Some of the best fishing is in the coves near the dam, where water conditions and structure offer many locations where fish rest and feed.

The lake is a warmwater fishery. Increasing numbers of walleyes are being taken along with catfish, black crappies, tiger muskie, largemouth bass and various panfish. Several species are stocked.

Look for bluegills in two to 15 feet of water near the shore along any bank, dropoff or rock point. Local experts say the big 'gills are taken with waxworms, red worms and mealworms. Still fish the worms and gently jig wax- and mealworms. Also try small minnows on dark-colored lures or tiny twister tails.

Gordon's Sport Supply, a nearby bait and tackle retailer, has excellent knowledge of the lake. Some 40-inch-long tiger muskie have been taken from the lake by trolling jumbo plugs at shallow depth.

BOATING: Windsurfers love the lake. Prevailing winds are funneled, and gust over the water offering exciting sailing for the colorful board craft. A section of the lake is a bowl-like area where winds are the most predictable and steady (this area is mid-lake). Water in this area can be quite choppy. Wind sailors use the small sandy beach next to the boat rental to stage and launch.

A hard-surfaced deck surrounds the busy boat rental, while a U.S. flag flaps in the wind greeting the many patrons who rent pedal boats, sailboards, kayaks, rowboats and other small craft. Also sold here are snack foods including corn dogs, hot dogs, cold drinks, pizza, chips, ice cream treats and nachos. Three umbrella tables are on the attractive wooden deck that links the small, neat facilities. Mooring spaces along the cove near the one-lane launch serve the rental operation.

The Marsh Creek Sailboard Shop rents boards and provides lessons on the lake. Directly across the lake from the boat rental is the 24-hour boat launch for pleasure boaters and fishermen.

Canoeing the main body of the clear lake can be quiet and the crowds small on weekdays or before Memorial Day weekend and after Labor Day. Try hugging the shoreline and watch for fish in the clear waters. Submerged vegetation and small floating material provide cover for bass and panfish. Often the slipping of a paddle into the water is just enough disturbance to send the fish darting off, only to hold momentarily until they take off for good–or merely nervously watch you cruise away.

Calm inlets and coves, away from the wind, are also favorite places to canoe, kayak or fish.

Non-powered and electric boats only are permitted on the lake.

HIKING: The park maintains about six miles of easy to moderately difficult trails on the west side of the lake. Hiker and horseback riders share the trail system that is composed of four concentric loops.

A covered bridge of the "Burr Arch" design was relocated to the northeast section of the park in 1972. The 45-ton Larkin Bridge is for pedestrian traffic only.

BRIDLE TRAILS: Six miles of riding trails west of the lake are open to equestrians.

DAY-USE AREAS: Hilly and terraced, the mowed spaces around the boat rental and snack shop are scattered with picnic tables and other amenities. About 150 tables and grills are also located around the swimming pool complex.

The lakeshore is gently rolling with interspersed mowed and grassy, meadow-like sections. Many picnic tables are accompanied by grills and nearby comfort stations.

SWIMMING POOL: The main swimming pool is L-shaped and ranges from 1.5 feet to five feet deep. All sides of the pool's deck are concrete and with grass borders perfect for sunbathing. For small children, a 1.5-foot-deep, round pool is near the main pool. The swimming pool is open from 11 a.m. - 6:45 p.m. (Wednesday 10 a.m. - 5:45 p.m.) daily from Memorial Day weekend to Labor Day. There is a small fee to swim.

Cement benches are positioned around the pools for parents to watch the action. At the end of the facility are angular block and wood changing buildings and a snack concession. The snack bar serves both pool patrons and walk-ups from the outside. A shady patio with tables is at the outside window of the concession stand.

NATURE: Environmental education programming is limited and depends on staff allocation. An effort to develop school-age programs is underway.

The park has a mix of fields and woodlands where white-tail deer, red fox, squirrels, cottontail rabbits, woodchuck and other common mammals can often be seen. Birding is also popular; and the spring migration period (March - May) often is punctuated with the haunting calls of the common loon, grebes, a variety of waterfowl (including ruddy duck, black duck, tundra swan, snow goose, widgeon, coot, wood duck, northern pintail, green-winged teal, black scoter, common goldeneye and others), gulls and two types of terns. Other songbirds including bluebirds, northern orioles, red-winged blackbirds and many sparrows can also be seen along trails, edges and the lakefront. The breast of the dam is one of the best places to view wildlife. Late October is one of the best times to observe waterfowl.

Visitors from nearby urban environs may also discover strong blooms of spring wildflowers, including bloodroot, spring beauties and coltsfoot. This colorful procession is followed by summer bloomers like steeplebush, grasses and shrubs. Finally, asters and goldenrods bloom in late summer and fall after a summer of sun and warmth.

HUNTING: Hunting is offered in loops A, B and C on about 1,000 acres. Call for additional information. Deer, small game and waterfowl hunting are offered.

WINTER: As weather permits, ice skating, ice fishing and sledding on about seven acres of slopes are encouraged.

INSIDERS TIP: Try windsurfing–take a lesson!

40 Memorial Lake State Park
Land: 145 acres   Water: 85-acre lake

Fort Indiantown Gap Military Reservation surrounds Memorial Lake State Park in Lebanon County near the southern base of Blue Mountain. Depending on the time of year, you can sometimes hear the booming guns in the military area practicing and maneuvering on the target ranges.

Small shade trees dot open spaces along the north shoreline of the placid lake and other day-use areas.

A large bronze plaque that commemorates veterans is in a shady grove of conifers and reads, "This lake, covering approximately 85 acres, created by a manmade dam, was constructed in 1945. It is dedicated to the memory of the officers, warrant officers, non-commissioned officers and guardsmen of the Pennsylvania National Guard who have served their state and nation during World War I and World War II, more especially to those who made the supreme sacrifice in these great struggles for freedom and democracy. Among them were members of the 28th Infantry Division which suffered losses in both wars. In World War I, 2,874 killed and 11,265 were wounded; World War II, 2,323 killed and 9,324 wounded and 943 missing in action." The plaque was presented by the Pennsylvania National Guard Veterans Association.

The day-use park with a great mountain view gets plenty of non-motorized action on the lake and many visitors from the nearby Indiantown Gap National Cemetery, one of 113 VA national cemeteries nationwide.

Information and Activities

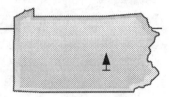

Memorial Lake State Park
R.R. Box 7045
Grantsville, PA 17028
(717) 865-6470

DIRECTIONS: The park, 30 minutes northeast of Harrisburg, is accessible from I-81 at exit 29 (Fort Indiantown Gap), PA Route 934 North. The park office is in a converted farmhouse. Memorial Lake also manages Swatara State Park.

EMERGENCY NUMBER: 911 system.

HIKING: A short, easy trail travels along the northern shore, dead ending at the lower parking lot. Along the trail hikers might see some of the 100 species of birds that visit or nest in the park.

FISHING: Families and beginning anglers will enjoy gentle shoreline fishing areas and many small panfish that will bite live baits (red worms, etc.) suspended under floating bobbers. In several areas around the lake, benches face the shimmering water or picnic tables nearby from which families can try their luck fishing while enjoying lunch. No fishing is allowed from the breast of the dam, but near the dam offers some good shallows and shady places to try.

Memorial Lake is a big bass lake. All large- and smallmouth bass must be 15 inches in length, with a daily creel limit of four combined species.

BOATING: Two boat launch ramps, one with a courtesy dock serve the lake for non-powered and electric motor boats. About 56 seasonal mooring spaces are available at the park for small boats.

In a small brown building, with a humming pop machine next to the service window, is the funky boat rental concession that has rowboats, canoes, kayaks, sailboards, sailboats and pedal boats.

Because Memorial Lake has good wind conditions, local windsurfers often ply the surfaces catching the breezes and criss-crossing the lake.

Sailboard and sailing lessons are offered during the week, 10 a.m. - 6 p.m. and weekends 10 a.m. - 7 p.m. Sign up at the small boat concession. Near the boat rental is a small, sandy, beach-like strip where beginning and experienced windsurfers can launch. The boat concession is open from Memorial Day weekend to Labor Day.

DAY-USE AREAS: The unit has picnic tables, three parking areas, grills and drinking water. The park's two tot lots with timber-outlined sandbox, swings and a nearby picnic shelter. A volleyball court with stand is nearby.

A fitness trail (Vita Course) follows part of the lakeshore and winds through the rest of the park, offering a variety of exercise stations next to a gravel pathway. You'll find step-ups, stretching bars, suspended rings, sit-up benches, elevated push-up stations and signs that describe various exercises you can do along the way.

INSIDERS TIP: One-on-one sailboard lessons are offered on an informal basis at the windy little lake. Also, an Olympic windsurfer from the area once trained on the lake and still visits.

Windsurfers and small sailboats share the quiet lake.

41 Moraine State Park
Land: 16,291 acres   Water: 3,225 acres

Only an hour from Pittsburgh, the ambitious idea to reclaim this scarred terrain for a state park originated in 1951 after a geological study of Muddy Creek Valley revealed glacial evidence dating back 14,000 years.

The study indicated the presence of a once large lake with significant glacial deposits of sand, gravel and rocks, known as a ground moraine (hence the park's name) lying west of the lake area. A few years later the Western Pennsylvania Conservancy proposed construction of an impoundment to create a water-based recreation area. By 1965 construction of the dam began, and in the years that followed a beautiful 3,225-acre reservoir was created.

Development of the area was not an easy task. Much of the work included restoration and reclamation of past mining operations and the plugging of 422 active and abandoned oil, gas and water wells. Contaminated soils were removed by the thousands of cubic yards, and the original contour of the lands were returned.

The impoundment was completed in 1969 and named Lake Arthur, for the late Edmund Watts Arthur, a partner in the geological study team. The lake has 40 miles of shoreline and is seven miles long. Today the north and south shore areas are active with land-based recreation areas, cabins, paved bicycling trails, boat ramps, open spaces and much more. Moraine State Park is one of the finest examples of land reclamation in the state. Once a pitted and scarred area, the park now boasts good fishing, marinas, winter activities, sprawling day-use areas and hunting.

Information and Activities

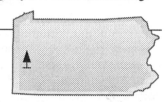

Moraine State Park
225 Pleasant Valley Road
Portersville, PA 16051
(412) 368-8811

DIRECTIONS: One hour north of Pittsburgh, off I-79 at U.S. 422 (exit 29). The park office (at the south shore) is on Pleasant Valley Road and open year-round, seven days a week during the summer. The north shore is about a seven-miles long; south shore is about a two mile loop with park amenities scattered along the park road and lakeshore.

CAMPGROUND: Although there is no family camping, the rolling and open Five Points Organized Group Camping Area and Muskrat Cove are popular with youth and other organized groups.

CABINS: Eleven modern cabins are perched on a ridge above the lake and available for rent year-round. Each cabin has it's own small dock and has two bedrooms to accommodate six people for sleeping, a bathroom with a shower, and a kitchen (seats six), and dining and living area. The wooden deck-like porch looks out upon the lake and is a relaxing place to watch the action on the water or a quiet sunset. Bring your own linens, towels, utensils and tableware. Each cabin has a picnic table, firebox grill and a place for a small campfire. Call well in advance for warm-season rentals.

Cabins no. 1 and 2 have a view of a small cover, while no. 3 is more open and has a broader view of the lake. A small children's play area is near the cabins. Cabin no. 11 is also in a less shady area and is handicapped accessible.

Cabin no. 7 sits above the lake with a narrow stairway down to the shady shoreline, where a small floating dock rests. Cabins no. 7 and 10 are excellent choices for a week or weekend.

Cabins no. 4 and 5 are close together and would be great for two families that are vacationing together. Cabin no. 6 is quite open, sitting on a large lot with plenty of open mowed lawn.

FISHING: The lake is part of the state's big bass program. Lake Arthur, which in the broadest sense is a restoration of a 10,000-acre glacial lake, has fair to good fishing for northern pike, walleye, muskie and panfish. Anglers also have good luck with channel catfish and bass. Staff observes the best catches are taken from Muddy Creek, Swamp Run, Shannon Run and other coves where underwater structure hold fish. A major walleye stocking program in the mid-1990s has improved angling. Jig minnows and crank baits during the spring are recommended. About 35 million walleye fry have been stocked in Lake Arthur since 1969. Muskie anglers are urged to use large jerk baits and slow trolling.

The unit maintains three fishing piers and 10 boat launches scattered around the irregularly shaped manmade lake. Ice rescue equipment is at some of the smaller boat launch access areas. Ice fishermen use jigging spoons and lead-head jigs tipped with minnows on the bottom.

BOATING: There is a 10-horsepower limit on the lake.

About one-half mile from the park office is the Pleasant Valley boat rental concession with a narrow one-lane launching ramp. For those who want to rent pontoons, paddleboats or larger boats, a concessionaire operates at the south shore of the park. He also sells larger watercraft. Complete with dry dock mooring, Moraine State Park and Lake Arthur are very popular with sailboaters. In fact, dozens of colorful wind-powered craft operate on typical summer weekends.

Barber's Point is a windsurfing launch. Windsurfers can bring their boards to this exclusive area and rig, stage and sail all day. There are 10 launching ramps in the park. Due to the popularity of sailing, served ramps have designated rigging and de-rigging areas.

Lake Arthur is also an excellent spot to canoe. The many quiet coves, cliffs and barn swallow colonies, kingfishers, wading birds and resident waterfowl make the lake a perfect place for family paddling.

HIKING: The nine-mile Glacier Ridge Trail extends from the neighboring Jennings Environmental Education Center to the northwest corner of Moraine. It is part of the North County National Scenic Trail. Both the Sunken Garden and Pleasant Valley both 3 mile trails are easy hiking or skiing.

The Hilltop Nature Trail is consists of two loops.

The Long Loop is an easy climb to fields high above the lake and takes about 1 hour and 15 minutes, while the Short Loop is a 45-minute trek through fields and along a number of habitats.

BIKING: Along the north shore drive is the green-colored and angular bicycle concession building (368-9011) where single-speed, youth bikes, 10-speeds and tandem bikes can be rented by the hour. Helmets, baskets and child seats are also available. In season (April 1-fall), the concession is open 10 a.m. - 6 p.m. weekdays and 9 a.m. to 6 p.m. weekends. Vending machines and rest rooms are at the rental concession.

The seven-mile paved bike trail departs from the rental station, travels along Lake Arthur and ends at the marina restaurant (full service/seasonal). A seven-mile mountain bike loop begins at the Mount Union Road trailhead and has some steep slopes and rough surfaces. Walkers also share the meandering hard-surfaced trail.

CROSS-COUNTRY SKIING: Sunken Garden and Pleasant Valley trails have been improved and connected to offer six terrific miles of ski trails. A heated rest room is at the trailhead of Pleasant Valley. The trails are suitable for all skill levels.

DAY-USE AREAS: Along the lightly wooded lakeshore are many day-use areas equipped with picnic tables, grills, cement block rest rooms and shelters. The park has more than 1,000 picnic tables (some are wheelchair accessible) and six reservable shelters. Family picnicking is very popular at Moraine.

Swimmers may use the beach only when lifeguards are on duty from Memorial Day to Labor Day. Food, beverages, showers and changing rooms are at the shoreline facilities.

WINTER ACTIVITIES: Aside from excellent cross-country skiing, the park offers ice boating, ice fishing, snowmobiling, sledding, winter hiking and ice skating.

NATURE NOTES: During late March and early April, Lake Arthur is a hotbed for migratory waterfowl activity. Like many of the once glaciated lakes in northwestern Pennsylvania, the area is often visited by snow geese, tundra swan, green-winged teal, northern pintail, lesser scaup, common goldeneye, red-breasted merganser, American black duck and others. Twenty-nine species have been recorded on the lake.

42 Mt. Pisgah State Park
Land: 1,302 acres Water: 75-acre lake

Stephen Foster Lake (named after the famous composer who died falling out of a window) and north shore day-use areas are the focal points of the park. The pleasant lake formed by a dam on Mill Creek offers fishing, non-powered and electric motor boating, skating, shoreline walking and picnicking.

Mt. Pisgah is a hilly, well-kept day-use park that is one of the best for family outings and reunions. The proximity of pavilions to the swimming pool and play areas makes the park especially appealing to families with lots of children. The reservable (small fee) pavilions are washed daily and are next to recycling stations and trash barrels. They always have a view of the lake.

The rolling tract that is now the state park was obtained in 1969, using bond funds. Foster Dam impounded the lake in 1977, and other facilities were added and opened in 1979.

These lands were first cleared for farming in the early 1800s. Many of the early settlers came from New England, and many of their descendants still reside in the area. These hearty pioneers cleared virgin pine and hardwood, and stacked the stumps in fence rows, which still border the old fields. Some displays in the park's nature center are dedicated to these settlers' spirit and hard work.

Information and Activities

Mt. Pisgah State Park
R. R. 3, Box 362
Troy, PA 16947-9448
(717) 297-2734

DIRECTIONS: In the scenic Endless Mountains region of Pennsylvania's northern tier, midway between Troy and Towanda in Bradford County. The park is along Mill Creek at the base of Mt. Pisgah (elevation 2,260 feet). The park is two miles north of U.S. Route 6. Inside the park office, that overlooks the swimming pool is a brochure rack that offers information about nearby attractions and other state park in the area.

EMERGENCY NUMBER: 911 system.

FISHING: Foster Lake is weedy and shallow in spots. Many bass anglers explore these areas with spinners and buzz baits, hoping to hook a lunker bass. Perch, bluegill and crappies are planted occasionally, and the small lake offers several shoreline fishing areas that are great for small children to use.

Many bass anglers use their boats powered only by an electric trolling motor to get to areas where rubber worms can be flipped into weedbeds.

BOATING: Pedal boats, V-bottom aluminum boats, and sometimes canoes are rented at a shed-like building at the north end of the lake. The concession is open seasonally, noon to 5 p.m. weekdays, noon to 7 p.m. weekends.

The single-lane boat launching ramp (small launching fee) has a gravel parking lot and seasonal mooring area for small fishing boats, and a small courtesy dock for loading and unloading. A tiny play area with tractor tires and swings near the boat ramp is a great place to entertain the kids and watch the antics at the launch.

HIKING: Mt. Pisgah has 10 miles of hiking trails. The trail emphasizes how man interacts with nature, and our role as stewards of the natural world. Most trails are on the south side of the lake and are moderately difficult to easy walking along the lakeshore and through open fields, wetland and mixed woodlands. Certain trails are open to cross-country skiing when the conditions permit.

DAY-USE AREAS: The primary day-use area is next to the swimming pool, offering your choice of sunny or shady picnic tables. Some of the park system's biggest grills are at the pavilions at Mt. Pisgah. The Hilltop Pavilion is one of the best places for a group picnic or reunion with a terrific view of the lake, shoreline activities and swimming pool.

SWIMMING POOL: Parking at the 5,676-square-foot swimming pool is on grassy lots. The popular pool has water depths from eight inches to five feet, and a blue wheelchair ramp with stainless steel railings is provided for people with disabilities. It is divided into two sections and watched over by as many as five lifeguards. Several deck-side benches are arranged around the pool for parents and sun bathers. The pool buildings are field stone, wood and barn-like. They house changing rooms, showers, rest rooms, lifeguard quarters and a first aid station. The pool temperature is advertised daily.

NATURE CENTER: Many seasonal environmental education programs, hikes and mini-classes are offered at the stone and vertical wood nature center. A cozy wood stove with nearby benches is a popular staging area for outdoor education lessons. Displays include furs, a coyote mount, brochure racks, touch table, photo displays, skulls and written material. The center is open 10 a.m. - 4 p.m. weekends. About a dozen picnic tables, bluebird nesting boxes, rest rooms and a horseshoe pit are near the small center.

Open meadows and regenerating fields offer places to view a variety of wildflowers, while the small lake attracts migrating osprey and loons in the spring. Red-tailed hawks are often seen soaring above the hilly tract, while great blue herons and other wading birds often stalk the shallows, plucking unfortunate minnows from the waters.

HUNTING: Permitted on about 1,100 acres, game hunted includes deer, rabbit, squirrel, grouse, turkey and pheasant.

WINTER: Snowmobiles are welcome on the signed trails, and skaters and ice fishermen may use the lake. Cross-country skiing is permitted on certain marked trails.

43 Neshaminy State Park
Land: 330 acres Water: Delaware River

Bring a big picnic basket and your swimsuit. Neshaminy is a popular boating and general day-use park. The park is and a day-use park complete with pool, playground, picnic tables, several game fields and walkways.

Dunks Ferry Road, forming the eastern boundary of the park, is one of the oldest roads in Pennsylvania. Beginning in 1679, Dunken Williams operated a ferry that crossed back and forth over the Delaware River. The small road provided access to his ferry operation, and today, more than 300 years later, Dunks Ferry Road perpetuates both his name and enterprise.

Around the mid-1770s, a large inn was built to serve travelers. Operated by many owners over the years, the Dunk's Ferry Inn has a colorful history. The most profitable owner was John Vandergrift, who also had a successful shad fishing business for 39 years during the 1800s.

Neshaminy is one of the few parks where you can see ocean tides. The waves won't knock you down, but patient river watching will reveal tides that sometimes rise and fall at a rate of an inch a minute. Indians used the rise and fall of the tides to trap fish. At high tide, the fish swam over the top of a fence. As the tide went out, the fish were trapped and easily speared. The small estuary is fresh water, not salt, unlike the lower estuary. It's a place where plants and animals from the two-water world meet, offering some interesting viewing.

These road-like waterways attracted millions of European immigrants a century ago. Many of them landed and settled in Philadelphia.

Information and Activities

NESHAMINY STATE PARK
3401 STATE ROAD
BENSALEM, PA 19020-5930
(215) 639-4538

DIRECTIONS: In Bucks County. At the intersection of State Road and Dunks Ferry Road, the park is accessible from PA Route 132 (Street Road) exit of I-95. The park is 1.5 miles from I-95. The park, in metro Philadelphia, has good directional signs. Camping is not available.

BOATING: The 35-acre marina across the Neshaminy Creek has 191 slips (six sets of gated docks) for larger boats that are rented seasonally. A large, hard-surfaced launching ramp that can accommodate larger boats is at the marina. A smaller launch, often populated by revving Jet Skiers, is also in the marina area. Tenant boaters may overnight at their slips. The slips are equipped with 30 amp and some 50 amp electrical services.

FISHING: Bass and muskie are the top game fish, especially near the marina. Mud Island is also a popular area where anglers often use live bait, twister tails and bright crankbaits. This area has strips of mud flats and good weed cover. Bass anglers often jig, rubber worm or pull spinner through the channels and along structures. Strippers hit red worms and the shad run (use white and yellow shad darts bounced off the bottom or in the current) can be very strong in the section of the river near the park. Some stripper anglers troll salt water lures, changing depths and colors often.

The river channel can be up to 45 feet deep. Boat control is a key to success when fishing a wide and deep river like the Delaware.

HIKING: The three-mile Neshaminy Trail follows the river and turns up the creek, offering hikers a gentle walk with a view of the river.

PLAYMASTER THEATER: Offering a variety of performances, the blue-gray theater has a large hard-surfaced parking area, with access off of State Road at the north end of the park. Most of the performances are scheduled during the winter. Call (215) 245-7850 for details.

DAY-USE AREAS: Hundreds of picnic tables and charcoal grills are scattered around the flat park that is open year-round. Mowed day-use areas surround the swimming pool, connecting to four large parking lots. Families or organized groups may also rent picnic pavilions by calling the park office. Some of the picnic areas are heavily wooded and outfitted with cement pedestal tables with wood-plank tops.

SWIMMING POOL: A small diving pool with two boards is inside the fenced main swimming facility. The main pool is 1.5 feet in the shallow end to 4.5 feet in the middle. A 40-foot-long, blue-tiled, shallow wading pool for toddlers is open near the main pool. Some shady, grassy areas and benches are near the sparkling swimming pool.

The pool is open early June to Labor Day, 10 a.m. - 5 p.m. weekdays and 10 a.m. 6 p.m. weekends and holidays There is a small admission fee.

The food concession stand has windows that serve the inside and outside (three walk-up windows) of the pool. The modernized red-brick building snack bar sells ice cream, fries, pizza, hot dogs, nachos and pretzels.

The theater offers performances during the winter.

44 Nockamixon State Park
Land: 5,283 acres   Water: 1,450-acre lake

Nockamixon is best known for its boating. Seven miles long, with 27 miles of irregular shoreline, the beautiful undeveloped lake serves the metropolitan areas of Bethlehem, Philadelphia, Allentown, Easton and Quakertown. Boats are limited to 10 horsepower or less, which keeps the lake quiet and dotted with dozens of sail boats and human-powered craft. Small rental boats are popular with visitors.

Tree-lined coves with occasional rock outcroppings are wonderful places to explore by canoe or other small boat. On most summer days, the quiet surface of the lake is only disturbed by a small boat puttering to a fishing hot spot. Slipping a canoe into the water at sunrise is simple pleasure that will guarantee some lovely surprises once out on the lake or along the rich shorelines and marsh.

Two deep covers (fingers) extending from Lake Nockamixon's northern and southern ends are the best areas for quiet water paddlers or small boat pilots. At these reaches, the water is interspersed with marshy areas, spots of thick vegetation, water pockets and puddle-like areas. There is a good chance you will encounter wildlife. The narrow coves also extend under vehicular bridges.

Stilt-like wading birds can often be seen probing the shallow, while kingfisher that look like World War II fighters make a rattling call and dive into the lake coming up with a minnow–and often, with just wet feathers. Green-backed and great blue herons are common.

From the water is also the best view of the rolling green hills that skirt the park lands. The hillside and fields in the distance are in the early stages of succession, slowly maturing from grassy meadows to shrub land, then woods.

The park was dedicated on Dec. 7, 1973, signaling the opening of a park that became known largely for its fishing and boating.

Information and Activities

Nockamixon State Park
1542 Mountain View Drive
Quakertown, PA 18951
(215) 529-7300 - park office
(215) 529-7308 - marina (seasonal)
(215) 538-1340 - boat rental

DIRECTIONS: Five miles east of Quakertown and nine miles west of Doylestown. The park is on PA Route 563 and may be reached via PA Rtes. 309, 313 or 412. The park office is an attractive two-story stone house with cream-colored shutters and burnt-red entrance door. A regional state park office (in a lovely old house with wrap-around porch and railing) is in the park, along the lake.

EMERGENCY NUMBER: 911 system.

VISITOR CENTER: In an octagonal stone building with wood-shake shingle roof. Inside the center is a large wall-mounted lake map that shows lake depths, structures, and launching ramps, access points and parking areas. The center also has a small brochure rack.

CABINS: Tucked along a sometimes dusty gravel road are ten family cabins, which were built by the Pennsylvania Conservation Corps in the mid-1980s. They are furnished with flush toilet/shower, living area, kitchen/dining room, two or three bedrooms and electric heat. The cabins are on the south side of Lake Nockamixon. Cabins are a considerable distance from other park amenities and facilities.

The cabins are on slightly different elevations, often surrounded by small lawn. A newer play structure is between cabins 1 and 2, making them ideal choices for families with small children. Cabins 2-4 are clustered in a shady area and share a driveway. Cabins 5-7 are also grouped together. Some of the cabins have handicapped accessible ramps and porch-side parking for two cars. Cabin 7 is on a low ridge, and cabin 6 sits in a hollow. Cabins 5 and 6 enjoy some direct sunshine during the afternoon.

Along a narrow gravel lane are cabins 8-10. Cabin 8 is sunny, cabin 9 is in a shallow valley and cabin 10 is the most private, located at the end of the spur.

YOUTH HOSTEL: The Weisel Youth Hostel, along Tohickon Creek in the northwest corner of the park, is operated by the Bucks County Department of Parks and Recreation. Contact the house parents at Weisel Youth Hostel, R.D. , Quakertown, PA 18951, or call (215) 536-8749.

BOATING: The main marina is a colorful series of floating docks along a half-mile cove near the visitors center. Brightly covered sailboats bob at their moorings, and busy sailors fiddle with ropes, tools and cleaning compounds. The marina can dock 576 boats up to 24 feet in length. There is also a 76-space dry storage area where boats on trailers may be kept. The waiting list for dock space is long. If you are interested in a slip, contact the marina office. Slips may be rented on a short-term basis, in the absence of a regular tenant. Rest rooms and plenty of parking and mowed spaces outline the busy marina.

The park has four boat launching ramps and a tan-colored concession that rents canoes, small sailboats, rowboats, pedal boats, pontoons and aluminum motorboats (8 hp engines). Three sets of floating finger docks along a small cove serve the boat rental concession. The concession also has rest rooms.

FISHING: Spring and fall angling can be good to very good on the lake–before and after the recreational boating season. The lake contains large- and smallmouth bass, muskie, striped hybrid bass, channel catfish, carp and panfish. Crappies can be big. The south end of the lake has received manmade fish-holding structures over the years and is one of the first areas anglers should explore. Small coves and points hold fish in this area. Local anglers like to fish near the bridges.

At about the mid-point of the lake off Route 563, is a well designed fishing pier (hard-surfaced peninsula) that is accessible for persons with disabilities. Anglers at the pier use live bait under bobbers, small spinners, spoons, white jigs and minnows. The pier has a narrow sandy shoreline where smaller children will trying to fish. A vault toilet is nearby.

A small children's fishing pond is near the main day-use area. Also along the main lake are many bank fishing access points.

HIKING: Hikers can use any of the park's equestrian trails or the 2.8-mile hard-surfaced bike trail that takes visitors to undeveloped areas of the park. Most of the trails are fairly close to the lake. About 3.5 miles of hiking trails on the southwest side of the lake are used by the seasonal naturalist to conduct guided hikes and other programs.

EQUESTRIAN TRAILS: A gravel parking lot offers horsemen staging and a trailer parking lot. Trail riders can use a 22-mile series of connected loops that stretch from the Elephant Road trailhead parking area to the Mink Road parking lot on the south side of the lake, and from the fishing pier to the Tohickon Creek cove on the north side. Rental horses are available from private operators.

DAY-USE AREAS: Shady picnic areas with pedestal grills and other amenities are near the swimming complex and scattered around the park. About 500 tables are maintained in the park. Comfort stations and parking are near virtually all of the day-use areas.

SWIMMING POOL: The pool is in the middle of a hilly, lawn-like area complete with three heavily used one-meter diving boards, narrow concrete decks, and teal-colored lifeguard chairs. Sunbathers can enjoy a grassy knoll near the pool, inside the fence and stone walls. The pool is open 11 a.m. - 7 p.m. Memorial Day weekend to Labor Day. Group rates, lessons and seasonal passes are available. No bottles, jugs or food are allowed in the pool area.

Unique to most public swimming pools is the diving well, where divers bounce off boards and are supervised by a lifeguard. No flips, back dives or inverted dives from the diving boards are allowed.

Towels, sunglasses, T-shirts, sunscreen and life jackets are available.

Stone and vertical wood-sided changing rooms and a snack bar (outside) serve swimmers. The walk-in food concession on a terrace above the pool sells hot dogs, candy, ice cream, ice water, homemade pizza, salads, popsicles and soft drinks. Day-use amenities around the pool are outlined by attractive low stone walls. Several picnic tables are scattered near the snack bar.

Swimming is not permitted in the lake.

NATURE: Near the youth hostel, the environmental study area is the scene of seasonal outdoor education programs. Habitats in the sprawling park include hardwoods, marsh, plantations of larch and white pine, and old fields.

Nockamixon is a good birding park. The area is especially good for viewing birds of prey that include visiting bald eagles (fall migration), osprey, turkey vultures, northern harrier, red-tailed hawk, Cooper's hawk, red-shouldered hawk, American kestrel and the occasional golden eagle (fall migration).

The quiet, largely tree-lined lake is also a popular stopover for waterfowl seeking a rest from biannual migrations. Many common ducks stop in. Other interesting sightings including snow goose, mute swan, tundra swan and cute little ruddy ducks. Birders will also find good numbers and adequate habitat for a variety of shorebirds, mostly sandpipers. Twenty-seven species of warblers have been recorded. Six types of thrush and several species of gulls and terns are seen.

WINTER: Cross-country skiers are welcome to use bike trails, day-use areas or roads closed to traffic during the winter. Ice skaters and ice fishermen may use the lake, with caution. The gentle slopes near the marina are ideal for family sledding and tobogganing. The park staff suggests that you call ahead for snow and ice conditions.

HUNTING: Clean your gun for hunting on about 3,000 acres during the season. Call the park office for details.

INSIDERS TIPS: Bring your canoe. Nearby State Game Lands No. 157 encompasses 2,010 acres north of the state park and offers hiking and hunting.

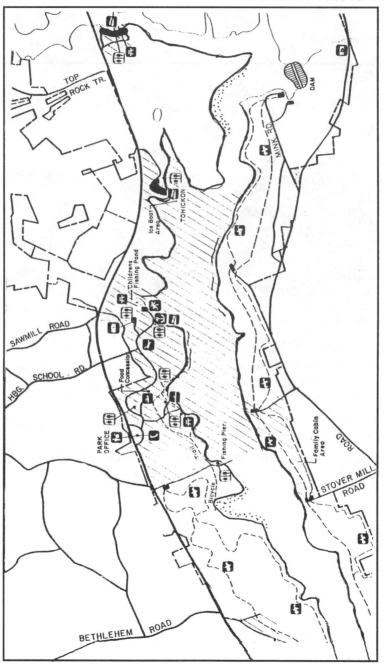

45 Nolde Forest Environmental Education Center

Land: 665 acres

Water: Two small ponds and streams

The Nolde Center marked the birth of the bureau's efforts to establish educational resource centers for formal environmental education. The center opened in 1970. After the opening of Nolde, the bureau further showed its commitment to environmental education by establishing the Environmental Education Section, which is responsible for curriculum development, management and programming in all state parks across the Commonwealth.

Nolde is open to casual visitors, but is best known as a destination for thousands of school-age students to participate in the center's discovery and problem solving approach to environmental studies. Teachers and students explore different aspects of the environment and develop concepts and skills that help them become effective environmental decision-makers. Students also engage in hands-on environmental education activities. Nolde specializes in comprehensive teacher in-service training and a variety of cooperative programs and training activities with local colleges, universities and school districts. Programs are also offered by the staff and guest teachers for the public.

A network of trails makes the center's streams, ponds and diverse habitats accessible to both students and visitors. Trail-side teaching stations offer places for students to work and learn. Benches are available for those who want to enjoy the sights and sounds associated with the natural world. Two short trails are accessible to wheelchairs.

In the early 1900s, Jacob Nolde began to develop a coniferous forest on abandoned farmland and scrub woodlots. Today, the area is covered by stands of red pine, white pine, Japanese larch, eastern hemlock, Douglass fir and Norway spruce. A mature second g.)wth of deciduous forest (oak, maple, beech and tulip poplar) make up another large part of the grounds. The center is remarkably scenic and properly maintained in a very natural state.

When Jacob Nolde, a hosiery baron, first saw this land of poor soil farms and clearings he saw potential. Most of the trees had been stripped off the tract to make charcoal.

Jacob found only one white pine growing by the sawmill about 500 yards from the house. He said, "if one white pine can grow here, why not others?" So he set out to create a beautiful pine forest. Jacob Nolde planted 500,000 evergreen trees (mainly Norway spruce and white and Scotch pine) by 1916. Some seedlings were planted in plantations, others were planted in the oak forest.

The Commonwealth purchased the house and land in 1966 after son of Hans Nolde's death. The house was renovated to accommodate offices and meeting rooms. The office is open 8 a.m. - 4 p.m. weekdays

Information and Activities

Nolde Forest Environmental
Education Center
2910 New Holland Road
Reading, PA 19607
(610) 775-1411

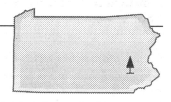

DIRECTIONS: Take Route 625 from south Reading (New Holland Road) about three miles from Route 625's junction with Rt. 222. The center is in Berks County. Trails are open sunrise to sunset daily.

Pennsylvania State Parks

C.H. MCCONNELL ENVIRONMENTAL EDUCATION HALL: The L-shaped brick hall is used as a classroom. Towering oaks shade the building, with a large wildlife feeding station at its rear. The building is named in honor of Clifford McConnell (1918-1980), a popular deputy secretary of resource management. He believed in the need for the public to develop a level of environmental awareness that would translate into sound environmental ethics.

NOLDE MANSION: The renovated stone mansion of English Tudor design provides offices and meeting rooms and houses the center's library. Colorful and interesting gardens surround the mansion, including a butterfly garden and a variety of native wildflowers. Plant materials include inkberry, Veronica, ilex, dogwoods, purple coneflower, lavender, buddleia and others. A small running fountain in the shape of a fish's mouth provides water for birds and wildlife.

The Nolde family wanted a homey house with simple lines and sunny exposure for the rooms. One side of the house gives the impression of an ancient castle with strong vertical composition. Horizontal lines in the front of the house portray ease, comfort and repose. The west wing of the house has a living room on the ground floor and master bedroom with a balcony above it. The living room ceiling is made of weathered oak beams salvaged from an old barn on the property. The fireplace overmantel, also of oak, is hand carved. The architects designed a terrace for privacy; it was shielded from the servants' quarters and the approach to the house.

From the tower, where a small library was tucked away, the Nolde family had a winter view of a sawmill, pond, dam and forester's house at the foot of the hill. The library floor is made of three-by- 14-inch hemlock planks salvaged from stable stall floors from the same barn that provided the living room beams. The three-story tower enclosed a winding stone staircase with a hand-wrought iron railing trimmed in brass. The family placed a 15-foot Douglass fir Christmas tree at the base of the towering steps each year.

The ground floor of the house held a billiard room and laundry room. The servants' quarters consisted of three bedrooms and bath. Part of the house is of Foxcroft stone, called gneiss by geologists, from a quarry in Bryn Mawr, Pa. It is an extremely hard and durable building rock because it has been exposed to heat and pressure within the earth. A varied-color slate roof tops off the building.

Nolde Forest Environmental Education Center

HIKING: The center is criss-crossed with a network of trails through extensively forested areas. Most of the trails at Nolde are well-used and easy walking. The area is laced with paths, and early morning or evening hikers have the best chance of spotting wildlife. Deer, forest birds, chipmunks and darting squirrels are most commonly seen.

NATURE: Many "new and improved" bluebird nesting boxes dot the edges of fields, offering the songbird five-star housing. Deer are common at the center, often seen feeding along the old woods roads. Around the two small ponds and three streams, visitors may see resident amphibians and reptiles (including the snapping turtle). The small ponds teem with activity in the spring, especially when the chorus frogs, vocal wood frogs and spring peepers awaken and call for mates. The center is also home to great-horned owls, screech owls and broadwing hawks.

A bird checklist that details the sightings of 117 species is available from the office. The checklist offers information of abundance, and whether particular species are commonly or rarely seen in the park. The list groups birds by type. Some of the most interesting species include golden-crowned kinglets, often seen in the conifers picking at tiny branches, 25 species of warblers, five types of woodpeckers, seven kinds of thrushes, four types of vireos and many others.

Enjoy violets, lush ferns and other woodland wildflowers during the spring and early summer.

INSIDERS TIP: Ask for directions to the "Inspiration Pine," which inspired Jacob Nolde to begin his plantings.

46 Ohiopyle State Park
Land: 19,046 acres Water: Youghiogheny River

A "wild" river runs through it. The sometimes foaming Youghiogheny River (pronounced *yok-a-GAY-nee*) carries about 100,000 thrill seekers each year and bisects the sprawling 19,000-acre park at the gateway of the Laurel Mountains.

Ohiopyle is among the state's most popular and beautiful natural attractions, hosting 2 million visitors annually who fish, hike, hunt, bike, camp, and, of course, ride nature's "roller coaster" in rubber rafts or high-tech kayaks.

The park area has been a popular destination for more than 100 years, but rafting trips have launched the park to super stardom among outdoor enthusiasts. Ohiopyle gets its name from the Indian word *"Ohiopehhle"*, meaning white frothy water, referring to the impressive falls and fast-running middle and lower sections of the river.

Other points of interest include Cumberland Falls and the Cumberland Run Ravine, which is blanketed with wildflowers and blooming rhododendron. Ferncliff Natural Area, a horseshoe-shaped peninsula formed by a bend in the river, is registered as a National Natural Landmark. The area contains four miles of easy hiking trails. The botanical treasures are wonderful.

Information and Activities

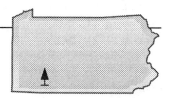

Ohiopyle State Park
P.O. Box 105
Ohiopyle, PA 15470
(412) 329-8591

DIRECTIONS: From the Pennsylvania Turnpike, take Exit 9 (Donegal) east on SR 31 to Jones Mills, right onto SR 381, then south 17 miles to the park entrance. The park office is south of the village of Ohiopyle on LR 2012.

INFORMATION: The park office is open from 8 a.m. - 4 p.m. daily. In the front of the park office (and inside) is a phone, maps and brochures. A small visitors center in an old railroad depot operates seasonally in the tiny village of Ohiopyle, where several raft and outdoor outfitters are located. There is also a popular trailhead here.

THE RIVER AND RAFTING: The "Yough," the most recreationally rafted river in the world, is considered the birthplace of rafting in the eastern United States. The first commercial whitewater rafting occurred on the river in 1963. Today, four large outfitters offer guided raft trips on the Yough in Ohiopyle State Park.

George Washington, who abandoned hopes of navigating the Youghiogheny as a route to Pittsburgh because of the falls and white-water, would certainly be amused–probably amazed–at the number of families that safely travel the foaming waters today.

Water levels in the river are nearly constant year-round, with the primary rafting season running April to October. The trip is a seven-mile run. About 1,920 rafters, canoeists and kayakers use the Yough daily. More people have experienced this mighty river than any other river in the world.

For a quieter river section, the more relaxing Middle Yough, upstream from the falls, is a good place for families and novice rafters. This 11-mile section, accessible only by boat or bike, features pristine scenery and excellent fishing. Wildlife along this section of the river is abundant, including increasing numbers of otter and other native species.

Pennsylvania State Parks

To preserve the natural beauty of the river way and avoid overcrowding of the river and park, daily quotas of river travelers are observed. Daily quotas of 960 unguided and 960 guided boaters have been in effect since the mid-1970s. The four commercial outfitters have regular launch times. Private paddlers with their own craft or a rental boat must obtain a launch permit, which may be reserved by calling the park office at (412) 329-8591. A small launch fee is charged on weekends, and advance reservations are strongly recommended. A changing house and parking area for those with their own boats are across the main road from the launch area.

The rafting outfitters are the White Water Adventures (800) WWA-RAFT, Laurel Highland River Tours (800) 4 RAFTIN, Wilderness Voyageurs (800) 272-4141 and the Mountain Streams and Outfitters. Outfitters can rent you kayaks, bikes and inflatable boats, as well as camping and outdoor equipment.

At the main day-use area and river launch area are a food concession and rest room and launching check-in station with parking nearby. Also in this area are the falls and a series of observation decks.

Many kayakers take "the loop," where after 3 p.m. they can make several trips around the Ferncliff peninsula, take out under the old trail bridge that towers 100 feet above, and walk about 600 yards back to the starting point.

HELPFUL HINTS: If big thrills are your goal, take to the whitewaters of the Yough in April or May. During the summer the river is very busy. Consider a trip during the weekdays, instead of Saturday or Sunday. Book ahead!

First-time rafters should take a couple of guided trips before tackling whitewater on their own. Wear tennis shoes and, bring dry clothes. Shorts and a T-shirt are great in the summer, while wool, windbreakers and wet suits (available to rent) are recommended during chilly times. Also, remember, the most dangerous part of whitewater rafting is the paddle. More people get hurt from flying paddles than anything else. Don't be a victim of "summer teeth," some are here...some are there!

CAMPGROUND: Open year-round, the 226 (44 of these are tent sites only) tent and trailer sites are especially busy on summer weekends and holidays. Quiet hours are 9 p.m. - 8 a.m. for the gently rolling campground that has comfort stations, picnic tables, grills and playgrounds. The park serves as the southern terminus of the 70-mile Laurel

Highlands Hiking Trail and of the 43-mile Youghiogheny River Trail, North Section. Eventually linkages will be developed for the trail system to stretch 315 miles from Pittsburgh to Washington, D.C.

All tents are to be set up in the vicinity of the picnic table and fire ring, and those coming in and setting up after 9 p.m. are urged to do so quietly, respecting the rights of others. A total of five people per site is allowed at Ohiopyle. Visitors must obtain a pass to enter the campground. Firewood is sold, and no cutting of firewood are allowed. Pets and alcohol are prohibited.

Camping sites have gravel and grass pads, picnic tables and grills. The campground is at least 70 percent shady, with many private and large sites for bigger RV rigs. Sites in the 190s are among some of the most private and shady. Ask at the angular check-in station about pull-through sites. Sites 216-221 are private, separated by some sparse vegetation and near the service buildings.

The Birch and Ivy loops are more open than the others.

Those RVers with large rigs should study the maps; many park roads are steep and winding. Campfire and nature programs are offered at the amphitheater in the campground during the summer.

A youth hostel on Ferncliff Road is open year-round. Call (412) 329-4476. Also in the area is a privately operated campground called Scarlet Knob, only two miles from the rafting. Call (412) 329-5200 for site reservations and fees (seasonal sites are available).

EMERGENCY NUMBERS: Ambulance, 437-4981; state police, 439-7111; fire, 437-5121.

HIKING: Ohiopyle has about 60 miles of trails, from easy and moderate to difficult. A full range of scenic and natural areas is along the many hiking loops. From sandstone water slides and waterfalls to rugged cliffs, huge boulders and rapids, Ohiopyle is a premier destination for hikers and backpackers. Some of the finest views are from Baughman's Rock and Sugarloaf Knob, both on the southeastern side of the sprawling park.

SUGARLOAF SNOWMOBILING/MOUNTAIN BIKING AREA: About 600 acres of meadowland are criss-crossed with 9.4 miles of maintained trails for mountain bikes and snowmobiles. The trails generally traverse the knob in a series of concentric loops. In this area visitors will find excellent hills for tobogganing and sledding. Bikes are allowed on designated trails only, including the trail on an old railway bed that starts in Confluence and goes to Connellsville. It will one day connect Pittsburgh to Washington, D.C.

Sugarloaf Trail (3.8 miles) rises from the trailhead at the head of the bike path lot to the edge of the Mountain Bike Trail–two moderate climbs and smooth surfaces. Baughman Trail (3.4 miles) rises from the trail, offering moderate to difficult hiking due to the rocky nature of the path and sometimes narrow twisting path with a rise of 900 feet over three miles. Meadow Run Trail (3.3 miles) provides access to natural water slides, descends to the Yough River and gives hikers a views of the Entrance and Cumberland rapids.

CROSS-COUNTRY SKI AREA: Near the river on the north end of the park by the campground, the Kentucky (2.5 miles) and Sproul (3.5 miles) trails are designed with skiing in mind. This area is closed to snowmobiles.

NATURE: Bear and bobcat are the glamour animals in the park, but are rarely seen. In the Ferncliff Natural Area, trails are open and park naturalists often conduct interpretive hikes there. This peninsula encompasses 100 acres of unique habitats and many rare and interesting plants. The peninsula's rock base is hard, durable Pottsville sandstone that has resisted the water erosion and forces of the Yough River to course around it, creating falls, potholes, scoured rock and turbulent waters.

The rich soils and location of Ferncliff between northern and southern forests have created a tremendous variety of ecological niches for wildlife. Visitors should pick up a copy of *A Field Guide to the Ferncliff Peninsula* from the park office or other contact stations. It details trail rules, life at every level of the forest (from the understory to treetops), plants, natural tidbits and facts, a map, information on the forest canopy, ferns, animal dens and a fun nature quiz.

The peninsula's wildflower display starts as early as February, when skunk cabbage appears in the bottomlands, often pushing through a blanket of snow. Coltsfoot, chickweed and spring beauties follow. Soon May apple, Dutchman's breeches and squirrel corn appear, and by mid-April to mid-May the botanical beauties bloom, offering a display among the finest in the region. Two very rare species–Carolina tassle-rue and large-flowered marshallia–can be found in the park.

Fifty-three tree species, 26 shrubs and 12 types of vines are also found in the park.

Songbirds are abundant, especially during migration times at Ohiopyle. Thirty-six species of warblers have been recorded including breeding species of golden-winged, northern parula, yellow, chestnut-sided, magnolia, Cape Map, black-throated blue, black-throated green, blackburnian, prairie, cerulean, black-and-white warblers and many others.

Other songbirds seen include flycatchers, eastern kingbirds, eastern phoebe, thrushes, swallows, 11 species of raptors, green-backed herons, seven species of woodpeckers, six species of vireos, three types of wrens and ruby-throated hummingbirds. A birding checklist is available from the office, naturalist or other contact points.

SPECIAL NOTES: The Bear Run Conservancy and the incredible Fallingwater house designed by Frank Lloyd Wright are only three miles from the park. More than 2 million people have visited Fallingwater since 1964 (open April 1 - mid-November, fee). This house is Wright's most widely acclaimed work. The house seemingly rises over a waterfall and fits perfectly into the cool, lush terrain.

Whitewater at Ohiopyle.

47 Oil Creek State Park
Land: 7,026 acres Water: Oil Creek

Today, excursion trains clatter through lush valleys past once-rich oil wells and boom towns that are now rusty and idle. The Oil Creek and Titusville Railroad runs from May - October (call 814-676-1733), with a stopping point at the restored depot in the park.

Oil Creek State Park is near Drake's Well, the birthplace of the world's oil industry. In the late summer of 1859 on the banks of Oil Creek in northwestern Pennsylvania, an event occurred that changed the world far more than any of the wars and revolutions that were to follow. On Aug. 27, Edwin L. Drake struck oil! His modest well and simple technology proved that oil could be obtained in large quantities by drilling. Amazingly, he found oil at a depth of only 69.5 feet. This discovery fueled U.S. growth and transportation, and cleared the way for the auto industry and commerce.

This was the first time oil was gathered by means other than scraping at small oil seeps and capturing at weak springs. With increased quantities, a number of inventors began refining the crude oil to improve its burning characteristics and to eliminate the foul smell. Soon the

Oil Creek State Park

demand for kerosene and other petroleum products outpaced the supply. Petroleum Centre became the hub of oil activity in the 1860s, as well as oil fields at Tarr Farm, Pioneer Farm and Miller Farm. But only 15 years later, the once whirling and smelly wells began to dry up and the towns along Oil Creek shrunk. Visitors won't see much evidence of their wild heyday. The wooded hills of Oil Creek Gorge, well-maintained trails, hemlock and broadleaf forest and park amenities offer natural beauty and terrific modern-day outdoor recreation for today's visitors.

A scattering of wells are still active in the park, but most visitors now are looking to discover birds, spring wildflowers or a trout breaking the surface. The park is adjacent to the Drake Well Museum and historic Pithole City (Pennsylvania's largest ghost town). Both the park and neighboring museum interpret the early petroleum industry by identifying oil boom towns, important oil wells, transportation points, cemeteries and comparing and contrasting past lifestyles with the present.

Information and Activities

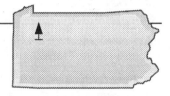

Oil Creek State Park
R.R. 1. Box 207
Oil City, PA 16301
(814) 676-5915

DIRECTIONS: South of Titusville, in Crawford and Venango counties, the main entrance is off PA Route 8, one mile north of the Borough of Rouseville. The park office is on a knoll above the main day-use area. It's open 8 a.m. - 4 p.m. daily.

VISITOR CENTER: Adjacent to the tan-park office is a large, brown carpeted visitor center filled with interpretive displays depicting the history of the region. The most interesting display is entitled, "Over a Century of Oil Later," which describes the impact of the oil industry on you. There are also graphics and quality displays that talk about oil well technology, the Tarr Farm, life in Petroleum Centre, transportation and oil, sources of oil and geology, Empire Well, a large globe that shows current worldwide oil production sites, and a recorded history lesson.

You will also learn about devastating fires that swept the towns, family life, the hardships and the abandonment of the valley and how it has grown back–scars being covered by forests and fields. Today the area is much like it was 140 years ago–forested, streams running clear and some settlement returned. The visitor center is open daily during the summer.

FISHING: Oil Creek is stocked with trout. The creek is also a very good bass fishery. The Oil Creek Outfitters, in a white clapboard-style building near the bike trailhead, rents bikes and sells fly fishing supplies. Inside the cramped shop are colorful fly lines, tiny flies of feathers and fur, delicate graphite rods, fly tying supplies, how-to books, maps, limited snacks and always a couple of fly fishermen with beige vests covered with tiny tools and rusting flies pinned to their fuzzy lapels.

Oil Creek is the largest trout stream in the state. Each year the state stocks 33 miles of the wide stream with up to 30,000 trout. Sections of the creek are delayed harvest, artificial lures only (a 1.5-mile section near the Petroleum Centre bridge downstream to the Tarrman bridge). Although there are many parking sites, some avid anglers bike or hike to quiet sections of the stream that is sometimes called Pennsylvania's Beaverkill.

Oil Creek, once polluted by the oil and timber industries, is now amazingly clean and benefits from preservation and quality improvement efforts by Trout Unlimited and other groups.

Local fly fishermen typically use a combination of emerging-pupa and dry-fly patterns. Matching a caddis fly or mayfly hatch is a promising and practical technique. Caddis hatches are almost ongoing on Oil Creek. In early May try tan- and cream-bodied caddis. Weeks later, emerging-caddis-pupae imitations work. By late May or very early June, mayflies hatch, then sulphurs offer some excellent dry-fly action. Later in the season watch for the white fly hatch. Wading Oil Creek is tricky–slippery, coated rocks are everywhere. Bring your chest waders, felt soles and wading staff.

Many intrepid fly fishermen use poppers and floating cork bugs for bass in the spring and early summer. Try white poppers with whiskers and twitch them through pools and around shade and structure.

HIKING/BICYCLING: From gentle day hikes of six or seven miles to trekking the entire 36 miles, the long and shorter connecting trails are popular, pleasant and rich in history. Oil Creek has 52 miles of hiking and interpretive trails. You can rent a bike or grab a snack at the concession below the park office. The paved trails are wheelchair accessible.

BIKE TRAIL: The nearly 10-mile biking trail is probably the main feature of the park during the summer. It has historical and informational signs along its entire length, taking riders along the creek to the Drake Well Museum. Bicyclists are asked to keep right in a single file, sound off when passing other riders, ride defensively, move completely off the trail when stopped, obey all traffic signs, watch your speeds and carry out everything you carry in.

The mostly shady, hard-surfaced trail winds through a scenic valley. There is parking at both ends of the trail in Drake Well at Titusville and near the park office and outfitter's bike rental shop. The trail is easy, low-grade and suitable for all members of the family. There are primitive rest room facilities at the half-way point. This is also a scenic overlook equipped with picnic tables. You will pass by Miller Farm and a trail to a nearby waterfall.

OIL CREEK HIKING TRAIL: The major hiking trail is 36 miles in length and marked with yellow paint blazes and five connecting loops with white blazes. It is a big loop that runs down the east and west sides of the Oil Creek valley. There are four trails that cross Oil Creek to connect the loop, enabling hikers to plan a wide range of hikes of different lengths. The historic Drake Well is at the north end and Rynd Farm is at the south. The trail passes through grassy areas, thickets of young birch, red oaks, thick forest floor ferns and wildflowers including jack-in-the-pulpit, mayapple, mayflower, wild geranium, violets and others.

The meandering trail passes many historic sites of interest including the Miller Farm, Shaffer Farm, Boughton, Pioneer and Petroleum Centre. Hikers will pass a small waterfall, scenic overlooks and hills and hollows.

Overnight camping is allowed in two designated areas by advance registration and payment of a small fee. Adirondack-style shelter with fireplace are for overnight backpackers. Trail shelters are at Wolfkill Run on the west side of the valley and Cow Run on the east. Each camping area has six shelters which can accommodate four people, plus rest rooms, water and firewood. Registration should be made well in advance by calling (814) 676-5915. A small fee must be paid in advance. One night's stay is limited to each shelter. Overnight parking at Wolfkill Access Road requires a permit from the park office. No overnight parking is allowed at Cow Run Access Road. A map and regulations are available from the park office.

The park also has two interpretive trails open to the public. Each takes less than an hour. The trail that begins at the office takes visitors to the old train station and interprets the impact of oil and the boom town.

One of the first signs says, "Return to the oil boom era of the 1860s. Follow these signs and let your mental time machine transport you to the noisy hustle and bustle of Washington and Main streets, major thoroughfares of the boom town Petroleum Centre. Petroleum Centre, with more than 5,000 residents, flourished from 1865 to 1873 on its twin livelihoods of oil and entertainment. Within a few years of its founding it hosted a theater, bank, three churches, 12 dry goods stores, seven hotels, three stables and an unknown number of saloons, brokerage offices, gambling houses and houses of ill repute. Because it was a company-owned town, it had no municipal government, no law enforcement except for the county sheriff and no sanitation or public works. The famous 'Coal Oil' Johnny set up the town for pure unadulterated wickedness. It eclipsed any town...for open flaunted vice and sin..."

Other signs talk about the old hotel, raceway and central railroad, and take you to the restored railroad depot with a ticket booth, benches and a potbellied stove. If you wish to board the train at Petroleum Centre Station you must pull the handle and activate the flag that tells the engineer to stop. The train runs a 26-mile round trip on certain weekends from May through October.

CANOEING: The quiet waters of Oil Creek provide beginners with a scenic float trip. Water levels and conditions can change, so always call the park office for conditions on the well-known trout stream. A canoe launch point is at the bike trail parking area near Drake Well. Take-out points are at Petroleum Centre, Blood Farm and Rynd farm. The distance between Drake Well and Rynd is 13.5 miles.

DAY-USE AREAS: The main day-use areas surround the park office and are across the creek toward the train station and Petroleum Centre historical site. Wide expanses of mowed areas, parking, bike rental, trailheads and picnicking sites are available. The two main picnic areas have drinking fountains, comfort stations, play fields, grills and rental shelters.

NATURE: The various habitats of wooded lowlands, steep hemlock ravines, bushy fields and thickets, mixed oak and maple forests and small cattail wetlands make bird watching along the many miles of trails fruitful and easy. The park's bike trail that runs parallel to Oil Creek provides access to remote sections of the park. The trail is good for vireos, warblers, thrushes, wild turkey and ruffed grouse.

The creek attracts kingfishers, herons, flycatchers and waterfowl, especially during the spring and fall migration. A birding checklist available at the park office details the 34 species of migrant warblers that have been seen including black-throated blues and breeding Blackburian, and other species like eastern bluebirds, wood duck, whip-poor-wills and common nighthawks. In the winter look for pine siskin, Eastern screech owl, evening grosbeak and purple finch. Bald eagles and osprey are also seen during seasonal migrations. The park has a short bluebird trail.

WILDCAT HOLLOW: Many school groups visit this interesting area and use the outdoor classroom near Petroleum Centre. There is a bus parking area, picnic shelter, rest rooms, activity fields and four themed trails.

HUNTING: About 6,250 acres of the rolling park are open to hunting. Common game species are rabbit, deer, squirrel, turkey and ruffed grouse. Call for details.

WINTER ACTIVITIES: A cross-country ski hut (heated by a wood fire on most weekends; rest rooms and maps are available) and staging area are at the trail head east of the park office. The park has nearly 20 miles of trails that can be skied when weather permits. The primary skiing area is one mile east of the office off of SR 1004. Skiers will see where a 1985 tornado flattened portions of the forest and how it is starting to regenerate.

NEARBY ATTRACTIONS: Tyred Museum has more than 5,000 miniature vehicles and 25 antique cars and planes. Call (814) 676-0756. Pithole, America's largest oil boom town, is now abandoned. Call (814) 827-2797.

INSIDERS TIPS: Oil Creek Outfitters has a large collection of dry and wet flies for Oil Creek. Bring a 6.5-foot rod. Bicycling helmets are required for children 12 years old and under.

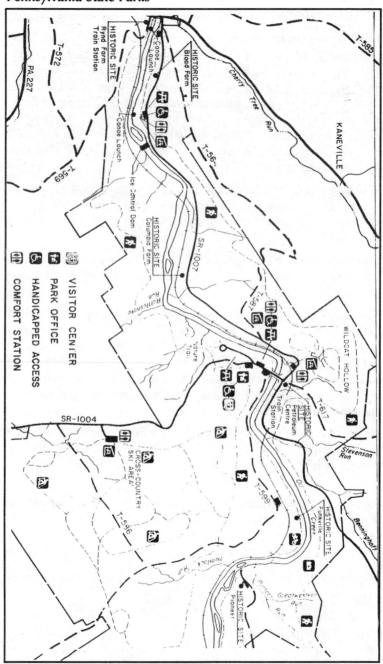

48 Parker Dam State Park
Land: 968 acres   Water: 20-acre lake

Altered by a powerful tornado that carved a record-breaking path through the densely wooded area, Parker Dam is still mostly wooded and in the heart of the spread-out Moshannon State Forest. The blowdown, one of the biggest in Pennsylvania history, felled a cathedral forest and ripped, tossed and destroyed native vegetation. At first the devastation was almost unbearable. Now the site is healing and new growth is creating rich habitats.

Today visitors might see deer, red, gray and flying squirrels, barred owls, great horned owls, and long-eared and screech owls. Bobcat, fox, coyote, salamanders, lots of beaver, wood ducks, raptors and great blue herons in the swamp meadow are also seen throughout the state park. For serious wildlife watcher, guided elk sighting tours are organized in the Elk State Forest north of the park. Contact the park office for details.

By the late 1800s, most of the white pine was removed from the Moshannon Forest, which is now a tract of upland hardwoods. In the early 1900s, the Central Pennsylvania Lumber Co. bought 4,597 acres of hemlock timber in the area and built a standard-gauge railroad. Some of the old railroad grades can still be seen. The lumbering company rapidly cut wood and loaded up to 45 rail cars daily for the trip to sawmills in Williamsport. By 1912 more than 30 million board feet of timber had been shipped.

In 1930 and 1931, the Commonwealth purchased the land holdings to become tracts in the Moshannon State Forest. By mid-1933, the Civilian Conservation Corps arrived in Penfield and set about building roads, dam and spillway that created the 20-acre lake that became the focal point of the state park.

The park remained largely unchanged until the 1960s, when the campground was renovated. Modern water and sanitary facilities were completed in 1976.

Information and Activities

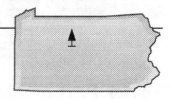

Parker Dam State Park
R. D. 1, Box 165
Penfield, PA 15849-9799
(814) 765-0630

DIRECTIONS: In Clearfield County, 17 miles north of Clearfield and five miles south of Penfield off PA Route 153.

The park office is in a brown wood frame building with wood roof shingles and a beautiful, varnished front door that welcomes visitors. It is open 8 a.m.- 4 p.m., weekdays, and 10 a.m. to 6 p.m. Saturdays and Sundays during the summer, 3 p.m. - 5 p.m. on Saturday and Sundays in the fall, winter and spring.

CAMPGROUND: Parker Dam has 110 family camping sites. All may be reserved during the summer. For campground reservation information for Parker Dam or Elliott State Park, call (814) 765-0639. 92 sites are large enough to accommodate trailers sized 21-35 feet. Two sites can handle big RV rigs of 36-50 feet in length. 13 sites (3, 7, 9, 13, 17, 25, 26, 34, 37, 39, 40, 46 and 107) have 80 amp electrical service in the rolling and wooded camping area northeast of the park office. 50 sites have electrical hookups. Most of the sites are private and separated by a wall of vegetation. All of the camping sites have picnic tables and fire rings. One showerhouse serves the area.

The campground, on a dry ridge, is shady with hard-surfaced pads. The campground has two wooded short walk-in tent sites, 109 and 110, near Fairview Road.

Families should consider sites 45 and 47 near the timber-structure play area that has benches for the adults. The amphitheater is down a foot-path near site 51. Sites 53 and 55 are terrific for smaller RV units. Sites 64-70 and 42-46 are more open than the others, offering direct sunlight for several hours each day. Sites on the outside of the main loop are backed up on a natural area. Sites 89 and 108 (gravel surfaced pad, private), the largest in the park, are roomy enough for an extra vehicle or boat and trailer.

EMERGENCY NUMBERS: State police, 1-371-4652; fire, 911.

CABINS: Along a ridge line is a pleasant grouping of cabins west of the park office. The 16 rustic cabins are open year-round and rented by the week during the summer, and daily during spring, fall and winter. Advance registration is required. Minimal furnishings include single bunk beds, chairs, tables, a modern stove, refrigerator, electric lights and fireplace. Cut firewood and private flush toilets and showers are in a separate building outdoors. Each cabin has a nearby picnic table and fire ring or grill.

Cabin 4, like many in the group, is a classic, square-shaped log cabin with fieldstone chimney, pleasant front porch and stacked stone pillars. Cabin 6 is private and in a small wooded ravine. Cabin 14, on the other hand, is along a rise, while cabin 13 sports a wide front deck and shade. Each cabin is at slightly different elevations and rests under a solid tree canopy. Down an almost private lane is cabin 7, with large porch and extra parking. Cabin 10 is accessible by wheelchair. Cabins 2 or 3 are good choices for families due to their proximity to a small play area and soft drink machine.

FISHING: Shoreline fishing is popular at the park. Using Powerbait, small spinners and other live bait (wax worms and red worms), locals take good numbers of brook trout, bluegills, crappie and channel cats from the small pond. A short wooden boardwalk and gravel path skirt the pond's west shoreline.

HIKING: An impressive elevated wooden boardwalk along the creek mouth was constructed by the Pennsylvania Conservation Corps and the St. Mary's High School Conservation & Ecology Club. The wind-ing walkway meanders over wetlands and along the cool creek bank. The trail is used for nature study and pleasure.

The Quehanna Trail, with a western trailhead near the campground entrance, was established to provide a foot travel route from Parker Dam to Susquehannock Trail. The entire trail system, including connector trails, surpasses 75 miles in length. Contact the park office for complete details. Overnight backpackers should register. Maps are available when you register. The entire loop takes you through the Quehanna Wilderness and into Sinnemanhoning and Potter counties. Five to seven days are required for the hike. Shorter loops provide one-two-and four-day hikes.

When camping along this trail, suspend your food between two trees, 10 feet above the ground. This is a wilderness hike; be sure to step on logs not over them, take and wear quality clothing and know your limits before starting. Small fires are permitted. Near the trailhead are a small outdoor display of lumbering tools, information about the white pine and a 75-foot log slide with attached chains. The long wood slides were used to skid logs out of the forest.

Beaver Dam Trail (2.3 miles) traverses an area set aside for the propagation of beavers. Keep a sharp eye out for signs of beavers (cuttings, tracks, ponds and dams) and beavers puttering about on land or in the water. Beaver watching is best done in the evening when there isn't much daylight. Approach them from downstream when possible and find a comfortable sitting spot...and wait. Station yourself near pond or dam entries and remain quiet and still. This trail was used by the Central Penna Lumber Co. to log Mud Run in the early 1900s.

Souder's Trail (.75 mile) is self-guided. Booklets are available from the park office or nature center.

Trail of the New Giants (1 mile) is a walk through brush and fallen giants (oaks, beech, sugar maple, ash) that were flattened by Pennsylvania's strongest tornado in May 1985. About 250 acres of cathedral-like trees were blown down in less than five minutes. The trail is cut though the middle of this area that is now being called the Windstorm Natural Area. Tornado Alley Trail and Abbot Hollow Trail also offer a close-up look at the damage and regeneration.

Stumpfield Trail (.5 mile) begins at the amphitheater in the campground and traverses a meadow that was once a mighty forest of pine and hemlock. Wildfires ravaged the area after it was logged in the 1880s and 1890s. The intense heat of the fire consumed the humus layer of the soil and set the succession of plants back to grasses and sedges. The hike now offers a chance to see advanced succession where aspen, cherry and maple are beginning to enclose the meadow.

CCC INTERPRETIVE CENTER: A CCC log-style building perched at lake's edge near the earthen dam and beautiful stone spillway is the small museum that is open on Sunday afternoons. Inside are displays, printed information and histories of the efforts and lifestyle of Civilian Conservation Corps workers. Aging photographs depict camp life, clothing and samples of their work. The porch on the white chinked building with small three-over-three windows is charming. An old CCC grader is also displayed outside the classic building.

DAY USE AREAS: The day-use areas are clustered around the lake (nature center, beach, concession), many in view of the park office. Picnicking is in wooded settings with ample parking, tables, massive timber and stone CCC pavilions and charcoal grills for your hot dogs. Pavilions are reservable on a first-come, first-served basis, with some having electricity. Playgrounds, shady volleyball courts and ballfields with wood-frame backstops are heavily used on summer weekends. Many small trees have been planted in the day-use areas and will enhance the open spaces as they grow tall and full.

BEACH: The 75-yard-long, light-colored sandy beach is on a point near the paddle/row boat rental concession. The guarded beach is open 11 a.m. - 7 p.m. daily from Memorial Day to Labor Day, unless posted otherwise. The deepest point in the corded-off beach is five feet. A handicapped accessible ramp goes into the water and is open when the beach is. A log cabin-style concession sells snacks and is open noon - 6 p.m. daily during the summer. The dam with stone retaining walls is in front of the beach.

NATURE: Seasonal naturalist programs offered to campers and the general public include educational programs, recreational games and outdoor activities. From interpretive hikes to beach games and snake hunts, all ages can participate. Visit the park office or small dark-brown log nature center near the beach for a schedule of activities. Slab log seats are in front of the nature center that houses interpretive displays and is often the focal point of programming and activities. How to watch beavers is one of the best displays in the center. An outdoor touch and learn board is soiled from heavy use by curious youngsters. The center's mission is to interpret the lake's natural communities.

Hummingbird feeders at the park office are busy, with the tiny birds hovering and cocking their heads from side to side as if sizing up the feeders and colored liquid food inside. Hummingbirds need high energy food because of their high body metabolism. Just hovering burns up 10 times the energy man uses. Because they need that much food, they must feed every 15-20 minutes, visiting feeding stations and blossoms many times daily. They feed with great intensity at dusk.

Hummingbirds can fly backwards, and use spider webs and saliva to construct a walnut-sized nest. Other interesting facts are that hummingbirds' legs are so short (how short are they?), they can't walk or climb, they just stand and sit (like my teenage son!). They can reach a speed of 27 mph, beating their wings 80 times per second. A hummingbird's flight muscles are proportionately the largest muscles in the animal kingdom. Hummingbirds can travel 500 miles on one gram of stored food. The only pigment found on a hummingbird's feathers are brown and black.

Other birds to look for include great blue herons and cedar waxwings in the fall. Northern shrike are sometimes seen in the deepest part of winter.

HUNTING: Only the north portion of the park is open to hunting from the fall archery season for deer to March 31. Call the park manager for information.

WINTER: Parker Dam is an oasis in the middle of the sprawling Moshannon State Forest, offering access to miles of snowmobile and cross-country ski trails. Parker Dam also offers ice skating and fishing on the lake (waxworms and minnows on light colored jigs are preferred). A sledding and toboggan run is popular as weather permits.

INSIDER TIPS: Clean and safe, Parker Dam is a launching point from which to explore the surrounding state forest lands and amenities. During warm weather months, watch the hummingbirds visit the feeders at the park office.

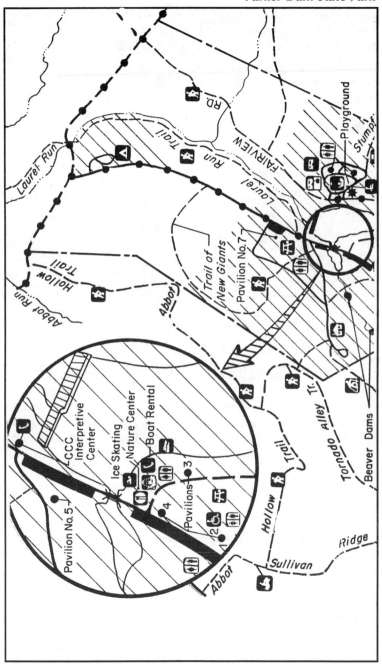

49 Pine Grove Furnace State Park

Land: 696 acres   Water: Two small lakes

Pine Grove Furnace is in the northernmost tract of the mountainous Blue Ridge province, locally known as South Mountain in the Michaux State Forest. For millions of years, creeks have drained these highlands by following paths in fractured and structurally weak rocks. They cut through and eroded a rock thickness of at least 600 feet. This process of weathering and erosion of the highlands, downstream transportation of sediment, and subsequent deposition have occurred throughout the geologic past as they do today.

The park is on Mountain Creek, which joins the popular trout stream, Yellow Breeches Creek and flows east to the Susquehanna River. Little Rocky Ridge and Piney Mountain overlook the park from opposite sides of the Mountain Creek valley. The scenic park owes its name to the discovery of iron ore deposits nearby and the rise of a busy iron industry which operated between 1764 and 1895.

Groves of towering pines, crystal clear streams and the mountains first attracted settlers to the secluded terrain around South Mountain. The sounds of axes and bucksaws were heard throughout the woodlands after the first sawmill was built in 1762. Within 10 years, lumbering activity dimmed and the new natural resource was iron.

Pine Grove State Park took its name from the Pine Grove Iron Furnace; its stone remains still stand. The furnace dates to 1764 and for 122 years manufactured cast iron products including ten-plate stoves, fireplace backs, iron kettles and heavy military supplies. Brick and slate works were also operated in the vicinity during the 1870s in an effort to keep the local economy strong after the iron works declined.

The small 1.7-acre Fuller Lake was once the quarry from which iron ore was mined to supply the huge furnace. When groundwater kept filling the quarry, mining ceased. Laurel Lake once supplied water power to Laurel Forge to reheat and hammer cast iron ingots from the furnace to produce wrought iron items. In 1977 the Pine Grove Furnace was listed on the National Register of Historical Places.

Recreational facilities were built by the iron furnace company and visitors came by steam locomotive. In 1913 the state purchased about 20,000 acres for public development. Part of the story of Pine Grove Furnace is that it has been reclaimed from a mine and lumbered area to a reforested, popular state park. During the period when the private recreation area was operating, an advertisement appeared that promoted the fact that the attendant in the ladies rest room had hot water.

Although the current park is as popular as the private operation 100 years ago, it still doesn't have hot water in the rest rooms. The hot water back then was used to freshen up after a long, dusty train or carriage ride to the park.

Information and Activities

Pine Grove Furnace State Park
1100 Pine Grove Road
Gardners, PA 17324
(717) 486-7174

DIRECTIONS: 12 miles northeast of Caledonia. Take exit 11 from I-81, south on SR 233 for eight miles to the headquarters. The park office was once a boarding house and now has a small meeting room and service counter. The visitor center, next to the park office, was once a stone grist mill. The park office is open 8 a.m. - 8 p.m. daily during the summer.

EMERGENCY NUMBERS: State police, 249-2121 or 911.

CAMPGROUND: Pine Grove Furnace features 74 primitive camping sites along two loops that is open year-round. No showers or utility hookups are available, but each site has a picnic table and ground-mounted fire ring. Many sites are separated by vegetation and are over-sized. Rest rooms are pit-type, but are clean and offer baby changing stations.

A narrow road serves the shady, flat tract. Larger trailers and motor homes may want to take a look at sites 4, 6, 7, 17, 21, 31. 23, 32 and 58, which are pull-through sites. Virtually no site in the campground gets direct sunlight. Many sites in the 40s and 50s are over-sized and backed up against natural areas. Sites 64 and 65 are extra-wide camping sites, perfect for large rigs or campers who like additional side-yard room. These types of sites are easy to back into.

PINE GROVE GENERAL STORE: The store was once a stable. Now it's renovated and restored, and sells firewood, bread, ice, snacks and interesting handmade items. The long, shady porch, which was probably added in the 1930s, is often a hang out for backpackers coming off the marathon trail system. The long-distance hikers are usually consuming soft drinks by the quart and grin from ear to ear.

Part of the building is a stable, where wagon and sleigh rides are proposed to be operated.

GROUP TENTING: Organized youth or adult groups can reserve the 160-capacity tent camping area at any time of the year. The gently rolling area is divided into six areas with capacities varying from 25 to 35 each. There is no vehicular access to the sites. It's a short walk. Sites are near an open field.

FISHING: Both warm and cold water species can be taken from Laurel Lake, depending on the time of year and weather conditions. Panfish, perch and rainbow trout are in the lakes, while Mountain Creek is stocked with brown, brook and rainbow trout. The creek also has a good number of native brook trout. The park has about four miles of streams.

Locals say that Mountain Creek is at least as good a stream as the popular Yellow Breeches and Falling Springs Run. The creek is stocked over a distance of 16 miles, from the park to Mount Holly Springs. Try

Ironmaster's Mansion is now a youth hostel near the Appalachian Trail.

Adams, royal coachmen, rusty caddis, common sulphurs and terrestrials. Watch for the white fly hatch.

BOATING: Leave your gasoline engine home. Only non-powered and electric-powered boats are permitted on Laurel Lake. Use caution on the very shallow lake. The tiny 1.7-acre Fuller Lake has no boating access.

Little Laurel Lake (25 acres) is a charming lake to paddle. The isolated lake is at the steep foot of mountains that provide wonderful views and protection from midday winds. A dam is in the northeast corner of the triangular lake with a single small island. Two small channels near the island lead to the point where Mountain Creek enters the cool lake.

Small boats can be rented near the launching ramp or, better yet, bring your own canoe and picnic lunch. Polarized sunglasses make fish watching in the gin-clear water a pleasing diversion. You can paddle the entire shoreline and more in less than two hours.

HIKING: The halfway point of the famous 2,000-mile Appalachian Trail is in the park. A tradition for long-distance hikers is to eat one-half gallon of ice cream in one-half hour or less when they reach this

277

scenic point. The record is five minutes and 30 seconds. Few, I'm told, resist the tradition–most use the entire half-hour savoring each bite. The halfway marker is just 100 yards form the southern park gate. The trail goes from Mt. Katahdin in central Maine to Springer Mountain in northern Georgia.

Koppenhaver Trail (1 mile) is a loop marked with yellow blazes that starts and ends at the Fuller ballfield. The path travels through stands of mature pines and hemlocks and crosses Tom's Run.

Pole Steeple Trail (.75 mile) is rugged. but the view from the quartzite rock outcropping is excellent.

HISTORIC WALKING TOUR: The 18-station historic walk (1.25 miles) takes about an hour and a half. Look for symbols along the trail that correspond to numbered paragraphs in a four-panel brochure available at the park office or visitor center.

The easy walk will take you by the remains of the village where water power was harnessed and large millstones grinded (where the current visitor center is located), near where the blacksmith shop once stood. Imagine, as you walk, the mules and horses at work providing the muscle power for pulling coal and ore-filled wagons and dragging wooden sleds loaded with logs for charcoal making.

At station 10, you'll learn about the cold-blast furnace that was the heart of Pine Grove. The furnace was modernized many times over the years, but the essential ingredients of iron production–iron ore, charcoal and limestone–remained the same. Native ore was the source of iron. Charcoal provided the heat to smelt the iron ore. Limestone acted as a flux to separate ore impurities from the molten iron.

Fillers loaded these three ingredients into the top of this stack. Near the base of the furnace, the tuyere arch provided a space through which blasts of air were forced. This sped the operation. At first, a water wheel powered the bellows; later, a steam-powered blowing engine was installed. When the founder tapped the furnace, he drew molten iron from the base of the stack into sand canals to form pig iron bars. Skilled moulders also ladled molten iron into tightly-packed sand molds to create hollow ware and decorative stove plates.

BICYCLING: Ambitious visitors can rent a bike at Laurel Lake for a spin on the gently rolling park roads. It's about three miles from the furnace to Laurel Lake.

Pennsylvania State Parks

AYH HOSTEL/IRONMASTER'S MANSION: White shutters gleam in the sunlight on the two-story, red-brick mansion perched on a ridge above the park. It once looked over a vast complex of iron producing facilities; now, it is the happy home to weary hikers trekking the Appalachian Trail. Today visitors sit on the long porch with cross-buck railing and watch the activity below and enjoy the vistas in the distance.

The hostel has overnight dormitory-style lodging. Cooking and dining facilities are available. Call (717) 486-7575 for details.

VISITOR CENTER: Once a stone grist mill, the center now houses a number of historical displays that include examples of the ten-plate stoves that were produced at the furnace. The stoves were made of cast and rolled iron. With timber framing overhead and creaking hardwood floors under foot, the historic center is an excellent first stop to learn about the industrial and natural history of the area. The overall theme of the visitor center is how man has used the resources in this part of the state. From ore and water to timber resources, the region is as productive as ever.

DAY-USE AREAS: Pick a table. Any one of the almost 400 picnic tables is a great place to meet and have lunch. The tables are scattered in several locations, usually with comfort stations, grills and water nearby. Two pavilions can be rented for a fee; when not reserved they are available on a first-come, first-served basis. A babbling creek carves its way around the day-use and other areas offering a delicate murmur and cool place where birds and other mammals often frequent in midday.

Several day-use areas have volleyball courts, horseshoe courts and game fields.

One area is set aside for overnight parking with proper registration at the park office for AT hikers.

BEACHES: Both lakes have small guarded sandy beaches that are open 11 a.m. - 7 p.m. daily from Memorial Day weekend to Labor Day, unless otherwise posted. The lakes can be very cold. Dressing stockades are at both lakes and picnic tables are scattered nearby. Concessions are at each beach near toilets and picnic areas.

NATURE: Interpretive programming is offered from Memorial Day to Labor Day. The visitor center is open during these months 1 p.m. - 4 p.m. Friday, Saturday and Sunday. Education programs are often historically-themed, while campfire programs might include stories and nature history lessons. A number of nature walks and tours of the historical areas are also scheduled. Pick up a calendar of events from contact points around the park.

BIRDING: Bounded by mountains and large tracts of oak, pine and hemlock forest and fields, Pine Grove Furnace has diverse habitats that appeal to birds. The two small lakes gather waterfowl visitors as a resting place on their biannual journey.

There are no endangered species nesting in the park; however, bald eagles are occasionally seen in the spring at Laurel Lake. Osprey are also seen in this manner. The park publishes a bird list that tells when certain birds might be in the park. Six species of woodpeckers, 10 species of bird of prey, five species of flycatchers, three species of swallows, many finches, nuthatches, creepers warblers and wrens are spotted. Whip-poor-wills are often heard at night during the summer. Winter feeder visitors include crow-sized pileated woodpeckers and red-breasted nuthatches. Frustrated black-crowned night herons have been seen eyeing the Huntdale Fish Hatchery, where large net-covered raceways contain thousands of fry and fingerling sized game fish.

HUNTING: 75 acres of the park are open from the fall archery season until March 31. Call the park office for additional details.

WINTER: Ice skaters can strap on the blades and use a maintained area on Laurel Lake. The rest of the lake is used by ice fishermen. Nordic skiers can enjoy the old railroad beds. When the park has lots of snow, many skiing opportunities exist.

INSIDERS TIPS: The outlook from Pole Steeple (south of Laurel Lake, .75 mile) is terrific. A World War II prison of war camp was once near the park property in the state forest. Check out the neighboring log cabins–a must see.

NEARBY ATTRACTIONS: A colony of charming log cabins with bright white chinking is scattered around the park. The cabins are beautiful, often surrounded by green ferns and towering trees that provide deep shade. You can bike, ride or walk these narrow gravel roads where you will discover some of the finest cabins east of the Mississippi River.

Michaux State Forest is an 84,912-acre forest that surrounds the state park. Hunting and hiking are top activities. Call (717) 352-2211 for additional information.

Huntdale Fish Hatchery off PA Route 233 North features an attractive visitor center that interprets the activities of the facility.

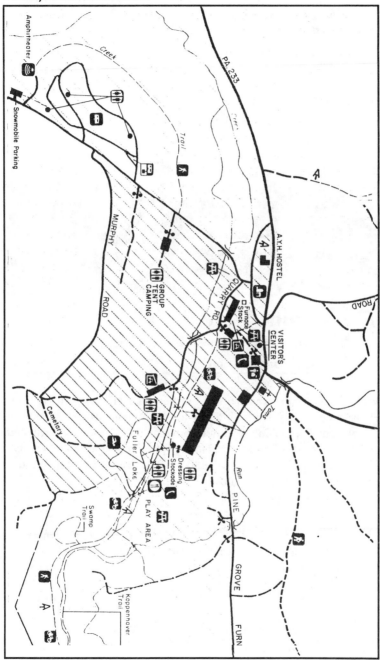

50 Point State Park
Land: 36 acres Water: Allegheny and Monogahela rivers

With the end of the war in 1945, Pittsburgh's civic and political leaders became acutely sensitive to the town's horrendous reputation as a "smoky city." Belching steel mills brought widespread prosperity and tens of thousands of good jobs, but they also brought air pollution on a scale unlike that anywhere else in the nation. Historic photos illustrated the fact, showing downtown streets at midday with street lights blazing as if it were midnight. These photos and a strong civic effort built public support for cleanups and a movement called "the Renaissance."

The bipartisan civic effort, which created the Allegheny Conference on Community Development, oversaw all kinds of urban renewal projects that were unprecedented among American cities. One of its first acts was to establish a park at the "Point"–the nub of land where the Allegheny and Monongahela rivers join to form the Ohio. The symbolic park helped rid the area of unsightly slums and railroad warehouses–a holdover form the days of the cross-state canal and railroads, where travelers and shippers headed for Cincinnati, St. Louis or New Orleans continued west from the Monongahela Wharf.

The triangular-shaped, 36-acre park contained the original Fort Pitt blockhouse, site of a pre-American Revolutionary military movement between French and British troops. They fought to control the "Gateway to the West"–the Ohio River. The French had controlled the site at Fort Duquesne, but fled when they learned that the British were coming to seize it. Historians consider their arrival in November 1758 to be the founding of Pittsburgh.

The blockhouse, built in 1764, was the focal point of the drive to install the new urban park. By July 1946, the Commonwealth assembled the land and started building the marquee park.

One of the most widely recognized fountains in the world is in the high urban park. The 150-foot-tall, computed-controlled fountain sits on a 200-foot-wide pedestal-like basin, dramatically lit by 24 white and gold lights for spectacular night viewing. Thousands of air passengers flying into Pittsburgh International Airport at night have enjoyed a dramatic view of the colorful circular fountain. Behind the fountain is the outline of Fort Duquesne and a walkway that tours the point of land at the river junction.

Information and Activities

Point State Park
101 Commonwealth Place
Pittsburgh, PA 15222
(412) 471-0235
(412) 281-9284 - museum

DIRECTIONS: In downtown Pittsburgh, the entrance to the park is on Commonwealth Place, across the street from the multi-story Hilton hotel. The park is open 7 a.m. - 11 p.m. daily. Picnics are allowed in the park. In-line skaters and bike riders are not allowed in the park.

FORT PITT MUSEUM (small fee): Two gray cannons guard the entrance to the red-brick museum. Visitors should begin by watching the 20-minute film that describes the settlement of the area including wars, explorers, fur trading, Indians and more. The museum is open 10 a.m. to 4:30 p.m. weekdays except Monday, noon to 4:30 p.m. Sunday.

The museum has lots of high-quality dioramas, artifacts (tools, arms, trading, products, etc.) and interpretive exhibits. The facility specializes in information about the French and Indian War and the Revolution to lifestyles of settlers and soldiers. The museum can hold the attention of all ages.

The round lobby inside the front doors of the museum offers a huge model of the old fort detailing the five points where armament were positioned, agricultural stations, how it was constructed, rivers and much more. The fort's walls were made of sod and timber, and the museum has many interesting exhibits that explain construction technology, period tools and techniques, and the reasons why the fort was built the way it was.

Curators have also developed educational displays that demonstrate how grist mills work, heavy manufacturing of the era, early printing techniques (including a sample of an ink ball and reversed type), ship building, iron making and foundries, glass production and many large paintings that depict pioneer life.

The museum operates a small gift shop that sells post cards, coon-skinned hats, novelty items, single-sheet historical information, books and more.

DAY-USE AREAS: The park offers open spaces, the famous fountain, benches, picnic tables, performance stage, blockhouse, fort outline, river walk and a view of Three Rivers Stadium and yellowish bridges that arch across the rivers. The park is a green space amid a dynamic high-rise downtown where many area employees often spend their lunch hour.

NATURE: About 50 bird species have been identified in the urban park. Night hawks are abundant, especially when the lights of Three Rivers Stadium are on for ballgames in the summer.

NEARBY ATTRACTIONS: Downtown Pittsburgh, Carnegie Science Center and much more.

INSIDERS TIPS: Visit the submarine, in the water, at the science center, just minutes from the state park. The park is also the site for outdoor concerts and other activities during the summer. Living history activities by period-dressed volunteers are held each Sunday afternoon during mid-summer.

51 Presque Isle State Park
Land: 3,200 acres Water: Lake Erie, Presque Isle Bay

Presque Isle is the only place in the state where waves break on sandy beaches. It is also one of the few places in the commonwealth where you can see evidence of the recent geologic past and watch geological process in action.

Waves and currents are constantly removing sand from parts of the seven-mile peninsula and depositing it in others. The wind-swept sandy beaches, the sheltered harbor behind the fragile, narrow-necked sandpit peninsula and the many environments supporting unusual plant and animal communities all exist because of lake-related processes and the movement of sand over many years. Presque Isle is a recurved sand spit. Waves, currents and wind have moved sand, creating a series of dune ridges, ponds and marshes.

Although the name "Presque Isle" means *almost an island* in French, the area has been a real island several times. Storm waves have broken through the neck isolating the spit at least four times since 1819. One of the gaps remained open for 32 years before being closed by natural situation. Today on the pork chop-shaped peninsula, much history can be seen in the pattern of dune ridges, swamps and ponds that commonly occupy the low areas between them. The older ridges show the location of earlier shorelines. These ridge lines run mostly east and west back from the water's edge near miles of beach that are among the most popular in the region.

Presque Isle has long been a popular recreation area. In fact, in 1934 more than 1.4 million visitors roamed the beaches and splashed in the lake's waters. Today about 4 million visitors come to the park annually. The fascinating park continues to be one of the most popular in the state. Presque Isle has the longest beach in the state and was acquired in 1921.

Information and Activities

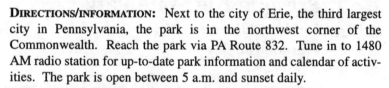

Presque Isle State Park
P.O. Box 8510
Erie, PA 16505-0510

(814) 871-4251

DIRECTIONS/INFORMATION: Next to the city of Erie, the third largest city in Pennsylvania, the park is in the northwest corner of the Commonwealth. Reach the park via PA Route 832. Tune in to 1480 AM radio station for up-to-date park information and calendar of activities. The park is open between 5 a.m. and sunset daily.

EMERGENCY PHONE: The park is part of the 911 system.

PERRY'S MONUMENT: On a tree-lined point, standing bolt-upright and firm against the lake winds, is Perry's monument, about five miles from the park office on the south shore. Commander Oliver Perry engaged the British fleet at Put-In-Bay, near Sandusky, Ohio, with both fleets having about equal firepower. Two hours into the battle, Perry lost his flagship, the Lawrence, and most of its crew. Transferring to the Niagara, Perry sailed into the midst of the British fleet and within an hour the Union Jack was lowered. Perry then penned a report with these immortal words: "We have met the enemy, and they are us."

Two ships, two brigs, one schooner and one sloop sunk in 1850 in Misery Bay. The Niagara was raised in 1913, reconstructed and stood at the foot of State Street in the city of Erie across the bay until the mid-1980s. Presently the Brig Niagara has been reconstructed and is Pennsylvania's flag ship, sailing in many tall ship events around the

Great Lakes and Eastern U.S. coast. There are a small day-use picnic shelter and tables near the tall stone monument.

HIKING: The firm multi-purpose trail that meanders along the water's edge is nearly six miles long. It begins at the park entrance and ends at Perry's monument. The popular trail is used by in-line skaters, bicyclists, joggers, cross-country skiers, wheelchairs and walkers. About 10 more miles of hiking-only trails are also marked and maintained at the park.

Many of the hiking trails start near the lighthouse:

SELF-GUIDED INTERPRETIVE TRAIL: This quarter-mile loop begins at Stull Interpretive Center, taking hikers from the beach to the forest with easy-to-read descriptive signs interpreting the natural succession.

FOX TRAIL: Used for cross-country skiing in the winter, during the warm weather season hikers will see the flora of an oak-maple forest and canopy-loving birds.

OLD GAS WELL TRAIL: Winding near the marina, the half-mile trail travels along a sand ridge past an old gas well that once produced fuel used by the park.

CANOE PORTAGE TRAIL: This one-quarter-mile trail connects Marina Lake to Pettinato Beach (beach No. 8) and takes walkers between sand dunes and forest lots.

RIDGE TRAIL: The easy half-mile trail follows the edge of Cranberry Pond along a portion of a ridge that was a former beach dune 300 years ago.

MARSH TRAIL: This short trail bisects Cranberry Pond, one of the many ponds in the park that was formed by waters trapped between two ridges.

SIDEWALK TRAIL: Built by a former lighthouse keeper to provide a path connecting the lighthouse to Misery Bay where his boat was docked, the 1.25-mile trail is now for recreation use.

DEAD POND TRAIL: One of the most interesting trails, this one leads over a former dune and through distinct ecological zones, including oak-maple forest, pines and sand plains. The trail is two miles long.

PINE TREE TRAIL: The trail passes the remains of the Biology Field Lab used by Dr. O. E. Jennings to study plant succession on the Isle. There are places on the trail where you can see full succession in a two-mile-long stretch.

GULL POINT TRAIL: This trail starts at the kiosk at the east end of Budny Beach (beach No. 10) parking lot and loops through the Gull Point Natural Area. At the southeast end of the loop, a spur leads to an elevated observation platform at the edge of the Special Management Area. Birders often see many species of wading and shorebirds from this vantage point.

NORTH PIER TRAIL: Along a sand ridge and shoreline between North Pier and Beach No. 11 is an old firing range that was used for training during World War II.

GRAVEYARD POND TRAIL: Scenic views of a lush lagoon and Big Pond are the rewards of this .75-mile trail which was the final resting place for many of Commodore Perry's men during the winter of 1813-1814.

LONG POND TRAIL: Along Long Pond's shoreline, one of the ponds within the lagoon, you pass the boat landing, scenic views and popular fishing spots.

BOATING: 473 seasonal slips, fuel, lifts and transient docks are available at the marina. There are no engine restrictions on the lake. Internal combustion engines are prohibited in the interior lagoons, which are defined as the continuous body of water between Misery Bay and Marina Bay, excluding Graveyard Pond. Beaching boats on the shore is permitted except within 100 feet of designated swimming areas and at the Gull Point Special Management Area between April 1 and Nov. 30.

A selection of by-the-hour rental boats is offered at the tiny watercraft concession at the north end of Misery Bay, including small aluminum fishing boats, rowboats, motorboats, electric powered boats, canoes, minnow buckets, landing nets and coolers. Live bait including grubs, minnows and crawlers are also sold. Call (814) 838-3938 for boat rental information during the season. Windsurfers prefer the Sunset Point area to ply the waves and catch the steady winds.

There are six launching ramps provided in five areas around the long park. Most of the launches are concrete ramps and improved with gravel lots and offer a floating courtesy dock, picnic tables and nearby rest rooms.

FISHING: Serious walleye anglers fill the launches in the spring and fall rigging up to troll. They use planner boards or jig and flutter lures near any type of underwater structure or points. Shoreline fishing sites are plentiful. During the spring, Misery Bay is fair or good for crappies, perch, sunfish or trout. From a boat, stay in the shallows during the early summer.

DAY-USE AREAS: More than 500 picnic tables and several rental shelters are scattered along the beaches and in shady areas. The Cookhouse Pavilion is a popular family reunion-type day-use area and shelter.

BEACHES/SWIMMING: The 18 guarded beaches are open 10 a.m. - 8 p.m. daily Memorial Day to Labor Day, unless posted otherwise. These are the longest beaches in the state, offering surf swimming in clear Lake Erie. Scuba diving is permitted in designated waters. Certified divers must register at the park office. Skin-diving with mask, fins and snorkel is NOT permitted. Volleyball courts are near beach No. 6 and other areas. The beaches are low, rolling and wide. Food concessions are operated at four beaches each summer: Beach No. 6, Beach No. 11, Pettinato Beach and Budny Beach.

NATURE: The natural significance of Presque Isle State Park–and Gull Point within it–can't be overstated. The fragile, ever-changing geological land forms are unique in Pennsylvania. Plant succession in a compressed setting for which the park is famous is most visible on Gull Point, an area of about 319 acres.

Gull Point, part of the Special Management Area that is protected and closed to the public, is a wonderful land form with varying topography and zones of natural succession of aquatic areas that provide diverse habitats. Many plant species are rare and of special concern, while fish species and freshwater mussel species are found just offshore. Gull Point's value for nesting and migrating shore and wading birds from April through November is known nationally and carefully preserved. 55 species of plants found at the park are listed as rare or endangered.

In fact, so important is this area for nesting, the Special Management Area has been designated on the eastern tip of the point. This protected area encompasses 67 acres and is closed to public from April 1 - Nov. 30. This includes water access and hiking. Boats are permitted to moor 100 feet from shore and beyond.

A full-time naturalist offers outdoor education programming and staffs the recently renovated brown clapboard Stull Interpretive/Visitor Center. The center also features a summer youth day camp, tours, interpretive pontoon boat ride and school group programs. The bird room that features excellent labeled bird mounts is of particular interest to amateur naturalists. Also popular is the bird banding station and banding activities that are conducted on select spring and fall weekends. The center is open seven days a week from 10 a.m. 6 p.m. Memorial Day to Labor Day and 10 a.m. 4 p.m. Thursday-Sunday during the spring and fall.

A central theme of the interpretive center is teaching about the forces of wind and water on the park and how the natural transportation of sand from west to east threatens the park's recreational areas. Efforts to stabilize the beaches continue, including the construction of groins and breakwaters which retard the drift of sand. Since 1955 enough sand to fill 50 football stadiums have been trucked in to replenish the beaches along the western shore of the peninsula.

Monarch butterflies migrate through the long linear park in large numbers each fall.

Behind the center is a small garden with many wildflowers, including spotted touch-me-nots, blue flag, royal fern, marsh fern, New England aster, winter cress, clover, wild raspberry, common milkweed and others. Botanists will also find beach pea, lupine, wormwood, lyre-leaved rock cress, two prairie grasses, horsetail, white-stem pondweed and many more interesting species.

INTERPRETIVE BOAT TOUR: The free 45-minute interpretive ride into the lagoon is led by a naturalist who discusses natural history, cultural history, geology and other ecology-based topics of local interest. The tour departs three times daily during the season. The tour takes 20 people per trip and you must register at the interpretive/visitor center on a first-come first-served basis. The tour runs Memorial Day weekend through Labor Day.

BIRDING: Presque Isle is one of the best birding spots in the country. A checklist and locator map are available at the park office or visitor center.

One of the best birding hot spots is from beach No. 11. Use your spotting scope to scan the shallows for nesting terns and other stealth-like wading and shorebirds. Other birding spots include the Lily Pond, on the point just past the park office across the road from Beach No. 2; along the eastern half of the Sidewalk Trail; the Pine Tree Trail; the east end of the Dead Pond Trail; and Frye Landing. The Thompson Circle-

Pennsylvania State Parks

Dead Pond Trail is an excellent place to view the spring raptor migration.

More than 300 avian species have been identified in the park's diverse habitats, including some interesting accidentals like northern gannet, white pelican, reddish egret, greater white-fronted goose, cinnamon teal, eurasion teal, Swainson's hawk, golden eagle, northern bobwhite, king rail, Wilson's plover, snowy plover, surfbird, pomarine jaeger, long-tailed jaeger, Arctic tern, three-toed woodpecker, boreal chickadee, bohemian waxwing, dickcissel, lark sparrow, Henslow's sparrow, Harris' sparrow and pine grosbeak.

Many other species also frequent or are residents at Presque Isle, such as 12 types of gulls, 11 types of herons and bittern, 10 species of flycatchers, seven kinds of woodpeckers, many sandpipers, 16 species of birds of prey, dozens of wood warblers, six types of vireos, thrushes, wrens and dozens more.

Shorebird viewing can be exceptional after storms. Two excellent winter birds, snowy owls and northern shrike, are often seen in January and February.

WINTER SPORTS: The park is open year-round and cross-country skiing is popular on the five-mile matrix of trails. Ice fishermen also jig atop Presque Isle and Misery Bay with minnows and small lead-head jigs.

NEARBY ATTRACTIONS: Nearby are water slides, carnival rides, restaurants, ice cream shops, go-cart tracks, zoo, 23 golf courses, Ashbury Woods Nature Center, Children's Museum, Erie Planetarium, 20 marinas, Erie Art Museum, Warner Theatre and The Exhibition Hall.

INSIDER TIPS: The second week of May is the peak season for warblers at Presque Isle. Although the structure is closed to the public, you may walk by the impressive lighthouse near Beach No. 9. A calendar of environmental education programs is posted at the interpretive center. The gift shop inside the interpretive center has some excellent field guides and books on dunes and ecology.

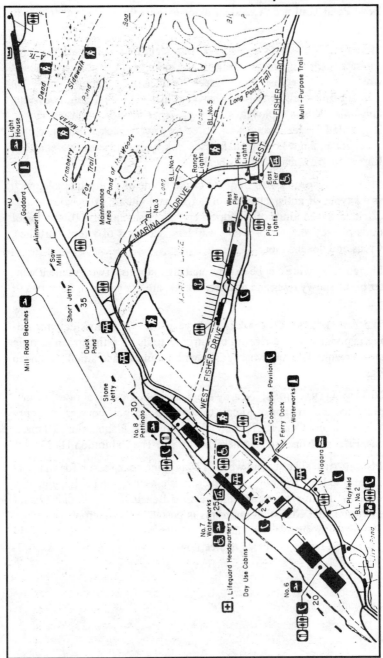

52 Prince Gallitzin State Park
Land: 6,249 acres   Water: 1,600-acre lake

Prince Gallitzin State Park is the focal point of an entire region of family attractions, breathtaking scenery, fascinating history, fun and recreation nestled in the Allegheny Mountains in western Pennsylvania.

Inside the park, the tree-lined, eight-mile Glendale Lake is the focal point. The lake can be up to 40 feet deep and helps to control the drainage of 42 square miles. It offers very good warm-water fishing, swimming, boating, camping, hiking and all kinds of winter recreation.

The park was named for Russian prince and Catholic priest Demetrius Gallitzin. He was born in Hague, Holland, in 1770 to a royal family. His father was a Russian prince and was serving as envoy to Hague when the prince was born. Young Demetrius was schooled by his mother and came to America in 1795 with a letter of introduction from Bishop Carroll. He entered Sulpician Seminary with the desire to become a priest. Father Gallitzin was the first Catholic priest to have received all his orders in the United States. In becoming a priest, he gave up his rights as Russian nobility and was assigned to the Conewago Mission in Pennsylvania some 60 miles from Baltimore.

Having an adventurous streak and a desire for his own parish, Gallitzin's wish was granted and he established a wilderness church called Saint Michael's, near Loretto.

Father Gallitzin was offered Bishophood in other areas of the United States, but he loved the area. He remained with his parish until his death in 1840.

Information and Activities

Prince Gallitzin State Park
966 Marina Road
Patton, PA 16668-6317
(814) 674-1000
(814) 674-1007 - campground, cabins, pavilion reservations

DIRECTIONS: In central Cambria County between Patton and Coalport, reach the park via PA Routes 36, 53 and U.S. Route 219. Under flapping state and U.S. flags, near a Smoky the Bear sign, large map and stump puller display is the angular park office that has a small brochure rack and information counter. The office is open 8 a.m. - 4 p.m. weekdays.

EMERGENCY NUMBERS: The park is on the 911 system; non-emergencies, call (800)-281-1680.

CAMPGROUND: Crooked Run Campground is one of the largest family-style campground in the state park system. And the campground contact station is the finest. It's comprised of 10 loops and 437 sites under tree-covered terrain on a number of contours and elevations. Sites have hard-surfaced pads, picnic tables and fire rings. Tent sites and others are intermingled. Prince Gallitzin is one of the most modern, well-kept and heavily used facilities in the system.

The park has seven bathhouses, one in the center of each main loop. All sites are reservable and the campground is open from the second Friday in April until the end of antlerless deer season in December. The campground is often full on weekends, with 80 percent of the sites booked in advance. Call ahead as soon as you know you plan to camp at this fine unit. There are five electrical sites, 421-425 for use by the physically challenged. Organized group camping for up to 120 people is available by advance registration.

In a large campground like this, users tend to cluster around amenities (beach, boat ramp, showers, store, etc.) that fit their needs. Campers who like open sites should inspect the Hemlock loop (sites 155-198) and a few sunny sites in the Hickory loop, 213, 215 and 216. Cherry loop, one of the flattest areas, is near a steep trail down to the lake where boats can be moored.

118 of the sites are large enough to accommodate RV rigs up to 50 feet in length; 135 sites can handle units up to 35 feet; and 184 sites are perfect for small units up to 20 feet in length.

Cherry loop is popular at the eastern end of the campground. Site 388 is a great place for tent camping. Many sites on the north outside perimeter of the loop have a partial view of the lake below and are small.

White Oak loop is shady and has a smaller interior loop near the modern showerhouse. Many campers choose sites in White Oak so they can moor their watercraft nearby. Sites 329 and 330 are excellent shady places for pop-up campers. Some of the sites like 335, 337, 339, 341, 343, 344 and 345 have a partial view of the sparkling lake through about 50 yards of small, scattered trees. Site 308 is a terrific large and open site for really big RVs.

Hemlock loop also has a small loop within it called the Spruce area that is near the showerhouse. Generally, sites in the Hemlock loop are spread out more than in some of the other loops. In fact, 188 is a big site for a trailer or motor home. The campground's only one-lane gravel boat launching area is between sites 175 and 177. A few of the sites in this loop will enjoy about one-half of the day in the sunlight. Fishermen and swimmers like the location of this loop, which is close to the beach and good fishing spots.

Hickory loop is heavily wooded with a small loop in the center that is near the showerhouse. Medium- to large-sized recreational vehicles can use most lots in this loop. Sites on the outside perimeter of the loop are backed up against a young-growth natural area.

Red Oak loop has pines overhead offering very shady and cool camping. The amphitheater is accessed from the back of this loop along a narrow walkway. Sites 131, 133 and 135 are especially shady and close to the showerhouse. Many tent campers choose this loop.

Maple loop, near the store and swimming beach, can accommodate larger RV rigs. Site 63 is near the water. Boats can also be temporarily moored along the shoreline. Many sites in the 70s have a view of the water and beach that is marked off with blue and white floating buoys and rope. Some play equipment is also around the mowed beach day-use area. The beach, playground, store and open spaces make this the ideal family loop.

Beech loop is the first loop upon entering the large campground. Sites 3 and 5 are popular, according to the campground host. Sites on the outside of the loop are backed up on a natural area. The mature trees and other aesthetics make this the most pleasing loop. Sites 19-35 have a good lake view. There's plenty of room between these sites and the lakeshore for children to play.

There is a three-mile bike trail that circles the campground. At the east end of the campground are a couple of camel-back dirt humps on the bike trail that the kids love to jump and drive over. Remember to bring the kids' bikes and helmets.

Just past the Beech loop is the camp store, which also has eight sets of washers and dryers. The cement block store is large as camp stores go, offering ice, toys, coolers, cold drinks, T-shirts, novelty items, cooking staples, small fishing supplies, firewood, public telephones, sunglasses, marshmallows and snacks.

CABINS: A split-rail fence outlines the entrance to the 10 modern family cabins that are open year-round. Also in the shady, rolling area above the marina is a fitness trail that offers warm-up equipment and a variety of exercise stations that combines science and imagination. There are warm-up games, strengthening games, cool-down games and other equipment.

Scattered at different elevations along a ridge above the lake are the popular cabins that are available by the week in the summer and nightly during the off-season. The newer modern cabins are log-style and have a hard-surfaced road and parking area.

Cabins are furnished and have a living area, kitchen/dining area, toilet/shower room and two and three bedrooms. The two-bedroom cabins can sleep six, while the three-bedrooms versions can sleep eight (one double and three bunks).

Cabin 10 is on the highest ground, while cabin 3 enjoys a view of the lake through some sapling-sized trees. Cabins 1 and 2 are near the water. Each cabin has newer picnic tables that are mounted on a single pillar, porch and a grill. Carved into the woods, cabin 8 is private and a good choice for families. If you like a lawn where small children might play, select cabin 7. With little car traffic, the cabins are ideal for family vacations. The cabins are within walking distance to the marina, but separate from the rest of the park.

FISHING: The children's bank fishing area is the perfect place to introduce kids to the joys of angling, especially in the evening when panfish will readily bite small live bait cast from the grassy shoreline.

Adult fishermen appreciate the many coves and 26 miles of shoreline along one of Pennsylvania's biggest lakes. During the spring, walleye are king. Local anglers recommend crawler rigs and crankbaits early in the season. Bass anglers tend to work the lower arms of the lake using spinners, some topwater lures in the spring and casting crankbaits near points and around underwater structures. Panfishermen do well with minnows, red worms and tiny jigs. Some good-sized perch and crappies are taken in deeper waters along the dam.

Glendale Lake offers some fair to good muskie. Visiting anglers should talk with locals and bait shop owners to learn the tricks and hot spots—if there are any. The key to hooking one of these monsters is to know the lake and be persistent. Because muskie feed only every two or three days, the key is to have your line in the water when they finally "turn on." Covering the water is also important. Try trolling between the main marina and main beach.

Ice fishermen take walleye with jigging spoons tipped with a minnow worked near the bottom. Panfish in the winter love waxworms. Ice fishermen will need to move regularly to find the fish. Go where you see other anglers catching fish.

BOATING: Pontoons, small sailboats and fishing craft bob at finger docks in the gentle waters of the narrow cove. The marina store (814-674-5029) offers boat rentals (pontoons, canoes, sailboats pedalboats, rowboats and motorboats), live bait, limited fishing tackle, sales, service, fuel, soft drink machine and marine supplies. The marina store is open 8 a.m. - 8 p.m. Monday - Friday and 7 a.m. - 8 p.m. weekends and holidays. A two-lane, hard-surfaced boat launch is at the marina. Non-powered boats and boats up to 10 hp are permitted on the 1,640-acre lake.

Beaver Valley boat launch, near the dam, offers mooring stations, eight sets of wooded-plank floating docks and a small one-lane ramp that is busy in the early spring. About 70 cars can park here.

Windsurfing is increasingly popular on the south end of the lake.

HIKING: Many trails at Prince Gallitzin are mowed, and some are challenging. The park has nine trails totaling nine miles in length, three miles of which are self-guided.

Turkey Ridge Trail (1.2 miles) begins at the main beach and is an easy walking loop that might bring you near deer, wild turkey and bleating songbirds.

Crooked Run Trail (1.5 miles) is along a cool mountain stream that has a scattering of rocks.

Point Trail (2.75 miles) is a rugged trail reached by following Crooked Run Trail. The trail is south of the campground, across the cove.

Poems Trail (.6 mile) is a unique nature trail that teaches nature lessons and more using poetry.

Obtain the self-guided booklet for the Forest Trail from the visitor center. Other trail information and simple trail maps are in print.

DAY-USE AREAS: More than 1,300 picnic tables are dispersed around the park, most of them in the swimming area and day-use areas 1, 2 and 3. Other picnic areas are in the boat mooring and launching ramps. Five picnic pavilions can be rented for a fee.

BEACH: The 200-yard sandy beach has a wonderful view of wooded mountains rolling off into the haze. The sectioned-off guarded beach is open from 11 a.m. to 7 p.m. daily Memorial Day weekend to Labor Day, unless otherwise posted. Adjoining spaces near the beach are grassy, shady and equipped with picnic tables, two sets of small play structures and benches, and busy picnic shelters.

NATURE: Overlooking the marina is the brown wood-framed visitor center, where a broad menu of seasonal environmental education and interpretive programs are provided to the public. Inside the center, spaced along the red tile floor, are educational displays, information about conservation programs, dioramas, bluebird nesting boxes, mounts, aquatic life displays, habitat samples, other natural history information and wall posters. A small feeding station is near a side door to the angular building.

Diverse habitats of standing dead timber, bog-like wetlands, mowed open areas, planted food plots, brushy fields and mixed hardwood forests offer wildlife and wildflower viewers an excellent chance to see many species along the network of hiking trails. From bear and deer to tiny wildflowers and shorebirds, every season has something special to offer.

Pennsylvania State Parks

Prince Gallitzin is an especially good state park for birding. A variety of interesting spring birds includes gadwall, common loon, lesser scaup, oldsquaw, bufflehead semipalmated sandpiper, least sandpiper, least flycatchers, Bonaparte's and ring-billed gull, and Acadian flycatcher. Staff reports that the spring warbler migration is strong and that shore birds like greater yellowlegs are often seen stabbing at the water's edge and running from the gentle lapping waves. Virginia and sora rails nest in the park.

The park also has a breeding population of cliff swallows that nest near the marina and other high grounds around the north end of the lake. Open grassland can yield sightings of grasshopper, vesper, field and Henslow's sparrows. Common raptors, Canada geese, Lapland longspurs, snow buntings, tree sparrow and evening grosbeak are often seen in the winter season. The beautiful migrating swans use Prince Gallitzin as a resting place in spring and fall.

HUNTING: Approximately 3,000 acres are open to hunting common game species like deer, turkey and rabbit. The area is known for quality deer hunting. Call the park for details about hunting.

WINTER: Ice skaters glide on the frozen waters of the marina cove during the winter, while cross-country skiers enjoy seven miles of mostly wooded trails. Ice boating (permit required) and fishing are also exciting cold-weather sports. Sledding and tobogganing take place on four acres of gentle slopes.

Snowmobilers may use the 20-mile trail network beginning the first day after antlerless deer season.

SPECIAL NOTE: In early August of each year is "Mountain Days," a celebration of art, crafts and food.

NEARBY ATTRACTIONS: Call the Cambria County Tourist Council for a list of area attractions at (814) 536-7993. They include Forest Zoo, Seldom Seen Valley Mine, Conemaugh Gap (the deepest gorge east of the Mississippi), Cambria County Historical Society, Johnstown Flood Museum and the famous Johnstown Inclined Plane, the steepest vehicular incline ride in the world.

INSIDERS TIPS: There are lots of small stores, private cabins and marinas around the lake. Walk the Poems Nature Trail and get inspired.

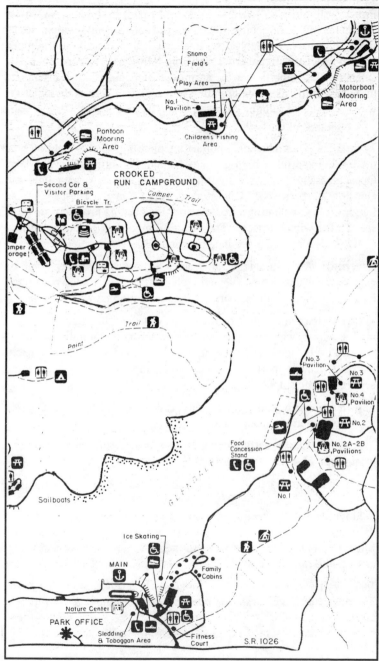

Shomo Field's

Play Area

No.1 Pavilion

Children's Fishing Area

Motorboat Mooring Area

Pontoon Mooring Area

CROOKED RUN CAMPGROUND

Second Car & Visitor Parking

Bicycle Tr.

Camper Trail

Camper Storage

Point Trail

No.3 Pavilion

No.3

No.4 Pavilion

No.2

No. 2A-2B Pavilions

Food Concession Stand

No. I

Sailboats

Ice Skating

MAIN

Family Cabins

Nature Center

PARK OFFICE

Sledding & Toboggan Area

Fitness Court

S.R. 1026

53 Promised Land State Park

Land: 2,971 acres Water: Two lakes, 615 acres

Fun is in full swing at Promised Land State Park.

But the park wasn't so much fun in the 1870s when Shakers settled to farm the area only to find rocky, poor soils, forcing them to move on. The name the religious group gave the area turned out to be a cruel joke. Today, the sprawling and scenic park is truly a promised land for campers, boaters, fishermen, swimmers, hikers, hunters and day users. The park is one of the busiest in the Commonwealth.

The land was purchased by the state and opened as a park in 1905. It was greatly expanded and developed by the Civilian Conservation Corps in the 1930s. The park is surrounded by the 8,039-acre Delaware State Forest which has many access sites, trailheads and outdoor recreation opportunities.

From May 10, 1933 until July 1, 1944, Promised Land State Park was also referred to as Camp Pocono and Camp S-139. One company of the Civilian Conservation Corps was established in the current Deerfield

Campground. Many worthwhile conservation and recreation projects were carried out during these years. The CCC boys constructed fire roads and trails, reforested areas, established campgrounds and built picnic shelters, buildings and bathhouses. In addition they built the park's 12 cabins on Bear Wallow Road. If you can still see wonderful evidence of CCC buildings and walkways throughout Promised Land.

Promised Land State Park is on a broad upland surface known as the Pocono Plateau. The high and low land surfaces are separated by only a couple dozen feet in elevation, and the slopes are rolling. However, the gentleness of the slopes doesn't mean that it is always easy walking. One of the outstanding features of the park is the abundance of boulders, rocks and outcroppings which lie in jumbled disarray throughout the tract.

After the ice melted from the last glacier, there were many depressions on the newly exposed surface. A few, such as Bruce Lake, filled with water and have remained lakes. Some of the depressions were shallow and remain as swamps, while other depressions went through a series of plant growth changes to become peat bogs, then firmer fields and forest covered lands that now characterize the park. (You can learn more about the geology of the park from a brochure called "*Ancient River and Ages of Ice,*" available at the park office).

Promised Land is the second or third most attended state park in the system. More than 75 percent of visitors to the park are from Pennsylvania.

Information and Activities

Promised Land State Park
R. R. 1, Box 96
Greentown, PA 18426
(717) 676-3428

DIRECTIONS: In Pike County, five miles south of I-84 along PA Route 390 or 10 miles north of Canadensis, along PA Route 390, the park is 100 miles from Philadelphia and New York City and a one-to three-hour drive from Allentown, Easton, Bethlehem, Reading, Harrisburg, Scranton and Wilkes-Barre. The park office is well-stocked with park and regional information. In-line skates and skateboards are not permitted in the park, restrictions exist on pets and firearms.

EMERGENCY NUMBERS: Fire, 676-9181; state police, 226-1862.

Pennsylvania State Parks

CAMPGROUND: 535 campsites are available in four tent and trailer areas (the Pines, Lower Lake, Pickerel Point and Deerfield). Campers have access to water and a dump station, but there are no hookups. More than 125,000 campers use the four areas annually. All of the areas are near swimming, boating, fishing, day-use areas and hiking trails. Pets are not permitted in the campground. The Pines Campground is at the northwestern end of Promised Land Lake. The Pickerel Point Campground is on a peninsula on Promised Land Lake and the Deerfield Campground is nearby nestled on a hillside of boulders and trees. Pickerel Point has a swimming beach. The Lower Lake Campground, at the western edge of Lower Lake, contains modern sanitary facilities with hot water, showers and its own beach.

Maximum stay in the camping areas is 14 days in the summer and 21 days in the fall. Pickerel Point Campground is open year-round, although the snow can get deep during the winter. All campgrounds are typically booked solid on the three summer holiday weekends.

The Lower Lake Campground, with a tiny boat ramp (and mooring) at its entrance, is comprised of four areas referred to as Beechwood, Northwoods, Hemlock Hill and Rhododendron. All four sections have flush toilets and hot showers.

The Beechwood area has its sites laid out in blocks, neatly trimmed and evenly spaced. The camping sites in Beechwood are paved. Sites are best for small to medium-sized RV rigs. Campers with larger travel trailers may want to inspect sites first, looking for the few that are wider than the others. Most of the sites are very much alike in this loop, mostly shaded, flat and along the hard-surfaced campground road. This is a modern camping area, with picnic tables and ground-mounted fire rings on top of a gravel bed.

Maybe the best sites in Beechwood are 329, 357, 366, 370, 374 (raspberry bushes next to this site!), 379, 384, 385, 405, 406 (near a fern-covered area) and sites along the outside perimeter. Sites 345, 347, 370, 372 and 414 are set aside as handicapped accessible sites. This camping loop has a huge population of chipmunks that scurry around, picking up food morsels and flicking their tails at oncoming bikes and slow-moving cars.

Northwoods Area is mostly a tent camping loop, with some sites on slightly varying elevations. Choose your site carefully; some of the sites are on an incline. This loop is more rustic and has a thicker canopy of mature shade trees, some of which are dead or dying. Site 444 is oversized, with a campfire-like fire ring. Sites 459, 461, 463, 465, 467 and 469 are well spaced out and backed up against a natural area.

Hemlock Hill is a fern-covered spur with hemlocks and maples offering dense shade. This is a quiet loop. The gravel pads are large enough for medium to large RV rigs. If you like full sun, try site 479. All of these sites are deep.

Rhododendron Area offers semi-random tent camping sites. Many of the nicely spaced sites allow you to park, then walk up the hillside a bit to flat tent camping spaces. Some of the best tent camping sites are in this secluded ridge-side section. A few sites have distant lake views, boulders strewn under light shade, and broader widths. Sites are grass and gravel, outfitted with picnic tables and fire rings. Some sites are thick with rock outcroppings and shaded by towering furry hemlocks. Sites 535 and 545 are the best sites in the section.

Deerfield Campground (opened in 1956) is a large, sloping rustic loop that is about 70 percent shady. At the entrance to the area is an attractive 40-foot clapboard auditorium with wood floors (piano and folding chairs inside). The CCC rectangular building is shaded by a huge oak tree. Stones are often piled up around the ground-mounted fire rings at sites that are shaded by younger trees. Campers can pitch a tent among the large boulders and rocks. Some sites also have a very distant view of the quiet lake. Some of the sites are also oversized allow for additional tents, chairs or other camping equipment. Site 307 allows campers to be among boulders and under thin trees. Campground 283 is set aside as an ADA sites, prepared for patrons with mobility limitations.

Pickerel Point (opened in 1934) is a long linear spur on a peninsula with shoreline camping sites at the water's edge. A small environmental education office is at the entrance to this popular, but sometimes crowded, loop.

Pads are of gravel and grass, with picnic tables and fire rings at each site. Virtually all of the sites are smaller than at the other campgrounds. The water-side sites (103 -126 and 219 - 249 are walk-in tent sites) are down a slope and popular. A tiny sandy beach with a grassy area and one lifeguard stand is at the tip of the peninsula and open seasonally. One of the best views in the park is from this beach.

The Pines Campground (which opened in 1950) is a single large loop off North Shore Road featuring 80 sites. This campground is open from Memorial Day to Labor Day. From site 40, campers can hike a hard-surfaced trail to the main beach and significant day-use amenities. A pencil-straight pine plantation and muffin-like boulders make up a large part of the area, offering visitors a chance to pitch a tent on pine needles and enjoy the airy environs. The tract is pleasant. Sunlight streaks between the tall pines and breezes can make their way to the ground, cooling off campers and keeping sites dry. Sites 8-31 are under huge pines; 76 and 78 are the deepest. All sites have gravel pads and picnic tables, but no hook-ups.

Sites along the outside perimeter are backed up against natural areas and often have a woodland view of a dipping ravine.

CABINS: Twelve rustic cabins (built by the CCC) are within walking distance to the beach. Cabins 3 and 4 are log and stone with green roofs and thick white chinking. They are tucked onto the hillside next to shady gravel parking places. Picnic tables are under the porches, and toilet facilities are nearby.

Cabins 5 and 6 have stone chimneys and are off the roadway about 40 yards. Cabin 7, called the Bald Eagle cabin, is near the rest rooms. Cabin 8, Kittaning cabin, and Cabin 9, the Moshannon are small wood frame cabins. Cabin 10 has the nicest porch, while Cabin 11, the Lackawanna, is nestled under a towering tree. Cabin 12, the most private, is at the end of the loop in a very shady section. Cabin guests can explore nearby wetland areas, a small creek, hilly tracts and nearby day-use areas.

FISHING: Lower Lake (173 acres) is stocked with trout. Common species to both of the lakes include large- and smallmouth bass, pickerel, muskie, yellow perch, sunfish and catfish. Many coves and weedy areas attract fishermen's attention during the spring and early summer. Fishing by the dam is also fair to good, where anglers crank spinners and drift live bait hung under bobbers. Ice anglers use small live bait and have the best luck in deep water.

The lakes have good underwater structures including stumps, weed beds and points along deep flats and shallow shaded covers. Many bank fishermen like areas near Conservation Island. The stumps and other shallows can be reached with shoreline casts in this area. Bank anglers like the small dam near the boat rental, says staff.

BOATING: The boat concession (717-676-4117), with porch and counter top-like window, is open seasonally 8 a.m. - 8 p.m. weekdays and 7 a.m. - 8 p.m. weekends, weather permitting. The park also offers seasonal boat mooring for small fishing boats. The small store also sells hats, limited fishing tackle, nets and soft drinks. Pedal boats, canoes and V-bottom boats are offered for hourly rental.

The two lakes offer paddlers a chance to explore deeply recessed coves, windy channels, an island, miles of wooded shoreline and clean waters.

There are four launches on Promised Lake and one on Lower Lake. Canoeists like the lakes because there are many places to beach and walk. Conservation Island is a favorite for canoeists to paddle around and eventually stop and explore. Paddlers might also see beaver and many active beaver lodges on the island's east shore. Try cruising the area in the evening for the best chance to see beaver and tall wading birds standing silently waiting and looking for their last meal of the day.

Paddlers will also find broad areas with dark water, lily pads and other aquatic plants like bladderwort. Many submerged plants that send flower stalks to the surface are fun to paddle near and examine.

Bruce Lake can be canoed, but only by a long portage.

HIKING: A total of 30 miles (on 16 trails) of mostly moderate hiking trails are in the park and Bruce Lake area.

Some of the more interesting trails include:

Little Falls Trail (1 mile) takes trekkers past a series of small waterfalls on the East Branch of the Wallenpaupack Creek. You will follow the creek for one-half mile and cross it on a wooden bridge.

Bruce Lake Road Trail (2.5 miles) is an old road that ends at Bruce Lake, a natural glacial lake formed when ice from the Wisconsin glacier gouged out bedrock and formed the depression. Glacial till was deposited at the south end of the lake, creating a natural dam. The lake is fed entirely by groundwater.

Egypt Meadows Road (.75 mile) passes Panther Swamp and ends at the Egypt Meadows Lake spillway. The lake was formed by the CCC in 1935. Before that time, the area was covered with hollow, soft meadow grass which was harvested and used as packing material for the famous Dorflinger's Glass Works in White Mills, Pa. The glass works began in 1865 and was the largest glassware center in the United States until after World War I, when competition from abroad made profitable manufacturing impossible.

Pennsylvania State Parks

Lower Lake Trail (.75 mile) meandering through hay-scented ferns, is used by deer as much as by hikers.

Bruce Lake Trail (5 miles each way) is swampy in areas, and you will see signs of beavers. Bring a lunch and spend a day hiking.

DAY-USE AREAS: Promised Land is a big, sprawling park with day-use areas scattered along the shores of both lakes. About 300 tables serve guests near parking areas, water, trash containers and comfort stations. The CCC planted more than 72,000 trees in the park during the mid-1930s.

SWIMMING BEACHES: Three guarded beaches are open 11 a.m. - 7 p.m. daily Memorial Day weekend to Labor Day. A small concession stand serves the main walk-in beach. The beach is on a sandy point and swimming lessons are occasionally offered. Many benches and picnic tables are clustered near there. The Pines camping area is near the main beach.

MUSEUM: The small museum is open 10 a.m. 4 p.m. daily in mid-summer and weekends during the rest of the year. The facility is staffed by volunteers. Inside are a one-man saw, 500-pound bear mount, nature videos, local history (including Civilian Conservation Corps), tools, historical photographs, wildlife identification, charts, firefighting equipment and other interpretive displays.

A renovated 20-row amphitheater is near the museum.

NATURE: Among the thick stands of rhododendron, mixed hardwoods, pine plantations and wetlands, many species of fauna can be viewed from the 30 miles of trails, edge areas and open fields.

The environmental education center, with small stone chimney, is in a brown building with shingled roof. During the summer nature walks and interpretive hikes, campground programs and other outdoor learning activities are scheduled. A blacksmith shop and small play area are nearby. All of this is at the entrance to the Pickerel Point camping area.

CONSERVATION ISLAND: Accessed by a stone bridge that water flows beneath and circulates through the aquatic vegetation, the scenic island has a high-quality self-guided nature trail (1 mile). The trail and its accompanying booklet describe forest communities, line art of various tree species describes mosses and lichen, rock ledges and geology, open areas, rhododendrons and the "mitten-like" foliage of sassafras, and has a poem by Joyce Kilmer. From the island visitors can observe thick aquatic vegetation and stump-filled waters that surround the island where a variety of wildlife nest, rest and feed.

About 145 species of birds have been recorded in the park including American bittern, bluebirds, bufflehead, indigo bunting, brown creepers, many ducks, flicker, three types of flycatcher, goshawk, northern harrier, kestrel, red- and whitebreasted nuthatches, three types of sandpipers, eight types of sparrow, five kinds of swallows, pine siskin, hermit and wood thrush, four species of vireo, many warblers and lots more.

The park has 30 species of reptiles and amphibians, 32 species of mammals, 94 kinds of trees and shrubs, dozens of mushrooms and fungi, and at least 150 species of wildflowers.

When walking through Promised Lane, be on the lookout for big trees. The park has five "champion trees," including a 74-foot-tall big tooth aspen with circumference of 56 inches; 96-foot-tall red maple with a crown spread of 45 feet; eastern hophornbeam with a height of 37 feet; 20-foot-tall rhododendron with a circumference of 16 inches; and an old apple tree that stands 39 feet with a crown spread of 40 feet.

The 2,765-acre Bruce Lake Natural Area has 2.5 miles of trails and contains two lakes: Bruce Lake, a natural glaciated lake of 48 acres, and Egypt Meadow Lake, an artificial lake of 60 acres adjacent to 100 acres of Balsam Swamp.

WINTER: Snowmobilers may use 27 miles of trails. Ice fishing and cross-country skiing are also popular in the park and neighboring forest lands.

HUNTING: More than 450 acres are open to hunting. Call the park for additional information.

INSIDERS TIPS: There are many neighboring attractions including mini-golf, shopping and cottage rentals. Check out the twig bench in the park office. The shoreline road that outlines the east side of the lake is a pleasant drive during all seasons.

NEARBY ATTRACTIONS: Call (800) 762-6667 for additional tourist information.

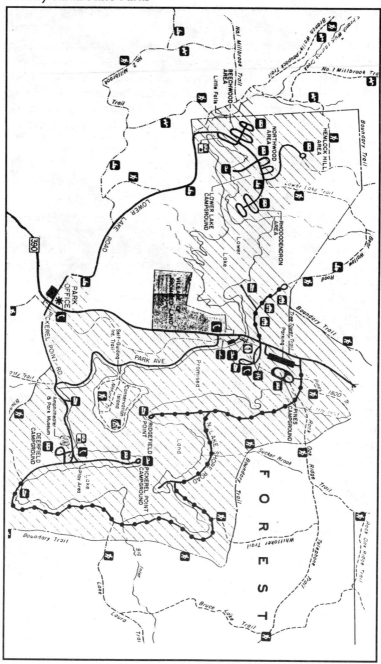

54 Pymatuning State Park
Land: 25,000 acres Water: 17,000-acre lake

Gov. Gifford Pinchot said at the 1934 Pymatuning Dam dedication, "All human accomplishments begin with a dream." The state began a dream by surveying and planning the Pymatuning Swamp in 1868. This historical "Pymatuning Act" was armed with $100,000 and a mission to conserve waters entering the Pymatuning Swamp and to regulate the flow of water in the Shenango and Beaver rivers. A secondary purpose is to use the dam and lake as a reservoir to impound flood waters during storms.

Today, Pymatuning State Park is the largest in the state. The surrounding lands, including a lake with 70 miles of shoreline, wildlife management areas and state gamelands, are visited by up to 4 million people annually. The region has incredible outdoor recreation facilities including 657 family camping sites in three areas, family cabins, hunting, fishing, boating, winter activities, wildlife museum, sightseeing, picnicking, hiking, eagle watching and nature study.

Pennsylvania State Parks

Pymatuning State Park lies on what was once a great swamp, and a popular Indian hunting area known to be inhabited by the Monogahela, Delaware, Seneca and other Indian tribes. By 1794, General Wayne defeated the Indians and the Treaty of Greenville was signed, clearing the way for the first settlers.

The earliest settlers were farmers who found the swamp a true hardship to clear, control and farm. Complete with quicksand, dangerous bogs, floating islands and predators, farmers soon fled the mosquitoes and tangled wetlands until technology advanced in the mid-1800s when draining the land was feasible. Onions proved to be the perfect crop for these moist, fertile soils.

About 50 years later the state began the major efforts of dam building, road improvements, advanced drainage systems and land purchases. Most of this work was completed by 1934, creating a reservoir 17 miles long with a capacity of 64 billion gallons. The park was dedicated in 1937.

One of the most popular activities at Pymatuning, which is an Iroquois Indian name for "the crooked-mouth man's dwelling place (which means a deceitful person), is fish watching along the Linesville Causeway and at the fish hatchery visitor center. The hatchery is one of the biggest in the country, producing an average of 100 million walleye fry each spring for distribution to lakes throughout the state.

Since the 1930s the park has continued to grow, adding the Tuttle beach area, a huge network of campgrounds, sprawling picnic areas and covered pavilions, boat launches, lake access, improvement for those with disabilities and much more.

Information and Activities

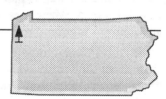

Pymatuning State Park
P. O. Box 425
Jamestown, PA 16134
(412) 932-3141

DIRECTIONS/INFORMATION: In northwest Pennsylvania on the Ohio border, take the Meadville exit from I-79. Travel west on U.S. 6/322 through Jamestown to the park office. Within a 100-mile radius are Erie, Pittsburgh, Youngstown, Meadville, Cleveland and New Castle. The small communities that surround Pymatuning are well stocked with bait shops, eateries, attractions and lodging.

EMERGENCY NUMBER: State police, (814)-336-6911.

CAMPGROUND: Pymatuning has 657 family camping sites in three areas.

Tuttle Camp Campground, open from the second Friday in April to the third Sunday in October, is on a point at the north end of the lake, near Tuttle Beach. Tuttle Camp has 139 non-electric sites and 62 electric sites. 17 of the electric sites and 33 of the non-electric sites can be reserved on holiday weekends. The small tan-colored camp office has a drinking fountain, picnic table and general park information near the small fitness trailhead.

The most popular camping sites are those near the water. Sites 445 and 447 are very sunny and near the water, while 327, 329 and 331 are non-electric sites also near the water. Virtually all of the sites in the 400s are separated by a wall of vegetation and are completely shady.

The camp store near site 419 features limited camping supplies, snacks, cold drinks, white gas, firewood and candy. Under a canopy of mature maples, oaks and scattered evergreens is a small spur of sites 413-420, near a short walking trail. Between sites 448 and 450 is a single-lane boat launch with a wooden mooring dock. If you like to be near a showerhouse, consider the heavily wooded sites 453 and 454. Sites 422 and 424 are partly sunny and back up against a natural area. Sites 99 and 101 have excellent morning sun.

All sites in Tuttle have picnic tables and ground-level fire rings. The 300-site loop offers good tent spots, especially sites 322, 324 and 325. They are level and have a partial view of the lake through the trees. Morning sun also warms sites 335, 336, 337, 339 and 340 at the north end of this loop. Many sites in Tuttle have enough parking space for an additional vehicle or boat and trailer.

LINESVILLE CAMPGROUND: A primitive but popular campground is open from the second Friday in April until the end of the antlerless deer season in December. Trailers up to 30 feet in length can use virtually any of the 125 sites in Linesville. During April and May, this campground is busy with anglers.

JAMESTOWN CAMPGROUND: One of the largest campgrounds in the state, Jamestown is also one of the busiest. Open from the second Friday in April to the third Sunday in October, Jamestown has 199 non-electric sites (55 of which can be reserved on holiday weekends) and 132 electric sites (27 can be reserved on holiday weekends).

The huge lake has many access points and shoreline day-use areas.

Maze-like, staff reports that two of the most popular areas are sites in the 300 and 600 loops. Many sites in these areas are dry and near the beach and lakefront. The rest rooms in the 600 loop are heated early and late in the season, making these popular areas for campers during the colder seasons. These are also the last rest rooms to be closed in the late fall. A double-car launch ramp and courtesy dock are behind site 615 and near good fishing areas on the lake.

The group camping area can accommodate up to 400 people.

CABINS: With knotty pine interiors, you'll be impressed with each of the 20 modern cabins. One cabin (No. 20) is completely accessible to people with disabilities. Five more such cabins are planned for the near future. Each cabin has a picnic table and grill on the small lawns surrounding them.

The cabins are all lakeside; 17 are two-bedrooms, sleeping up to six and three are three-bedroom sleeping up to eight they have no phone or televisions; a coin laundry is next to cabin No. 20. They may be rented by the week in the summer, and nightly in the off-season. Cabins have modern bathrooms, electric heat, carpeting and modern conveniences.

Cabin 7 is private and shady, 10 has a partial view of the lake, and cabins 11 and 12 are on a knoll that overlooks the sparkling lake below. Cabins 13-15 have a mostly obscured view of the water, but are more log-style and cozy. Cabins 17 and 19 are at the end of the loop and quiet.

HIKING: The park rarely leaves the shoreline, limiting much serious hiking. About three miles of trails are offered. You can ride horses or bikes on park roads. A small wildlife observation station is on the hiking trail. The longest trail starts in Tuttle Campground

BOATING: Three boat liveries operate on the lake offering full service, rental boats and some fishing information. Seasonal boat mooring is offered at the park. Non-powered and boats with up to 10 hp. motors are permitted on the lake. Boats with large engines are allowed, as long as the engines aren't used.

Windsurfers and small sailboats are becoming increasing popular on the lake.

FISHING: Walleye fishing has improved dramatically in the past 10 years on Pymatuning Lake. With stocked walleye, each spring is getting better and better. Early season walleye will chase crankbaits. Anglers who troll the points and cover plenty of water will find the ever-moving marble eyes. Anglers love Pymatuning because they catch a lot of fish. Granted, many are undersized, but the action can be fast.

Crappie fishing is very good in the coves during the spring and fall, and in deeper water as the summer warms up. The best crappie fishing is the last two weeks of May. Youngsters can have lots of fun catching crappies on just about any live bait with a bobber from shore in most day-use areas of the sprawling park. Large- and smallmouth bass, some muskie and carp are also taken from the lake. Ice fishing can be very good for walleye at twilight using jigs tipped with minnows about six inches off the bottom.

Waters near the hatchery are no-fishing areas. Many anglers congregate near the causeways, around Clark Island, in the north and south coves at Padaharam, and in other sheltered coves and small bays around the entire lake. Check with area bait and tackle shops for the latest hot spots and techniques.

DAY-USE AREAS: From the stone wall-lined road on top of the dam, day-use visitors can choose many excellent areas that are equipped with table, grill and rest rooms. At the south end of the park near the dam are pavilions, ball fields, open spaces, boat mooring, park office and good fishing.

Pymatuning has eight rental pavilions with electricity and four without.

BEACHES: Like most of the beaches in the system, they are open 11 a.m. to 7 p.m. daily from Memorial Day to Labor Day, weather and staff permitting. Four guarded beaches are operated in the park and are complete with bathhouses, sanitary facilities and food concession stands.

NATURE: The Pymatuning Laboratory of Ecology, operated by the University of Pennsylvania, and the fish hatchery are near Ford Island on the north end of the lake off U.S. 6. The park offers seasonal interpretive programs that include hikes, nature films, youth fishing and much more. Pick up a bulletin at contact stations.

Waterfowl watching is great at the park. Fall migrants include American black duck, northern pintail, northern shoveled, gadwall, American widgeon, canvasback, redhead, ring-necked duck, green-winged teal, and probably 20,000 Canada geese pass through biannually. Osprey and bald eagle watching is also very good. In the summer, shorebirds can be seen in ponds probing the shoreline and shallows for insects.

WILDLIFE MUSEUM: On a shady knoll in the center of Ford Island, the deep brown clapboard museum, now called the visitor's center, was built in 1938 to house a massive collection of more than 400 mounted bird specimens. Visitors should stop at the center immediately upon entering the park for orientation, rules, up-to-date wildlife sightings and other park information.

The museum is free and open 8 a.m. to 4 p.m. March 1 - November, often longer during the summer months. Standing along the edge of the patio are five telescopes and rustic log chairs. The popular facility is surrounded by an expansive mowed area and looks out over a huge marsh and lake where bald eagles are often seen nesting and soaring in the distance.

Inside is one of the most impressive displays of mounts in the eastern United States. Most of the specimens are behind glass and grouped by type. From songbirds to wading birds, raptors and ducks, you can see the birds up close–an excellent identification aid when you see live birds darting by in the field.

The diversity of specimens is too long to list, but there are rare birds like golden eagles, bitterns and smaller song birds. Owls, some common mammals and an entire display devoted to eggs are also in the well-lighted natural history museum near the information desk. One favorite display is the adult Canada goose cupping its wings as if it's on a glide path down to the lake's surface. The museum also interprets the need for nesting and resting areas for migratory waterfowl and the importance of wetlands preservation. Management techniques for these special lands are also discussed via interesting displays and posters.

Inside the multi-purpose room are red folding chairs, audio-visual equipment and a feeding station outside its window. The visitor center should be your first stop!

HUNTING: Call for details about waterfowl hunting.

WINTER ACTIVITIES: The fun doesn't stop when the snow flies. Try ice fishing, sledding, ice boating, cross-county skiing (4.7 miles of trails), snowmobiling or ice skating. Some winter sports equipment can be rented.

NEARBY ATTRACTIONS: they include a Fish commission hatchery, Baldwin-Reynolds House Museum, Drake Well Museum, Great Lakes Museum and Coast Guard Memorial Museum, Railroad Museum, Ohio state park (Pymatuning State Park) on the west bank of the lake, and the Andover Recreation Park playground for smaller children.

INSIDERS TIPS: Bald eagle watching from the wildlife museum/visitor's center on Ford Island is best in April, before the leaves come out. Spotting scopes are set up then. Spring and summer fish feeding at the spillway is a local tradition.

55 Raccoon Creek State Park
Land: 7,323 acres   Water: 101 acres

Raccoon Creek is nestled in a wooded valley in southern Beaver County, less than 30 miles from downtown Pittsburgh in a place where one of the finest wildflower reserves in the region can be found. More than 500 species of wildflowers have been identified in the 314-acre tract that offers an ongoing blooming season from late March to October.

Long before the park was developed, the historic Frankfort Mineral Spring was a popular gathering spot for those seeking a healthful vacation offered by the "healing powers" of the mineral waters. The health spa-like resort operated during the 1800s, and the shallow mineral pool and falls can still be viewed today. The Frankfort House served patrons to the springs for more than 100 years, closing in 1912. Fifteen minerals have been found in the waters. A short seven-minute hike along the stream from the parking lot takes visitors to the cool and shady falls.

The eastern half of the park is managed for low impact use, while the west—or middle—part of the park, with the wildflower reserve on the far west, is the site for camping, lake access, swimming, large day-use areas, playgrounds and much more.

The park has rich bottomlands, lots of standing dead timbers and significant populations of songbirds and other wildlife. The manmade lake offers fair to good fishing, lots of shoreline access and excellent springtime trout fishing. Traverse Creek, not Raccoon Creek, travels the entire length of the park. Raccoon Creek is located a few hundred feet to the west, making a horseshoe-shaped loop through the wildflower preserve.

Information and Activities

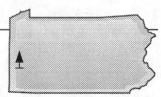

Raccoon Creek State Park
3000 State Route 18
Hookstown, PA 15050
(412) 899-2200

DIRECTIONS: From Pittsburgh take U.S. Route 22 or 30, or from the north take PA Route 18, which bisects the park. The park is on U.S. 30 seven miles west of Imperial. The park is open 8 a.m. to sunset daily.

CAMPGROUND: Spread through a wooded valley, Raccoon Creek family campground is composed of five loops offering 26 tent sites and about 150 sites for trailers. A playground near loop F is a busy area for family campers. Three showerhouses service the campground. The amphitheater in the campground is often used by the full-time parks naturalist for day and evening programs during the busy summer.

The campground is 80 percent shady. Three sites are accessible to persons with disabilities. The campground is typically full on holidays and weekends during the summer. The campground is open from the second Friday in April until the third Sunday in October.

The organized group camping area, much of which consist of terrific rustic Civilian Conservation Corps (CCC) buildings (this was once a CCC camp itself in the late 1930s), are near the cabins in the eastern portion of the unit. The proximity to Pittsburgh keeps the park busy during the entire season.

EMERGENCY NUMBERS: State police, 773-7400; ambulance, 899-2511.

CABINS: Located in the western, more quiet part of the park, the 10 modern cabins are booked solid during the warm weather period.

Pennsylvania State Parks

FISHING: In the spring, trout anglers gather along the banks of the lake casting Powerbait, a doughball-like bait sold in small jars. Most anglers roll the sticky and colorful floating compound into a pear-shape and place a slip sinker ahead of it. Many local experts say about 18 inches between the sinker and the floating bait work well in the springtime. The tree-lined narrow lake is only about 175 yards wide in most places.

BOATING: Boats are restricted to paddles or batteries and may launch from the one-launch ramp that has 42 mooring spaces. A small boat rental concession operates seasonally at the ramp, featuring ice and minor supplies.

HIKING/BRIDLE TRAILS: A Trail Guide to Raccoon Creek State Park available at the office details seven hiking and bridle trails that wander through the park. Complete with maps, legend, rules and regulations, the booklet is simple to use along the generally easy trails at the park. As mentioned, the trails in the wildflower reserve are excellent.

DAY-USE AREAS: More than 500 picnic tables and two large and four small shelters are scattered around the middle section of the rolling park. Many picnicking sites are under large trees and have newer rest rooms, grills and water hydrants nearby. Shelters can be reserved in advance. The renovated recreation hall is often rented out for weddings and receptions.

KINGS CREEK CEMETERY: Many pioneers are buried in the small, old cemetery.

BEACH: The small beach is a narrow band of clean sand about 25 yards wide and 100 yards long. The beach is guarded and open 11 a.m. - 7 p.m. Memorial Day to Labor Day unless otherwise posted. A newer cement block bathhouse, small food concession stand and day-use area look across the lake to the wooded shoreline in the distance. A small pier that extends into the lake is also nearby.

NATURE CENTER/WILDFLOWER RESERVE: The gray nature center was once an open-sided picnic shelter. Inside the interpretive building, which is at the trailhead to the wildflower reserve, are educational displays, a floor painted with animal tracks, interpretive posters, mounts, books and an observation room.

Complete with a large Ben Franklin wood stove, the center offers many types of environmental education programs year-round.

The wildflower reserve was developed by the Hickory Club (a sportsmen's club) and then sold to the Western Pennsylvania Conservancy in the early 1960s for preservation. The conservancy added adjoining properties to equal the present 314 acres. In the late 1960s, it sold the property to the state. The oak-hickory forest, with pine plantations, abandoned fields and floodplain forest, is the perfect place for hundreds of species of wildflowers to prosper.

Birding is very good at the park, including 11 birds of prey and other sightings like the common loon, pied-billed grebe, horned grebe, and during the migrations waterfowl like tundra swan, snow geese, Canada geese, wood duck, American black duck, northern pintail, gadwall, common goldeneye and many others. The eastern wood pewee is common in the spring, and 33 warblers have been sighted over the years.

SPECIAL NOTES: Universal Soldier and Pioneer Day is in May when military reenactments, pioneer craft demonstrations, musical entertainment and refreshments are offered.

A Guide to Raccoon State Park is available at the office. The park has seven hiking and birding trails.

56 R.B. Winter State Park
Land: 695 acres Water: 7-acre lake

Surrounded by 195,000 acres of rugged Bald Eagle State Forest, R.B. Winter State Park is a perfect launching point from which visitors can explore extensive natural areas or a vast craggy network of trails, visit a nearby buggy museum, trek the damp Shrouded Forest, snowmobile, cross-country ski, butterfly watch or just camp out and relax.

The unit originally was known as Halfway State Forest Park, because it was the halfway point through Brush Valley on the 14-mile Narrows Road. The winding settlers' road was struck before the turn of the 18th century, and is now a twisting state forest road called Sand Mountain Road. The Halfway House, near the park office, was a tavern where teamsters stopped to feed and water their horses and stay overnight. The dusty road was a primary route for transporting farm produce to the Susquehanna River and on to the barge canal system.

Some of the finest white pines ever cut in Pennsylvania came from this fertile area. Trees six feet across at the stump and 200 feet tall would provide enough wood to build a good-sized modern home today. Hikers can still find stumps of these giants in Pine Swamp. It took only a few years for the area to be stripped clean of timber however, spurring the Commonwealth to purchase the scarred land in 1905. Just four years later, during the drought of 1909, the area burned, completing the destruction. A few untouched areas remain in the park.

Minor improvements to the tract took place after these years, including the construction of a stone arch bridge that can still be seen today. But in 1933 the builders and rescuers came, and they were called the Civilian Conservation Corps. About 200 young men comprised the camp and began the task of clearing stumps and building a dam. The CCC also cleared the land of debris left by slashing lumbermen, developed good roads and built many public buildings and shelters.

The pleasant park was further improved by Raymond B. Winter, a young forester who came to the region to resurrect the forests and improve the lands. He worked for 45 years to bring back the area we now enjoy. After reading about Winter, I was delighted that the park is named for him.

Information and Activities

R. B. Winter State Park
R. D. 2, Box 355
Mifflinburg, PA 17844
(717) 966-1455

DIRECTIONS: In central Pennsylvania, Union County on PA Route 192, 18 miles west of Lewisburg. The park office is in the stone and wood Robert E. Klingman office building, open 8 a.m. - 4 p.m. daily.

R. B. Winter State Park manages three other properties: McCall Dam (day-use), Sand Bridge (day-use) and Ravensburg state park.

EMERGENCY PHONES: State police, 524-2662; ambulance, 911.

CAMPGROUND: Half of the 60 family camp sites are reservable between Memorial Day weekend and Labor Day. The northern section of the campground loop and the east spur have sites that can be reserved up to 30 days in advance. Sites have gravel pads, picnic tables and ground-mounted fire rings. Early summer campers will enjoy massive blooms of painted trilliums that dot the shady campground. Campers might also see and hear a variety of wildlife along the hillsides and cool ravines. The campground playground features a small wooden play cabin and other apparatus accessed by a small foot bridge. Many sites are different elevations and stretched along narrow low ridges.

According to staff, sites 30, 35 (easy to back into) and 50 are the most sought after (long trailers can use these sites). They are shady, like all sites, but more scenic and oversized. The upper sites along the south portion of the main loop are excellent tent sites (38, 40, 42, 44, 46, 53, 54 and 56). They are along the rocky hillside, private and set up on pads formed by lap-jointed landscape timbers. Site No. 9 is a terrific tent camping place that is backed up against a natural area and rock-strewn water gap. Sites 27-30 are at the bend of the loop and private. The campground also has a horseshoe pit and a drinking fountain near site 39. Site 57 is a deep site near the pit toilet building.

LODGE: The lodge is a modern log-style two-story house, with a full front and back porch. It sleeps eight with four bedrooms and a full bathroom upstairs. Downstairs guests will enjoy a living room, half-bath, dining room and kitchen. The house has modern appliances and wall-to-wall carpeting. Guests should bring their own cookware and utensils. The lodge is available to rent by the week in the summer, and daily in the off-seasons. Near the lodge are a basketball goal and volleyball court. Firewood is provided for lodge guests.

FISHING: The seven-acre stream-fed lake is impounded by a native sandstone dam on Rapid Run, offering fair to good cold-water fishing. The dam is situated just upstream of a deep-water gap through which Rapid Run exits from Brush Valley. In the distance, anglers will enjoy the 300-foot-tall mountain ridges that shadow the valley floor. Many anglers, both summer and winter, congregate near the breast of the dam or on the handicapped accessible fishing dock.

BOATING: No boating (including canoes) is allowed on the small lake.

HIKING: Most lake-related facilities and a hard-surfaced pathway are handicapped accessible. Walkers can circumnavigate the small lake, with most of the hiking on good trails. Some areas are soft and can be wet.

The park has 6.3 miles of easy trails, with only short stretches of steep inclines. The unit is an excellent starting point for backpacking treks into the sizable Bald Eagle State Forest. The Rapid Run Nature Trail connects to Lookout Trail, which leads to the lookout and its 300-foot elevation above the park. The mountaintops are about 500 feet above the valley. Lookout Trail is very difficult, with many high steps. My knees are still sore!

The Rapid Run Trail travels through the 39-acre Rapid Run Natural Area, where visitors will discover a bog, virgin wetlands, second-growth white pine, hemlock forest and many diverse habitats. Many large stands of oak are along the upper ridges of the entire park.

Along the Ridge Run Trail is the shrouded forest tract of the hemlock and white pine forests that once covered much of the state. Information available from the visitor center or park office describes the one-mile loop and has excellent line art of some of the flora and fauna you might see along the way.

In places, "the wood is so thick, that for a mile at a time we cannot find a place the size of a hand where the sunshine could penetrate, even in the clearest day...It is such a desolate region that I have often thought I might die of oppression," Conrad Weiser said in 1737, an early explorer of the area. The dense forest is a wonderful excursion for campers and day visitors to learn about the cool, damp woodlands. You will see white pine and hemlock regenerating, fast waters and still waters where tadpoles and salamanders wriggle, chances to see deep-woods birds like the crow-sized pileated woodpecker, flying squirrels or the dark-eyed barred owl that often sit on a branch near the trunk. If you listen carefully in the spring, wild turkey might also be heard clucking and crunching in the distance.

NATURE: The park naturalist offers evening programs, talks, hikes and youth programs for campers and park visitors in the campground and at the visitor/nature center that was built in 1995. The 52-foot-square center with pyramid-style skylights features an open teaching area, outdoor wildlife feeding station, interpretive displays, office, porch with benches, animal mounts, aquariums, lots of counter tops, hands-on learning area, fireplace, a place for small children, books and a quiet sitting area with cushions and an outdoor view.

Near the park office is a well-maintained butterfly garden (also a colonial herb garden) composed of bright-colored annuals and various wildflowers known to attract or provide food and habitat for fluttering butterflies and hummingbirds.

Butterflies depend on plants in many ways. The most successful gardens include plants which meet the needs of butterflies during all four stages of their life cycle: egg, caterpillar, chrysalis and adult.

After mating, female butterflies search for specific kinds of "host plants" on which to lay their tiny eggs. For example, monarchs lay eggs on milkweed; black swallowtails on parsley; and Eastern tiger swallowtails on tulip trees or wild cherry.

In only days, caterpillars emerge from the carefully placed eggs and begin to eat and eat and eat. They are very selective eaters, however, and feed only on specific kinds of plants. If the desired plants aren't available, the slow moving caterpillars starve rather than eat another type of vegetation. My dog seems to be like this, too. Usually female butterflies lay eggs on or near the plants their offspring prefer to eat. Most caterpillars feed on native plants and are not considered agricultural or ornamental pests.

In a few weeks when the caterpillars are fully grown, they shed their skin for the final time and change into chrysalises. Inside each chrysalis, the body of an adult butterfly is almost magically formed. Often chrysalises are attached to plant stems and protected by surrounding vegetation.

After emerging from the chrysalis, the adult butterflies gain their wits–assuming they have wits–and soon begin to search for nectar-rich flowers to feed upon. Plants are important to butterflies during each stage of their life cycle. A garden designed with this in mind attracts the largest number and greatest variety of butterfly visitors.

R.B. Winter's garden features plants that offer nectar and a food source for caterpillars. Home gardeners can learn a lot from visiting the small garden, including some practical suggestions on which plants attract the beautiful insects. Nectar plants include goldenrod, milkweeds, asters, red clover, buddelia, phlox, red clover, Joe-pye weed, bergamot, lilac, thistle and black-eyed Susan. Caterpillar food plants include dogbane, milkweed, wild carrot, rue, willows, birch, cherry, nettle, rose, apple and violets.

Other plants that round out the garden might include yarrow, salvia, lavender, coneflower, butterfly bush, queen Anne's lace, sweet William, bee balm, daylilly, zinnia, verbena, cosmos, daisy, fleabane, sedum and fennel.

Many plants that attract hummingbirds are also mingled into the design of the garden. Like butterflies, hummers are attracted to nectar producing plants, especially those that are red. Talk to the staff naturalist about butterfly and hummingbird garden design. They are simple and easy to maintain.

Other birds that you might see in the park include hermit thrush, scarlet tanagers, wood thrushes and breeding birds like eastern phoebe, hummingbirds, swallows, at least four types of warblers, veery, belted kingfishers and many others.

Interesting migrant birds seen in the spring or autumn are fox sparrow, bufflehead, common merganser, yellow-bellied sapsucker and a variety of warblers. Year-round residents include pileated woodpeckers, barred owl, brown creeper, nuthatches, cedar waxwings, song sparrows and sharp-shinned hawk.

Nature buffs might also want to hike park roads southwest of the lake and see some wonderful examples of succession and dark, damp woodland tracts.

DAY-USE AREAS: Three bulky picnic pavilions grace the grounds and are often busy with hungry visitors and family groups gathering on weekends. About 350 tables and many grills are scattered around the park. Many of these are in shady areas near the lakeshore.

The scenic stone masonry dam at R.B. Winters is the first dam built by the Civilian Conservation Corps in the country. It was completed in 1934. The rushing spillway is pretty and cool place to visit on hot summer days. Staff says the dam is equally beautiful in the winter. It never freezes and the cascade of moving water splashes cold and icy, leaving interesting ice formations and a pleasing snowy view.

A Keystone-shaped warming hut near the beach is used by winter hikers and cross-country skiers. It is equipped with two picnic tables, skylights and a wide fireplace.

BEACH: You can spread you toes in the sandy along the 125-yard long guarded beach that is open from Memorial Day weekend to Labor, 11 a.m. - 7 p.m. The water is divided into patrol sections by a white rope and yellow buoys. Two lifeguard stands and a handicapped ramp are along the small swimming area. The changing house has chemical toilets.

Behind the changing house, the food concession serves hot dogs, hamburgers, chips, cold drinks, bulk ice and ice cream treats. Three horseshoe courts stand ready for action close to the yellow sandy beach. Handicapped accessible picnic tables are also scattered around the many day-use areas, including the shady and scenic spots near the lakeshore and swimming area.

WINTER: Snowmobiling is permitted on 30 miles of trails in the neigh-

Fishing and relaxing are popular at the tidy park.

boring state forest. Cross-country skiers can also use the rolling five miles of trails inside the park.

INSIDERS TIPS: Watch acrobatic hummingbirds hover at the park office's red feeding station. Mountain bikers should pick up a copy of the *Mountain Biking Guide to the Bald Eagle State Forest*, Central Region (a free pamphlet with map) from the office. The area also hosts a yearly autumn mountain bike jamboree.

McCall Dam State Park
(717) 966-1455

At the east end of Centre County off PA Route 192, McCall Dam has a small day-use area with a few grills, comfort station and a lightly used organized group tent camping areas. The tiny tract is four miles from R. B. Winter State Park. The park was once the site of a saw and shingle mill, which ranked among the largest of its day.

Ravensburg State Park
(717) 966-1455

To reach the park, take PA Route 880, eight miles southeast of Jersey Shore or eight miles north of Carroll, exit 28 on I-80. The park is in a steep-walled, rocky gorge carved by Rauchtown Creek on the side of Nippenose Mountain. The park was named for ravens that roosted on the rock ledge at the southern end of the park. Raven are still seen in good numbers at the park.

Camping at 76-acre Ravensburg State Park is primitive. The wooded area is outfitted with pit latrines and is near the Rauch Creek. The campground is open on the second Friday of April until the third Sunday in October. Future plans for a showerhouse will make this campground more popular. But for now, it's a great secluded getaway camping area. There is no office at Ravensburg; friendly park rangers monitor and help campers. There are four pavilions and more than 100 tables at Ravensburg State Park.

Rauch Creek (pronounced "rock" creek) has stream-bred trout and often has holdovers from club-stocked fish. The creek, like Cold Run and Locust, is a sleeper, depending on the time of year, water quality and hatches. Not many anglers froth the improving waters. Dunes and various colored caddis patterns work the cool, shaded streams.

A small playground, trails, open spaces and picnic tables are the major features of the wilderness park. Hikers can access the Mid State Trail that bisects the linear park. The park is bordered on three sides by the Tiadaghton State Forest.

The most interesting connector trail at the park is Castle Rock. It offers geology-minded hikers a chance to see rock outcroppings and other exposed strata that were deposited, eroded and are still changing. The view is wide and worth the semi-vertical trek. Wildflowers enthusiasts will love the spring season and the large population of Canadian yew.

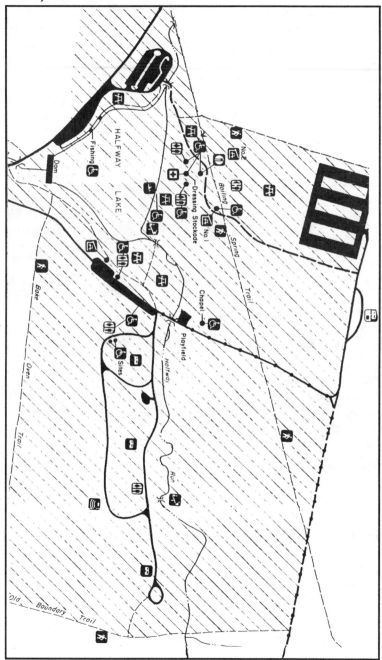

57 Reeds Gap State Park
Land: 220 acres Water: Honey Creek

Scenic mountain streams strewn with smooth boulders run year-round, offering great fishing and a tranquil atmosphere. The shady streams carved around the park and throughout the region attract visitors today–and did so for settlers 200 years ago. In fact, the park is named for pioneers Edward and Nancy Reed.

Native Americans from the village of Ohesson, near today's Lewistown, used this valley as a hunting ground. Later, European settlers came to the valley for the same reason, naming it New Lancaster Valley.

The first day-users to the area were homesteaders and others in the 1700s, who used the area as a bush meeting ground. The settlers would pack lunches and travel in their horse-drawn wagons to hear a circuit preacher and enjoy pioneer fellowship. These meetings, also known as homecomings, were held through the mid-1920s.

Honey Creek was the site of a water-powered sawmill set up in the mid-1800s by Edward Reed just inside the western park boundary. Part of the dam remains and is still visible along Honey Creek Trail. About 1900, a steam-powered sawmill was located by the park's maintenance building. Only four years later, the Commonwealth bought large tracts of depleted forest lands to become Reeds Gap and Poe Valley state parks.

In the early 1930s, enterprising small business people began selling 5-cent soft drinks cooled in Reeds Gap Run to attract picnickers. By 1933, the Civilian Conservation Corps established a camp for 200 men, and Reeds Gap was soon being developed for recreational purposes. By the late 1930s, the area featured play equipment, picnic pavilions and a bandstand. Swimmers began enjoying the small lake formed by a CCC-built dam on Honey Creek.

These days swimmers are restricted to the pool that was built in 1965. Also during this time, many upgrades were completed, including flush toilets, a modern bathhouse, concession stand, water system and maintenance buildings.

Information and Activities

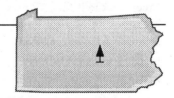

Reeds Gap State Park
483 Park Drive
Milroy, PA 17063-9735
(717) 667-3622

DIRECTIONS: Follow U.S. Route 322 from Milroy by following park signs for seven miles. Regular office hours are 8 a.m. -4 p.m. daily, 8 a.m. to 7 p.m. Saturday and 11 a.m. to 7 p.m. Sunday. Warning: Many Amish people live in the region. Watch for horse-drawn buggies.

EMERGENCY NUMBER: 911 system.

CAMPGROUND: The park has 14 tent sites. The shady area is between parking lots D and E. The most popular site is 7 because it's an extra private walk-in site. Sites 11-13 are also excellent, shady sites. Two wooden bridges connect the campground to the day-use areas.

HIKING: the Reeds Gap interpretive trail has eight aluminum signs along its 1.7-mile length along the creek explain a variety of natural history features and concepts, including the forest floor, tree canopy, diversity of wildlife, the role of the forest and more. The trail starts near the food concession stand and is easy walking. The Flicker Trail (.5 mile), Blue Jay Trail (1.3 miles) and Honey Tree (1.8 miles) are moderately difficult trails inside the park.

The Reeds Gap Spur is the longest side trail in the Mid State Trail system. The spur uses existing trails and marked in blue blazes. The spur is rugged going, demanding long pants and sturdy boots. It goes across the grain of the ridge and valley, requiring more than 3,100 feet of climbing. The spur is not a one-day hike. Primary campsites are at Little Wiekert Run and in Bear Gap. A forestry map may be available at the park office for the spur.

FISHING: Honey Creek is stocked with rainbow and brown trout. Shoreline fishing places are abundant. You may wade this stream.

Penns Creek is the most famous limestone stream in middle Pennsylvania. The stream, near Reeds Gap, cuts through Poe Paddy State Park. The creek has it all—strong hatches, open spaces, good water conditions year-round and terrific scenery. Locals say the action slows after June 1. Fly fishermen who stick around for the Golden Drake hatch in late June, and other drakes and mayflies the rest of the summer, can have great fun. The stream can get very warm around Poe Creek after mid-July. Some of the best action on Penns Creek is in the lower section around Wiekert in late April, while big caddis hatches come off for many weeks to follow.

DAY-USE AREAS: Four pavilions (three are reservable), open spaces and a swimming pool (free) are the major attractions.

The slightly elevated pool is two to five feet deep. The green block showerhouse and food concession with two picnic tables are stationed nearby. Benches and a sunning deck accommodate parents and spectators. A small wading pool is enclosed in a fence for smaller children to splash in. The pools total about 4,000 square feet.

The seasonal eatery serves hot dogs, burgers, subs, onion rings, chips, soft drinks and ice cream.

NATURE: Nature lovers will relish the quiet and pristine nature of the area. Birding is good in the park. Expect to see barred owls, and listen for pileated woodpeckers banging away in the distance. Other avians include barn swallow, black-and-white warbler, flicker, red-tailed and red-shouldered hawk and a variety of smaller woodpeckers. No bird or flora lists are available.

WINTER: Snowmobiling and cross-country skiing are offered on service roads and open spaces.

INSIDERS TIP: Some of the most scenic mountain streams are in and near Reed Gap State Park. Penns Creek is nationally known.

Poe Valley
(814) 349-8778

There is no paved access to either Poe Valley or Poe Paddy. Each park requires about eight to 10 miles of travel on good gravel forestry roads. The parks are worth the ride.

Campers cluster around the breast of the dam that retains the 26-acre lake at primitive Poe Valley State Park. The first sites to go, according to staff, are 69, 71, 73, 75 and 77. The campground is mostly shady, with sites near the dam getting more sunlight than others. The campground is open the second Friday in April to the end of the antlerless deer season. There are pit latrines only at this rolling campground.

This 630-acre unit has a small boat rental, seasonal naturalist programs and a 600-foot groomed beach. The facility has about 150 picnic tables. Lake fishing is popular during the early part of trout season. Hikers can connect to the Mid State Trail or other hugged foot trails that wander the neighboring Bald Eagle State Forest.

Day-trippers can discover caverns, a railroad tunnel and other nearby rustic attractions in this remote part of the state.

Poe Paddy State Park

At the confluence of Big Poe Creek and Penns Creek, four miles east of Poe Valley State Park (on gravel road Big Poe Road), the 25-acre park is located on the site of Poe Mills, a prosperous, but short-lived, lumbering town of the 1880s and 1890s. A railroad once served the community of about 300 people. The park was constructed by the CCC in the 1930s.

Campers will like sites 121-125 along the excellent trout stream, Penns Creek. Poe Paddy has two organized group tent areas that are popular with school and church groups. The park has 43 flat, primitive sites with gravel pads and two Adirondack lean-tos. The park has about five acres of forested wetlands, a ravine and mixed deciduous/coniferous forest. About 10 picnic tables are in the tiny park.

Tubers often take the cutoff from Penns Creek through an old railroad tunnel for some fun summertime floating.

58 Ricketts Glen State Park
Land: 13,050 acres Water: Two lakes

Ricketts Glen, which almost became a national park in the 1930s, is the crown jewel of the Keystone State's parks system. It will take several days to properly explore the state park and Glens Natural Area, a Registered National Natural Landmark. A scenic and huge park, it is best known for 22 beautiful waterfalls that lie along two branches of Kitchen Creek in the Glens Natural Area. The highest waterfall exceeds 90 feet, and others tower to 40 feet in height.

Ricketts Glen is named for Col. Robert Bruce Ricketts, who enlisted as a private in 1861. Eventually, he fought in the Battle of Gettysburg, leading Battery F, one of the units that turned back Picketts Charge. After the war, he bought vast tracts of virgin timberland in the region, seeking peace and the solitude of nature. On his first deed, he listed his address as "Army of the Potomac." Ricketts bought heather from Scotland and planted it, and eventually his land holdings totaled more than 80,000 acres. The Colonel was buried beneath soaring hemlocks.

His heirs sold much of the land to the state Game Commission in the

1920s. The first transaction authorized by the legislation covered 1,261 acres, and subsequent sales by Rickets' son in 1943 and 1949 raised the size of the park to about 10,000 acres (later expanded to 13,000 acres).

The famous falls on Kitchen Creek were discovered about 1865 by two fishermen staying at the Stone House Tavern, a sporting lodge owned by Ricketts. Col. Ricketts named several of the falls for friends and relatives before he died. The highest falls, Ganoga at near 100 feet, was named after Ganoga Lake. Because it was so hard to fish the falls, Ricketts hired Matt Hirlinger and six other men in 1889 to build the present trail and stops around the falls. This monumental task wasn't completed until 1893, four years of hard work later.

Ricketts Glen State Park is a wonderful park. It is perfect in all seasons. In the spring the waterfalls run full. During the summer the glen is cool on the hottest days, and in autumn the sun begins to penetrate colorful foliage. Each falls seems surrounded in a swirl of color. Few people visit the trails that are laid out in virgin timber along the waterfalls in the winter.

Information and Activities

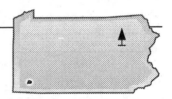

Ricketts Glen State Park
R. R. 2, Box 130
Benton, PA 17814-8900
(717) 477-5675

DIRECTIONS: 30 miles north of Bloomsburg on PA Route 487. This section of Route 487 is steep from Red Rock to Lake Jean. Caution should be used if you are towing a large travel trailer. The park sprawls across Columbia, Luzerne and Sullivan counties.

Park elevation is 2,400 feet. The brown clapboard park office has a variety of visitor services and a listing of nearby service providers (churches, markets, laundry, kennels, etc.). A naturalist and other staff are often in the office to answer questions.

EMERGENCY NUMBERS: State police, 542-4117 or 928-8126.

CAMPGROUND: Open year around, sites have gravel pads, picnic tables and fire rings.

Loop 1-73 is segmented into small groups of camping sites. The loop is on a peninsula, with perimeter sites having a distant, sometimes

The park has 22 scenic waterfalls and wide trails that access them.

obscured view of the lake. One of the big advantages of the sites in this loop is their large size. Many of the sites are also separated by varying widths of vegetation and shrubs.

Sites 64 and 65 are at the end of the loop and next to the water's edge. Site 64 would be an especially good tent camping site, or a place where a smaller RV unit could be parked. Bring you cartop boat and hand launch it from your camping site.

Some sites near the water also have large boulders, offering extra seating and visual pleasure. The shoreline is soft in places, but the view is excellent of waterfowl and small boats with fishermen putting back and forth in boats powered by electric motors on Lake Jean. Many campers choose the small lakeside spur with sites 35-39 that are gently elevated and near the lake. This small spur is airy and has reasonable access to the water. Other excellent water sites are 20 (very private), 22, 29 and 31. Site 26 is oversized and deep, great for an extra tent or large RV rig.

Loop 75-120 is shady. Sites on the outside perimeter are backed up against natural areas. Most sites in this loop are adequate for medium-sized RV rigs. Airy, breezy and fern covered, the young forest in this tract is pleasant, cool and appealing for tent or RV campers. Sites 94 and 120 have an obscured view of the lake. Temporary boat mooring is allowed along the shoreline in the campground. Sites 115 and 117 can be damp; 106-113 are scattered up the grade and said to remain dry after showers and spring melts.

Organized group camping for about 125 people is available in the park.

CABINS: You can walk to the falls from the modern cabin area, where 10 of the units are at the east side of the park. The cabins, open year-round, are furnished with a living area, kitchen/dining, toilet/shower and two or three bedrooms. A young forest surrounds the cabins, offering more sunlight than is often found around woodland cabins. Advance registration is required.

Cabin E is in an airy spot, about half shaded. Cabins A, D, G, E, F, and J share driveways. Each cabin a small porch, picnic table and fire ring. Cabin C is on a knoll and gets sunlight during much of the day. The small road that serves them is quiet, making the cabins an excellent vacation spot for families with small children.

THE FALLS: You'll hear them before you see them, and you won't forget them for a long time. Moss covered and well-worn, the trail along the falls helps build excitement for the sometimes challenging walk next to them. Some of the steps are steep and can be slippery. A trailhead sign describes the elevations of the falls and other information.

As you descend along the falls, the cool mist from several of the cascades can be felt and the rush of water tumbling over the rocks heard louder and louder. A series of trails, covering a total of five miles, parallel the streams as they course their way down the glens.

"As long as I live, I'll hear waterfalls and birds sing, and get as near the heart of the woods as I can." John Muir.

Each of the falls is different than the next. The first waterfall is Murray Reynolds, divided and rippling more than 16 feet wide. Sheldon Reynolds is next, a wide sheet of water cascading 27 feet down a smooth rock face, splashing and sending a thin mist above the pool. Like eating potato chips, once you start it's hard to stop wanting to race to the next cascade, which doesn't remotely resembles the last.

PHOTO TIPS: To freeze the falls, use a camera shutter setting of 1/250 or faster. At this speed you'll get crisp, stop-action photos. For soft, dreamlike, milky falls, shoot pictures at 1/15 or slower. Use a tripod at these slower shutter speeds.

FISHING: Half-log benches near the dam are a common place for anglers to toss live bait, bobbers and warm-water denizens. Bait is available at the Red Rock store or at the beach concession. Bass, muskie, rough fish and panfish are taken from the lake. Nearby streams and the adjacent 40-acre Mountain Springs Lake has fair to good trout fishing.

BOATING: Electric or human-powered boats only are permitted on 245-acre Lake Jean. Thirty seasonal mooring slips and one launching ramp serves the park. A small boat rental is near the beach.

HIKING: At the base of the park on Route 118, the half-mile Evergreen Trail is a wonderful pathway to explore, observe and discover natural communities. The Evergreen Trail offers an excellent view of the final series of falls as it meanders through a majestic stand of towering white pine and wispy conifers.

"Nature will bear the closest inspection: She invites us to lay our eyes level with the smallest leaf, and take an insect view of its plain. Every part is full of life." Henry David Thoreau.

BRIDLE TRAILS: Trail riders can mosey along five miles of horse trails.

DAY-USE AREAS: Extensive picnic facilities are scattered around the park, at Lake Jean and the lower areas off Route 118.

SWIMMING BEACH: The sandy guarded beach is about 130 yards long and 30 yards wide along a gentle, broad cove. A small block-style food concession serves the usual snack foods plus some limited camping supplies including paper plates, charcoal lighter fluid and ice. The swimming area is open from 11 a.m. to 7 p.m. Memorial Day weekend to Labor Day. Lifeguards patrol the swimming area, while grassy areas nearby provide for a variety of day-use activities. Children 9 years and under must be accompanied by an adult. The beach, with a wonderful view of the surrounding tree-lined shore, features a hard-surfaced handicapped access ramp into the water.

The modern bathhouse with wood shake roof has a telephone, stump-like benches and picnic tables around it. The beach is one of the cleanest, sandiest, and nicest in the parks system.

NATURE: Ricketts Glen is best known for its spectacular waterfalls. Yet knowledgeable outdoor visitors will know the area (Glens Natural Area) to also be where northern and southern hardwood trees meet, making the diversity of habitat, flora and fauna extraordinary. Some of the giant pines, hemlocks and oaks are more than five centuries years old, with some fallen trees dated more than 900 years old, having a diameter more than five feet.

The park is also well-known for its terrific wildflower population that includes trilliums, various orchids, white baneberry, gentians, hawkweeds, wake robin, blue flags, turtleheads and meadows full of goldenrod and aster in the fall.

Two branches of Kitchen Creek cut through the deep gorge of Ganoga (which means *"water on the mountain"*) Glen and Glen Leigh, unite at "Waters Meet," and then flow through Ricketts Glen among the giant hemlocks and oaks.

The Glens is a wild, Y-shaped gorge cut back into the resistant rocks of North Mountain by Kitchen Creek. The elevation drop within the Glens area is about 1,000 feet in a distance of 2.25 miles. Most of the drop takes place in Ganoga Glen and Glen Leigh above their junction at Waters Meet.

Erosion of the Kitchen Creek gorge began several million years ago. Ganoga Glen, Glen Leigh and Ricketts Glen owe their present rugged configuration mainly to the erosion power of glacial meltwaters that rushed down these ravines during retreat of the last huge ice sheet. The youthful nature of the Glens is shown by the fact that they contain at least 25 distinct waterfalls (22 of them named). At least three times in the last million years, continental glaciers buried northeastern Pennsylvania under hundreds of feet of ice.

Although evidence of the first two glaciations is sparse in the park, the last left an extensive record as it advanced in a south-southwesterly direction about 15,000 years ago. The glacier scoured up loose soil and rock, plucked large blocks of sandstone and conglomerate from outcropping ledges, and abraded grooves and fine striations into the underlying bedrock pavement. When the ice front retreated to the northeast, a layer of bouldery glacial till was left behind, filling in old valleys and creating swamps, flat uplands and, of course, waterfalls.

While each falls in the Glens has it owns unique beauty, two general types can be recognized. Where the creek descends over thick sandstone in the Huntley Mountain formation, distinctive "wedding cake" falls result, as exemplified by F. L. Ricketts Falls. Typical falls in the Catskill formation, on the other hand, are of the "bridle veil" type and consist of a relatively hard caprock (usually gray sandstone) overlying a softer layer (red shale) that commonly forms a recess at the base of the falls. An example of this latter type is Harrison Wright Falls.

Environmental education programming is offered, including campfire programs, guided hikes and others.

Naturalists often teach about the waterfalls, geology and aquatic life. How could anything live in a waterfall? Some things do, according to staff. For example, the met-winged midge larva looks like a row of six tiny black beads stuck on a rock. Six suction cups, complete with oozing cement and waterproof hairs, help the little midges cling to rocks. Female midges dive in the fastest water to lay eggs that they glue to the rocks. The larvae hatches from the eggs.

The caddisfly larvae builds a net to snare food as it rushes by. The insect hides in a rock crevice near the net and waits for prey to get caught. Sometimes the caddisfly loses its footing, floats downstream and tries to take over another caddisfly net. The two insects battle until one, usually the intruder, backs off.

Mayfly larvae, as most fly fishermen know, have built-in filter baskets. They face upstream and hold bristle-covered front legs together to strain food.

WINTER: Ricketts Glen is open year-round. More and more winter-season visitors are coming to the park to cross-country ski, ice fish on Lake Jean, camp, hike the falls trail or snowmobile on designated trails.

HUNTING: More than 83,000 acres of state game lands to the west and north of the park, plus 9,000 acres in the park, are open for hunting. Call the park for details.

INSIDERS TIPS: From the Grand View Lookout, visitors can see 11 counties and three states. Its elevation is 2,449 feet.

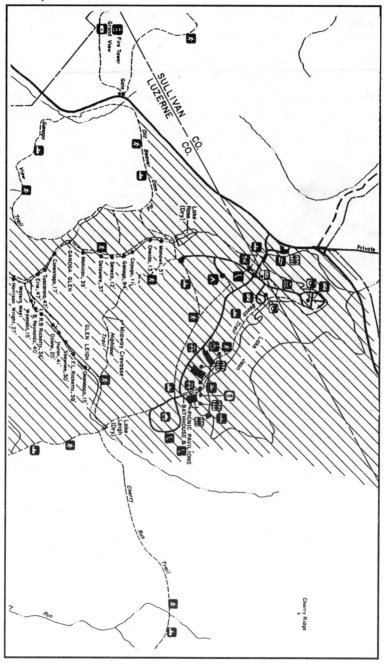

59 Ridley Creek State Park
Land: 2,606 acres Water: Ridley Creek

The park has an interesting history. As you drive through Ridley Creek you are traveling on what is called "Sandy Flash Drive." This is the main park road that was named for James Fitzpatrick (born in 1748), the son of Irish immigrants.

Fitzpatrick was a tall, handsome blacksmith and mechanic with blond hair and blue eyes. James attended many "frolics" (dance) parties–often riding 20 miles, dancing all night and riding back to work at the crack of dawn. A local farmer, seeing the youth dash by on his horse, dubbed him "Sandy Flash," and the name stuck.

This cute story turned sour, however. Fitzpatrick eventually became a deserter of the Continental Army, ending up being savagely beaten, chased as a fugitive and finally caught. After an escape he return to his native community, living quietly for a time until he began robbing people and savagely beating many of them. Accounts say he seemed obsessed with his beating and desertion from the military and developed a preference for robbing tax collectors, whose dollars he saw as supporting the American cause, which he came to hate and fight against. He also robbed affluent people, gaining a misplaced Robin Hood-like status. The instances were rare when Sandy's spoils were shared with those less fortunate.

After a series of daring raids upon men and communities, the Supreme Executive Council posted a $1,000 reward. Sandy Flash's last robbery attempt was on the home of William McAfee. Captain Robert McAfee was having tea with his parents at there home when Fitzpatrick crashed the doors and demanded their cash. Mrs. McAfee was able to sneak upstairs and empty the strong box, hiding their money. When the box was shown to the outlaw he became enraged and herded the entire family and a serving girl up into a small bedroom over the old kitchen.

Meanwhile, the truly wacky Fitzpatrick has been trotting around the house in a pair of fancy ladies boots. Stumbling about, he momentarily sat on the bed to adjust the frilly boots and Captain McAfee, seeing his chance, jumped upon him. The brave serving girl, Rachel Walker, acted fast seizing Fitz's pistol, which he had sat beside him while fiddling with the boots. As she grabbed the gun she also tossed a thick coverlet over his head. In an instant he was bound by a hired man, named David Cunningham.

Taken to jail and tried, Sandy was sentenced to death by hanging. On a September day in 1778, a rope was placed around his neck under the gallows. The cart in which he was standing was driven out from under his feet, but because of his extreme height (six foot, four-inches), his toes still touched the ground and the hangman had to tightened the noose to insure death. Wild and handsome, he created a legend and bragged on his way to the gallows that he had "enough (gold) to buy Chesten County." If you hear hoof beats at the private riding stable that's adjacent to the park, you might think of Sandy Flash.

The park opened in August 1972.

Information and Activities

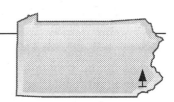

Ridley Creek State Park
Sycamore Mills Road
Media, PA 19063-4398
(610) 892-3900

DIRECTIONS: Sixteen miles from the center of the city Philadelphia. On PA Route 3, 2.5 miles west of Newtown Square. The park may also be entered from Gradyville Road, east from PA Route 352 or west from

PA Route 252. The park office is in Jeffords Mansion. The park closes at sunset and those times are posted.

JEFFORDS MANSION: The mansion, which houses the park office, is one of the most beautiful buildings in the state park system. Huge granite steps, tall stone arches and lush mounded courtyards frame the massive building that was once the home of Walter and Sarah Jeffords. The main house was actually built around an earlier 18th century stone house.

The original house was constructed by George Green in the 1770s and is now surrounded by mature terraced garden, broad oaks, landscaped spaces and graceful stone walls and quiet patio spaces. The stone work around the grounds are often moss-covered and shady. Touring the mansion and grounds is a wonderful experience. Look for the huge empress tree in front of the mansion. It has giant leaves and broad branches that shade a large part of the opulent entrance.

When you are standing at the park's reception desk, you are actually in the old section of the house with fireplaces at each end of the room, open beam ceilings and a winding staircase to the floor above. To the right of the reception desk was the formal dining room. Imagine the rich family entertaining large groups–or dining alone with their only child. This huge 30-foot-long space is now used for natural history exhibits and environmental education programs. Exhibits include a touch table, native wood section, animal mounts, flip boards that test your nature knowledge, butterflies of Ridley Creek and geology display.

Also notice the dark oak paneling with wood pegs that cover the walls where historical photographs, gleaming light fixtures and other unique artifacts are hung. Upon entering the "new" (1915) section of the mansion you'll discover a room with a wide stairway and an 18th century mantle fireplace. The next room has the grand staircase, patterned after one in a European castle, more oak paneling that was cut from the property, a leaded-window alcove, elk antlers and a broad, shinny chandelier.

Finally, visitors may enter the ballroom with wood floors that was used by the Jeffords for over 50 years. One story about the huge room is that Mr. Jeffords was fond of having a stable hand bring one of his top horses right into the room to show off to guests. The white textured ceiling is molded plaster that was made in six-foot sections. The painting over the huge fireplace (you can stand up inside the large fireplace) is of Jeremiah Bishop. His family owned "Bishop's Mill" (in the area that is now referred to as Sycamore Mills) in the 18th and 19th century.

THE COLONIAL PENNSYLVANIA PLANTATION: Three jumbo hard-surfaced parking lots serve the 112 acres of farmland that was first opened in 1974. The tract has been a working farm for more than 300 years. It is open 10 a.m. - 5 p.m.. from mid-April to November on Saturday and Sunday. There is an admission charge, but children under four years are free. A wooden boardwalk takes you into the farm, past a tiny log gift stop, to where a wide view of wooden outbuildings and fences stand near pastures and cultivated acres.

The plantation is a research and educational facility dedicated to the discovery and preservation of knowledge about the ordinary man of the 18th century. The mission of the rustic plantation is historical interpretation and recreation of the lifestyles of an Edgmont township family farm. Surrounded by a variety of farm animals and a landscape remarkably like that of 200 years ago. Interpreters go about their daily routines dictated by custom and season.

Guests may visit the farmhouse, stillroom, stable, springhouse, rest room, sheepfold, pig pen, crop fields, stone cabin, wagon shed and barns, kitchen garden and orchard. The plantation represents over one million dollars in investment. During the weekdays hundreds of school children learn of rural life in colonial Pennsylvania and, in particular, a children's place in that world through tours and workshops. Workshops offer hands-on experience with hearth cooking, farm chores, candle dipping, carding, spinning and more.

You'll also learn about the "worm fence." Englishmen called it a "worm fence" because of a series of crooks that were commonly used in New Jersey, Pennsylvania and New England. In this type of fence, posts are not used, just rails of equal length. The rails are stacked on top of each other as in a log building, but not notched. Sometimes the fence becomes so high, it must be braced with an angle rod. This crude, zig-zag fence outlines the farm spaces.

A number of special events are held annually includes a May Craft Show, October Feast. Memberships are available. Classes might include hearth cooking, basketry, chair rushing and archaeology.

CAMPGROUND: Organized groups may register in advance to use the 120 person group campground. The facility is open April - October.

FISHING: A small handicapped accessible fishing pier is on Ridley Creek, a tributary of the Delaware River. The creek is stocked with trout several times a year. The creek is basically a put-and-take stream where dark-colored flies work the best. Sections of the stream have a heavy canopy of beech and sycamores. At the lower end of the park there is a one mile stretch that is a delayed harvest section that runs downstream to Dismal Run. When water temperatures climb in July, anglers should try the Dismal or Jeffers runs. Look for deep pools and riffles.

HIKING: Many trailheads are complete with parking lots for many cars and are off the main park roads. The park has 12 miles of easy to moderately difficult trails.

Other trails include the White Trail (3 mile loop) that is almost all wooded; Yellow Trail (2 mile loop) connecting the park office with Picnic Area 17, which passes through fields and forest; Blue Trail (1.5 miles) and the paved office area trail.

BIKING: A five mile paved path along Sycamore Mills and Forge Roads is designated for bicycles, joggers and walkers. Many families bring their bikes to explore the rolling park. Bikes are not permitted on unpaved hiking trails.

DAY-USE AREAS: Nearly 1,000 picnic tables are in 14 picnic areas. Each is equipped with a comfort station and grills. Several areas have large fields suitable for games. Areas 8, 11, and 17 have playground equipment. Picnic areas 8, 11 and 17 have pavilions that can be reserved.

NATURE: A large percentage of the rocks in the rolling tract are metamorphic. The Grandville orogeny, a period of mountain building, occurred over one billion years ago. The orogeny caused depressions which resulted in increases of temperature forcing the pre-existing rock to metamorphous (change), producing new rock types. Subsequently, 460 million years ago this area was subjected to Taconic orogeny which caused new rocks beds to change again.

Ridley Creek maintains a tree identification course along the multi-purpose trail where 48 trees are marked with numbered disks. You can test your tree identification knowledge by picking up a quiz sheet from the park office. You will find the answers posted on the bulletin board near the reception desk at the office.

The environmental education effort at the park revolves around teacher education and day programs for area school groups. Occasional public programs are offered during the summer. Many years ago, the success of interpretive programs actually led to the dedication of the Nolde Forest Environmental Education Center near Reading in 1971.

Ridley Creek has a wonderful bird check list that is grid-like, offering information about seasonal occurrences and relative abundance. The list has over 190 species. The Bridle Path Trail is considered one of the best paths from which to see wildflower and many avian species. Spring offers an excellent warbler migration of about 30 species. Breeding birds include willow flycatcher and swamp sparrow, along with dozens of other more common species including woodpeckers, various finches, nuthatches, wrens, thrushes and vireos. Birders can spot a variety of birds of prey over fields, hummingbirds at flowers and woodcock in the brush.

Nearby Tyler Arboretum has a list of 154 bird species seen and 25 accidentals.

WINTER: Bring your cross-country skies to tour the multi-use trail. Sledding is permitted on the grassy slope near the park office.

HUNTING: The first hunt was in 1984 to control the deer population. Today, hunts are for management purposes only.

NEARBY ATTRACTIONS: Adjacent to the park is the 650-acre Tyler Arboretum, a non-profit institution dedicated to preserving, developing and maintaining the plant collection and natural environment in order to encourage the study and enjoyment of horticulture and natural science. The arboretum is one of the oldest in the northeastern United States. There are marked hiking trails, greenhouse, Pinetum, gardens and museum collection in Lachford Hall (begun in 1738). Call (215) 566-5431 for details.

INSIDERS TIP: The English Tudor-style Manorhouse (Jeffords Mansion) is a wonderful building, both inside and out.

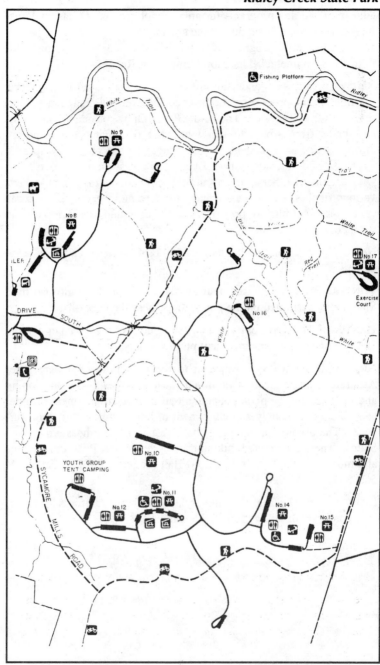

60 Ryerson Station State Park
Land: 1,164 acres Water: 62-acre lake

About 14,000 years ago, glaciers carved new drainage pathways in the southwest corner of the state, leaving deep valleys and sharp hills. Today, after many years of erosion, the rolling hills are gently rounded and lush with towering trees and all types of fauna. Interestingly, drainage patterns vary greatly from one hillside to another.

While the layout of the terrain in Greene County is interesting, it causes some sedimentation in the lake. The lake has been dredged twice over the years, and fishing and water conditions have improved.

The dam crosses the North Fork of the Dunkard Fork, a tributary of Wheeling Creek, contains the small lake that is fed by the stream and offers many wildlife viewing opportunities. This wetland area that feeds the lake is inhabited by beaver (who cut too many trees down near the shoreline), muskrats, deer, squirrels, skunks and rabbits.

The fertile and rolling area is also home to many species of reptiles and amphibians, including an assortment of salamanders, frogs and turtles. Box and snapping turtles are common, as are the eastern spiney soft-shell. Birders will enjoy the chance to see osprey during the spring migration. Year-round, great blue herons have a nesting rookery in a grove of sycamore trees that can be seen from Bristoria Road in the early spring. Other interesting bird species include the Carolina chickadee, Acadian flycatchers and willow flycatcher, which can often be seen in open areas.

The park got is name from a small fort built in 1792 to protect westward moving settlers.

Information and Activities

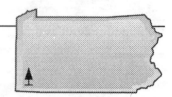

Ryerson Station State Park
R.R. 1, Box 77
Wind Ridge, PA 15380
(412) 428-4254

DIRECTIONS: On both sides of PA Route 3022, off PA Route 21, three miles from Wind Ridge.

CAMPGROUND: Ryerson has both family camping and organized group camping for youth, church or scouting groups for up to 80 people. The group campground has composting toilets, pavilion, tables and plenty of open spaces for outdoor activities. The family campground is open from the second Friday in April through antlerless deer season in December.

The 50-site family campground has gravel pads and is on a ridge northeast of the small lake, where cooling breezes help keep insects to a minimum in the summer. The hilltop soils drain quickly and make for dry, comfortable camping. Sixteen sites have electrical hookups. There are both pull-through and back-in sites, all equipped with picnic tables and fire rings.

There are no showers at the class B Ryerson Station campground. Pull-through sites on the outer loop are the most popular sites. Sites 21 and 22 are always busy, as are electrical sites 8, 9, 10 and 11. Spruce trees are carefully planted in strategic locations that will one day provide ample privacy and visual barriers for family campers. Ryerson has two sites that are accessible for people with disabilities.

EMERGENCY NUMBERS: State police, 627-6151; ambulance and fire, 428-4242.

FISHING: Trout are stocked annually. Warm-water game fishing can be fair to good in the lake. The stream runs strong in the springtime and offers good fishing, but by late July its flow can often be greatly reduced. Local trout anglers prefer small spinners, flies and natural baits.

BOATING: Ryerson has a one-lane launching ramp and shoreline mooring that can accommodate 25 small boats. Mooring sites can be rented seasonally; several sites are also available for campers who bring a small fishing boat with them. No gasoline motors are allowed on the lake.

Canoeists can paddle quiet Duke Lake and explore small streams in this park only three miles from the West Virginia border.

HIKING: From hilltop to valley, Ryerson does have great length of trails. The unique geology and topography are popular with many hikers and backpackers who sometimes use the park for training.

One self-guided interpretive trail and about 10 miles of moderately difficult trails wind through the state park.

Lazaer Trail, named after a former landowner, travels through spruce plantings and huge oaks thought to be more than 300 years old. The two-mile Fox Feather Trail crosses the stream at the bottom of a hollow and emerges along the lake's shoreline. From the old iron bridge near the center of the park, Pine Box Trail (2.5 miles) makes a loop along the stream's edge, along a hillside and by a field and ravine. More than 40 people came up this hill in pine boxes to their final resting spot in Stahl Cemetery

DAY-USE AREAS: Most of the 380 picnic tables are in the main day-use areas near the swimming pool, but plenty are scattered along the quiet stream and nestled under shady trees. The park operates the rentable picnic pavilions that are very busy during June, July and August. Pavilions can be rented up to one year in advance and two are outfitted with electrical hookups. The main picnic and day-use area has toilet facilities, children's play apparatus, sand volleyball court, grills and shady views of the lake and nearby swimming pool.

A small boat rental concession and food stand are in the main day-use area that serves the community-like swimming pool. The food concession sells hamburgers, hot dogs, pizza and cold drinks, plus limited camping supplies.

The unit has a small nature center where seasonal environmental education programs are offered. The building also is a greeting center for visiting school groups.

SWIMMING POOL: The fenced-in blue swimming pool with deck-side seating is open from 11 a.m. - 7 p.m. daily Memorial Day weekend to Labor Day. The pool is three feet deep on each end and five feet deep in the middle. The larger nearby wading pool is popular with small children. Admission to the pool is free, and there is no diving allowed.

NATURE: A seasonal environmental educator offers interpretive programs in the evening for campers. He or she also works with visiting school groups.

HUNTING: About 900 acres are managed for deer and small game hunting. Call the park office for details.

WINTER: Ice skating, ice fishing, cross-country skiing and sledding are popular winter activities at the small park.

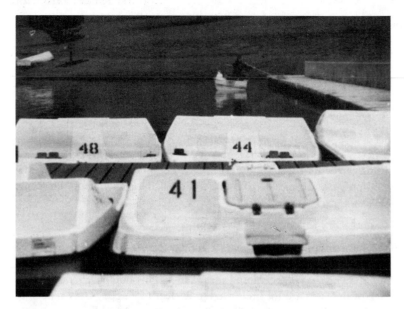

61 Shawnee State Park
Land: 3,983 acres Water: 451-acre lake

Shawnee State Park draws visitors from Harrisburg and Pittsburgh, and points north and south.

It is a good family-style park with a well-kept campground, quiet park roads, rental boats and bikes, shoreline fishing, day-use amenities and the attraction of nearby historic Bedford. The park is well-known for being a wonderful place for all types of reunions—and its location between the capital and Pittsburgh brings large groups to the park on weekends throughout the summer.

Many natural destinations are neighbors of Shawnee like Koon Lake, Lake Gordon, Yellow Creek and many trout streams including Towne Creek, Bob's Creek, Wills Creek, Evitts Creek and others.

The 451-acre Lake Shawnee, the focal point of the park, is one of the top fishing and canoeing lakes in the state. From the rocky and tree-lined shore to one of the best swimming areas in the park system, the park is easy-to find off the interstate.

Also in the area are antique shops, old fashioned country auctions, tav-

353

erns, great restaurants, bed and breakfasts, Bedford Springs and lots of shopping for all ages.

Information and Activities

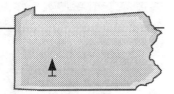

Shawnee State Park
R. R. 2, Box 142B
Schellsburg, PA 15559
(814) 733-4218

DIRECTIONS: In Bedford County, 87 miles east of Pittsburgh on I-70. From I-70, Exit 11, follow U.S. 220 south to Rt. 30 west. From Bedford, take Route 30 10 miles to Schellsburg. then south on Route 96 to the park.

EMERGENCY NUMBERS: 911 system.

CAMPGROUND: In recent years a number of sites have been improved with electrical hook-up service, including sites 1-5 and parts of Section A. Shawnee has 300 camping sites in the highly contoured tract. Some 212 of the sites are for trailers up to 20 feet in length. Only nine sites can handle RV rigs of 36 feet or more. Sections B and F, equaling one-fourth of the sites, can be reserved on holiday weekends. The large campground is open from the second Friday in April until the end of antlerless deer season in December. The showerhouses have exterior sinks.

The clapboard campground store is geared for fun, selling fishing bait (meal worms, redworms, crawlers, etc.), firewood, ice and loads of snacks. It also rents bicycles.

In Section B, site 116 is private. Sites on the outer perimeter are against a wooded buffer zone. Site 126 is deep and wooded, where a tent would work perfectly.

In Section A, sites 30, 32, 33 and 34 (large and flat) have a thickly wooded natural area behind them. Section C has some shady but smaller sites. The amphitheater is accessed down a hard-surfaced footpath between sites 154-156.

Site 163 is a pull-through site in Section D, where some of the larger sites are. Site 179 is private and good for tent campers. Electrical sites in the D loop are level, shady and busy. Site 217 is a pull-through.

In Section F, many of the outside perimeter sites are backed up against a natural area with a view into a dark wooded valley.

The spur with sites 256-264 has the most secluded camping pads for smaller units. Section G is set off on its own, away from the other loops and not as shady along the hillside. As is often the case, the outside of the loop is backed up against a wooded area. Sites 279 and 280 are high and dry. Site 296 is a pull-through. The ground in this loop is almost sandy.

As you enter the campground, many of the first 15 sites are backed up against a natural area and shady. Most sites have gravel pads, picnic tables and fire rings or grills.

Organized primitive group camping for 120 people is available by advance registration.

COTTAGE: On the island, near the handsome white barns that house the regional park office, is a lovely white cottage that is available to rent by the week during the summer. The cottage has a lake view, lawn and plenty of parking.

FISHING: Several underwater structures were placed when the lake was drawn down in the past. Many bass anglers have sounded the waters to determine points, stumps, cribs and other fish-holding places. The lake receives strong fishing pressure with most anglers using live bait (minnows, mostly). Ice fishermen also dunk lots of minnows and waxworms in the frigid water during the winter.

Plugging for muskie near the Colvin boat launch is popular at the park. Thirty-five-pound muskies have been taken from the lake by trolling. Many local bass anglers concentrate efforts south of the large island. Some bass anglers find success in front of the swimming area using crankbaits, spinnerbait, jigs and live bait.

Fly fishermen will enjoy the challenge of the Raytown Branch that flows through a shale deposit near the park. It can be very good fishing before the water warms in early June. Try Cahills and blue and dark quills early in the season, after dinner. A fly fishing packet for the general area is available by calling (800) 765-3331.

Staff says the kids can have lots of fun from shore casting a waxworm under a bobber in the evening. Plenty of small, but fun to catch, panfish are easily caught.

HIKING: Twelve miles of mostly easy trails loop around the park. The most popular of the loops is the Lakeshore Trail/Forbes Trail (3.5 miles) that traces the northern shoreline. Mountain bikes are allowed

The large cottage has a lake view, lawn and plenty of parking.

on the Lakeshore Trail.

BIKING: From a cement block building with a low flat roof is a small bike rental concession near the main beach. The concession is open about 9 a.m. - 8 p.m. daily during the season. You may rent bikes by the hour or the day. The concession has tandem bikes, mountain bikes and bikes with baby seats. Aside from certain trails (in the northwest section of the park), the bikes (and walkers) can use the winding park roads that pass scenic vistas for riding.

BOATING: West of the beach, connected by a footpath, are a modern rest room, small boat rental concession and busy launching ramp near the bridge to the island. Eighteen tan and blue pedalboats, a dozen or so aluminum fishing boats and electric motors are offered for rent. The park has 183 mooring spaces and two launches. Non-powered and electric-powered boats only are permitted on the lake.

CANOEING: Shawnee Lake is named for the Shawnee Indians who briefly inhabited the region during the early 1700s. The unusual configuration of the lake and lack of motor boats make it one of the top 10 lakes in the state to paddle. From the large dam at the east end to the western shallows is about 1.5 miles, with two branches northeast and southwest of each other.

An island with two plank bridges for access divides the placid lake into three sections. In spring the water is clear and cold. Anglers often laze on the banks or in boats trying to catch trout. Later in the year, when the waters warm, typical species caught include perch, bluegills, pike, walleye, carp, large- and smallmouth bass, muskie and crappies. This is the time when canoeing is the best. Warm breezes are gentle and the entire lake is yours to explore.

From a canoe you might see nesting swallows, wood ducks and stealth-like kingfishers watching the surface. Cattail marshes, sedges and water lilies fill small coves and sun-drenched bays. You can also paddle around the two small wooded islands near the Colvin launch area at the north end of the lake.

DAY-USE AREAS: The park needs more picnic pavilions. With expansive day-use areas and increasing demand, family reunions and day-use are on the rise. Yet hundreds of single tables are scattered along the lake and open spaces.

BEACH: More parks should have walk-in beaches like Shawnee. The large parking lot along a low ridge is about 200 yards from the beach, separating traffic and noise from the delightful beach and day-use turf on the north shore. The ample hard-surfaced walkway down to the beach is handicapped accessible and gently winds down to the sandy cove past benches and shade trees perfect to picnic under. The sand and turf beach is at least 250 yards long by 40 yards wide. The water is cordoned-off by orange and white buoys, making two large guarded swimming areas. Lifeguard stands are on the beach and in the five-foot-deep waters at the edge of the buoy line.

The two-window concession stand offers basic snack foods and cold treats, plus volleyballs for rent. The first aid station is near, in a small building. Two sand volleyball courts near the beach are busy with tanned spikers all summer.

The beach is open 11 a.m. - 7 p.m. daily, Memorial Day weekend to Labor Day, unless otherwise posted. No swimming is allowed when the beach is not guarded. Shawnee is one of the best beaches in the system, complete with a terrific view of the tree-lined shores and bass boats that often move in slow motion, sneaking up on the denizens. Two large bathhouses have flush toilets and showers.

NATURE: Shawnee is a balance of successional woodland and developed recreational spaces with large mowed areas and open shorelines. Songbirds are abundant, as are common mammals like deer, squirrels, woodchucks, raccoons, skunks and fox. Serious nature lovers should venture to the west side of the lake beyond Route 96, where rich wetlands offer habitat for marsh and water birds, muskrats, snapping turtles and a good variety of marsh wildflowers. Small boats can penetrate the area during most of the year.

The three-part lake is heavily visited by migrating waterfowl each spring and fall. Birders should know that double-crested cormorants have been recorded at the park. Other birds seen include dunlin, short-billed dowitcher, Virginia and sora rail, spotted sandpiper and two types of terns, Caspian and black. Early May is the best time for a much better than average warbler migration, featuring golden-wing, Nashville, yellow, chestnut sided black-throated greens, hooded, Wilson's and many others.

WINTER: Ice skating, ice fishing, sledding on the hillsides and ice boating are popular winter activities. Cross-country skiers can use most of the trails at Shawnee as weather permits. Warriors Path, in Saxton, has an additional 5.3 miles of ski trails. About 11 miles of trails are open for snowmobiling during the winter.

HUNTING: About 3,000 acres are open to hunting from the fall archery season through the spring turkey season. Call the park office for details.

NEARBY ATTRACTIONS: Bedford County has excellent day-trip opportunities for park users. Many attractions are along U.S. Route 30, which was the main highway between Fort Bedford and Fort Ligonier in the 1700s. Original inns and other unique historical buildings can be seen along the road and in small settlements. Old Bedford Village, on old U.S. Route 220 north of Bedford, is a group of historical buildings collected from all over the country. Period artisans demonstrate crafts and lifestyles of blacksmiths, broom makers, leather workers, coopers and potters. Contact the Bedford County Travel Promotion Agency at (814) 623-1771 for additional information about attractions and activities.

INSIDERS TIPS: The well-kept park is great for family reunions and muskie fishing at the north end of the lake. Take the 51-building walking tour of historic old Bedford.

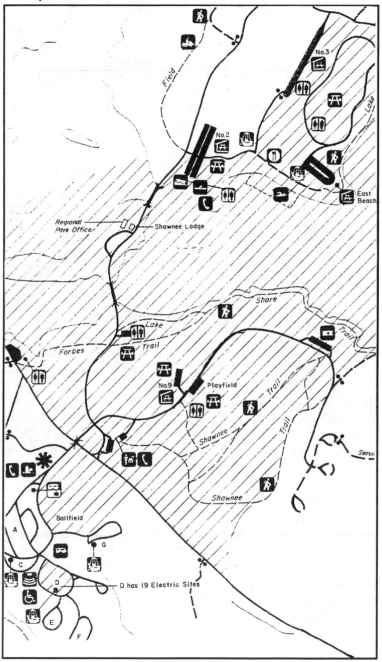

62 Shikellamy State Park
Land: 131.5 acres Water: Susquehanna River

Two quite different parcels make up Shikellamy, both strongly relating to the confluence of the Susquehanna River. The two areas face each other across the 3,060-acre Lake Augusta, which is a seasonally dammed section of the Susquehanna. In fact, it's behind the world's largest inflatable dam three miles downstream from the park. The average depth of the lake is less than seven feet, and when the river dam is open, the river runs slow and shallow.

Two overlooks on the lightly wooded Blue Hill (west area, off U.S. 11) 360 feet above the river junction offer spectacular views of Sunbury, Northumberland and surrounding areas. From these vantage points visitors can also see boat traffic, house tops, smoke stacks, Packer's Island, marina and cars and trains. One picnic pavilion, some gravel parking lots and a scattering of picnic tables serve this scenic hill top day-use area. A one-mile nature trail offers visitors a chance to see flora, fauna and interesting geological formations.

Pennsylvania State Parks

Boating and fishing are popular activities. The main park area, where parking lots, play areas, marina and restaurant are located, is at the southern tip of Packer's Island at the confluence of the Susquehanna River. In this section of the park are a one-mile-long paved bike trail, boat rental and small marine supply, boat launching ramp, and shoreline fishing.

Information and Activities

Shikellamy State Park
Bridge Avenue
Sunbury, PA 17801
(717) 286-7880

Milton State Park is managed by the staff of Shikellamy. Milton is on an island about 13 miles from Shikellamy. The 43-acre island park has soccer fields, a small boat access, bank fishing, plenty of picnic tables, short trails, playground and rest rooms.

DIRECTIONS: The park is two parcels. One is across the Susquehanna River from Sunbury on Blue Hill and can be reached from the town of Shamokin Dam by going north on U.S. Route 11. The portion of the park in Northumberland County is between the Borough of Northumberland and city of Sunbury off Route 147 on the southern tip of Packer's Island. The park office is on Packer's Island.

RESTAURANT: Elevated on heavy piers above the 100-year floodplain, the white and blue restaurant and lounge has scenic views up and down the waterway and over the small marina. A full entree of fine foods is served in the round, heavily windowed eatery that has bright rose-colored carpet and brass lamps. The restaurant has banquet rooms and private dining rooms. It is open seven day a week, 11 a.m. - 9 p.m. Sunday -Thursday and 11 a.m. - 10 p.m. Friday and Saturday. Steaks and seafood dishes are the featured dinner choices. A number of historical photos line the walls and interpret Pennsylvania history.

Many window-side tables are available for diners to enjoy the view. Jet Skiers, fishermen and boaters are often using the lake and wide quiet rivers.

Outside, under the main dining room, is a patio area with picnic tables. Near this cement patio is a board with a description and photograph of the various floods that the park and building have survived. In June 1972, the deepest flood in the area covered the entire bottom floor of the elevated restaurant.

BOATING: The boat rental concession (286-6758), in a low brown building near the railroad bridge at the lake's edge, is open seasonally 9 a.m. - 9 p.m. The store sells soft drinks and ice, and rents pontoon boats, canoes, pedal boats and aluminum fishing boats. The concession also rents water skis, wet bikes, ski boats and sells marine supplies, fuel and safety equipment. A single land launching ramp for small boats is adjacent to the rental concession. The park also has a larger three-lane, hard-surfaced boat ramp on the south side of the point, where two courtesy docks welcome boaters. From the boat ramp you can get a good view of the gray flood wall that has been built around the low central city.

DAY-USE AREAS: About 25 acres in the middle of the main park on Packer's Island are dedicated to picnicking. Plenty of parking, water and rest rooms are in the vicinity. Open spaces and play equipment (tube slides, climbers, sand box and tire swings) are popular during weekend family reunions and other outings in the urban park.

63 Sinnemahoning State Park
Land: 1,910 acres Water: 142-acre reservoir

On the east side of the well-known trout steam, Sinnemahoning Creek, the park jets from the water and climbs steeply into the state forest. The rest of the linear park, however, lies on the west of the rocky creek along bottomlands, open fields and a mixed forest.

Sinnemahoning (which means "rocky lick") is in the 200,000-acre Elk State Forest, which derives its name from the great number of elk that once thrived in the region. The state forest has a number of amenities including Memorial Springs, Noble-Chambers Memorial Forest, Quehanna Wild Area, two dams, several state parks within its borders, rugged trails, clear running trout streams and hunting lands.

Elk once lived throughout Pennsylvania. By the mid-1800s the range was reduced to a small area in Elk County. The last native Pennsylvania Eastern elk was killed in 1867 near Ridgeway. Between 1913 and 1926, the game commission attempted to restore an elk herd by releasing 177 western elk.

The current elk range is in southwestern Cameron and southeastern Elk counties, with most mature bulls in St. Mary's, except during the two-month rutting season when they travel to meet cows and their young just north of Benezette.

To maintain the elk herd and to keep them from agricultural areas, the game commission has carefully clear-cut small areas to provide browsing, maintains grassy strips for grazing and plants select trees and shrubs to provide food variety.

Elk are much larger than whitetail deer. In fact, a mature bull stands about five feet at the shoulder, can weigh 700-1,000 pounds, and has a set of backward curving antlers which may sport as many as 14 points. Cows are smaller, antlerless and can weigh between 500 and 600 pounds. The big animals' coats vary in color from dark brown to reddish, depending on the season, but the large buff-colored patch covering the rump is unmistakable.

Elk tours are offered in the area, and visitors can often see them from roads throughout the range. Elk can been heard and seen during the mating season in September.

The park, along with Hyner Run and Gouldsboro state parks, were opened in 1958 and were incorporated into the state park system in 1962. Sinnemahoning was one of the state's first attempts to develop multi-purpose use of an impoundment area. The 1,198-foot-long earthen dam was completely operational in 1955.

Information and Activities

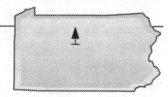

Sinnemahoning State Park
R. R. 1, Box 172
Austin, PA 16720
(814) 647-8401

DIRECTIONS: In Potter and Cameron counties, eight miles north on PA Route 872 from its junction with PA Route 120 in Sinnemahoning, or 35 miles south of its junction with U.S. Route 6 in Coudersport. The tiny office is open 8 a.m. - 4 p.m. Monday - Friday.

EMERGENCY NUMBERS: Hospital, 274-9300; fire, 1-486-3426; state police, 1-486-3321.

CAMPGROUND: No reservations are taken at Sinnemahoning. The many repeat campers are a testament to the quality of the small 35-site family campground with 12 electrical sites and a bed of pine needles under foot. The electrical hook-up sites are always the most popular. Staff says that sites 10 and 30-35 are the most requested. The campground is about half open, sunny and grassy. Sites 21-29 are wide open and sunny. All of the gravel pad sites have ground-mounted fire rings and picnic tables.

Sites 12 and 14 are private, notched into the woods with vegetation separating them. Sites 16 and 17 are under large conifers, while site 19 is peacefully situated at the end of the loop. Sites 24 and 26 are backed up against a wooded ravine and shady. A small timber-style play apparatus and sandbox are in the campground and popular with younger children. Two tiny kids' seats are carved out of tree stumps with names scratched all over the inside of them near the playground area.

The campground is open the second Friday in April until the end of antlerless deer season in December. About one-half of the sites at the unit are for small-to medium-sized camping rigs. The campground has nine 30-amp electrical sites and three sites that have 50-amp service.

Cabin: The Brooks Run Ranger Cabin is adjacent to Brooks Run one mile from the park office. The two-story, aluminum sided structure features a modern kitchen with a refrigerator, electric range and storage cabinets, a bathroom with a shower, a dining room, living room with a fireplace and attached sun porch, and four bedrooms with two queen beds and four bunks. There is sleeping for up to 12.

Bring your own bed linens, towels, cleaning supplies and ax/handsaw for cutting firewood. The White House-like cabin with large lawn is available year-round, by the week and half-week. The cabins is rented only by the week in the summer.

FISHING: Disabled anglers need to stop by the park office before using the accessible fishing pier. Trout are stocked in the lake, but many local anglers are excellent catfish and bass fishermen. The lake also supports a small population of muskie and good numbers of small panfish.

Youthful shoreline anglers often try their luck in Brooks Run creek that runs through the main day-use area. Bobbers and live bait (red worms, mostly) are a good combination for evening fishing along the creek or lake's edge. Many shoreline anglers also fish on a small point near the boat launch.

At the park, there is a delayed harvest-artificial lures only regulation area from the mouth of Bailey Run south 2.1 miles on First Fork

Sinnemahoning Creek.

This area represents some of the best scenery and fishing in the state. The steep mountains in the distance, grassy bottomlands and scattered islands along the relatively quiet waters attract many anglers all year.

One of the most popular lures is the gold, one-eighth-ounce Cast Master spinner made in Massachusetts. Many anglers fish in the morning around the island, using a spinner and retrieving it slowly, or tossing a host of dry and wet flies. Local anglers say colors are very important in this creek. Try different colors until you find one that turns on the fish. Wading in about two miles north of the campground is easy and fairly safe.

Certain sections along the First Fork are like fishing a Montana stream–if scenery is important you, this is your stream. Open grassy shorelines, freestone waters, steep mountains, thick hatches and terrific spring fly fishing are found here. April, May and early June hatches are well-known. Hendrickson emerge in mid-April until the first week in May. Later in the spring, try brown and green drake imitators, sulphurs and blue-winged olive patterns. Bring lots of dun patters and nymphs later in the season.

Local fly fishermen advise visiting anglers to move around. Try different riffles and pools, but be careful wading in some of the big waters.

BOATING: Non-powered and electric-powered boats can use the single hand-surfaced launch. Sixth seasonal mooring sites are nearby, five of which are handicapped accessible. A courtesy dock is also available for temporary mooring and launching. Four benches face the lake and are near the boat ramp, from which you can watch boaters struggle with their trailers, boats, fishing poles, coolers, hats, sandwiches and other necessary stuff.

HIKING: Bring your bike (or in-line skates) for rides on the long park road, or hike some of the remote and often rugged park trails. Try the one-mile Red Spruce connector trail or the Low Lands Trail along the creek. Many other hiking opportunities are in neighboring Elk State Forest.

DAY-USE AREAS: The Forty Maples Day-Use Area, named after 40 maples planted there, has two reservable pavilions (small fee), comfort station and shady picnicking along the First Fork Sinnemahoning Creek.

Pennsylvania State Parks

SWIMMING BEACH: The guarded area is divided into two segments with floating buoys and patrolled by two lifeguards from 11 a.m. - 7 p.m. Thursday - Monday, Memorial Day weekend to Labor Day. A brown block changing room is nearby with rest rooms. The lake is only 100 yards wide at this point, and the beach has about 50 yards of sandy frontage. The actual swimming area is about 11,000 square feet. The lake is cool, with temperatures rarely exceeding 70 degrees.

NATURE: Staff says they often see "vacationing bald eagles" in the park. Seemingly the birds are just out for some scenic flights and hunting for an occasional dinner over the deep valleys and mountain peaks. Often, especially on the weekends, volunteer eagle watchers set up spotting scopes under a canopy and share chances to see the majestic birds soar over the lake. The eagle watching station is usually set up at the boat launch.

Deer are often seen grazing along park roads, while wild turkey, rabbits and squirrels are common along forest edges and brushy fields. Skunk, mink and long-tailed weasels are also spotted around the creek, sometimes sharing the same stretch of the scenic waterway with great blue herons, kingfishers and many other songbirds and common waterfowl. Osprey are also routinely seen in the spring and summer, hunting the shallows and perched atop standing dead timber.

WINTER: Ice fishing is popular on the lake. There is even an annual ice fishing contest sponsored by the local sportsmen's club. Local experts say wax worms and minnows on white or yellow jigging spoons work the best in the deep lake. Snowmobilers can use more than four miles of joint-use roads and trails in the park when snow condition permit. There are about 25 miles of snowmobile trails in Elk State Forest.

HUNTING: Nearly 1,400 acres are open to hunting, trapping and dog training in the fall. Call for more details about the very good hunting opportunities at Sinnemahoning State Park and the surrounding Elk State Forest.

INSIDERS TIP: Join the eagle watchers on the weekends and use their high-powered spotting scopes to view the national symbol.

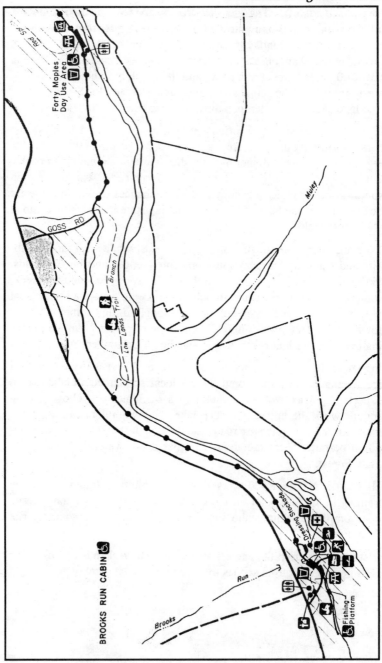

64 Sizerville State Park
Land: 386 acres Water: creeks

Sizerville is a small, enchanting park in the "Endless Mountains" of north central Pennsylvania in Cameron County. Geologists call this area the Mountainous High Plateau Section of the Appalachian Plateaus Physiographic Province. It's also at the confluence of the West Branch Cowley Run and East Branch Cowley Run, and is surrounded by 460,000 acres of state forest and state game lands.

The state park is a great starting point to explore the narrow valleys and steep-sloped mountainsides that make up the scenic region.

This rugged section of the Commonwealth was one of the last permanently settled areas in the entire United States, even though it was purchased from the Iroquois Indian nation in 1784. Early pioneers bypassed the undulating north central part of the state for better agricultural areas to the west.

Sizerville has abundant varieties of wildflowers, native hemlock and plantations of pine and spruce combined with northern hardwoods. The remoteness of the area has lent itself as the place where beaver and elk were reintroduced–and now thrive–more than 75 years ago. Today the elk herd draws many visitors who camp, hike, ski, snowmobile, swim, fish and enjoy the quiet mountainside roads, small towns and pristine parks.

The unit opened for public use in 1924, with the first facilities built in 1927. The name Sizerville comes from a logging boom town of the same name which flourished around the turn of the century. Sizerville is now a ghost town. The park was furthered developed by the Civilian Conservation Corps in the 1930s, and thousands of acres of pines were planted in an effort to replace massive tracts of virgin timber logged in the early part of the century.

Information and Activities

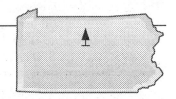

Sizerville State Park
R. R. 1 Box 238-A
Emporium, PA 15834
(814) 486-5605

DIRECTIONS: Seven miles north of Emporium on PA Route 155 in Cameron and Potter counties.

EMERGENCY NUMBERS: State police, 486-3321 or 274-8694.

CAMPGROUND: Down a winding road, the 23-site campground is more or less one big shady loop with five walk-in tent sites scattered streamside along Cowley Run.

Sites have gravel pads, picnic tables, fire rings and trash cans. Firewood may be available for campers. Eighteen sites have 50 amp electric services and can accommodate trailers up to 35 feet long. Almost all of the sites are shady. A blue chip-gravel walkway to the amphitheater is lit by a lamppost. The small facility is near site 15.

If you are a light sleeper, site 17, which is near the road, might be a bit noisy.

Camping sites 11 and 12 are oversized and directly across from the recycling station. A small timber-structure play apparatus is near the very clean maroon-colored showerhouse.

A great user-friendly amenity in the campground is wire lantern holders at each site.

Organized group tenting for up to 100 persons is open from May 1 through November. The area is quite open and mowed.

FISHING: The park road follows much of Cowley Run, a babbling, high-quality mountain freestone fishery that is stocked with brook and brown trout. It's also not unusual to catch a native brook trout in the pools and riffles of the scenic creek. Some of the finest trout streams in the state are in the region. Fly fishermen should consult with area bait and tackle shops for additional information about hatches and local rules.

Excellent area creeks include Portage, Driftwood and branches of the Sinnemahoning Creek. Warmwater anglers may want to try the 142-acre lake at Sinnemahoning State Park 40 minutes away.

HIKING: Sizerville has five hiking loops, three of which (Bottomlands, Campground and North Slope) are easy to moderate in difficulty. Nady Hollow Trail (1.5 miles) ascends a 1,900-foot mountain. The "Cutback" section takes the hiker halfway up the mountain and then gradually runs down along the treed mountainside. This trail is for properly prepared and dressed hikers.

Sizerville is also a trailhead for the Bucktail Path Trail, an extensive and rugged trail system throughout the northern region of central Pennsylvania. The Bucktail Trail extends from the village of Sinnemahoning on PA 155 to Sizerville and is not heavily traveled. In fact, finding the path sometimes is challenging.

Hikers have extensive opportunities in nearby Elk State Forest; a map is available.

VISITOR CENTER/NATURE CENTER: A stone walkway and arched trellis winding through natural plantings of shrubs and wildflowers attract butterflies and greet visitors at the entrance of the two-story, wood-frame center. The carefully designed and colorful butterfly garden is the perfect welcome to the busy center, which offers extensive environmental education programs year-round. Sizerville is fortunate to have one of the top naturalists in the business, and the creative and popular programming prove it. I am very impressed with their comprehensive and heads-up programs for visitors, kids and teachers.

Staff has established a strong outdoor education curriculum for area teachers (in-service training) and schools. Each year, K-6th graders visit and learn about a different concept that includes valuing and problem-solving skills–and many opportunities to learn about the outdoors along the park's trail system.

The center is adaptable and well-used, with chairs and tables scattered around learning centers. Staff believes in hands-on learning, and the many touch boxes and displays invite environmental learning opportunities for all ages. The single-room center also displays some animals mounts (beaver, great horned owl, osprey, female sharp-shinned hawk and fawn for example, animal tracks poster, audio/visual equipment, pileated woodpecker box, pelt samples and hand-out materials.

June through August is when most general public programs are set. School groups flock to the park in the spring and fall to learn about man's role in the natural world and lots more. The naturalist also produces a well-designed newsletter/calendar that details program information. The publication also has fun nature tips and trivia. Programs include elk workshops, all types of programs about butterflies (Sizerville is one of the pioneers in butterfly gardening, watching and interpreting), junior naturalist, touch-n-grow, crafts, puppet theater, incredible edibles, fly fishing clinics, elk watch trips, wildflower wonders, bird hikes and many others.

The North Slope Trailhead is behind the center, while a variety of native plants grow around the building and blend into the butterfly garden at the front entrance.

DAY-USE AREAS: Some fine Civilian Conservation Corps work is still in good repair and used at Sizerville. Eight shady day-use pavilions are stocked with nearly 300 picnic tables and plenty of grills and other amenities. Expect the area to be 80 percent shady, covered by tall white pines, hemlock and sturdy hardwoods. Most day-use amenities are conveniently grouped together, making Sizerville a perfect small state park destination for families, with smaller children.

SWIMMING POOL: Just west of the visitor center is the 105-foot-long rectangular swimming pool with an adjacent wading pool. The popular pool is a regional favorite featuring a maximum depth of five feet, nearby changing facility and small food concession that has all your favorite snacks and soft drinks. The pool is open 11 a.m. - 7 p.m. daily, Memorial Day weekend to Labor Day.

The pool has a wide cement deck for sunning, not running. The guarded pool has four ladders and a bench at one end. There are also a few benches and picnic tables along the perimeter and on a knoll to the east for day-users to watch the swimmers splash about on hot days. Across from the changing rooms, outside the pool fence, are a set of Civilian Conservation Corps-constructed rest rooms. Sizerville is the site of the

Pennsylvania State Parks

"S-85 Sizerville 1933-1935 Civilian Conservation Corps camp."

NATURE: Confirmed nesters at the park include wild turkey, ruby-throated hummingbird, yellow-bellied sapsucker, eastern phoebe, indigo bunting, blue jay, red-eyed vireo, robin, magnolia warbler, blackburian warbler, ovenbird, northern waterthrush, chipping sparrow, northern junco, northern saw-whet owl, house wren, American redstart, rose-breasted grosbeak and chickadee.

The park has a strong spring warbler migration that includes species like magnolia warblers, yellow-rumps and black-throated greens. Noisy pileated woodpeckers are also seen and heard rapping on trees along the park's trails and roads.

HUNTING: About 200 acres inside the park are open to hunting from the fall dove season through March 31. Call the park manager for additional information.

WINTER: The mountainous park gets 60-70 inches of snow annually, making a terrific base for 66 miles of snowmobile trails adjoining park grounds. Cross-country skiing is also popular at the park. Ice skaters will enjoy a lighted area and benches, weather permitting.

INSIDERS TIPS: Sit quietly in the colorful butterfly garden at the visitor center. *"To make a wish come true, whisper to a butterfly. Upon these wings it will be taken to Heaven and granted. For they are the messengers of the Great Spirit."* (North American Indian legend)

The 70-square-mile elk range is about 35 minutes from Sizerville. Plan to participate in an organized tour to learn about elks' natural history, etiquette, habitat management and viewing on private lands.

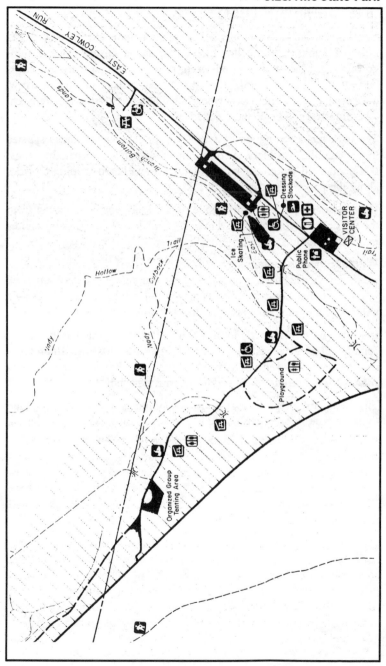

65 Tyler State Park
Land: 1,711 acres Water: Neshaminy Creek

Tyler State Park is a hilly woodland interspersed with agricultural fields that are leased by farmers. Corn, beans, hay and other crops are grown offering a pastoral beauty, generating income and enhancing certain habitats in the unit. The land is cared for and kept in production using modern conservation practices. Farming is a good neighbor to the well-kept park facility. The area has been farmed for more than 300 years. Today the park is surrounded by housing developments and community-owned lands.

The unit is a day-use park near Philadelphia. Before it became a state park, the property was owned by George F. Tyler. He accumulated the land over a nine-year period starting with the Solly farm at the north end of the park that is now leased to the Hosteling International Organization. The Solly house served as the Tylers' country home until a mansion was constructed. The mansion is now part of Bucks County Community College.

The Tylers were well-known for their fine herd of Ayrshire dairy cattle, a stable of 25 horses, pigs, sheep, poultry and lush fields that grew crops to feed the livestock.

Several stone dwellings in the park are fine examples of early farm houses of rural Pennsylvania. Some of the structures date to the early 1700s. One of the best to see is on the bike path north of the pedestrian causeway in the middle of the park.

Tyler State Park was opened to the public in May 1974.

Information and Activities

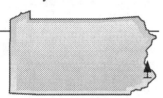

Tyler State Park
101 Swamp Road
Newtown, PA 18940-1151
(215) 968-2021

DIRECTIONS: In Bucks County. From the Pennsylvania Turnpike take exit 27 or 28. From exit 27 follow PA Route 332 east from Willow Grove through Richboro, and from exit 28 follow U.S. Route 1 north to Interstate Highway 95. Follow I-95 north to Newtown-Yardley exit 30, then drive west on the four-lane bypass around Newtown. The park entrance is at intersection of Swamp Road and the four-lane bypass.

The park office is in a renovated white farmhouse. The office contains park information, a small display of period historical artifacts and various natural artifacts.. Educational items change seasonally.

There is no swimming at Tyler State Park.

YOUTH HOSTEL: An early Pennsylvania farmhouse, the Tyler State Park AYH-Hostel is a great place to stay and enjoy all the recreational activities of the surrounding park. Bike, horseback ride, cross-county ski, sled, boat or fish in the area. Visitors may also enjoy the nearby Mercer Museum of pre-industrial tools, Peddler's Village or Washington's Crossing Historic Park where George Washington made his famous Christmas-night crossing of the Delaware River in Trenton. Call (215) 968-0927 for details. Write AYH Hostel, Tyler State Park, P.O. Box 94, Newtown, PA 18940. The facility is open year-round.

BOATING: The small canoe rental offers the craft by the hour, half day or full day. It is open between Memorial Day and Labor Day. A single pier serves the small canoe livery. A boat dock is maintained by the park for visitors wishing to use their own small boat. The gentle creek

A miniature barnyard is a popular play area for youngsters.

has four large zig-zag curves along its length inside the park.

The boat rental office is next to a tiny park store that sells T-shirts, hats, sunglasses, sunscreen and other small items. The building is a lovely stone structure with flagstone floor and shake roof. Picnic tables are also scattered in this busy area.

FISHING: You may fish along the gentle banks of the Neshaminy Creek or from a canoe. The warm creek offers fair panfishing during the spring. Some smallmouth bass and medium-sized crappies are also taken from the wide, slow-flowing creek.

HIKING: The park has 24 miles of trails, four miles of which are gravel hiking-only trails. Serious hikers should cross the causeway at the ford in the center of the park to access a variety of multi-use trails. Many points along the trails are high, offering good views and interesting walking.

Ambitious visitors may want to try the exercise trail (constructed by area Jaycees) that includes places to do arm swings, toe touches, knee bends, waist stretches, deep stretches, chin-ups, sit ups, long jumps and more. The trail is a simple one-mile loop.

BIKE TRAILS: More than 10 miles of paved bike trails wind throughout the park near fields, through wooded areas, along the creek and by day-use amenities. The eight-foot-wide bike paths are part of the 24-mile trail network that goes off in every direction. The park map is necessary to guide riders around the gently rolling park. Picnic tables are in key locations along the winding bike trails.

BRIDLE TRAILS: Some trail riders use the Guild of Craftsman Craft Center parking lots as a staging area and easy access to the nine miles of dirt trails. Many of the bridle trails were originally marked and established by the park's namesake, Mr. Tyler, who purchased the land between 1919 and 1928. Trees along the trails he rode were marked with a strip of white paint. The more difficult trails are marked with short posts cut with a horseshoe design. Riders should stay on marked trails. A nearby (off park property) riding stable rents horses by the hour. Call Sunset Stables at 860-1791.

A second parking lot on PA Route 332 across from the Spring Garden Mill is available.

CRAFT CENTER: Juried arts and crafts are sold at the large center at the south end of the park off of Newtown Road. Two annual (spring and fall) arts and craft showings and sales are featured each year. A wide variety of arts and handiwork is displayed including paintings, fabrics, photography, jewelry, woodworking and lots more. The large white buildings with red chimneys are outlined by split-rail fences, offering an attractive home to the high-quality crafts and artisans inside.

SPRING GARDEN MILL THEATER: Once an active grain and feed mill, the theater is now operated by a local group called the Landhorne Players. They have developed the large structure into a working theater offering cultural activities and performances.

DAY-USE AREAS: Six play areas have been developed for younger visitors. Two are built to look like miniature farm buildings. Two others have rustic log "observation towers" and other climbing structures. The other play areas were made using recycled materials.

The causeway (near the three-foot dam and canoe concession) is one of the most popular places in the park. Children may fish and enjoy the quiet waters, ride the bike path and walk over the bridge to the main trail system. A Frisbee golf course (complete with map available at the park office) is also near the main day-use area and tests the skill of disc throwers.

Pennsylvania State Parks

The most interesting and fun play area is the maze. An actual maze constructed of four-foot-tall walls is an inviting adventure for children. The maze is next to a two-level miniature barnyard, with tractor and silo that houses a spiral slide. A big sandbox is also here, ready for play—remember to empty those shoes after a foray into the sand.

Most of the day-use picnic areas are outlined by conifer trees, open spaces and plenty of parking.

On summer weekends, a mobile snack bar truck serves the causeway day-use area and other sections of the unit.

NATURE: Seasonal (nine-month) outdoor education classes offer all ages a chance to learn more about the area by joining a guided hike, attending scheduled mini-classes or participating in interpretive talks.

The park is comprised of mixed woodlots, thickets, hedgerows and open fields in various stages of regeneration and succession. About 185 birds have been sighted in the park . Common mammals like deer, raccoon, squirrel, fox, rabbit and others are often seen along the 24 miles of trails or park roads, especially in the evening.

WINTER: When the creek freezes, ice skaters can lace 'em up and skate during daylight hours near the boathouse warming area. Ice fishing is also permitted on the lake (look for the deep channel). Sledders can use the slopes, while cross-country skiers may stride on the hiking and bridle trails.

INSIDERS TIP: Call the Bucks County Tourist Commission for additional visitor information at (800) 836-Bucks. Ten historical homes are on the park property and visible from the trails (tenants live in the homes).

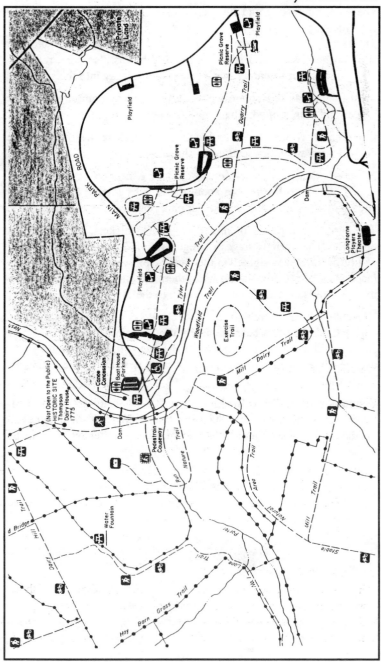

66 White Clay Creek Preserve
Land: 1,255 acres Water: Creek

On June 26, 1984, the Pennsylvania state park system added a site when the DuPont Company donated 1,700 acres–1,200 in Pennsylvania and 500 in Delaware–worth $8.5 million. The rolling wooded tracts and scattered wetlands were part of the holdings that the company had assembled in the early 1950s for a potential 1,000-acre reservoir. The need did not materialize.

Long before large industry or the state had control of the land, Native Americans lived in the White Clay Creek valley some 12,000 years ago. They settled on the higher knolls of the floodplain to hunt, fish and gather plants for food, medicine, dyes and fibers. Groups also moved into adjacent uplands to hunt or to make projectile points and other tools from the milky quartz found there. Later, groups began farming simple crops like squash and beans.

The first European settlers came to the fertile area in the late 17th century and began clearing the oak and hickory forest, opening up agricultural spaces to plant wheat and corn and to develop meadows for cattle grazing. Most of these early farmsteads were on the floodplain, taking advantage of the naturally rich soils and using any cleared logs for construction materials for houses and farm buildings.

White Clay Creek and its tributaries provided water power to saw lumber and grind grain into flour. The farms produced well, and many gristmills operated through the 1700s and the early part of the 1800s. By the end of the 19th century, most of the custom mills had closed.

Although the region is now rapidly developing, the White Clay Preserve ensure that portions of the natural environment, much like it was 200 years ago, will survive for future generations to enjoy. The entire preserve is managed for low intensity day-use activities.

Information and Activities

White Clay Creek Preserve
P.O. Box 172
Landenberg, PA 19350
(610) 255-5415

DIRECTIONS: The Pennsylvania section of the park is in Chester County. It can be reached by U.S. 1 south to SR 41. .

HIKING: The Pennsylvania side of the park has three miles of hiking trails and 5.5 miles of equestrian trails. On the Delaware portion of the park are 16 miles of trails that lead to scenic vistas overlooking stream valleys and impressive rock outcroppings. Gristmill grindstones were once made from the rocks exposed along Millstone Trail. The Logger's Trail chronicles the history of lumbering in the area, while the Lifecourse fitness trail offers a more strenuous workout. Visitors to the sprawling park may also visit the Arc Corner Monument, which punctuates the curved boundary between Pennsylvania and Delaware.

FISHING: Trout fishing is popular in White Clay Creek, but the action is seasonal (fish are stocked in the spring, summer and fall). Many anglers have better luck trying for bass, bluegill and crappie in the Delaware on the Pennsylvania side. White Clay Creek can flow slowly and warm up by June. Try a variety of warmwater fishing patterns.

CEMETERY: The entire old cemetery is surrounded by a five-foot-tall stone wall with wooden gates that have large iron hinges. A Minguannan Indian town was once located here. Chief Macholoha Owhala and his people of the Unami group also lived here. The land between the Delaware River and the Chesapeake Bay to the falls of the Susquehanna River was sold to William Penn October 18, 1683.

Pennsylvania State Parks

The former Baptist church, now a learning center, is a two-story stone building at the corner of the cemetery. Inside the building with gray shutters are seating, simple nature study items, Indian artifacts, rocks, animals mounts and other teaching supplies.

It's an interesting walk around the small cemetery. Many tombstones are heavily worn from the cycles of the weather, but some are still readable and date to the early 1800s. Sadly, there are many tiny stones that mark the graves of small children. The largest stone marks the grave of Dr. John Boyde (1813-1884).

The park uses the cemetery for an annual non-scary, almost educational Halloween program. Costumed actors greet children, offer treats, and often talk about period history and local customs. Many of the players are ancestors of the deceased who are resting in the cemetery.

DAY-USE AREAS: On the Delaware side of the park, a series of summer concerts are often conducted in the park including big band music, bluegrass, oldies, rock and roll, Irish-style, dance tunes, show music and marches. Other programming include youth natural history classes, arts and crafts, kite day and other entertaining family-style activities.

The Delaware side of the park has plenty of picnic tables, pavilions and open spaces for non-organized family fun. There is even a disc golf course to challenge your flying skills. The Delaware state park offers plastic litter bags to help keep the preserve that is jointly managed with Pennsylvania clean.

NATURE: The lush protected park is the perfect setting for the many environmental education learning programs offered. Learning opportunities include wildflower rambles, fern, tree and wildflower identification, let's go fishing, cultural history, tombstone rubbing, bees and hornets, butterfly survey, how to grow healthy house plants, bird walks, sunset walks, seasonal walks and lots more.

The quiet preserve offers excellent birding and lessons in geology. At one time the White Clay landscape has been flooded, folded, heated and eroded, creating the scenery we see today. Thousands of years ago, the preserve was part of a large continental area that was covered by a shallow sea. Through time, sediment composed of sand, silt and mud spread over the sea floor. At various intervals, volcanoes poured lava onto these deposits. Gradually the sediments hardened into sedimentary rock.

About 460 million years ago, an immense mountain-building episode folded and heated the rocks and completely changed their character. The rocks in the preserve "cooked" at elevated temperatures and pressures for some 70 million years, long enough for new minerals to develop.

About 390 million years ago, the preserve was uplifted and cooled, which halted the metamorphism. Since then, the minerals have remained largely unchanged. Minerals such as quartz and calcite are common. Pick up a copy of the Trail of Geology from the park office for more information.

HUMMINGBIRDS: One of the most fascinating and handsome visitors to the preserve is the helicopter-like hummingbird. Each spring, ruby-throated hummingbirds, the only hummingbirds found east of the Mississippi River, move north from their winter ranges in Central and South America. On the way, they fly nonstop across the Gulf of Mexico–at least 500 miles–and zip and dart from one flower or flower garden to the next on their journey to breeding areas like the White Clay valley. The birds arrive here in late April and early May.

As hummingbirds trickle into the area (they don't migrate in groups), some head for familiar nesting areas, while others, especially yearlings, look for backyards or other new territories they can stake out as their own. Yards, parks and gardens with plenty of edge habitat and spring-blooming flowers tend to have the best chance of attracting these migrants as summertime settlers. A well-maintained hummingbird feeder will also increase a backyards appeal.

Hummingbirds are nature's speedsters. They are capable of moving up to 60 miles per hour, with a heart that beats up to 600 times per minute and wings that beat 75 per second. Because of this high energy level, the whirlybirds must eat almost constantly. The hyper birds lap sugary liquid nectar from the base of preferred flowers with their long, slender tongues. They also eat tiny insects as they travel from blossom to blossom.

Plants that attract hummers include trumpet vine, honeysuckle, gladiolus, jasmine, begonias, scarlet morning glory, paintbrush, salvia, petunias, coral bells and trumpet-creeper. Black locust and horse chestnut trees can also put the brakes on the little birds.

The birds are easy to attract to backyard feeders, and the word is spreading that commercially bought feeders, filled with one part granulated sugar and four parts water, is all you need. The mixture should be boiled and cooled before filling your feeder reservoir. Store any unused feed mixture in the refrigerator until needed. Never use honey; it ferments and can make the tiny birds sick. Buy a feeder that is red.

Locate the feeder in a somewhat shady area near a flower bed by suspending it with a wire or string from a tree branch or stand. Smear petroleum jelly on the string or wire to stoop ants from reaching the feeder. If the feeder fails to attract birds in a week or two, move it.

Clean the feeders once a week in hot water and dishwashing liquid. Wash it like you would dishes. Keep an eye on your feeder; the birds feed every 10 to 15 minutes. Once birds begin using your feed, you can move it a bit each day toward the area you'd like to observe them from (if it isn't already there).

After the tiny birds start feeding in your yard, a male may stake the territory and nest there. Females, the dull-colored ones, build the half-dollar-sized nests, constructed with soft plant fiber and spider web, among twigs or branches or deciduous trees. Nests are often camouflaged with lichens. The two pea-sized eggs laid in the nest hatch after about two weeks of incubation. The hatchlings are under their mother's care for about 25 days–then young birds strike out on their own with all the skills needed to feed, breed, build nests and migrate hundreds (even thousands) of miles.

DID YOU KNOW:

- that hummingbirds can fly backwards?

- that they build their nests using saliva and spider silk?

- that hummingbirds' legs are so short that they can't walk or climb, just land and sit?

- that their flight muscles are proportionally the largest in the animal kingdom?

- that a hummingbird can travel 500 miles on one gram (the weight of a paper clip) of stored fat?

67 Worlds End State Park
Land: 780 acres Water: Loyalsock Creek

The name Worlds End reflects the fear of pioneers who traveled the first road into the primeval pine forested gorge on the banks of wide Loyalsock Creek (meaning *"middle creek"*). The remote park is located is a narrow S-shaped valley beneath steep slopes, near wide-throated canyons, cascading waterfalls and foaming whitewater. The isolated park is an excellent place to explore nature's best offerings. Already well-known to trout fishermen, kayakers and whitewater canoeists, hikers, campers and nature lovers, the park is also an excellent family destination.

During the summer the thick hemlock forest reverberates with the songs of breeding birds. Mountain slopes display rocky gardens of wildflowers and hay-scented ferns. Worlds End is your starting point to explore a region famous for its haystack boulders (huge rounded steam boulders) made of burgoon sandstone that has resisted water erosion. You, and children, will have trouble resisting the temptation to climb the enormous coarse-grained rocks.

Worlds End is on the east end of the 42,000-acre Wyoming State

Forest. Most of the forest is in Sullivan County. The Susquehanna River winds through 70 miles of neighboring state forest and game lands. Much of the land was purchased by the state in the 1930s from the Central Pennsylvania Lumber Company, putting a close to the great lumbering era that stripped the region of timber.

Before the lumbering era, the pristine forests, waterfalls and pure creeks were virtually unexplored by Indians or early European explorers. The rugged terrain was almost impenetrable. Fortunately, Mother Nature has rejuvenated herself from the wasteland of the lumber barons, returning to the picturesque streams and resplendent solitude the region now offers.

The forest now has some excellent hardwood tracts and game areas. The forest is primarily of second growth northern hardwoods including maple, cherry, ash and beech. One of the assets of the park and state forest is its network of well-maintained roads that provide access to places like Fern Rock Nature Trail, 50 miles of fishable streams, mountain ponds, day-use areas, forested mountains and cool lonely valleys.

Information and Activities

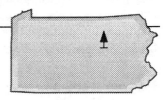

Worlds End State Park
P.O. Box 62
Forksville, PA 18616-0062
(717) 924-3287

DIRECTIONS: South of Forksville in Sullivan County. The park is on PA Route 154 and is reached via PA Route 87 from Williamsport and west; PA Route 42 from I-80 and south; and PA Route 87 from Dushore and the north and east. Park elevation is 1,135 feet.

EMERGENCY NUMBER: 911 system.

OFFICE/VISITOR CENTER: Sharing a sheet metal-sided small building near the creek are the office and visitor center packed with natural history displays and park information. From the silhouettes of birds of prey taped to the ceiling to free-standing displays, your first stop should be at the center for maps and other regional information. The walls are covered with posters (birds, frogs, snakes, etc.), nature photographs and more. Maybe the most interesting photo was of the S-95 Civilian Conservation Corps camp with workers lined up, backs straight and only a hint of a smile at the corner of their mouths.

Naturalist programs often begin at the facility. Typical programs include nature crafts, campground talks, amphitheater lectures and slide shows, guided hikes, discovery hikes, story hours for small children and campfire talks.

CAMPGROUND: Services are held at a simple outdoor chapel on Route 154 south of the campground entrance. The 70-site family campground is open through mid-December. Tent camping and small RV units are the biggest users of the narrow campground. Some sites are near PA 154. On busy weekends, when traffic is heavy, you may want to avoid these sites (15-25).

Loop A, sites 1-43, are wooded and shady and have gravel pads and picnic tables. Sites 1-13 are at the bottom of a hill, but dry. Many sites are divided by a thin wall of vegetation and oversized. Site 7 is oversized and often used, according to campground staff.

Loop B, sites 44-70, are above the A loop along the shady, tree-covered mountainside. Private sites include 45, 55, 64 and the walk-ins, 58-61 and 70. Site 70 is one of the prettiest sites in the campground.

Some of the walk-in sites are elevated and near the campground lane, while others require a short trek to reach. All of the walk-in sites are along the mountainside, dry and heavily used. The campground is very popular with families.

Three group tent camping areas maintained at Worlds End can accommodate about 30 individuals, each. Advance registration is required.

CABINS: All 19 of the wood-frame cabins can be rented by the day, half-week or weekly, spring, fall and winter–and by the full week in the summer. Cabins are outfitted with a refrigerator, range, fireplace insert, table, chairs and beds.

The "yards" of many cabins are strewn with rounded boulders and patches of waving ferns. Almost completely shaded, the gently rolling cabin area is along a bend in the rocky creek and very pleasant. Some cabins are just above the rushing stream that has short rapids, riffles and side pools along a sweeping curve. Directly on the Loyalsock are some of the more scenic and sought-after in the entire park system. All of the soothing cabins have stone chimneys that puff smoke from the wood stove on cold evenings.

The cabins have porches, picnic tables and fire rings or grills. The park store is about a half-mile from the inviting cluster of log-style and rough-sawn cabins.

Cabins on the stream are 1-7, 13 and 14. Cabin 4 (handicapped accessible) is the closest to the creek and charming. There are no bathrooms in the cabins, so if you have a small bladder, like me, consider cabin 1, 7 or 18, near the brown heated rest room building with a soft drink machine humming at its side. Firewood (near cabin 5) is usually available for cabin guests. Cabin 7, is log-style with wide white chinking, is along the sometimes noisy creek notched out of the forest and very private. Cabin 19, at the foot of the mountain, faces the road and is very shady with parking for two cars. The most private cabin, on the hillside above the rest, is rough-sawn clapboard sided cabin 12.

Both cabins 11 and 17 are perched on a hillside near the entrance to the three small organized group tent camping areas, north of the main cabin loop.

FISHING: Fly fishermen are often seen flailing high-priced rod and line, tossing a tiny feather-wrapped hook along the rocky Loyalsock Creek that winds through the entire length of the scenic park. Many fly fishermen rent cabins on the creek, camp, and flock to the area in April and early May. Loyalsock is stocked with brown and rainbow trout.

Loyalsock Creek has a rich history well-known to trout fishing devotees. From fishing clubs started a century ago to the Whistle Pig Club that calls the stream home today, anglers have waded the mighty stream and its dozens of quality tributaries for many years. The 25-member Whistle Pig Club is an eclectic group, mostly professionals, from Harrisburg. A small lodge three miles south of Hillsgrove hosts the group's slightly wacky activities and the more serious enjoyment of the many great hatches and waterways of the area.

The big creek has excellent early hatches (stoneflies, some mayflies, etc.) and good fall fishing. June and July can be productive over slate drake patterns. Often by mid-April, dry fly angling is at its peak. Wading is dangerous in some sections of the free flowing creek, which has a bottom littered with huge boulders and varying water levels.

After the water warms in June, smallmouth bass fishing can be terrific in the lower half of the stream. Mid-summer anglers should scout for cooler waters by fishing below Big Bear and other smaller tributaries that are shaded. Standard patterns that local anglers suggest as the water warms to include royal coachmen, Adams, minnow imitators, black gnats, Hendricksons, light Cahills and various terrestrials.

BOATING: Whitewater boaters may use the river year-round. The swimming area is closed to kayakers and other boats during the summer. Water levels fluctuate often; kayakers should inquire about conditions before coming.

HIKING: The park has about 12 miles of moderate to difficult trails, including a nature trail that is popular with campers and day-users. High Rock Trail winds along the north creek bank and connects the main day-use area to the cabin loop.

Backpackers can access one of the most rugged but scenic trails in the state, the Loyalsock Trail. Overnight hikers must register at the park office. The demanding trail is 60 miles of up and down trekking, offering views of cliffs carved by the creek, waterfalls, several steep areas (there have been two deaths from falling), rocky spurs, railroad grades, forested logging roads, steep hills, small streams and rocky edges. Wear your heavy duty boots, be in shape and be careful on this hike. Much of the trail is covered by hemlock, beech, chestnut, oak and white pine. The trail has a 2,720-foot vertical rise.

Most backpackers can complete the 17 mile loop in two days, leaving their car near the park office where it is watched by the park ranger. The park has maps, but for additional information contact the Alpine Hiking Club, P.O. Box 501, Williamsport, PA 17703.

DAY-USE AREAS: The "Food and Stuff" park store (open 11 a.m. 7 p.m. weekdays, Memorial Day to Labor Day 9 a.m. - 7 p.m. weekends) is directly across the lumpy parking lot from the park office and sells ice, T-shirts, cold drinks, snacks, candy, limited camping supplies (cereal, paper plates, propane, etc.) and simple grill items from the walk-up window.

Picnicking locations are along the flowing stream, mostly often under canopies, but some are streamside in sunny locations. Most picnic areas are equipped with grills and are within walking distance to rest rooms and other amenities. Four picnic pavilions are reservable.

SWIMMING AREA: A small guarded swimming area is open from Memorial Day weekend to Labor Day. The water is usually cold, but hearty children like to splash and wade in the exhilarating mountain stream waters.

NATURE: Along the park's 12 miles of trails are excellent woodland habitats bisected by the creek and some open spaces. Northern parula and yellow-bellied flycatchers are often seen. Interesting breeders include northern waterthrush, black-throated green warblers, blackburnian, black-throated blues, chestnut-sided warbler and others. Other common wildlife is also seen along the roads and trails.

WINTER: Several miles of park roads that connect to neighboring state forest lands are popular snowmobile and cross-country skiing routes. Skiers may use park trails or link to the state forests eight miles of trails.

HUNTING: A large portion of the park is open to hunting. Call the park office for details.

INSIDER TIPS: Rent cabin 4; it is one of the nicest streamside cabins in the entire state park system. Majestic vistas abound. Visit the Canyon Vista, reached via Mineral Spring and Cold Run roads, and nearby High Knob Overlook. Scenery is especially grand during the June mountain laurel bloom and during the fall foliage period.

NEARBY ATTRACTIONS: Call the Sullivan County Chamber of Commerce for additional information at (717) 946-4160.

Some cabins are along the rushing stream.

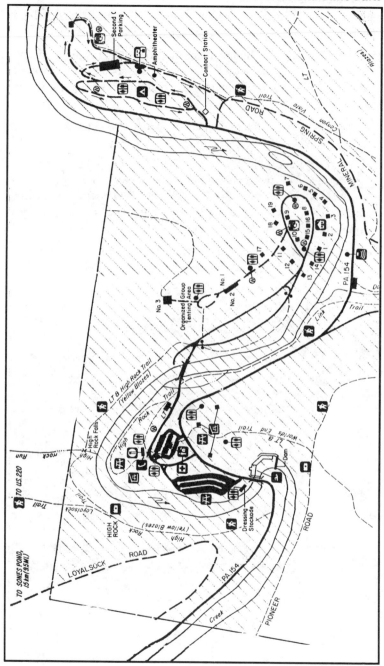

68 Yellow Creek State Park
Land: 3,140 acres   Water: 720-acre lake

The drive along Route 422 rambles pass gently rounded hills, rolling farmlands, through mixed deciduous woodlands and small towns. Yellow Creek, in Indiana County, is a family-style park nestled along the low wooded hills that roll off into the distance, beckoning vacationers from around the state and nation. Here you will find year-round recreational facilities and activities for the entire family.

The tract of land that stretches along these fertile valleys was once a major trail used by Delaware and Shawnee tribes and early settlers. The corridor, called Kittanning Path, roughly follows Route 422, the main access road to the park from Indiana and Ebensburg.

The state began purchasing and development of the park in 1963 using funds from the Project 70 park expansion program. An earth and rock dam creating a 720-acre lake was completed by the end of 1969. Day-use areas were dedicated to public use in 1976, and additional land acquisitions were made in 1982.

Information and Activities

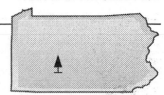

Yellow Creek State Park
R.D. 1, Box 145-D
Penn Run, PA 15765
(412) 357-7913

DIRECTIONS: Drive east from Indiana on U.S. 422 about 10 miles to SR 259, turn right on SR 259 to the park office. Its about 12 miles from the city of Indiana.

Next to the brown cement block park office is a handy three-sided reader board that features information about Yellow Creek and other nearby parks and attractions. Inside the small office are a number of animal mounts, a map of the area and brochure rack near the counter. There is no overnight camping at Yellow Creek. However, there are two private family campgrounds (Yellow Creek Campground with 50 sites at (412) 463-3860 or the L & M Campground with 200 sites at (412) 479-3264) nearby.

FISHING: Yellow Creek Lake is a state designated big bass lake. The following rules apply: large- and smallmouth bass minimum size is 15 inches, and you may take no more than four daily of combined species. There are lots of convenient shoreline fishing opportunities around the lake.

The lake is considered a very good panfishing lake, where youngsters can easily catch them from the bank. The lake also has fair populations of muskie, walleye, catfish and northern pike.

Yellow Creek, heavily fly-fished since the mid-1950s, has significant angling pressure in the delayed harvest waters and near public access points. Trout anglers do very well in April during Hendricksons and caddis hatch times. Later in the summer, hoppers and other terrestrials produce trout in the creek. Yellow Creek is named for its coloration, rarely attaining clarity. Avid fly fishermen recommend that you change patterns often, try the wild-trout waters near Woodbury, and make an effort to hit the creek when the green drake, March browns and caddis are emerging. The stream is scenic, difficult wading in sections and has deep pools, riffles and slow-moving flats.

Laurel Run, Yellow Creek and Little Yellow Creek are stocked with brown and brook trout. Ice fishing is also popular at the state park.

BOATING: Four small, one-lane launches, some with floating mooring

The park has many modern day-use facilities.

docks, are located around the lake. A seasonal boat rental is operated near the day-use area. At this launch, the best on the lake, there are floating docks and a retaining wall near day-use and beach areas. Gasoline is sold at the concession. Canoes and rowboats are for rent.

Canoeists will find two areas on the lake excellent quiet areas to slip their paddle into the waters. The first is at the east end of the lake close to the park office. Put in and head east along the marshy shoreline, heading to the headwaters of Yellow Creek. Once you find Yellow Creek, which flows cold and deep, you can paddle at least to the Route 422 bridge before the water becomes too shallow.

Another excellent paddle is in the southwest portion of the lake at Grampa's Cove. Ply west to explore expansive marshes and neighboring Gramma's Cove and some excellent birding areas. Fall is a terrific time to canoe this section of the lake.

HIKING: Laurel Run Trail begins at the park office and is half-mile long of level and easy walking. The trail follows the Laurel Run stream for which it was named, to its junction with the lake and then returns through reforested fields. This trail is one of the best for viewing spring wildflowers, especially during the first week in May.

Fishermen also use this trailway.

Ridgetop Trail (2 miles)starts near the beach. About two miles long, the trail winds its way through a variety of habitats of open fields and forest, to many stages in between. With several ups and downs, the trails is considered moderately difficult hiking. At least 1 1/2 hours should be allowed for a leisurely pace.

The Wildlife Observation Trail starts in main part of the park. If you are interested in spotting waterfowl, this trail is for you! You will meander through forested areas to the elevated wildlife observation tower.

The Damsite Trail is the longest in the park and leads to an overlook near the dam. The 660-foot-long dam is of rock and earth and contains the quiet lake. The 2.5-mile trail follows an abandoned road and passes pine plantations, old coal mines and fields.

Snowshoers and cross-country skiers explore the park when weather permits.

DAY-USE AREAS: Yellow Creek State Park is in two parts, a north and south unit. Yellow Creek has one of the finest day-use areas in the state park system.

The north unit features a small boat launch on a cove, rest rooms, picnic pavilion and open spaces on a low ridge above the lake. A Boy Scout camp, a large developed area, is also in this vicinity. Shoreline boat mooring and good fishing are in this part of the small lake, that features many tiny coves and a jagged shoreline.

The south day-use area is more developed than the north, featuring sets of play equipment, significant parking and open spaces. Small wooden walkways help day-users roam the playground that stretches more than 100 yards and has timber play apparatus, sand volleyball court and other interesting play structures. There are about one dozen pieces of play apparatus in this mowed area.

The popular 150-yard-long guarded beach (open 11 a.m. - 7 p.m. daily, Memorial Day to Labor Day) at Yellow Creek is complete with brick changing rooms/bathhouse, a lifeguard and first aid station and chairs, food concession with nearby picnic tables and plenty of room. A sign on the rest room door at the beach is worth remembering if you have small children: "Please check and change your children's diapers frequently. This is a natural body of water, without the benefit of bacteria or infection controls. We regularly test and monitor the water's bacterial levels. Swimmers need to also assist with, good personal hygiene. Please respect your fellow swimmers and follow these suggestions to protect the body of water from human waste that may result in illness. 1) babies should be checked and changed frequently, 2) soiled diapers should be disposed properly, 3) if you have a gastrointestinal illness known to transmit in a body of water, please do not enter the swimming area."

Ice skating is also offered at the park when weather permits. Large areas are managed for hunting during the fall; call the park superintendent for details. About 350 acres of the parks are managed for snowmobiling.

NATURE NOTES: Seasonal interpretive programs explore the diverse areas' natural communities.

Birding at Yellow Creek is excellent and may be the best in the state. The active Todd Bird Club has maintained careful records of the 243 species identified in the park. Dozens of birding hikes are offered annually at the park for beginners and advanced birders.

The park enjoys strong migrations of waterfowl; 28 species have been spotted over the years including tundra swans, surf scoter, common loons, ruddy duck, American widgeon and other more common types. Both Gramma's and Grampa's coves are good places to see the waterfowl raft, while certain shore birds can also be seen wading about, like solitary and spotted sandpipers. November is the best month to see migratory waterfowl.

The diverse habitats of mixed fields, marsh grass, young oak-hickory forests, shorelines with sheltered coves, thickets and various wetlands are excellent places to see some of the 35 species of warblers, brown creepers, thrushes, red-eyed vireos, clay-colored sparrows and others. Rare species sometimes seen include red knots, godwit, Swainson's warbler, Franklin's gull and others.

Much of the habitat can also support upland ground birds and common mammals like red and gray fox, black bear, woodchucks, eastern cottontail rabbits, and red and gray squirrels.

Other great books available from
Glovebox Guidebooks of America . . .

Indiana State Parks Guidebook
A Hoosier's Guide to Parks, Recreation Areas and Reserves.
by John Goll
Indiana's only comprehensive guide to the great state parks! All the details about camping, hiking scenic areas, lodges, fishing and family recreation opportunities. Maps, photos, directions, 268 pages, $14.95.

Michigan State Parks Guidebook
A complete recreation guide for campers, boaters, anglers, hikers and skiers.
by Jim DuFresne
Complete information on Michigan's 92 diverse state parks. Welcome to Michigan's playground! Wilderness retreats, great fishing and the nation's longest freshwater shoreline. Maps, photos, 287 pages, $12.95.

Ohio State Parks Guidebook
A complete outdoor recreation guide to the Buckeye state.
by Art Weber and Bill Bailey
With 65 maps and 90 photographs. Complete park descriptions, camping, hiking trails, handicapped accessibilities, boating, fishing, rent-a-camps, rentals, lodges, beaches and nature notes. Everything you need to know to enjoy Ohio's terrific state parks! 384 pages, directions, phone numbers, $14.95.

Illinois State Parks Guidebook
A complete outdoor recreation guide
by Bill Bailey
Detailed guide to the natural features and facilities of the great Illinois state park system. Where to camp, fishing tips and hot spots, trails, watersports, historical and educational attractions, lodging, beaches, cabins, day-use areas, natural history, skiing and more. Photos, maps, 352 pages, $14.95.